GERMAN BAROQUE LITERATURE

The European Perspective

Edited by **GERHART HOFFMEISTER**

Frederick Ungar Publishing Co.
New York

Copyright ©1983 by Frederick Ungar Publishing Co., Inc.
Printed in the United States of America
Design by Anita Duncan

Library of Congress Cataloging in Publication Data
Main entry under title:

German Baroque literature.

  Bibliography: p.
  Includes index.
  1. German literature—Early modern, 1500-1700—History and criticism—
Addresses, essays, lectures. 2. Baroque literature—History and criticism—
Addresses, essays, lectures. I. Hoffmeister, Gerhart.
PT273.G47 1982   830'.9'004   80-5341
ISBN 0-8044-2394-6 (cloth)   AACR2
ISBN 0-8044-6279-8 (paper)

Contents

Preface

The study of German baroque literature flourished after each of the two world wars. This may in part be due to an affinity with an age that experienced a devastation through war and ensuing political-economic fragmentation on a larger scale than ever before known and yet demonstrated its resilience and proved its creativity through a surprising productivity in the arts. But research into the baroque has also developed a momentum of its own—particularly since Kurt von Faber du Faur laid the bibliographical foundations for it with his work *German Baroque Literature, I* (New Haven, 1958)—a momentum that still seems to be gaining ground. Two probable reasons for this intensified interest are the apparently endless possibilities for the investigation of lacunae and desiderata on the map of seventeenth-century German literature and the fact that the international dimension of baroque culture has turned the age into one of the more exciting areas of research.

The field's attractiveness as an academic discipline is evident from the recent foundation of large associations such as the Internationale Arbeitskreis für Barockliteratur at Wolfenbüttel in Germany and the American Association for Renaissance and Baroque Literature associated with the MLA in New York.

The present volume—with its combination of background studies, analyses of specific topics, and comparative viewpoints, written by distinguished contributors from universities in the United States, Canada, and England—should provide stimulating and rewarding reading to the student of the era, not only to the one seeking an introduction to or an overview of the baroque, but also to the scholar who needs expert advice on a specific question. In addition, this collection of essays gives an indication of the current status of "baroque studies" in the

English-speaking world. It also serves as a continuation of and counter-part to the editor's previous volume, *The Renaissance and Reformation in Germany* (New York: Frederick Ungar, 1977), though on a more demanding level.

The arrangement of the book and its spectrum of topics are the editor's; he is responsible for any shortcomings in this area. Unfortunately, not every desirable topic could be taken into consideration when planning this volume. For instance, a special chapter on Opitz's poetics is missing, although a considerable portion of Janis Solomon's chapter, "The French Model," is devoted to this subject. To the editor's great disappointment, a chapter on Italian-German relations in the baroque, originally planned for inclusion, did not materialize.* In these and other cases, however, pertinent items will be listed in the index. During the final stage of manuscript preparation, a scholar commissioned to write the essay on the baroque novel opted out. Only this, and not personal vanity, prompted the editor to substitute his own version.

Apart from this, the appeal for contributions from scholars met with an immediate and positive response when the project was announced several years ago. The editor is grateful to all the contributing authors, and above all to Professors Leonard Foster and Gerald Gillespie for their encouragement and helpful suggestions, as well as to the publisher, Frederick Ungar, and to his executive editor, Ruth Selden, who thought it worth the risk to publish this volume.

May the book be a welcome aid for classwork as well as a useful research tool for Germanists, comparativists, and students of European literature.

Gerhart Hoffmeister
University of California, Santa Barbara

---

*Those who wish further to pursue this topic are referred to Italo M. Battafarano, *Von Andreae zu Vico. Untersuchungen zur Beziehung zwischen deutscher und italienischer Literatur im 16. und 17. Jahrhundert*, Stuttgart 1979.

I

The Background to the Literary Epoch

1

Renaissance, Mannerism, Baroque

Gerald Gillespie

Any attempt to discriminate an epochal Renaissance, Mannerism, or baroque must, by necessity, involve circular definition. For the Renaissance (our starting term) decisively reshaped Western historical thought by the comprehensive way leading humanists set their ideals apart from the supposed intervening era of long decline they called the Middle Ages. The idea of a succession of ages was fundamental to Christianity, but by positing a new course to recover from the collapse of ancient civilization and loss of direction after the pristine centuries of the church, the Renaissance itself established our habit of historical periodization. Major subsequent moments and movements, e.g., the Enlightenment, Romanticism, and Modernism, may in turn have redefined the temporal zones, the cultural characteristics, and the developmental meanings of various "periods"—traditionally including those designated by the Renaissance—but every significant revision has confirmed a basic paradigm of a progression of new beginnings. Writers as diverse as Lessing, Rousseau, Schiller, Coleridge, and Novalis eventually recognized, in addition, that the arrival of anthropological and psychological views of culture in the eighteenth century was linked with the maturation of the Renaissance.

In the wake of Romanticism, Heine, Burckhardt, Pater, Ruskin, and innumerable other philosophers of culture regarded the Renaissance as the matrix or turning point of modern consciousness. Whether believing in larger organic rhythms (e.g., Taine) or some governing dialectic (e.g., Marx), nineteenth-century historians by and large presumed that forces of secularization became a cardinal factor when released in the Renaissance from about 1480 to 1720. It is not surprising that many British, French, and German writers, whose nations more profoundly experienced Protestantism, have focused on the interaction of the Renaissance and Reformation for an explanatory key. Perhaps the best-known German example is Nietzsche's polemic in the essay *Zur Genealogie der Moral* (1887), opposing his classical ideal to "degenerative" Christianity and tracing European decline over the intermediate conflict between the Renaissance, with its healthy restoration of tragic values, and the Reformation, a movement of "resentment" restoring slave mentality and stirring a Catholic response in the Counter-Reformation. Or, from a contrary perspective, one could cite seminal Modernists such as T. E. Hulme and T. S. Eliot, who viewed the secular unfolding of the Renaissance as the model of crisis, the traumatic "dissociation of sensibility," from which our contemporary world supposedly once again or still suffers. Postwar analysts have placed the accent variously on entry into or resolution of the critical juncture of the late Renaissance (ca. 1580–1660). For example, whereas Hazard (30) traces the triumph of a secular ethos emerging from intellectual turmoil, Haydn (29) explores the breakup of the early Renaissance synthesis under the pressure of trends it engendered.

The term baroque applied to literature first became well established in German and Italian usage and thus is still widely associated with the foibles of German "intellectual history" (*Geistesgeschichte*) in the minds of many non-Germans. Its German fortunes have been thoroughly recounted by Barner (5) and Brauneck (8). Two tendencies which began to affect German criticism around 1900 eventually worked their way into the English and Romanic spheres. One was the transference of categories from art history to literature spurred by Wölfflin's seminal book *Renaissance und Barock* (1888), which actually reasserted the contrast—already apparent to Galileo and others by 1660—between Ariosto's *Orlando furioso* (1516) and Tasso's *Gerusalemme liberata* (1575). The other was a general rehabilitation of pre-Lessing literature, marked by such critical efforts as Strich's on behalf of German seventeenth-century poetry (70), and Benjamin's on behalf of German seventeenth-century drama (6). Initially, Anglo-American criticism was satisfied to revive period terms from the British eighteenth century for describing the contrast between "Renaissance" and "metaphysical" style in poetry, and between Elizabethan, Jacobean, and Caroline playwrights. The relatively easier assimilation of the term baroque by modern Hispanic scholarship can be explained in part by the closeness of Spanish to Italian culture throughout the sixteenth and seventeenth centuries, just as Dutch acceptance was induced in part by a sense of the greatness of the Netherlandic *Gouden Eeuw* (Golden Age) paralleling the Iberian *Siglo de Oro*, whereas French conviction in the centrality of their classical age during the reign of Louis XIV fostered resistance to the idea of baroque literature until the end of World War II.

The differing rhythms and experiences of the European nations add a perplexing dimension to attempts to describe a baroque age for all Europe. Among the most eloquent and comprehensive recent books on this subject in English are Warnke's *Versions of Baroque* (77), surveying terms, genres, and themes, and Skrine's *The Baroque* (66), surveying literature, art, thought, and civic life under thematic headings. Approaches may be grouped under three broad divisions. First, there is the abiding question of *style*, which most critics find difficult to separate from a discussion of thematics. Second, there is the call for a more adequate *social theory*, proponents of which divide, so far, mainly along the lines of cultural psychology or anthropology, analysis of class structures, and reception aesthetics. Third, there is the effort to revive the study of *rhetoric* as a less pretentious instrument for rigorous scrutiny of theory and practice in the baroque, bypassing modern structuralism, phenomenology, etc.

I

Renaissance has remained a quite general label covering the aggregate of humanist literary interests and subjects, and not just neoclassical currents, in Europe from the late fifteenth well into or even beyond the sixteenth century. It applies to both vernacular and Neo-Latin writings, and the various national languages were affected by Renaissance impulses originally spread from Italy. Baroque has enjoyed ever wider acceptance for designating the stylistic or also cultural orientation of the seventeenth century, despite attempts to introduce Mannerism as a separate period between Renaissance and baroque, or in place of baroque (see section II, below). One consequence of the origin of the term baroque in art history has been the persistence of metaphoric or abstract associations such as "theatrical," "irrational," "irregular," "tense," "dynamic," etc. Another has been the survival of once pejorative associations, often rehabilitated as positive attributes of baroque style by current critics, e.g., "excessive," "outrageous," "disordered," "unnatural."

What distinguishes baroque from neoclassical unity in much of literary as well as plastic art in the view of current scholarship is the employment of multiple perspectives, fluidity of form, oblique and sinuous movements, delight in effects, deliberate illusioning and disillusioning, all-embracing theatricality, artistic wit. Baroque writers often strive to explore and expand the elements of their cultural and poetic repertory, to parade and multiply values and relationships, and to link their ideas in surprising trains of ornaments and imagery, but all the while exhibiting the instability and evanescence of their constructs. Spitzer (69) and others have noted a double movement — the interaction of contraries — as the hallmark of baroque writing. German criticism has focused on the antitheses of spirit and flesh, eternity and temporality, which generate the inherent tensions. Rousset (60) is among those who relate specific thematic clusters to characteristic processes of baroque imagination. Although formal features are often noted, most anthologies are nevertheless organized into categories based on favorite themes (e.g., Proteus, Eros, *Theatrum mundi*, *Homo christianus*). Critics as diverse as Buffum (10) and Jantz (36) have argued that in its essence baroque art is integrative and synthesizing, an art that attempts to establish or affirm a new order envisioned in the complexities and perplexities of the world.

Once scholars such as Grierson (24) and Leishman (40) had carefully defined the metaphysicals, Anglo-American criticism was reluctant to concede members of this class to the rival foreign concept, baroque. The high Renaissance, represented in Spenser and Sidney, was contrasted with the meditative wit of Donne and Marvell and the related meditative strain of Vaughan and Traherne (45). One of the first major shifts was Warren's (78) insistence, set forth in 1939, that Crashaw clearly could and should be aligned with his baroque counterparts. Eventually Petersson (55) would compare Crashaw as poet with Saint Teresa as mystic and with Bernini as sculptor in a cross disciplinary appreciation of high baroque art. Tuve (74) distinguished Elizabethan (i.e., Renaissance) from metaphysical imagery and related the new developments to the rise of altered attitudes about rhetoric (see section III, below). De Mourgues (48) recognized English metaphysical, French précieux, and Spanish-Italian baroque styles as an interrelated constellation of the early seventeenth century. Nelson (50) singled out intense "time" consciousness and "drama" as cardinal principles of baroque literature and argued that the greatest achievements of baroque poetry were registered in England and Spain. After a long eclipse, Milton was steadily rehabilitated in modern scholarship as a poet of stature, and gradually his grandiloquence, theatrical imagination, and cosmological vision came to be associated with the European high baroque climax (18). Warnke extended the particularly English term metaphysical to cover Dutch, French, German, Italian, and Spanish poets of the period 1580–1680 in his influential anthology (76) but continued to argue that one should designate the same poets baroque in the European context (77).

The Renaissance has traditionally been described as showing its exuberant phase in Rabelais and its high moment in the poets of the Pléiade during the French sixteenth century, before the elaboration of a dominant classical ethos in France during the seventeenth century. But Raymond (56), claiming authors who inconvenienced standard French literary history of these centuries were habitually devalorized, has argued that there is another line of development from Jodelle (1532–73) to d'Aubigné (1552–1630). He also points out that many French — not just British, Dutch, and German — baroque authors are Protestant, in refutation of the thesis of Counter-Reformation dominance. By the late 1580s, anti-Ciceronian impulses and baroque thematics are in evidence in both prose and poetry. Montaigne's *Essays* exhibit a new way of experiencing the life of the mind in action, with the temporal perspectivism of the baroque meditation. Their affinity to religious forms of meditation such as *Los ejercicios spirituales* of St. Ignatius Loyola has long been remarked. The French baroque also exhibits a scientific side and the Cartesian will to omniscience, balancing the regulative imperatives of purists, grammarians, and academicians. Current French scholarship admits resemblances to English metaphysical writing in the spiritual probes, multiple levels and points of view, and emblematics of Sponde (1557–95) or in the sometimes grim naturalism, theatricality, and irony of La Ceppède (1550–1622). But there are frequent disagreements about the exact division between more rugged, conceptualist poetry and preciosity associated with the influence on France of the great Italian poet Marino, as well as about assigning specific works to the category mannerist rather than baroque. Quite moot is the attempt by Buffum (10) to include conflictual, tragic writers like d'Aubigné under his thesis of the positive cultural vision of the baroque.

The collapse of the traditional French idea of seventeenth-century drama seems extensive. The young Corneille has received penetrating attention as a baroque playwright, and investigators such as Jacquot (35) assert the appropriateness of comparisons with Spanish and English dramatists who dealt with similar themes and structures. Rotrou and

Tristan L'Hermite, playwrights fascinated by the concept of the world as theater, have enjoyed a critical renascence. The presence of baroque impulses in French theater is now detected throughout the seventeenth century; for example, Butler (11) has discovered both classical and baroque traits in Racine, and Fumaroli has illustrated the survival of the baroque play-in-the-play in Molière (21). Lebègue (39) has designated the French theater of the late sixteenth and early seventeenth centuries as baroque, the rest of the seventeenth as classical. Others such as Tapié (72) think of the baroque as a main current of French seventeenth-century culture, shared within a larger European context, even though succeeded by a Classical age. De Reynold (59) and Graham (23), in contrast, deem classicism to be "essentially a French phenomenon," and baroque "more universal, although one finds the origins of both in the same sources." Although a strong advocate of the term baroque, Rousset (61) has cautioned against trying to make it interchangeable for the seventeenth century as a whole, either in France or in Europe; that would be to disregard the diversity of tendencies and differing rhythms of creativity in the arts and literature.

Perhaps because Spanish literature consequently enjoys an exemplary status, Hispanicists such as d'Ors (54) and Macrì (42) have more enthusiastically accepted the idea of a baroque period. Ordinarily, Spanish scholarship distinguishes two related strains in Iberian poetry. Quevedo represents that of "conceptualism" (*conceptualismo*), exhibiting baroque wit, intellectual force. Góngora represents that of "cultism" (*culteranismo*), exhibiting the drive for verbal elegance, artifice that rivals the glory of nature. Whereas the first bears some analogy to metaphysical style, the second bears analogy to French "preciosity" or, on a higher plane, to Marino's aesthetic imperative. In the drama, Lope de Vega furnishes not only countless plays with baroque themes and structure, but also a revealing treatise on the "new" art in existence by 1600; and Calderón carries the theater to an intellectual summit in the 1630s. Although disappointed as a spokesman of neoclassicism in drama, Cervantes lays the foundations of the novel in *Don Quijote*, which explores self-reflectively the baroque sense of a contest between reality and fiction, illusion and disillusionment.

Cioranescu (12) has built an explanatory thesis on the Spanish and European "discovery of drama" as the cardinal shaping idea of the baroque (cf. both L. Nelson [50] and R. J. Nelson [51]). Even in their choice of metaphors, baroque authors tend to express people's sense of finding themselves actors in a dreamlike script, searching amid multiple appearances for true being. The seventeenth-century Spanish theoretician Gracián's educational program and prudentialist world view reveal a radical disillusionism. The older Renaissance ethos of the courtier is replaced by a self-cultivation based on total theatricality, which is necessary, however, in order to serve higher principles in a fallen, deceptive, villainous world; accordingly, in the highest reaches, the ideal is the sublime prince who plays so artfully in the theater of actual history that he becomes in tune with the secret script of divine Providence. The title of the second edition of Gracián's treatise on poetics, *Agudeza y arte de ingenio en que se explican todos los modos y diferencias de conceptos* (1649), contains the key words *agudeza* ("sharpness" of wit or inventive "acuity"), *ingenio* ("genius" or "ingenuity"), and *concepto* ("concept" or "conceit"). In their baroque, Italian critics have identified similar emphases on surprise, elegant dissimulation, and wonder at the ingenious outcome in the poetics of Tesauro or in the practice of Marino, poet of *meraviglie* (47).

German usage of the term baroque has reflected the confusing conjunction of special historical factors. As Spitz (68) has shown, literary humanism was vigorous in the German sixteenth century, but Latin provided a main channel of expression and the introduction of Protestantism absorbed considerable energies as German poets sought to establish a national cultural identity rivaling that of Italy and France. A creative redirection of humanist writing and late Renaissance poetics, flowing out of Latin and into an ennobled vernacular, took place definitively only by the 1620s. The picture is further complicated by the fact that the influx of ideas from Italy, France, and the Netherlands was virtually simultaneous. In rejecting most of their own late-medieval and sixteenth-century poetic heritage in favor of "modern" Romanic prosody and subjects, German poets were receptive around 1600 to influences from various European waves (22). Thus Opitz, author of the pacesetting *Buch von der deutschen Poeterey* (1624), felt himself to be an heir of the great Hessian Neo-Latinist Johannes Lotichius Secundus, of Renaissance theoreticians such as Vida, Scaliger, and Heinsius, of the Italian tradition, and of the French Pléiade, even though he soon sadly acknowledged the waning of the latter as a present force in European letters. It is not surprising that one can distinguish classical and baroque attributes and phases in Opitz. In addition, the vast German-speaking territories eventually comprised a quilt of Catholic, Lutheran, and Calvinist states, often locked in combat but also with areas where the orthodoxies and sometimes dissident minorities were jumbled together. Inevitably, this led to the interpenetration of cultural streams, so that—for example—a chiliast Protestant like Kuhlmann reinterpreted the Spanish mystic St. John of the Cross, and the rationalist Lutheran Lohenstein translated and appreciated the prudentialist Catholic Gracián.

Hence the founders of modern baroque research such as Strich have underscored the influence of Spain and the Counter-Reformation. In exaggerated form, some critics have proposed that the Counter-Reformation, led by the Jesuits, determined the essence of the baroque (14). While Catholic authors played a large part in the German lyric (Spee), mysticism (Angelus Silesius), and drama (Bidermann), they were by far outnumbered by major Protestant figures, some of whom—like Fleming—lack any marked affinities with Catholic writing. That certainly does not mean, however, that German literati of different religious and political persuasions were neatly compartmentalized; on the contrary, common views of genre and common thematic interests cut across all sectarian lines. The deeply religious Lutheran lawyer Gryphius thus epitomizes baroque tragic sentiment in the martyr drama, even though his sources were often Catholic. Because Gryphius had fared better at the hands of moralizing Enlightenment theoreticians, he emerged rapidly for early twentieth-century scholarship as the initial model writer for the thematics of vanity, transcience, and deceptive appearance in conflict with eternal values. Reversing the Counter-Reformation argument, numerous scholars down to the present have defined the norms of the German baroque as stamped by Protestant religiosity (73). Fleming is adduced as the vibrant humanist counterpart to the basic Gryphian ethos. (On an anticourtly stream in the German baroque, as well as orientation to the courtly elite, see essay 15 in this volume.)

But eventually attention to other models, with other emphases, has enriched the picture, and today no single author or small group claims unchallenged centrality. The theatrical urge informed all aspects of society, especially the courts, which both housed important theaters and constituted a kind of drama themselves with their festivals, pomp, and pageantry. The widespread establishment of the opera through the German lands dates from the baroque, and contemporaneous drama of the later seventeenth century (Lohenstein, Avancini, Hallmann) exhibits many "operatic" traits in its structure and its employment of the means of the illusionistic stage. In poetry, the division into "healthy" earlier "schools" and later "decadent" worldly ones—the followers of Opitz, the Nuremberg school, the so-called First and Second Silesian vogues, leading to hypertrophic "gallant" wit—is now more sensibly described.

Detailed research has demonstrated the significance of new linguistic theories and of new poetics for literary experimentation in the baroque. There is more awareness of the carrythrough of secular traditions from the sixteenth to the eighteenth century, more fully explaining German participation in the larger flow of the European lyric and tending to rehabilitate late figures such as Hofmannswaldau.

Interest in the transition from the baroque has centered especially on Günther and Hagedorn, in whom Enlightenment sentimental views, a communal ethos, and a shift to less ornate, low-keyed, graceful expression are evident in the 1720s. Whereas some French critics have tried to assert the sway of a "pre-classical" moment encompassing much of the baroque in the early and mid-1600s, German scholarship has tended to argue for a "post-baroque" interlude usually termed the Rokoko, from approximately 1680 to 1730, and characterized by the overlapping of the older courtly ethos and newer bourgeois attitudes (1). R. Müller (49) has shown that the various baroque arts achieved their climaxes almost serially in the German lands, so that, for example, the baroque composer J. S. Bach was at a peak in the 1730s, whereas German architecture had meanwhile already achieved a distinct new phase of lightness and grace deemed rococo, as epitomized in the famous Wieskirche in Bavaria. In poetry, the successful introduction of Milton by the religious camp by the early eighteenth century diverted attention from the native baroque grandiloquence. In any case, the shadows and pathos of the baroque proper are missing from Brockes's prolix and flamboyant cosmological hymn of the 1720s, *Irdisches Vergnügen in Gott*, celebrating theodicy. Even though the heroic tensions that the baroque cultivated are gone, nonetheless the radiance of Marino's secular vision of the universe in the *Adone* (1624 ff.) still survives in the miracles, large and small, painted by Brockes in intense rococo colors.

The rise of an additional debate concerning Mannerism demonstrates the fecundity of German scholarship in the field of sixteenth- and seventeenth-century studies. It also shows how stylistic and thematological definitions could readily be interchanged with categories of cultural history.

II

Sixteenth-century theorists such as Vasari were conscious of the evolution of Renaissance art, which had come about through brilliant additions. Originally the term "manner" (*maniera*) was associated with style itself, represented by culminating geniuses such as Michelangelo, who pushed Renaissance ideas to their limits. Later it became pejorative, signifying a stilted or failed use of means, something "mannered" rather than truly sophisticated and elegant. Hence when, like baroque, Mannerism was transposed from the visual arts to literature, it kept the basic sense of the deliberate breaking of rules—rules deduced from classical art and prevailing in the Renaissance proper. But the modern use of Mannerism instead of baroque for a stylistic type occurring throughout seventeenth-century literature and beyond has tended, in German criticism, to be linked with the theory of cultural crisis.

This negative approach derives mainly from the tenets put forth by Curtius in his seminal book *Europäische Literatur und lateinisches Mittelalter* (16). Curtius proposed emptying the term mannerist of its specific art-historical content and applying it to any period as a common denominator for all literary tendencies opposed to "classical," whether appearing before, during, or after a major moment of classicism. He also proposed substituting Mannerism for baroque, which he felt was too vague and dubious as a period concept. Instead, Mannerism would serve to designate the aberrant or diseased strains of literature that flourished starting in the late Renaissance, but also in ancient authors such as Seneca, in certain medieval writings, and in modern times. Certain literary techniques and figures were presumed to be negative analogues of foreshortening, exaggeration, dramatization, emotional heightening, and irony in the visual arts. Curtius envisioned a process in which the privileged moments of ideal classicism, evidencing harmony and serenity, tended to give way to regularized norms upheld by academicians. Through too great reliance on rhetoric, normative classicism supposedly then was predisposed to spawn Mannerism as a reaction to obsession with formalistic matters.

Curtius's disciple Hocke next worked out, in two influential books (33, 34), a cultural explanation for artistic Mannerism, with ethical ramifications. Literary documents, in his view, offered a key to characteristics of the "manneristic type" of *homo europeus*, in a "specific intellectual history" of the "irregular," "disharmonious," "problematic," "subjective, heterodox, nonconformist." Tracing Mannerism back to the polarity of the Asian and Attic styles and seeing its recurrence in such modern writers as Mallarmé and Joyce, Hocke nonetheless conceded the existence of baroque art as a variant "mixed form" in moments when Mannerism and classicism meet.

Hauser (28), however, rejected Curtius's and Hocke's premise of periodicity in favor of a sociological thesis of an epochal breakthrough coincident with the inroads of early capitalism; the altered conditions of existence were reflected in a "psychology of alienation." The arguments and selections in Henniger's comparative anthology *Beispiele manieristischer Lyrik* (31) illustrate the narrow base of the "anthropological" counterpart to the Marxist thesis of alienation. About one-third of the poems derive from Góngora and Marino, namesake exemplars of distinct styles, the latter more widely influential in Europe. Another third are written by just two exemplars of the English metaphysicals, Donne and Marvell; the annexing of a few poems by Scève, Adimari, and Sor Juana maintains the historical focus on the ending sixteenth and early seventeenth centuries. The complementary German third consists of Nürnberg and Silesian poets of the mid- to late-seventeenth century (Klaj, Birken, Greiffenberg, Kuhlmann, Lohenstein, Hofmannswaldau). Henniger associates them with the Romanic and British authors in thematic clusters common to so many anthologies of the baroque because he accepts the Curtius-Hocke thesis of the broad oppositions Renaissance-Mannerism and Classicism-Romanticism as crucial stages in Western development. But for him Mannerism acquires the glamor of spiritual striving. Although again repressed by bourgeois ideals during the Enlightenment, Mannerism returns in a new form as Romanticism; then, in turn, Romanticism is repressed or shouldered aside by nineteenth-century Realism. But Henniger contends that the mannerist-romantic impulses recur as the central impulses of modern literature, flowing back mainly through such channels as Decadence and Symbolism in the Romanic nations.

Once Croce (15) had extended the inquiry, Italian scholarship proceeded as in Germany to participate in the general debate over the meaning and relative merits of baroque and mannerist. Thus it was appropriate that the Accademia dei Licei sponsored and published the proceedings (42) of an international congress in Rome in 1960 on Mannerism, baroque, and rococo, bringing together experts in the fine arts, literature, and music; notable critics such as Weise, Raimondi, and Praz sorted out the issues as applicable to Italy and other nations, but it is clear that the interpretations of particular authors or aspects of authors often stand in contradiction. An ambivalent figure such as Tasso is assigned variously to classicism, baroque, and Mannerism according to his apparent devotion to rules or use of particular means (e.g., elaborate conceits, hyperbole) in specific works, and the same problem obtains in the fine arts regarding the "phases" of Michelangelo.

While some theoreticians appropriate authors to bolster the

prestige of their preferred term, others invent further subdivisions to account for the richness of the age. For example, Sypher (71) has proposed not only the acceptance of a period of Mannerism intervening between Renaissance and baroque, but also a late baroque as the transitional period to a neoclassicism. German criticism, as noted, seems to stand virtually alone in entertaining a rather well defined concept of a rococo period between baroque and classicism. In the Romanic literatures, however, Hatzfeld (26) discerns four successive subperiods and stylistic complexes — Renaissance, Mannerism, baroque, and baroquism, the last a late baroque — occurring in different time waves from nation to nation. It is difficult to see how one could label the diverse English Restoration and Augustan period "baroquist"; however, figures such as Dryden certainly fit the general rubric of a neoclassicism still tinged with baroque traits, yet often exhibiting the moralizing sentimentalism of the early Enlightenment. Hatzfeld has also tried to extend the German concept of the rococo as a literary term specifically to the times of Louis XV, finding equivalent French aspects for the humanized softened art after the baroque.

More recent comparatist scholarship has tended to settle on one of three views of Mannerism. Mirollo (46) has complained against the inadequacy of certain national terms (e.g., the English hodgepodge of metaphysical, Ramist,* Tribe of Ben [Jonson], Elizabethan) or of European terms (e.g., Renaissance often loosely applied to Italy after mid-sixteenth century, to France after the Pléiade, to Spain after Garcilaso). He believes that in reaching a near consensus on the baroque as a more emotional, emphatic recapitulation of the Renaissance, many critics have transferred to the term Mannerism the negative features of alleged preciosity and complexity once attached to baroque. But it still remains necessary to distinguish good from bad mannerist works, if the response to "ideal classical values" of "order, symmetry, balance, clarity, and restraint . . . by reveling in excessive verbal artifice and complex meaning" is itself traditional since antiquity. He proposes using "mannered" for mere reflexive imitation of classical sources or exaggeration of previous rhetorical manners, mere stylish aberration; but "mannerist" for the deeper responses to felt crisis in the arts. This kind of discrimination would have to be applied to specific works, rather than authors or decades.

---

*Follower of Ramus, i.e., Pierre de la Ramée (1515-72), who was famous as an adversary of Aristotle and scholasticism and wrote *Dialectique* (1555).

The second view, articulated by Shearman (65), posits that rather than expressing anxiety and strain, mannerist art was a striving for elegant refinement and represented the aestheticism of a high moment in civilization when writers and artists delighted in experiment and artifice, seeking "grace" (*grazia*). The third view, represented by Warnke (77), suggests that since Mannerism "does not designate a clearly discernible literary period intervening between Renaissance and Baroque," we should restrict mannerist to label "one tendency found recurrently throughout the Baroque." This stylistic option, Mannerism — "the spare, witty, intellectual, paradoxical trend typified by Donne, Herbert, Marvell, Sponde, Quevedo, Huygens, and Fleming," also by "Webster, Gracián, Thomas Browne, Pascal, and the early Corneille" — contrasts with the "quintessential" or "high" baroque option — "the ornate, exclamatory, emotional, and extravagant trend typified by Crashaw, Gryphius, Marino, d'Aubigné, Góngora, and Vondel." Spahr (67) maintains a comparable distinction with respect to German letters.

Mirollo is willing to concede considerable substance to the viewpoint of German Expressionism, promoted by Hauser, Sypher, and others, that elements of a religious, political, intellectual, and social crisis contributed to the phenomena of mannerist art and literature. He cites from Hauser the key words "tension, anxiety, ambiguity, neurosis, strain, discord," which seem at times "prophetic anticipations of the abstract art of the twentieth century." Marxist criticism has readily adapted the favorite Western thematics of crisis to serve a theory according to which the first stages of capitalism and the rise of competitive nation states were reflected in the troubled art and writing after the climax of the medieval system and feudalism in the Renaissance. This framework is elaborated by Bahner (3). Very little hard positivistic analysis of the correlation of social milieux and means in Germany in the Renaissance and baroque has yet been achieved with respect to literary life. However, the way has been pointed by Martino (44) in his study of the transformations of the reading public, the production and distribution of books, the influence of dominant social strata, and variations from region to region, in connection with the larger patterns of generic and thematic interests.

As mentioned, an antiromantic British critic, Hulme, saw behind the aberrant phenomena of Modernism explicitly the impulses of Romanticism, itself a yet more virulent and degenerate wave of "Humanism" (i.e., of the crucial break toward secularism); other conservative thinkers of the turn of the century — Babbitt, Eliot, etc. — could be cited in similar vein. Kermode (37) has eloquently demonstrated that certain "traditional" Modernists were trying to restate and rescue the Western heritage in the face of a perceived crisis for civilization, while modern art at large directly exhibited the accelerated disintegration of common values. In a more recent examination of the pathway since Virgil, over which cultural piety has survived in layers of accommodative reconstitution of the "imperial" heritage, Kermode (38) argues that Milton finally represents the pursuit of revolutionary particularism.

German critics have often associated with Mannerism and baroque the radical social and stylistic impulses of Expressionism after the wrenching catastrophe of the Great War (41). The further trauma of Nazism and World War II has revived this thesis of parallels in the situation of writers during the prolonged turmoil of the Reformation, Thirty Years War, and civil wars lasting to mid-seventeenth century, and that of the Romantics undergoing the epochal upheaval of the French Revolution and of Modernists in a time of universal war and revolution.

III

On the basis of Vickers's claim (75) of a far longer tradition of rhetoric stretching from the Renaissance to the eighteenth century, one may well question the thesis that Romanticism recapitulated Mannerism. At least, it is far from clear that Mannerism was striving for a breakdown of distinct genres, even though the central principle of *ingenium* today suggests an earlier version of Romantic supergeneric imagination. If all writers of the late sixteenth and seventeenth centuries were trained in core subjects of rhetoric, then mannerist experiments and elaborations could have arisen through a natural process of exhausting the more central formulae and craving variant figures and vocabulary. Tuve (74) has suggested that the Ramian antipathy for Cicero and Aristotle during the sixteenth century and the emphasis on the invention of new figures current in England, especially at Cambridge University, were a stimulus for the rugged intellectual line that at once characterizes a metaphysical poem. Boase (7) reiterates the idea of an anti-Ciceronian or Senecan movement in prose styles, starting with Ramus and spreading even more widely by 1600 through the influence of Lipsius on the vernacular language at large. Curtius (16) reserves special admiration for the originality of Gracián as the first theoretician to declare the system of ancient rhetoric insufficient and to attempt replacing it with the gamesmanship of wit.

Barner (4) believes that certain insights of Nietzsche offer a fresh start, permitting us to supersede the German Classical tradition—the doctrine that art should be organic and mimetic—and to accept the devising of artifices as a profound human urge with its own laws. From Nietzsche, one arrives again at a view of the human being as a rhetorical creature, using language instrumentally. The approach to the baroque via rhetoric is more directly consonant, too, with the training and attitudes of sixteenth- and seventeenth-century writers. Thus we are liberated to judge according to the modern reality of having witnessed a tumultuous series of revisionary waves in art since the nineteenth century, and we do not fall into the error of blindly applying criteria (such as "organic" cohesion) of the Goethean age as if they possess some normative validity, but again pay closer attention to original baroque poetics. Barner sees four principal virtues in this change of course: In the first place, the identification of rhetorical structures in baroque theory and practice is compatible with reception aesthetics and a search for sociological clues; in fact, the analysis of possible "levels" or segments of the audience cannot dispense with such primary discriminations of the habits and modes of communication. In the second place, such discriminations often are specifically compatible with Marxian identifications on a formalistic plane—at least before one imposes any ideological interpretation of habits and modes as "reflections" of a hypothetical sociocultural reality. In the third place, description according to rhetorical elements obviates problems of rigid periodization, e.g., the problem of simultaneity or sequential appearance of traits in one figure or moment. And so, in the fourth place, the approach through rhetoric allows "vertical" (diachronic), as well as "horizontal" (synchronic), comparisons within and among nations; it is more adequate for coping with the actual complexities of intellectual life and artistic creation.

Buck (9) has argued in a similar vein that an approach to the baroque through rhetoric will help complete a longer-range process of theoretical revision. Although Romantic aesthetics did much to loosen the grip of older genre concepts, these were to a great extent still carried over from classicism in the surviving normative fixation on the triad "epic," "drama," and "lyric" but are finally being relegated to a vaster scheme. The fading quarrel of the ancients and moderns stems, in Buck's view, from the historical logic of Renaissance art as "rebirth," a renewal that finally altered the vernaculars, too, and raised them to a stature rivaling that of revered ancient models. In the maturing Renaissance, to the dominant polar principles *delectare* (delight) and *docere* (teach) was added again the ancient third principle, *movere* (move). The progressive sentimentalization of human existence understood to be under the power of Time, consciousness of which the Renaissance keenly awakened, culminated in baroque pathos.

In a complicated interaction of these factors, Buck observes, Renaissance writers pursued some tempting implications of the role of the poetic renewer who was participating in the emergence out of the muddle and error of the past. Renaissance syncretism and esoterics had already worked up considerable materials, and the existence of a newer range of motifs and formal mastery of them fed the cultivation of deliberate "obscurity" as the hallmark of elevated complexity, poetic worthiness. This momentum provided sufficient logic for imitation and appeal to sophistication. A concomitant expectation of intellectual capacity on the part of readers asserted the ideal social rank of all participants in the creation and appreciation of the new high art. This is self-evident, for example, in baroque dramas demanding quick recognition of generic features from multiple realms that are openly internalized in the work itself, most notably in the device of the play-in-the-play (4, 12, 21, 51). Beginning with the imperative to produce a probable or verisimilar art, the maker of this rival order was regarded in a classical way as a channel of knowledge and even wisdom, the *doctus poeta*. Inevitably, the exalted Renaissance role of the *vates*, a priestlike maker of "dark conceits," would lead toward the *genius* theory of the later eighteenth century. But in retrospect, as we know, the later role would be only selectively bestowed on giants such as Ariosto, Shakespeare, and Cervantes, since intervening doctrines of "naturalness" made most earlier authors less acceptable to the eighteenth century.

As Buck points out, however, one of the most significant experiences of the baroque proper was the reaction to, and digestion of, newer literary phenomena that travestied outmoded literature or strained the neater neoclassical boundaries of genres. Not least among these triumphs were Renaissance works such as Ariosto's pseudoromance *Orlando furioso*, to which newer designations—baroque, grotesque—became applied very early. Coping with the nature of new kinds of writing—the prose "romains," the "novella," the "tragicomoedia," etc.—had a liberating impact on the practice of great writers, not just on theoreticians. Besides the voluminous early discourses of learned societies in Italy on the attributes of modern classics (e.g., of Dante, Petrarch, Boccaccio), we have the thorough airing of these questions internally in popular works of stature (e.g., *Don Quijote*) in the core decades of the baroque. Before the eighteenth century, there was greater use of Aristotle's rhetoric than his poetic; the baroque aesthetics of *ingenium* stressed discovery and invention, freed of the constraints of ordinary logic, and evolved an aesthetic nonrational basis for elitist taste. More recent investigations of the appeal of a combinatory art to many writers in the German tradition and the working out of baroque speculations about a calculus of language in Romantic and Symbolist versions indeed suggest the merit of a fresh look at the serious interest in "artifice" as a surviving impulse from pre-Goethean times (52).

There is motive enough to turn aside from the abstractions of ideological approaches, if one accepts the observation by Barner that a direct linkage exists between the neglected rhetorical foundation of the baroque and its favorite thematics—e.g., the world as theater, man as a political animal. Of course, the implication is that in the baroque it was the acceptance of man as a "rhetorical" creature, maker of artifices and masks, which prompted a surge of poetic interpretations, because the intensity of this insight somehow altered the nature of the world. If one combines Barner's (Nietzschean) thesis of a radical acceptance of artifice with the historical evidence of a qualitative explosion of scientific knowledge in the baroque, then it does not seem farfetched that in the seventeenth century people took seriously poetic statements about the dislocation of man from his assured place established by the older cosmology and religious belief. By the same token, though, we must pay serious attention to statements about divine, cosmological, and human order that evidence the creation of a positive world view, as reflected eventually in Germany in Leibniz's philosophy of theodicy. In addition, the plethora of seemingly lesser forms—the epigram, letter, sermon, speech, mask, pastoral, etc., ignored when later generations lost sight of the centrality of rhetoric and concentrated on a three-branched schema—acquire new significance, because older rhetorical poetics did indeed recognize and describe them. Hence Barner and Buck are closer to Curtius as analysts of stylistic impetus, because they take a longer view of what "literature" has actually been in practice.

Defining the effective relationship of German writing both to ancient classical and to contemporaneous Romanic (and also coeval northern) writing is indispensable to a proper understanding. The rhetorical approach can thereby clarify whether indeed there is some crucial European common denominator, such as the apparently universal interest in "acuity" (what Opitz calls *Scharfsinnigkeit*). In a magisterial survey published two years before Curtius's major book, Wellek (79) proposed

that "most baroque poets live with a world picture suggested by traditional Christian gradualism, and have found an aesthetic method where
the imagery and the figures link seemingly alien, discontinuous spheres."
The attempt to define a common basis for such an attitude has been the
ruling obsession of German baroque scholarship to date. American com-
paratists have sought to expand the scope of such investigations to embrace the Scandinavian and Slavic worlds, too. The recent anthology
with a monographic introduction prepared by Segel (64) lends some
credence to Friedrich's (20) claim of a baroque culture stretching from
the Atlantic into the Slavic area in the decades 1610-60.

NOTES AND SELECTED BIBLIOGRAPHY

Secondary Literature

1. Anger, Alfred. *Literarisches Rokoko*. Stuttgart: Metzler, 1962.
2. Angyal, Andreas. *Die slawische Barockwelt*. Leipzig: Seemann, 1961.
3. Bahner, Werner. *Renaissance, Barock, Aufklärung: Epochen- und Periodisierungsfragen*. Berlin: Akademie Verlag, 1976.
4. Barner, Wilfried. *Barockrhetorik: Untersuchungen zu ihren geschicht-lichen Grundlagen*. Tübingen: Niemeyer, 1970.
5. ——. *Der literarische Barockbegriff*. Darmstadt: Wissenschaftliche Buchgesellschaft, 1975.
6. Benjamin, Walter. *Ursprung des deutschen Trauerspiels*. Berlin: Ernst Rowohlt, 1928; rpt. Frankfurt a.M.: Suhrkamp, 1969.
7. Boase, A. M. "The Definition of Mannerism." In *Proceedings of the Third Congress of the International Comparative Literature Association*. The Hague: Mouton, 1962, pp. 143-55.
8. Brauneck, Manfred. "Deutsche Literatur des 17. Jahrhunderts—Revision eines Epochenbildes: Ein Forschungsbericht 1945-1970." *Deutsche Viertel-jahrsschrift für Literaturwissenschaft und Geistesgeschichte*, 45, Sonder-heft (1971), 378-468.
9. Buck, August. *Renaissance und Barock*. 2 vols. Frankfurt a.M.: Akademische Verlagsgesellschaft Athenaion, 1972.
10. Buffum, Imbrie. *Studies in the Baroque from Montaigne to Rotrou*. New Haven, Conn.: Yale University Press, 1957.
11. Butler, Philip. *Classicisme et Baroque dans l'oeuvre de Racine*. Paris: Nizet, 1959.
12. Cioranescu, Alejandro. *El Barroco; o, el descubrimiento del drama*. La Laguna de Tenerife: Universidad de La Laguna, 1957.
13. Coutinho, Afrânio. *Aspectos da literatura barroca*. Rio de Janeiro: [n.p.], 1950.

14. Croce, Benedetto. *Der Begriff des Barock: Die Gegenreformation.* Zürich: Rasch, 1925.

15. ———. *Storia della età baròcca in Italia: Pensiero, poesia, e letteratura, vita morale.* Bari: G. Laterza, 1929.

16. Curtius, Ernst Robert. *Europäische Literatur und lateinisches Mittelalter.* Bern: Francke, 1948. Transl.: *European Literature and the Latin Middle Ages.* New York: Harper, 1953.

17. Cysarz, Herbert. *Deutsche Barockdichtung: Renaissance, Barock, Rokoko.* Leipzig: H. Haessel, 1924.

18. Daniells, Roy. *Milton, Mannerism and Baroque.* Toronto: University of Toronto Press, 1964.

19. *L'Esprit Créateur*, 1 (1961). Special number on "Poetry of the Baroque Age."

20. Friedrich, Carl Joachim. *The Age of the Baroque, 1610–1660.* New York: Harper, 1952.

21. Fumaroli, Marc, ed. *Revue des Sciences Humaines*, 37 (1972). Special number on "Théâtre dans le théâtre."

22. Gillespie, Gerald. *German Baroque Poetry.* New York: Twayne, 1971.

23. Graham, Victor E. "Aspects du maniérisme et du baroque en littérature." *Neohelicon*, 3 (1976), 361–74.

24. Grierson, Herbert J. C. *Metaphysical Lyrics and Poems of the Seventeenth Century, Donne to Butler.* Oxford: Clarendon, 1921.

25. Hatzfeld, Helmut. "The Baroque from the Viewpoint of the Literary Historian." *Journal of Aesthetics and Art Criticism*, 14 (1955–56), 156–64.

26. ———. *Estudios sobre el Barroco.* 2nd ed. Madrid: Editorial Gredos, 1966.

27. ———. "Problems of the Baroque in 1975." *Thesaurus*, 30 (1975), 209–24.

28. Hauser, Arnold. *Der Manierismus: Die Krise der Renaissance und der Ursprung der modernen Kunst.* München: Beck, 1964. Transl.: *Mannerism: The Crisis of the Renaissance and the Origin of Modern Art.* 2 vols. New York: Knopf, 1965.

29. Haydn, Hiram. *The Counter-Renaissance.* New York: Scribner, 1950.

30. Hazard, Paul. *La crise de la conscience européenne, 1680–1715.* Paris: Bovin, 1935. Transl.: *The European Mind: The Critical Years, 1680–1715.* New Haven, Conn.: Yale University Press, 1953.

31. Henniger, Gerd. *Beispiele manieristischer Lyrik.* München: Deutscher Taschenbuch Verlag, 1970.

32. Heusser, Nelly. *Barock und Romantik: Versuch einer vergleichenden Darstellung.* Frauenfeld: Huber, 1942.

33. Hocke, Gustav René. *Manierismus in der Literatur: Sprach-Alchimie und esoterische Kombinationskunst. Beiträge zur vergleichenden europäischen Literaturgeschichte.* Hamburg: Rowohlt, 1959.

34. ———. *Die Welt als Labyrinth, Manier und Manie in der europäischen Kunst: Beiträge zur Ikonographie und Formgeschichte der europäischen Kunst von 1520 bis 1650 und der Gegenwart.* Hamburg: Rowohlt, 1957.

35. Jacquot, Jean, ed. *Le théâtre tragique*. Paris: CNRS, 1962.

36. Jantz, Harold. "German Baroque Literature." *Modern Language Notes*, 77 (1962), 398–410.

37. Kermode, Frank. *The Sense of an Ending*. New York: Oxford, 1967.

38. ——. *The Classic*. London: Faber, 1973.

39. Lebègue, Raymond. *La tragédie française de la Renaissance*. Bruxelles: Office de publicité, 1944.

40. Leishman, James Blair. *The Metaphysical Poets: Donne, Herbert, Vaughan, Traherne*. Oxford: Clarendon, 1934.

41. Luther, Gisela. *Barocker Expressionismus? Zur Problematik der Beziehung zwischen der Bildlichkeit expressionistischer und barocker Lyrik*. The Hague: Mouton, 1969.

42. *Manierismo, baròcco, rococò: Concetti e termini*. Roma: Accademia Nazionale dei Licei, 1962. Includes among other notable articles: Georg Weise, "Storia del termine 'Manierismo,' " pp. 27–38; Ezio Raimondi, "Per la nozione di Manierismo letterario," pp. 57–79; Giovanni Getto, "Il Baròcco in Italia," pp. 81–103; Marcel Raymond, "Le Baroque littéraire française," pp. 107–26; Mario Praz, "Il Baròcco in Inghilterra," pp. 129–46; Oreste Macrì, "La storiografia sul Baròcco letterario spagnolo," pp. 149–98; Victor-Lucien Tapié, "Baroque slave et d'Europe centrale," pp. 353–58.

43. Maravall, José Antonio. *La cultura del Barroco: análisis de una estructura histórica*. Barcelona: Editorial Ariel, 1975.

44. Martino, Alberto. "Barockpoesie, Publikum und Verbürgerlichung der literarischen Intelligenz." *Internationales Archiv für Sozialgeschichte der deutschen Literatur*, 1 (1976), 107–45.

45. Martz, Louis L. *The Poetry of Meditation: A Study of English Religious Literature of the Seventeenth Century*. New Haven, Conn.: Yale University Press, 1954.

46. *The Meaning of Mannerism*, F. W. Robinson and S. G. Nichols, eds. Hanover, N.H.: University Press of New England, 1972. Includes among other notable articles: James V. Mirollo, "The Mannered and the Mannerist in Late Renaissance Literature," pp. 7–24; Henri Zerner, "Observations on the Use of the Concept of Mannerism," pp. 105–21.

47. Mirollo, James V. *The Poet of the Marvelous: Giambattista Marino*. New York: Columbia University Press, 1963.

48. Mourgues, Odette de. *Metaphysical, Baroque and Précieux Poetry*. Oxford: Clarendon, 1953.

49. Müller, Richard. *Dichtung und bildende Kunst im Zeitalter des deutschen Barock*. Frauenfeld: Huber, 1937.

50. Nelson, Lowry. *Baroque Lyric Poetry*. New Haven, Conn.: Yale University Press, 1961.

51. Nelson, Robert J. *Play within a Play: The Dramatist's Conception of His*

Art, Shakespeare to Anouilh. New Haven, Conn.: Yale University Press, 1958.

52. Neubauer, John. *Symbolismus und symbolische Logik: Die Idee der ars combinatoria in der Entwicklung der modernen Dichtung*. München: Wilhelm Fink, 1978.

53. Orozco, Emilio Diaz. *Manierismo y barroco*. Madrid: Ediciones Cátedra, 1979.

54. d'Ors, Eugenio. *Lo barroco*. Madrid: Aguilar, 1944.

55. Petersson, Robert T. *The Art of Ecstasy: Teresa, Bernini, and Crashaw*. New York: Atheneum, 1970.

56. Raymond, Marcel, ed. *La poésie française et le maniérisme 1546–1610*. Genève: Droz, 1971.

57. *Renaissance, Maniérisme, Baroque*. Actes du XIe stage international de Tours. Paris: Vrin, 1972.

58. *Revue des Sciences Humaines*, 55–56 (1949). Special number on the baroque.

59. Reynold, Gonzague de. *Synthèse du XVIIe siècle: La France classique et l'Europe baroque*. Paris: Conquistador, 1962.

60. Rousset, Jean. *Anthologie de la poésie baroque*. Paris: Colin, 1961.

61. ——. "Lé définition du term 'Baroque.' " In *Proceedings of the Third Congress of the International Comparative Literature Association*. The Hague: Mouton, 1962, pp. 167–78.

62. ——. *La littérature de l'âge baroque en France: Circé et le paon*. Paris: J. Corti, 1953.

63. Sayce, R. A. "The Use of the Term Baroque in French Literary History." *Comparative Literature*, 10 (1958), 246–53.

64. Segel, Harold B. *The Baroque Poem: A Comparative Survey*. New York: Dutton, 1974.

65. Shearman, John. *Mannerism*. Hammondsport: Penguin, 1967.

66. Skrine, Peter N. *The Baroque: Literature and Culture in Seventeenth-Century Europe*. London: Methuen, 1978.

67. Spahr, Blake L. "Baroque and Mannerism: Epoch and Style." *Colloquia Germanica*, 1 (1967), 78–100.

68. Spitz, Lewis W. "The Course of German Humanism." In *Itinerarium Italicum: Festschrift für Paul Oskar Kristeller*. Leiden: Brill, 1975, pp. 371–436.

69. Spitzer, Leo. "El barroco español." *Boletín del Instituto de Investigaciones Históricas*, 28 (1944), 17–30.

70. Strich, Fritz. "Der lyrische Stil des siebzehnten Jahrhunderts." In *Abhandlungen zur deutschen Literaturgeschichte: Fritz Muncker zum 60. Geburtstage*. München: Beck, 1916, pp. 21–53.

71. Sypher, Wylie. *Four Stages of Renaissance Style: Transformations in Art and Literature, 1400–1700*. New York: Doubleday, 1955.

72. Tapié, Victor-Lucien. *Le Baroque*. Paris: Presses Universitaires de France, 1961. Transl.: *The Age of Grandeur: Baroque Art and Architecture*. New York: Grove Press, 1960.

73. Tisch, J. Hermann, "Baroque." In *Periods in German Literature*, J. M. Ritchie, ed. London: Oswald Wolff, 1968, pp. 17-39.

74. Tuve, Rosemond. *Elizabethan and Metaphysical Imagery: Renaissance Poetic and Twentieth-Century Critics*. Chicago: University of Chicago Press, 1947.

75. Vickers, Brian. *Classical Rhetoric in English Prose*. New York: St. Martin's Press, 1970.

76. Warnke, Frank. *European Metaphysical Poetry*. New Haven, Conn.: Yale University Press, 1961.

77. ——. *Versions of Baroque: European Literature in the Seventeenth Century*. New Haven, Conn.: Yale University Press, 1972.

78. Warren, Austin. *Richard Crashaw: A Study in Baroque Sensibility*. Baton Rouge: Louisiana State University Press, 1939.

79. Wellek, René. "The Concept of Baroque in Literary Scholarship." *Journal of Aesthetics and Art Criticism*, 5 (1946), 77-97. Rpt. in *Concepts of Criticism*. New Haven, Conn.: Yale University Press, 1963.

2

Poetic Theory
and Logical Tradition

Friedrich Gaede

According to G. P. Harsdörffer, human reason consists of creative power, memory, and the ability to judge, and each of the three refers to one of the three forms of artistic expression: painting, music, and poetry. In Harsdörffer's view painting depends on creation, music on memory, and poetry completely on the faculty of judgment: "Die Urtheilskraft wird vereinbaret mit der Poeterey / welche nach Ihrer Übertrefflichkeit die Dichtkunst benamet werden mag. . . . Gebrauchet sich der mündlichen und schriftlichen Anzeig / zu zeiten auch der Deutungen und Geberden: Bestehend in einem kalten und trokknen Gehirn / wie die Alten haben / und hat ihren Sitz mitten in dem Haubt."[1] Harsdörffer's equation of poetry and faculty of judgment does not represent a personal point of view: rather, he makes explicit what has to be regarded as the implied main principle of baroque literature and poetics in general. The principle appears—and often hides itself—in a multitude of aspects.

Faculty of judgment—also called *iudicium*—has traditionally been regarded as the author's ability adequately to apply the principles of the *aptum*, i.e., to observe the correspondence of literary genres to characters, of characters to the style of their speech, etc. This important function of the *iudicium* has not escaped scholarly interest.[2] As a corrective of the poetic *ingenium* and as a guardian over the rules of the *aptum*, the *iudicium* is only the tip of an iceberg. The real weight that the faculty of judgment has for the literary development since the Renaissance remains

25

hidden as long as the understanding of the *iudicium* is only based on the definitions that appeared in the documents of the poetical and rhetorical tradition.[3] With few exceptions these definitions do not explain or even refer to the complex nature of the *iudicium*, which can only be understood with the help of contemporary documents of the logical tradition.

Connecting the discipline of poetics with the discipline of logic is justified not only by the fact that the *iudicium* is one of the three *operationes mentis* in classical logic, but also because the disciplines of poetics, rhetoric, and logic have been interrelated since Aristotle. In recent years Wilbur S. Howell has demonstrated that the history of literary, rhetorical, and logical theories have to be seen as a unity.[4] Howell's intention to combat the major current critical attitude, which excludes rhetoric and logic from literary theory, ought to be supported. But it should also be seen that the three disciplines are not on an equal footing. The discipline of logic is not just one of the three theories of communication. It also fulfills the function of epistemology before Kant. Therefore, the close historical relationship between the discipline of logic and literary theory enables us not only to understand that the faculty of judgment plays an important role in the literary development between the Renaissance and Enlightenment, but also to understand why it plays this kind of role.

Harsdörffer's equation of poetry and the faculty of judgment is anticipated in the pioneer work of modern literary theory, J. C. Scaliger's *Poetices Libri Septem* (1561), and in the Roman tradition of rhetoric and poetics on which Scaliger's work is based. Since all aspects—including the concept of imitation—of Horace's *Ars Poetica* refer to the principle of judgment, this principle provides the link between the Roman and the modern literary theories.[5] Quintilian wrote: "For my own part I do not believe that invention can exist apart from judgment. . . .judgment is inextricably mingled with the first three departments of rhetoric"[6] (i.e., with *inventio*, *dispositio*, and *elocutio*). Accordingly, Scaliger said: "Judicium has to be applied in two ways: first, it helps one to select the best for imitation; secondly, it helps one to criticize what he has created as if it would be alien to him."[7]

As stated by Scaliger and Roman writers, an author who is inventing is applying his judgment. When explaining his concept of imitation, Scaliger reveals how the inventing judgment works. He refers to the activities of painters and sculptors: "Sculptors and those who use colour take their ideas from things themselves, of which they imitate the lines, light, shade, and relief. Whatever they find most excellent in everything, they carry over from many things into one of their works."[8] By finding out and carrying over "the most excellent" of a thing, the artists are analyzing it. Isolating a single element out of a totality of elements, they abstract and proceed in the same way one does with a singular proposition: e.g., in statements like "this tree is green" or "Peter is a student," the predicate isolates one aspect of the totality of aspects inherent to the subject of the proposition. The result of this kind of abstracting or analyzing approach, the creation that is built out of the isolated and carried-over elements, is of an abstract-ideal nature.

Scaliger's concept of invention and imitation reflects the contemporary mode of logical reasoning, itself a reflection of the metaphysical situation of the time. From the Renaissance to the early Enlightenment, philosophers who wrote on logic emphasized the role of the proposition—mostly at the expense of the syllogism. Already serving as a basis of Petrus Ramus's system of argumentation, the proposition is in Locke's view still the foundation of truth: "Truth then, seems to me . . . to signify nothing but the joining or separating of Signs, as the Things signified by them do agree or disagree one with another. The joining and separating of signs here meant is what by another name we call proposition. So that truth properly belongs only to proposition."[9] Antoine Arnauld therefore summarizes the basic ideas of the logicians of his epoch when he writes: "Our principal task is to train the judgment, rendering it as exact as we can. To this end the greatest part of our studies should be devoted."[10]

By connecting the concept of truth with that of judgment, the modern philosophers refer to that ancient philosophy which also focuses its epistemological interest on the nature and function of the proposition, namely, Stoicism. This connection gives an initial explanation of why the period of Renaissance and baroque is also the period of Neostoicism—and why the literary development of this time constitutes the "Roman phase" of modern European literature, which is determined rather by Horatian concepts than by Aristotelian principles. For the Stoics the faculty of judgment is not only an epistemological problem; it is also the focal point of their ethics. The Stoic concept of virtue and wisdom is based on the principle of the proposition. The virtuous and the wise are qualified by their faculty of judgment. Seneca wrote: "Virtue itself is situated in our nobler part, the rational part. And what will that virtue be? A true and never swerving judgment"; and, "The happy man is one who has right judgment."[11] Hegel concluded that this kind of happiness "means nothing more than the feeling of harmony with self."[12] The wise see themselves as free and independent, but it is an abstract freedom which only means the separation of the intellectual self from everything concrete or physical.

Thus, the wise person embodies the Stoic theory of knowledge with its separation of the understanding and the object of the understanding. This separation is the core of the famous tripartite epistemological system according to which the Stoics discern between an empirical thing, the intellectual concept of the same, i.e., the significate, and the words expressing this concept, i.e., the signs. The intellectual concept of the thing, which the Stoics call *Lekton*, is in its complete form a proposition, and since it concerns a particular thing it is a singular proposition.[13] Because of the abstracting nature of any singular proposition, this leads to a situation of paradoxy as G. Watson observed: "The truth was in the Lekton they [the Stoics] said, and the perfect truth consequently requires the perfect Lekton, and this in turn is the perfection of Logos. . . . The paradox of the perfection of Logos is that the perfect Lekton even as unexpected implies selection whereas perfection denies it."[14] Because a singular proposition is always abstracting and unable to express the totality of the object to which it refers, it contradicts by its very nature the intention to depict the object as a whole and to state its "truth." This kind of contradiction has become relevant again in the modern time since the Renaissance because of revived interest in the proposition. The contradiction is reflected upon in all aspects of German baroque literature, e.g., in its antithetical style and in the concept of the world as vanity. The world is vain and cannot contain truth or spirit as long as it is being judged, i.e., as long as the spirit or the understanding of the world and the world itself, as object of the understanding, are separated.

This separation, which is the foundation of an unresolvable contradiction, determines also the main principle of Renaissance and baroque literature, the *ut-pictura-poesis* postulate. The principle has to be regarded as a literary application of the singular judgment. The idea that poetry should be like a picture is another way to express the above-mentioned imitative activity as Scaliger described it and as other authors of poetics repeated it. This imitative activity is in direct opposition to Aristotle's concept of mimesis. Aristotle's concept presupposes his idea of universality and unity. The *ut-pictura-poesis* principle, however, like painting, concerns individual objects only; moreover, it concerns only aspects of the objects. Literary imitation of particular objects can only be pursued by descriptive sentences that are characterized by the main criterion of all singular propositions: because of their abstracting function they cannot reproduce nature as it is, but they can create a *secunda natura* (Scaliger). The intention to systemize the selective process that aims at the second nature leads to the collection of "topoi."[15]

Since the *ut-pictura-poesis* postulate and the system of topoi determine the creative activity of writers during the Renaissance and baroque, the problem of the faculty of judgment must be present in their literary works. Three representative examples from poetry (Opitz), drama (Gryphius), and prose fiction (Grimmelshausen) will demonstrate the problem. The first example is the beginning of a sonnet by Martin Opitz:

> Ein jeder spricht zu mir / dein Lieb ist nicht dergleichen
> Wie du sie zwar beschreibst: ich weiß es warlich nicht /
> Ich bin fast nicht mehr klug; der scharffen Sinnen Liecht
> Vermag gar kaum was weiß und schwartz ist zu erreichen.
> Der so im lieben noch was weiß herauß zu streichen /
> Durch urtheil und verstandt / und kennt auch was gebricht,
> Der liebet noch nicht recht. Wo war ist was man spricht /
> So hat der welcher liebt der sinnen gar kein zeichen /
> Und ist ein lauter Kind . . .[16]

Opitz contrasts two states of mind, that of "being fallen in love" with that of the faculty of judgment. Only discerning reason, which can recognize and work with alternatives (black and white), is able to describe or to write. The lover, however, who is subjected to his passions and has therefore lost his faculty of judgment, cannot describe this situation. He cannot be a poet, and—vice versa—the poet who writes about love cannot be in this state of mind. The ironical self-comment of the poet matches perfectly with the antithetical structure of the sonnet.

In his poem Opitz not only equates—as Harsdörffer does—poetical writing with the faculty of judgment, he also equates the loss of this faculty with dependence upon passions. This originally Stoic alternative of either judgment or passions was revived by Descartes and other modern thinkers and became the basic anthropological assumption in the periods of Renaissance and baroque. In his treatise, *The Passions of the Soul*, Descartes made the judgment a weapon to fight dependence on passions: "That which I call its proper arms consists of the firm and determinate judments respecting the knowledge of good and evil . . . and the most feeble souls of all are those whose will does not thus determine itself to follow certain judgments, but allows itself continually to be carried away by present passions, which, being frequently contrary to one another, draw the will first to one side, then to the other, and, by employing it in striving against itself, place the soul in the most deplorable possible condition."[17]

This concept became the foundation of the drama of the epoch. Gryphius embodied it in the dialectical confrontation of martyr and tyrant. Shakespeare made it into the internal conflicts of heroes such as Othello. Judgment and passions are not simply alternatives: according to the Stoic tradition passion is corrupted Logos.[18] Under the impact of passion reason fails and produces misjudgments which then lead to vicious actions. It is the function of the intriguer to provoke the main characters to such actions by inciting their passions. Those, however, who resist such scheming or other temptations and stick firmly to their judgment are the Neostoic-Protestant heroes such as Gryphius created for his dramas. These heroes prove with their rejection of the world and with their contempt for emotional and physical sufferings the abstractness of their purely intellectual freedom, which is the abstractness of their judgment.

Not only dramatic tensions and actions are based on the principle of judgment. The leitmotif of Germany's most important example of prose fiction in the seventeenth century, *Simplicius Simplicissimus*, expresses the same idea. The statement "Der Wahn betrüget" has to be read: the judgment is deceptive. Judgment as false imagination refers to the proposition that is based on sensual perception. The leitmotif "Der Wahn betrüegt" summarizes the life experience of the novel's hero. On several occasions he finds out that the same empirical phenomenon is evaluated and judged in opposing terms. Grimmelshausen embodies this experience in his allegorical character Baldanders. When Baldanders says "Magst glauben was der Wahrheit ähnlich ist," he repeats what Justus Lipsius already has said about the judgment that is founded on sensual perception: "Der Wahn . . . ist . . . ein unnütz und betrieglich Urtheil . . . hat seinen Ursprung aus dem Leibe, das ist, aus der Erden, derhalben es auch nicht anders als irdisch gesinnet ist."[19] For Lipsius this kind of proposition is a misjudgment, an expression of inconstancy, and has to be opposed by the right judgment, which has its origin "in God" and is as firm as it is constant—and consequently never "baldanders."

Grimmelshausen's novel characteristically emphasizes the questionable application of the judgment rather than the appropriate or firm proposition in the Stoic sense.[20] Grimmelshausen, therefore, applies the sceptical treatment of the proposition—which is to refrain from judgment. One of his most important statements gives the reason: "ich grübelte der Ursach nach warumb doch die Menschliche Urtheil gemeiniglich so betrüglich wären? und hielte darvor / daß weil die blinde Urtheil oder der Menschen Wahn nach der Beschaffenheit deß innerlichen Gemüths passionirten Affecten geschöpft würden / daß sie deßwegen selten eintreffen könnten."[21] This sentence is a key to Grimmelshausen's work because it allows us to refer it to the philosophical background of the time. It is obvious that Grimmelshausen's concept of the judgment as subjective opinion means the misjudgment that is based on passion rather than on reason. Grimmelshausen does not offer the Stoic alternative of the "firm judgment." He is only able to present the sceptic-fideistic solution as it is shown in the sixth book of his *Simplicius Simplicissimus*.

So far two facts have been established: first, the faculty of judgment, or *iudicium*, became the common denominator of Renaissance and baroque thought and literature; secondly, *iudicium* has its origin in the post-Aristotelian time and found its first climax in the world of Roman Stoicism. This provokes the question about the cause of the *iudicium*'s revival in the modern world. The answer is contained in Hegel's comment on the proposition "The judgment is an expression of finitude."[22] The time between Renaissance and Enlightenment is the time of analytical thought or finite reasoning. The triumphal progress of analytical thought is reflected in the renewed and exclusive interest in the proposition. When Arnauld says "Our minds are finite; and blinded by the infinite, they are lost in it,"[23] he is indirectly explaining why he wants to concentrate all his logical efforts on the training of the judgment.

It was, however, Hegel who revealed the basic principles of finite reasoning by being its best critic. According to Hegel, finite reasoning (*Verstandesdenken*) takes a "separating and abstracting attitude towards its objects" by giving its subject matter the form of abstract universality. This is the process of judging or analyzing in general. By judging or analyzing an object, finite reasoning is subjecting it to its principles: the object has to correspond to thought and not the reverse. This means that finite reasoning is not only based on the assumption of a subject-object dualism, but also that, in this dualism, the recognizing subject rather than the recognized object plays the active and dominating part. In Hegel's words: "The finitude of Cognition lies in the presupposition of a world already in existence. . . . Finite Cognition . . . pre-supposes what is distinguished from it to be something already existing and confronting it—to be the various facts of external nature or of consciousness."[24]

Accordingly, poets who apply the *ut-pictura-poesis* postulate do not copy reality as such, but refer to an already existing object such as a historical figure or a work of art which they "depict" by subjecting it to their analyzing or judging activities. By this kind of creation of a *secunda natura* the poet becomes the *alter deus*, a "second god" (Scaliger). This acknowledgment of the poet's judicial subjectivity reflects the subjective foundation of propositional activities in general. Therefore, the main principles of Scaliger's and his followers' poetics cannot be separated from the main principles of contemporary logic or philosophy. There is no *kunst-immanent* development but simply the general development of mind with its philosophical or artistic expressions.

Finite reasoning and its logical consequence—the emphasized faculty of judgment—are present not only in the various applications of the *iudicium* in poetics and literary works but also in the system of poetics as such. This system is of a discriminating nature. It is a sequence of discernments which move from the more general to the more particular by dividing it up. At the end the totality of the literary work disappears behind a collection of single fixations, which then have to be coordinated again. The fact that there has to be *iudicium* to guide this coordination—of topics, characters, genres, etc.—is, therefore, the necessary result of the whole propositional structure of Renaissance and baroque poetics. It begins with the separation of *res* (objects) and *verba* (words), which is followed by the division between the invention of *res* and their disposition. Then *res* are divided into *persona* and *extra persona*, and so on. It is a system of abstraction in the original meaning of the word: dividing and reducing.

In this regard a statement of Opitz reveals the essence of the literary theory of his epoch: "Weil aber die dinge von denen wir schreiben unterschieden sind, als gehöret sich auch zue einem jeglichen ein eigener und von den andern unterschiedener character oder merckzeichen der worte."[25] Opitz's statement, and with it the whole system of baroque poetics, shows what, according to Hegel, is the main function of finite reasoning or "understanding" (*Verstand*): to establish the differences in things. In Hegel's words: "Thought, as Understanding, sticks to the fixity of characters and their distinctness from one another." As far as Opitz is concerned one would have to modify this statement in the following way: poetics, based on understanding, establishes the fixity of characters of literary works and "their distinctness from one another. Every such

limited abstract it treats as having a subsistence and being of its own."[26]
Whether it is a tragedy, comedy, or any other literary genre, it is treated
according to the complete system: the whole genre is reduced to partic-
ulars. For example: "Die Comedie bestehet in schlechtem [schlichtem]
wesen und personen; redet von hochzeiten, gastgeboten, spielen, betrug
und schalckheit der knechte, ruhmrätigen landtsknechten, buhler-
sachen, leichtfertigkeit der jugend, geitze des alters . . ."[27] This kind of
description could be continued infinitely, but a conclusive definition of
the genre that would reveal its essence is lacking. The analytic approach
is unable to seek or find this kind of definition.

The common denominator of the whole poetical system must also
determine the purpose of the literary work as far as this purpose is expressed in the poetics. Scaliger writes: "Imitation, however, is not the
end of poetry, but it is intermediate to the end. The end is the giving of
instruction in pleasurable form. . . . Now is there not one end, and one
only, in philosophical exposition, in oratory, and in the drama? As-
suredly such is the case. All have one and the same end — persuasion. . . . Persuasion, again means that the hearer accepts the words
of the speaker."[28] Thus, poetry is given the same function that we find in
the judicial and in the political speech: the function of influencing and
teaching the audience.

This implies the division between the "case" and the way this case is
talked about. We already know this division as the basic assumption of
finite reasoning, as subject-object dualism. In the tradition of rhetorics
this situation is known as the "dialectical character" of rhetorics, which
implies that there are two opposing views about the same case.[29] This
concerns especially the iudicial use of rhetorics and is present in the an-
tagonism of plaintiff and defending counsel. It is also present in the
political speech and in the rather literary *genus demonstrativum*. A good
example of the latter is Grimmelshausen's *Satyrischer Pilgram*, where
the author says and proves that there is nothing in the world, with the exception of the Lord and the devil, that cannot be praised and condemned at the same time. The opposing views about the same thing or
case are the result of abstract or finite reasoning (*Verstandesdenken*),
since "calling a thing finite is that it has an end, that it exists up to a certain point only, where it comes into contact with, and is limited by, its
other. The finite, therefore, subsists in reference to its other, which is its
negation."[30] It is the singular judgment that ascribes the limited formulae of understanding to the objects. Because the singular judgment is
one-sided by its nature, it provokes the contradicting judgment. The an-

cients already knew about the abstracting function of the judgment—Cicero wrote: "A proposition is a part of a case."[31]

Because rhetorical dialectic, or contradicting propositions about the same case, is the result of finite reasoning, we are now able to understand why rhetorical concepts have so strongly influenced the development of modern poetics since Scaliger. These concepts are influential as long as the principles of finite reasoning, especially the proposition, are dominant. Their influence ends with Leibniz and his omnipotent effect on German theorists and writers of literature in the eighteenth century. Leibniz becomes the critic of analytical thought and of the leading role of the proposition: "Man would be found without direction in the greater part of the arts of his life, if he had nothing to conduct him from the point where certain knowledge fails him. He must often be contented with a simple twilight of probability. The faculty of using this is judgment."[32] With Leibniz begins the twilight of the judgment and, therefore, a new chapter not only of the history of logic but also of the history of literature.[33]

NOTES

1. Georg Philipp Harsdörffer, *Frauenzimmer Gesprächsspiele*, V (Tübingen: Niemeyer, 1969), p. 103.

2. See Joachim Dyck, *Ticht-Kunst* (Bad Homburg: Gehlen, 1966), p. 118; Ludwig Fischer, *Gebundene Rede* (Tübingen: Niemeyer, 1968), p. 204.

3. See Dyck, *Ticht-Kunst*, p. 118.

4. Wilbur Samuel Howell, *Logic and Rhetoric in England, 1500–1700* (Princeton, N.J.: Princeton University Press, 1956); and *Poetics, Rhetoric and Logic* (Ithaca, N.Y., and London: Cornell University Press, 1975).

5. See Friedrich Gaede, *Poetik und Logik—Zu den Grundlagen der literarischen Entwicklung im 17. und 18. Jahrhundert* (Bern and München: Francke, 1978), pp. 38 ff.

6. Quintilian, *The Institutio Oratoria*, I, trans. H. E Butler (London: Heinemann, 1969), 385.

7. Julius Caesar Scaliger, *Poetices Libri Septem* (Stuttgart-Bad Cannstatt: Frommann-Holzboog, 1964), p. 214 (quotation translated by the author).

8. Quoted from Bernard Weinberg, "Scaliger versus Aristotle on Poetics," *Modern Philology*, 39 (1942-43), 349.

9. John Locke, *An Essay concerning Human Understanding*, ed. A. D. Woozley (London and Glasgow: Collins, 1964), p. 354.

10. Antoine Arnauld, *The Art of Thinking*, trans. J. Dickoff and P. James (New York: Bobbs-Merrill, 1964), p. 7.

11. Seneca, *Ad Lucilium Epistulae Morales*, II, trans. R. M. Gummere (London: Heineman, 1930), 93; "On the happy life," in *Moral Essays*, trans. J. W. Basore (London: Heinemann, 1935), p. 115.

12. Georg W. F. Hegel, *Lectures on the History of Philosophy*, trans. E. S. Haldane and F. H. Simson (New York and London: The Humanities Press, 1955), p. 265.

13. See Benson Mates, *Stoic Logic* (Berkeley: University of California Press, 1953), p. 28; and Gerard Watson, *The Stoic Theory of Knowledge* (Belfast: Queen's University Press, 1966), p. 52.

14. Watson, p. 84.

15. See Gaede, *Poetik und Logik*, pp. 42-47.

16. Martin Opitz, *Weltliche Poemata* (1644), II, ed. Erich Trunz (Tübingen: Niemeyer, 1975), p. 380.

17. René Descartes, "The Passions of the Soul," in *The Philosophical Works of Descartes*, I, trans. E. S. Haldane and G. R. T. Ross (London: Cambridge University Press, 1967), p. 354.

18. See Erika Geisenhof, "Die Darstellung der Leidenschaften in den Trauerspielen des Andreas Gryphius" (diss. Heidelberg 1957), pp. 27-32.

19. Justus Lipsius, *Von der Bestendigkeit*, ed. Leonard W. Forster (Stuttgart: Metzler, 1965), pp. 11-14.

20. See Gaede, *Poetik und Logik*, pp. 69-82.

21. H. J. C. von Grimmelshausen, *Das wunderbarliche Vogel-Nest*, ed. Rolf Tarot (Tübingen: Niemeyer, 1970), p. 71.

22. Georg W. F. Hegel, *The Encyclopaedia of the Philosophical Sciences*, trans. William Wallace (London: Oxford University Press, 1972), p. 300.

23. Arnauld, *The Art of Thinking*, p. 297.

24. Hegel, *The Encyclopaedia*, p. 143.

25. Martin Opitz, *Buch von der deutschen Poeterei*, ed. Wilhelm Braune (Tübingen: Niemeyer, 1954), p. 29.

26. Hegel, *The Encyclopaedia*, p. 143.

27. Opitz, *Buch von der deutschen Poeterei*, p. 20.

28. F. M. Padelford, *Select Translations from Scaliger's Poetics* (New York: Holt, 1905), pp. 2 ff.

29. See Heinrich Lausberg, *Handbuch der literarischen Rhetorik* (München: Hueber, 1960), p. 56.

30. Hegel, *The Encyclopaedia*, p. 62.

31. Cicero, *Topica*, trans. H. M. Hubbell (London and Cambridge, Mass.: Harvard University Press, 1968), p. 455.

32. Gottfried W. Leibniz, *New Essays concerning Human Understanding*, trans. A. G. Langley (New York: Macmillan, 1896), p. 528.

33. See Friedrich Gaede, "Leibniz' Urteilsreform und das Ende der Barockliteratur," *Simpliciana—Schriften der Grimmelshausen-Gesellschaft* III (1980), pp. 43-52.

SELECTED BIBLIOGRAPHY

Primary Sources

Arnauld, Antoine. *The Art of Thinking*. Trans. J. Dickoff and P. James. New York: Bobbs-Merrill, 1964.

Aristotle. *On the Art of Poetry*. Trans. Ingram Bywater. Oxford: Clarendon Press, 1909.

Cicero. *Topica*. Trans. H. M. Hubbell. London and Cambridge, Mass.: Harvard University Press, 1968.

Descartes, René. "The Passions of the Soul." In *The Philosophical Works of Descartes*, I. Trans. E. S. Haldane and G. R. T. Ross. London: Cambridge University Press, 1967.

Grimmelshausen, Hans Jakob Christoffel von. *Das wunderbarliche Vogel-Nest*. Rolf Tarot, ed. Tübingen: Niemeyer, 1970.

Harsdörffer, Georg Philipp. *Frauenzimmer Gesprächsspiele*, V. Tübingen: Niemeyer, 1969.

Hegel, Georg W. F. *The Encyclopaedia of the Philosophical Sciences*. Trans. William Wallace. London: Oxford University Press, 1972.

——. *Lectures on the History of Philosophy*. Trans. E. S. Haldane and F. H. Simson. New York and London: The Humanities Press, 1955.

Horatius, Flaccus Quintus. *Select Epodes and Ars poetica*. H. A. Dalton, ed. London: Macmillan, 1884.

Leibniz, Gottfried W. *New Essays concerning Human Understanding*. Trans. A. G. Langley. New York: Macmillan, 1896.

Locke, John. *An Essay concerning Human Understanding*. A. D. Woozley, ed. London and Glasgow: Collins, 1964.

Opitz, Martin. *Buch von der deutschen Poeterei,* ed. Wilhelm Braune. Tübingen: Niemeyer, 1954.

Quintilian, *The Institutio Oratoria*, I. Trans. H. E. Butler. London and Cambridge: Heinemann, 1969.

Scaliger, Julius Caesar. *Poetices Libri Septem* (1561). Stuttgart-Bad Cannstatt: Frommann-Holzboog, 1964.

Padelford, F. M. *Select Translations from Scaliger's Poetics*. New York: Holt, 1905.

Seneca. *Ad Lucilium Epistulae Morales*. Vol. II. Trans. R. M. Gummere. London: Heinemann, 1930.

——. *Moral Essays*. Trans. J. W. Basore. London: Heinemann, 1935.

Secondary Literature

Beetz, Manfred. *Rhetorische Logik*. Tübingen: Niemeyer, 1980.

Bochenski, J. M. *Formale Logik*. München: Karl Alber, 1970.

Dyck, Joachim. *Ticht-Kunst*. Bad Homburg: Gehlen, 1966.

Fischer, Ludwig. *Gebundene Rede*. Tübingen: Niemeyer, 1968.

Gaede, Friedrich. *Poetik und Logik—Zu den Grundlagen der literarischen Entwicklung im 17. und 18. Jahrhundert*. Bern and München: Francke, 1978.

——. "Leibniz' Urteilsreform und das Ende der Barockliteratur." *Simpliciana—Schriften der Grimmelshausen-Gesellschaft*, III (1980).

Geisenhof, Erika. "Die Darstellung der Leidenschaften in den Trauerspielen des Andreas Gryphius." Diss. Heidelberg, 1957.

Howell, Wilbur Samuel. *Logic and Rhetoric in England, 1500–1700*. Princeton, N.J.: Princeton University Press, 1956.

——. *Poetics, Rhetoric and Logic*. Ithaca, N.Y., and London: Cornell University Press, 1975.

Lausberg, Heinrich. *Handbuch der literarischen Rhetorik*. München: Hueber, 1960.

Mates, Benson. *Stoic Logic*. Berkeley: University of California Press, 1953.

Risse, Wilhelm. *Die Logik der Neuzeit*. Stuttgart-Bad Cannstatt: Frommann-Holzboog, 1964–1970.

Watson, Gerard. *The Stoic Theory of Knowledge*. Belfast: Queen's University Press, 1966.

Weinberg, Bernard. "Scaliger versus Aristotle on Poetics." *Modern Philology*, 39 (1942–43).

3

The Thirty Years War and Its Impact on Literature

Michael M. Metzger and Erika A. Metzger

Recent historical scholarship and reinterpretation have sharply questioned the validity of the terms "Counter-Reformation" and "Thirty Years War."[1] Chroniclers of German cultural, religious, and political life have tended to treat these complex events dominating the first half of the seventeenth century almost exclusively in terms of their effects on Germany. The very name "Counter-Reformation" implies that this powerful and differentiated phenomenon was motivated mainly by reaction to Lutheranism, suppressing the reality that strong desires for radical reform had been current for more than a century previously. "Thirty Years War" defines the term of hostilities for the German lands, but the Peace of Westphalia also brought to a close the war between Spain and the United Provinces of the Netherlands, which had lasted for eighty years; the struggle between the Habsburgs and the Bourbons, of which the last part of the war was a major episode, was to continue for decades. The present essay will do only marginal justice to these larger implications. Because the Counter-Reformation and the Thirty Years War were international in scope, and despite the terrible physical, political, and moral toll they took, Germany was drawn by them more deeply into the larger European sphere than ever before; to such an extent, so some would argue, as almost to lose her cultural identity. From the crucible of these events, however, German writers, creatively adapting new thematic and poetic impulses, brought forth culturally distinctive works stating authentic truths of their age and establishing definitively the German "baroque" temperament.

"During the whole course of the seventeenth century there were only seven complete calendar years in which there was no war between European states, the years 1610, 1669–71, 1680–2."[2] In European terms at least, even the twentieth century cannot match this record. The period saw some of the most wrenching geopolitical changes in history. At its outset, the Spanish and Austrian branches of the Habsburg dynasty seemed almost invincible, holding sway over Spain, parts of France, the Netherlands, northern and southern Italy, Austria, Bohemia, Christian Hungary, and, through the institutions of the Holy Roman Empire, the many territories of Germany, even the Protestant states of which were still associated in this ancient bond. At the close of the century, France was the dominant continental power, having broken out of Habsburg encirclement and pushing its boundaries to the Pyrenees and the Rhine. War was the catalyst for this epochal change, or rather a series of wars in which the major contenders, the Bourbons and the Habsburgs, only rarely confronted each other directly in their struggle for hegemony and dynastic survival, preferring to let allies and client states with ambitions of their own do much of the fighting for them. The political fortunes of many states rose and fell precipitously during the century, most notably of Sweden, Denmark, the United Provinces, and Poland.

Surrounded by ambitious and contentious neighbors, Germany in 1600 represented a vacuum into which their conflicts were destined to intrude. The constitutional structure linking Germany's hundreds of principalities was still medieval. The Imperial Diet was only seldom in session, and its rules were better suited to obstructing action by any of its constituencies than to providing a consensus about common aims and means to achieve them. In addition, the confessional division of the country into Catholic, Lutheran, and Calvinist lands was a formidable barrier to concerted political action. Having only the good of their respective territories and dynasties at heart, the German princes were easy prey to the manipulations of the great powers around them, which is not to say that some of them, such as the Duke of Bavaria, did not profit greatly from the needs of the warring parties for their services.

Germany played a strategic role in the plans of almost all of her neighbors, although these plans were not fully developed at the outset of the Thirty Years War. For Spain, routes through Germany from Italy, bypassing hostile France and England, were essential to maintaining her possessions in the Netherlands. For Sweden under Gustavus II Adolphus

(1594-1632), emerging as the dominant force in the Baltic, the German coastline was the vital southern boundary of her sphere of power and had to be withheld from enemies at all costs. For France, especially for Cardinal Richelieu (1585-1642), the chief minister to Louis XIII (1601-43), the divided German lands were a rich area for potential aggrandizement, and because of their very importance to Spain, French policy aimed at controlling events there. And the Habsburg Emperor Ferdinand II (1578-1637) had the dream, which was almost within his grasp for a time, of establishing an imperial monarchy in Germany in which the Catholic faith would be restored almost entirely.

Religious and political questions were inextricably intertwined throughout the Thirty Years War, although it became increasingly a struggle for territorial control. From the very outset, Catholic rulers were at odds with one another, and Lutheran princes did not scruple to help them if they stood to profit from it. The war began in 1618, when the Protestant nobility of Bohemia, Moravia, and Silesia, angered over a dispute on the rights of Lutherans to build churches in Catholic areas, overthrew the regents of Ferdinand II, who was also King of Bohemia, and, in August 1619, deposed the emperor as king, electing in his stead the leader of the Protestant Union in Germany, the Calvinist Elector Palatine Frederick V (1596-1632), later to be known as the "Winter King." Ferdinand II, who had just been elected emperor, could not tolerate the loss of one of the richest provinces of his crown lands, much less to a Calvinist prince. An imperial ban was announced against Frederick, and an army provided by Maximilian I of Bavaria (1573-1661) invaded Bohemia and defeated the Protestant forces in the Battle of the White Mountain in 1620. Frederick fled, the rebelling Bohemian nobles were stripped of their lands, and a relentless campaign of recatholicization was undertaken. The war was not restricted to Bohemia, however, for imperial armies occupied both the Rhenish and Upper Palatinates, Heidelberg being taken in 1622.

The penetration of Catholic, imperial forces into middle German regions that had previously been Protestant upset the precarious balance of power in Germany and made further war inevitable. But the emperor's armies were largely victorious until 1635, defeating a coalition led by Christian IV of Denmark in 1626, planting the emperor's standards on the shores of the Baltic by 1627. Much of the credit for this victory went to Ferdinand's general, Albrecht von Wallenstein (1583-1634). A wealthy Bohemian nobleman and convert to Catholicism, he had been created Duke of Friedland in 1623 for his vast financial and military aid to the emperor, for whom he had created his own army. In 1627, Wallenstein drove the Danes out of northern Germany and pursued them into Jutland. He was named Duke of Mecklenburg, thus holding a strategic base for the emperor in the north.

With his power in Germany at its zenith, Ferdinand permitted imperial ambition and religious zeal to triumph over political judgment and issued the Edict of Restitution in 1629, which would have forced the German Protestant princes to return to Catholic control all ecclesiastical territories secularized since 1552, seriously undermining the political and economic situations of most of them. Antagonized by this and other clearly monarchical moves of the emperor and fearing that he would use Wallenstein's powerful armies to subjugate them completely, they forced Ferdinand to dismiss Wallenstein at the Diet of Regensburg in 1630. In that year, however, Gustavus Adolphus, supported by French subsidies and considering his domination of the Baltic imperiled by the Catholic presence in the north, invaded Germany, rallying or coercing several Protestant powers to his side and quickly marching southwards into Bavaria. Wallenstein had to be recalled, and he, especially following the death of Gustavus Adolphus in battle in 1632, was able to drive the Swedish forces northwards. Wallenstein's position was now so strong that it seemed he would become the arbiter of German affairs, intriguing even against the emperor. He was murdered by officers loyal to Ferdinand in 1634. By 1635, Ferdinand was able to conclude the Peace of Prague, coming to an accommodation with most of the Protestant rulers.

During the final phase of the war, a French-Swedish alliance was arrayed against the Habsburgs, who were weakened by the increasing internal difficulties of Spain and the death of Ferdinand in 1637. Although marked by victories on both sides, the war became increasingly sporadic and indecisive, and it was to the satisfaction of the Electors that the Habsburg emperors had lost their ascendancy in Germany. Territorial questions now became dominant in the war, and all sides hoped for peace while continuing to fight. After eight years of negotiations, an agreement was finally reached early in 1648 in the Treaties of Münster and Osnabrück. In regard to the religious settlement, the "Peace of Westphalia" provided that the Augsburg Settlement of 1555 should be reinstated, but that the Calvinists were to be included and that, except for the Habsburg lands, minorities were to be tolerated in all principalities. France made significant territorial gains in Germany, as did Sweden and such German states as Bavaria, Brandenburg, and Saxony. Switzerland and the United Provinces received their independence from the empire. Most significantly, the privileges and independence of the territorial states in relation to the emperor, as they had historically existed before 1618, were reconfirmed, a situation which was to remain fundamentally unchanged until 1806.

Although the Thirty Years War was undoubtedly the worst catastrophe to befall Germany as a whole before World War II, its effects were evidently not as devastating as was formerly thought. The depopulation of whole regions of the country, for example, has recently been found to have been caused by temporary evacuations rather than wholesale slaughter or death from famine and disease. For in the decades after the war, apparently through the return of former inhabitants, populations again rose sharply, a trend augmented also by the very high birth rates of the time. Improved analysis of the scanty statistical evidence on demography and economic life indicates that the impact of the war, especially in areas that were hardly touched by it, was typical for wars of the time, and that recovery proceeded at a rapid rate.[3] Further, it is argued, armies were generally small, between 12,000 and 15,000 men, the largest having about 20,000, and, due to the seasons and lack of money, campaigns tended to be of short duration. Certainly less damage and suffering to the common people, especially those outside of cities, was caused by the fighting than by the movements and quartering of armies. Camp followers doubled or even trebled their size, and even "friendly" troops were allowed to live off the countryside, buying— generally taking—what they needed from the peasantry and townspeople, not seldom by force. Retreating troops wantonly destroyed crops, animals, and dwellings to leave nothing their pursuers could use. Typhoid and plague, which were epidemic in Germany throughout the war, were spread by refugees and troops alike, as were venereal disease and other afflictions.

Although we may relativize the objective effects of the war, its subjective impact on the people of Germany at the time cannot be denied. During its long and terrible course, which touched almost every district sooner or later, hardly a person alive at the time was unaffected by the war. Of all the arts in Germany, literature of the seventeenth century reflects this experience in the most varied and profound ways.

As in the case of other great themes of the time, it would be misleading to approach the depiction and discussion of the war in literature with the postulation that we are dealing with direct transformations of personal experience. Although this may be the case with autobiographical documents and journalistic or diplomatic reports,[4] artistic literary expression in this period, particularly in the Humanistic tradition, represents at best a highly refracted image of a pragmatic experience that has been largely depersonalized and reshaped by considerations of function, rhetoric, and convention. As is true of almost all other literary effort in this period, the depiction of the war is never an expressive end in itself, as it so frequently is in our time. Rather, despite the apparent immediacy of certain depictions, the war was made by poets to reveal its exemplary, emblematic nature, to become in its microcosmic entity part of a universal truth. There can be no doubt that the war, in its seemingly unending and arbitrary course, confirmed and deepened the pessimistic tendencies, at least as far as life in this world is concerned, of Christian, Neostoic thought to which so much of the moral philosophy and literature of the time can be related.

The lives of Martin Opitz (1597-1639) and Andreas Gryphius (1616-64), the greatest German poets of their age, may serve to illustrate the relationship of history, personality, and art during the Thirty Years War. Through his *Buch von der deutschen Poeterey* (1624), Opitz became the father of modern poetics in Germany, establishing at one thrust the European Renaissance conventions since Petrarch as the norm for literature in his homeland. Through his numerous translations of poetry, prose, drama, and opera from Greek, Latin, Italian, Dutch, and English, in addition to his own exemplary creations, he provided models and criteria that set the style and standard for much of the German poetic literature of his century.

Reaching adulthood and leaving his native Silesia just as the war broke out, Opitz became one of the most widely traveled poets of his age, remaining peripatetic almost all of his life, usually, beginning with Heidelberg in 1620, just one step ahead of the war, and sometimes, indeed, in danger of being overtaken by its action. Talented and evidently endowed with a magnetic personality, Opitz not only won the wreath of a *poeta laureatus* and a patent of nobility in recognition of his literary activities, but he also served successively as a teacher and diplomat, the latter career taking him to Holland, Denmark, Poland, Transylvania, and almost all regions of Germany. Although a Calvinist, Opitz became the secretary of Karl Hannibal von Dohna, the Catholic imperial governor of Silesia, a position that involved missions requiring the ability to gain the confidence of Catholics and Protestants alike. Following Dohna's death, never at a loss for employment, he served the Dukes of Brieg and Liegnitz and the King of Poland. More than any poet of his day Opitz could be said to have ridden the crest of events as a respected scholar, artist, and

diplomat, and he surely saw and understood much at first hand that was
withheld from his contemporaries. Yet, due to the confessional conflict,
his father was exiled from Silesia, and it was after a trip to visit him that
Opitz succumbed to the plague in Danzig.

Aside from scattered poems such as "Ein Gebet / daß Gott die
Spanier widerumb vom Rheinstrom wolle treiben. 1620," Opitz treated
the war in two major works: *Trostgedichte in Widerwertigkeit des
Krieges* and *Lob des Krieges Gottes Martis*. Four books of the *Trostgedichte*, begun in 1620 and completed in 1633, interpret the war as
God's retribution for human sinfulness and exhort the reader to courage,
virtue, and faith, an argument simple enough, but presented with a
dazzling wealth of rhetoric and exempla. In the first book, however,
Opitz includes graphic descriptions of the war in its most brutalizing
aspects to dramatize his complaint:

> Ja / die auch nicht geborn / die wurden umbgebracht /
> Die Kinder so umbringt gelegen mit der Nacht
> In jhrer Mutter Schoß: Ehe sie zum Leben kommen /
> Da hat man jhnen schon das Leben hingenommen:
> Viel sind / auch Weib und Kind / von Felsen abgestürtzt /
> Und haben jhnen selbst die schwere Zeit verkürtzt /
> Dem Feinde zu entgehn. Was darff ich aber sagen /
> Was die für Hertzenleyd / so noch gelebt / ertragen?
> Ihr Heyden reicht nicht zu mit ewrer Grausamkeit:
> Was jhr noch nicht gethan das thut die Christenheit /
> Wo solcher Mensch auch kan den Christen-Namen haben /
> Die Leichen haben sie / die Leichen auffgegraben /
> Die Glieder / so die Erd' und die Natur versteckt /
> Sind worden unverschämt von jhnen auffgedeckt.[5]

The containment in these lines of a vision of barbarous reality within a
tightly formal structure that is epigrammatically terse on the level of the
individual couplet and yet cumulatively flexible, extensive, and powerful, is quite typical of poetry about the war. Rarely, if ever, does one find
"expressionistic" techniques that seek a form appropriate to the horror of
the contents, least of all with a classicistic writer like Opitz, whose aim is
perhaps rather a grimly ironic tension between the regularity of the form
and the terrifying perversity of the action described within it.

It was the childhood of Andreas Gryphius, born almost two decades
after Opitz, that was most deeply affected by the war. His father, an
archdeacon of Glogau in Silesia, died in 1621, one day after Frederick V,
the "Winter King" of Bohemia, passed through the town on his flight

and demanded the silver implements from the church, and it is not unlikely that the shock of this occurrence led to the death of the arch-deacon.[6] Gryphius's mother married again, but died in 1628, and thereafter the poet's education, despite help from his stepfather, was constantly interrupted by the severe restrictions placed on Protestants because of the imperial efforts to recatholicize Silesia, only very few Prot-estant churches and schools being tolerated. Severe disruptions occurred also because of fires, the presence of troops in the country, and outbreaks of the plague. Later Gryphius was able to study at Danzig and take a position as tutor in the house of a Silesian nobleman, with whose sons he later traveled to Holland, where he stayed from 1638 until 1644, a period followed by travels in France and Italy. He did not return to Silesia until late in 1647. The last years of Gryphius's life were spent as an official of his native Glogau. Already in Holland Gryphius had published his first volumes of poetry, and he continued his literary endeavors after his return, concentrating particularly on the tragedies that have gained him the reputation as the greatest German dramatist of his generation.

The dominant theme of the poetry of Gryphius is the transiency of life, the vanity of human wishes before implacable death. Certainly this is a common theme of the time, but Gryphius was its most obsessive and penetrating poetic spokesman. Martial imagery occurring throughout his works, there can be little doubt that Gryphius's wartime experiences did much to condition this deeply tragic view. Through its controlled pathos and grandiose depiction of physical and spiritual devastation, Gryphius's sonnet "Threnen des Vatterlandes / Anno 1636" is justly con-sidered the poem that most poignantly expresses the war's meaning for Germany.

His metaphysically tragic sensibility combined in Gryphius with an acute sense for the historical moment in which he lived. For example, in 1650 he composed the tragedy *Carolus Stuardus*, which concerns the ex-ecution of Charles I of England, less than a year after the event. In the closing days of the Thirty Years War, between 1647 and 1650, Gryphius wrote a comedy, *Horribilicribrifax. Teutsch*, which demonstrates the same immediacy on quite another level. Two bragging, cowardly, cheating examples of the type of the miles gloriosus, traditional since Plautus and seen by Gryphius in Italy in the commedia dell'arte, stand at the center of an involved comic plot of courtship, money, intrigue, and marriage. Horribilicribrifax, the satirically prototypical soldier who has been master of all things for thirty years, is nearing the end of his reign, threatened with an end of the hostilities. For all of the humor of the delineation of the characters — a tour de force of German contaminated with all of the languages of Europe — there is detectable, too, a sense of bitterness and outrage on Gryphius's part toward this figure who has dominated his age. Here, Horribilicribrifax has just been informed that the emperor has made peace with the king of Sweden, and he rages:

Friede zu machen sonder mich? à qvaesto modo si! [*Auf diese Art!*] hat er nicht alle seine Victorien mir zu dancken? hab ich nicht den König in Schweden niedergeschossen? bin ich nicht Ursach / daß die Schlacht von Nördlingen erhalten? habe ich nicht den Sachsen sein Land eingenommen? hab ich nicht in Dennemarck solche Reputation eingelegt? was wer es auff dem Weissen Berge gewesen / sonder mich? E che fama non m'acquistai, quando contesi col Gran Turca? [*Und welchen Ruhm habe ich nicht erworben, als ich gegen den Großen Türken gestritten habe?*] Pfui! trit mir aus den Augen / denn ich erzürne mich zu tode / wo ich mich recht erbittere / Vinto dal ira calda e bollente e dallo sdegno arrabiato [*Beherrscht von heißer, kochender Wut und vom wütenden Zorn*], so erwische ich den Stephans-Thurm zu Wien bey der Spitzen / und drück ihn so hart darnieder / si fortè in terra [*so gewaltsam in die Erde*], daß sich die gantze Welt mit demselben umkehret / als eine Kegel-Kaul.[7]

The novels of Hans Jakob Christoffel von Grimmelshausen (ca. 1622–76) are the prose works in which the Thirty Years War is most intensively reflected, in particular his *Der abentheurliche Simplicissimus Teutsch* (1669) and *Trutz Simplex: Oder . . . Lebensbeschreibung der Ertzbetrügerin und Landstörtzerin Courasche* (1670). From his early youth, Grimmelshausen had been directly involved in the war, serving as a groom, soldier, and secretary on various sides by the time the conflict ended. Although clearly influenced by the Spanish picaresque tradition and set within the religious, didactic framework of a soul's pilgrimage through the follies and travails of the world to wisdom and eremitical devotion to God, many of his descriptions of incidents in the war in *Simplicissimus* are at once realistic and earthily humorous. The novel was popular in Germany already in the seventeenth century, and its great richness of incidents and characters, the narrative technique at once simple and subtle, and its masterfully contrived use of the colloquial language have justly caused it to be esteemed as the first great German novel. It is certainly the finest work to come out of the war.

References more or less extensive to the Thirty Years War are to be found in the works of practically all of the major writers in Germany during the first half of the seventeenth century. To name only the works of the best-known authors, the war is a theme in the poems of Georg Rudolf Weckherlin (1584–1653), Paul Fleming (1609–40), and Paul Gerhardt (1607–76), and in the epigrams of Friedrich von Logau (1604–55).

In *Coridon und Phyllis* by Daniel von Czepko (1605-60), we find graphic descriptions of the life of a soldier that clearly refer to the experience of the war. Johann Michael Moscherosch (1601-69) alluded to the subject frequently in his *Wunderbarliche und Wahrhaftige Gesichte Philanders von Sittewald*, and Johann Rist (1607-67) devoted several dramas to it, including *Irenaromachia, Das Friedewünschende Teutschland*, and *Das Friedejauchzende Teutschland*. Georg Greflinger (ca. 1620-77) wrote an epic entitled *Der Deutschen Dreyßigjähriger Krieg*.

There exists also a very much larger body of anonymous popular literature in the form of broadsheets and pamphlets containing songs, ballads, descriptions, and polemics written by authors on all sides of the conflict. Although many examples have been lost, much of this popular literature is still held in libraries and archives, and some of it has appeared in collections.[8] It is instructive to compare a work by a recognized and academic writer with a popular poem in order to gain insight into the ideological and formal differences between the two types. Johann Rist, a Protestant pastor and teacher in Holstein, who was later crowned poet laureate and ennobled by the emperor, wrote the following poem upon the death of Wallenstein in 1634:

> Was ist dies Leben doch? Ein Traurspiel ist's zu nennen,
> Da ist der Anfang gut, auch wie wir's wünschen können,
> Das Mittel voller Angst, das End ist Herzeleid,
> Ja, wohl der bittre Tod; O kurze Fröhlichkeit!
>
> Dies tut uns Wallenstein in seinem Spiel erweisen,
> Der Kaiser pflag ihn selbst anfänglich hoch zu preisen
> Als eine Säul des Reichs (so nannt' ihn Ferdinand),
> Der Teutschen Furcht und Zwang, des Kaisers rechter Hand.
>
> Bald aber, wie sein Glaub und Treu fing an zu wanken,
> Verkehrte sich das Spiel, man wandte die Gedanken
> Auf seinen Untergang, der Tag gebar die Nacht,
> Das Traurspiel hatt' ein End und er ward umgebracht.
>
> So tummlet sich das Glück, so läuft es hin und wieder,
> Den einen macht es groß, den andren drückt es nieder,
> Sein End ist oft der Tod. O selig ist der Mann,
> Der sich der Eitelkeit des Glücks entschlagen kann.[9]

For Rist, Wallenstein's fate is less of interest in itself than as a demonstration of the misery and transiency of life, the arbitrariness of fortune. Wallenstein's rise and fall are already literary for Rist, an exemplary tragedy contained rhetorically within the confines of a proposition argued and proved. As is the case with so much similar poetry, there is little partisan passion to be felt here.

The popular poem, evidently copied from a broadsheet, also draws a moralizing conclusion, but devotes far more time to immediate and polemical condemnation:

Neue wallensteinische Grabschrifft.

Hie liegt der Wallnstein ohne Fried,
Des Reichs ein Fürst und doch kein Glied,
War ohne Schiff ein Admiral,
Und ohne [(?)] Schlacht ein General,
Ein Landsaß in dem Herzogstand,
Im Kopf ein Herr in keinem Land,
Gut römisch und ein Mameluck,
Aufrichtig voll der Untreu Stuck,
Mit Krieg im Sinn ein Friedenmann,
Von süßen Worten ein Tyrann,
Wollt endlich mehr als Kaiser sein,
Büßt drüber mit einander ein
Leib, Ehr, Gut, fast Seel dazu —
Ei seht doch, was die Ehrsucht thu![10]

How quickly the events of the Thirty Years War lost their resonance and emblematic function, not only in the minds of the populace but also in those of the poets, is evidenced by the humorous epitaph on Wallenstein written about four decades after his death by Christian Hofmann von Hofmannswaldau (1617-79):

Hier liegt das große haupt / so itzt wird ausgelacht;
Viel wissen mehr von mir / als ich iemahls gedacht.
Doch wust ich / daß ein stein nicht leicht ein stern kan werden /
Ein stein / wie hoch er steigt / fällt endlich zu der erden.[11]

The poem clearly betrays satiation with the great volume of dramas and poems that centered on the general even during his lifetime, but especially after his death.[12] For Hofmannswaldau, Wallenstein is now only a subject for a witty play on words. Not until more than a century later, beginning with Schiller's tragic trilogy on Wallenstein and the rising historical sensibility, was the Thirty Years War to become again a question of engrossing interest to German writers, beginning a tradition that found expression in Ricarda Huch's *Der dreißigjährige Krieg*, Alfred Döblin's *Wallenstein*, and most recently in *Das Treffen in Telgte* by Günter Grass.

NOTES

1. A. G. Dickens, *The Counter Reformation* (New York: Harcourt, Brace & World, 1969), p. 7 and passim; S. H. Steinberg, *The Thirty Years War and the Conflict for European Hegemony, 1600–1660* (New York: Norton, 1966), pp. 1 ff. See also Carl J. Friedrich, *The Age of the Baroque, 1610–1660* (New York: Harper & Row, 1952), especially the bibliographical essay, pp. 327 ff.

2. Sir George Clark, *The Seventeenth Century*, 2d ed. (Oxford: Oxford University Press, 1969), p. 98.

3. Steinberg, pp. 103-16.

4. Marianne Beyer-Fröhlich, ed., *Selbstzeugnisse aus dem Dreißigjährigen Krieg und dem Barock* (Leipzig: Reclam, 1930); Hans Jessen, ed., *Der Dreißigjährige Krieg in Augenzeugenberichten* (München: Deutscher Taschenbuch Verlag, 1971).

5. Martin Opitz, *Geistliche Poemata* (1638), ed. Erich Trunz (Tübingen: Niemeyer, 1975), p. 341.

6. Eberhard Mannack, *Andreas Gryphius* (Stuttgart: Metzler, 1968), p. 3.

7. Andreas Gryphius, *Lustspiele*, ed. Hugh Powell, I (Tübingen: Niemeyer, 1969), 58-59.

8. Julius Opel and Adolf Cohn, eds., *Der Dreißigjährige Krieg: Eine Sammlung von historischen Gedichten und Prosadarstellungen* (Halle: Buchhandlung des Waisenhauses, 1862); Emil Weller, ed., *Die Lieder des Dreißigjährigen Krieges* (Basel: Neukirch, 1855; rpt. Hildesheim: Olms, 1968).

9. Karl Otto Conrady, ed., *Das große deutsche Gedichtbuch* (Kronberg/Ts.: Athenäum, 1977), p. 106.

10. Opel and Cohn, p. 346.

11. *Benjamin Neukirchs Anthologie Herrn von Hofmannswaldau und andrer Deutschen auserlesener und bißher ungedruckter Gedichte erster theil*, ed. Angelo George de Capua and Ernst Alfred Philippson (Tübingen: Niemeyer, 1961), p. 127.

12. Cf. Elisabeth Frenzel, *Stoffe der Weltliteratur* (Stuttgart: Kröner, 1962), pp. 656-58.

SELECTED BIBLIOGRAPHY

Primary Sources

Beller, Elmer A. *Propaganda in Germany during the Thirty Years War*. Princeton, N.J.: Princeton University Press, 1940.

Beyer-Fröhlich, Marianne, ed. *Selbstzeugnisse aus dem Dreißigjährigen Krieg und dem Barock.* Deutsche Literatur in Entwicklungsreihen. Reihe Deutsche Selbstzeugnisse, 6. Leipzig: Reclam, 1930.

Conrady, Karl Otto, ed. *Das große deutsche Gedichtbuch.* Kronberg/Ts.: Athenäum, 1977.

Czepko, Daniel von. *Weltliche Dichtungen.* Werner Milch, ed. Rpt. Darmstadt: Wissenschaftliche Buchgesellschaft, 1963.

de Capua, Angelo George, and Ernst Alfred Philippson, eds. *Benjamin Neukirchs Anthologie Herrn von Hofmannswaldau und andrer Deutschen auserlesener und bißher ungedruckter Gedichte erster theil.* Tübingen: Niemeyer, 1961.

Frenzel, Elisabeth. *Stoffe der Weltliteratur.* Stuttgart: Kröner, 1962.

Gryphius, Andreas. *Gesamtausgabe der deutschsprachigen Werke.* Marian Szyrocki and Hugh Powell, eds. 8 vols. Tübingen: Niemeyer, 1963 ff.

Jessen, Hans, ed. *Der Dreißigjährige Krieg in Augenzeugenberichten.* München: Deutscher Taschenbuch Verlag, 1971.

Logau, Friedrich von. *Sinngedichte.* C. W. Ramler and G. E. Lessing, eds. In Gotthold Ephraim Lessing, *Sämtliche Schriften.* Karl Lachmann and Franz Muncker, eds. Vol. VII. 3rd ed. Stuttgart: Göschen, 1891.

Moscherosch, Johann Michael. *Visiones de Don Quevedo: Wunderbarliche und Warhaftige Gesichte Philanders von Sittewalt . . .* Strassburg: Johann Philipp Mülben, 1642.

Mueller, Guenther Herbert Siegfried. "Georg Greflinger, *Der Deutschen Dreyszig-Jähriger Krieg*: Ausgabe und Kommentar." Diss. University of North Carolina, Chapel Hill, 1974.

Opel, Julius, and Adolf Cohn, eds. *Der Dreißigjährige Krieg: Eine Sammlung von historischen Gedichten und Prosadarstellungen.* Halle: Buchhandlung des Waisenhauses, 1862.

Opitz, Martin. *Geistliche Poemata* (1638). Erich Trunz, ed. Tübingen: Niemeyer, 1975.

——. *Weltliche Poemata* (1644). Erich Trunz, ed. Tübingen: Niemeyer, 1967.

Rist, Johann. *Sämtliche Werke.* Eberhard Mannack, ed. Berlin: de Gruyter, 1967 ff.

Wagenknecht, Christian, ed. *Epochen der deutschen Lyrik: 1600–1700.* München: Deutscher Taschenbuch Verlag, 1969.

Weller, Emil, ed. *Die Lieder des Dreißigjährigen Krieges.* Basel: Neukirch, 1855; rpt. Hildesheim: Olms, 1968.

Secondary Literature

Clark, Sir George. *The Seventeenth Century.* 2nd ed. Oxford: Oxford University Press, 1969.

Dickens, A. G. *The Counter Reformation.* New York: Harcourt, Brace & World, 1969.

Friedrich, Carl J. *The Age of the Baroque, 1610–1660*. New York: Harper & Row, 1952.

Geulen, Hans. " 'Arkadische' Simpliciana: Zu einer Quelle Grimmelshausens und ihrer strukturellen Bedeutung für seinen Roman." *Euphorion*, 63 (1969), 426–37.

Hinderer, Walter, ed. *Geschichte der politischen Lyrik in Deutschland*. Stuttgart: Reclam, 1978.

Langer, Herbert. *Thirty Years War*. New York: Hippocrene, 1980.

Maland, David. *Europe at War, 1600–1650*. Totowa: Rowman and Littlefield, 1980.

Mannack, Eberhard. *Andreas Gryphius*. Stuttgart: Metzler, 1968.

Newald, Richard. *Die deutsche Literatur vom Späthumanismus zur Empfindsamkeit, 1570–1750*. 2nd ed. München: Beck, 1957.

Paas, John Roger. "The Seventeenth-Century Verse Broadsheet: A Study of Its Character and Literary Historical Significance." Diss. Bryn Mawr College, Pennsylvania, 1973.

Pagès, Georges. *The Thirty Years War, 1618–1648*. New York: Harper & Row, 1970.

Steinberg, S. H. *The Thirty Years War and the Conflict for European Hegemony, 1600–1660*. New York: Norton, 1966.

Weber, Willi Erich. "Die Motive Krieg und Frieden in der Dichtung des deutschen Barock." Diss. Marburg 1950.

Wedgwood, C. V. *The Thirty Years War*. Garden City, N.Y.: Doubleday, 1961.

Weithase, Irmgard. *Die Darstellung von Krieg und Frieden in der deutschen Barockdichtung*. Weimar: Böhlau, 1953.

Willey, Basil. *The Seventeenth Century Background*. Garden City, N.Y.: Doubleday, 1953.

4

The Emblematic Tradition and Baroque Poetry

Peter M. Daly

In 1531 the famous Italian lawyer Andreas Alciatus published a small book of emblems which he had probably compiled during the seven years that he was without university employment. It was an epidemic of plague, not government cutbacks, that closed the doors of Avignon University in 1521, sending Alciatus back to Milan, from which town he vainly sought another position. One of the fruits of this period of enforced leisure was a collection of emblems. Alciatus could not have known that with his *Emblematum liber* (Augsburg, 1531) he had launched a new genre; in fact a new form of book that would become immensely popular. Alciatus's book itself has gone through over 170 editions, Francis Quarles's *Emblems* have appeared nearly 50 times, Hermann Hugo's *Pia Desideria* accounts for over 44 Latin editions, and Otto van Veen's *Moralia Horatiana* runs to at least 34 editions. Emblem collections were frequently reprinted, often with learned commentary, and translated into various languages. According to the bibliographies of Mario Praz[1] and John Landwehr,[2] over six hundred authors produced about a thousand titles which were issued in over two thousand editions. The emblem book was big business.

The book is, however, only one of the many media that disseminated the emblematic combination of symbolic picture and interpretative text. Emblematic designs were incorporated into almost every artistic form; they are found in stained-glass windows, jewelry, tapestry, needlework, painting, and architecture. Veritable emblem programmes may be found adorning the walls of private residences[3] and ecclesiastical buildings.[4] Emblems were used as theatrical properties in dramas and street processions. Poets and preachers, writers and dramatists frequently employed emblems and emblemlike structures in both the spoken and the written word. The emblem informed and helped to shape virtually every form of verbal and visual communication during the sixteenth and seventeenth centuries. The emblem may thus be regarded as a cultural phenomenon of major significance.

Like other baroque forms the emblem fell into disrepute and then into total neglect during the eighteenth and nineteenth centuries. In the twentieth century critics have denounced the emblem as capricious and arbitrary. Such judgments, however, often betray the prejudice of the writer more than they describe the phenomenon itself.

Henry Green[5] rediscovered the emblem for literary studies in the 1870s and 1880s. He not only reprinted editions of Alciatus and compiled an Alciatus bibliography, but he also attempted to show, if somewhat uncritically, the influence of emblems on Shakespeare. Praz produced what is still the best bibliography and an important study (see note 1) both of the emblem and of emblematic images in literature. The long article by Heckscher and Wirth in the *Reallexikon zur Deutschen Kunstgeschichte* offers a wealth of material and many insights into the emblem; its art-historical perspective is a valuable corrective to some of the one-sided treatments by literary scholars. In 1964 Albrecht Schöne published what has become a standard work on the subject of the emblem and drama, *Emblematik und Drama im Zeitalter des Barock* (2nd ed., München 1968). Schöne's new theory of the emblem has been largely accepted by German scholars.

Although we can date precisely the emergence of the new emblem genre to the year of 1531, Alciatus did not create something new out of nothing. The emblem has its forerunners. Indeed, the many different kinds of illustrated literature that precede the emblem book explain both the richness and variety of the new genre and the many different developments that followed during the later sixteenth and seventeenth centuries. In addition to such precursors as the illustrated broadsheet, dance of death sequences, *biblia pauperum*, book illustrations in general, and *tituli* in particular, there are the even more important traditions of heraldry, devices, and hieroglyphics. When we add to these illustrated forms the picture-thinking inherent in medieval traditions of Bible allegory and nature symbolism, then the range of the emblem is more clearly appreciated. And we have not yet mentioned the important role played by classical mythology, history, and literature, as well as the Greek Anthology and collections of *loci communes*.

The emblem is a mixed form that combines a motto (*inscriptio*, or lemma), a picture (*pictura*, or icon), and an epigram (*subscriptio*). The motto introduces the emblem and usually indicates its theme. The picture, which embodies that theme, may depict one or more objects, persons, and events, often set against a real or imaginary background. Beneath the picture is printed an epigram or short prose statement that functions as a *subscriptio*. The relationship of words to picture has been a subject of some disagreement over the years, which is hardly surprising given the great variety of emblem books, the different modes of combination possible, and the different perspectives of critics. Suffice it to say, the idea that the emblem is necessarily arbitrary or capricious must be abandoned.

Both the variety of emblems and the different traditions that led to the creation of the emblem genre can be illustrated by characteristic examples from Alciatus. Alciatus's literary model was the Greek epigram. In the early 1520s he was translating the *Anthologia Palatina cum Planudeis*, and the first reference to his *Emblemata* dates from this period. According to Henkel nearly half of the 103 emblems that comprise the first edition are either translations or imitations of Greek epigrams;[6] in the final enlarged collection containing 212 emblems the portion deriving from this source accounts for about one quarter. For instance, emblem 38 in the Paris editions bears the motto "Gerechtigkeyt sigt doch zu letsten" in Hunger's translation. The *pictura* shows a tomb, with the name Ajax (Aiacis) on the side, next to a body of water upon which a shield is floating (see Illustration 1).

The epigram relates briefly the story of how both Ulysses and Ajax had claimed Achilles' armor after his death. The Greeks presented Ulysses with the trophy, whereupon Ajax grew so incensed that in his insanity he killed himself. However, after his death Neptune intervened to redress the injustice by returning the shield to Ajax's grave. This account is taken directly from the Greek Anthology (Book VII, 115 ff.). The Ajax emblem is quite characteristic insofar as a general moral is enunciated in the *inscriptio*, embodied in the *pictura* through the particular fate of Ajax, which in turn is elucidated in the *subscriptio*.

Another tradition equally influential in the development of the emblem was the Renaissance hieroglyph. During the Renaissance, hieroglyphs were associated with ancient Egypt and above all with a book

Tandem tandem iuſtitia obtinet. XXXVIII.

Gerechtigkeyt ſigt doch zu letſten,
XXXVIII.
Die Griechen des Achillis ſchilt
Dem Aiax namen wider recht,
Neptunus ſagt, wie iſt das gſpilt?
Lont man alſo dem gueten knecht?
Drumb in des Aiax grab er ſchlecht
Den ſchilt durch gwalt des mers, das
ſchreyt,
O Aiax, dier gſchach groß vnrecht,
Doch finndt ſich dwarheyt mit der zeit.

Aeaidæ Hectoreo perfuſum ſanguine ſcutum,
Quod Græcorum Ithaco condo iniqua dedit,
Iuſtior arripuit Neptunus in æquora iactum
Naufragio, ut dominum poſſet adir ſuum:
Littoreo Aiads tumulo namq; intulit unda:
Quæ boat, & tali uoce ſepulchra ferit.
Viaſti Telamoniade tu dignior armis,
Affectus ſis eſt ædere iuſtitiæ.

Illustration 1: Andreas Alciatus, *Emblematum libellus* (Paris, 1540), p. 92.

known as the *Horapollo*. Nothing is known about its author and the book itself consists of two parts containing 70 and 119 chapters, respectively, each chapter dealing with one hieroglyph, such as falcon, goose, or a man with no head, or a concept such as "eternity." Probably written in the fourth century A.D., the *Horapollo* was discovered in 1419 and first printed in 1505. It became one of the most influential books of the Renaissance, with at least thirty editions of the Latin translation. These hieroglyphs entered the stream of the emblem directly through the *Horapollo*, indirectly through the *Physiologus*, the most important book of Christian nature allegory, and also through books of *imprese* (see below). Cultural traditions and symbolic lore overlap and interact to such an extent that it is virtually impossible to determine the source of a given emblem motif. Loosely speaking, hieroglyphic emblems are those in which motifs are strangely combined in a way that defies nature or logic. Thus, for the idea of "The Impossible," *Horapollo* has a man walking on water and a headless man. Possibly the most famous of Alciatus's hieroglyphic emblems depicts a dolphin entwined around the shaft of an anchor (see Illustration 2).

Princeps subditorum incolumi-
tatem procurans,

Titanij quoties conturbant æquora fratres,
Tum miseros nautas ancora iacta iuuat.
Hanc pius erga homines Delphin côplectitur, imis
Tutius ut possit figer illa uadis.
Quàm deæt hæc memores gestare insignia Reges,
Anchora quod nautis, se populo esse suo.

Illustration 2: Andreas Alciatus, *Emblematum libellus* (Paris, 1540), p. 25.

Another important precursor of the emblem is the *impresa*, or device. The *impresa*, from the Italian for "undertaking," combines a symbolic picture with a short motto, usually no more than three words in length. Originally these devices were personal badges invented by princes of the church and state to express a certain commitment, a personal aim or ambition, or even a situation, such as widowhood.[7] According to the rules for the perfect *impresa*, the motifs should be strange but true, and the motto was to be brief and in a foreign tongue.[8] The *impresa* had, then, a somewhat exclusive and esoteric character. However, many of the motifs—and indeed some mottoes—that were incorporated into the *impresa* reappeared in emblems. Claude Paradin reproduced the device of Maecenas, a powerful figure under the Emperor Augustus, whose seal ring bore the picture of a frog accompanied by the motto "Mihi terra, lacusque," thereby symbolizing his power on land and sea, as well as his commitment to secrecy.[9] Joachim Camerarius later adopted the frog and its motto for a general moral emblem with lightly political overtones. In the second line of the couplet-epigram, Camerarius's frog allows himself the rhetorical question whether he is not more powerful than a great prince.[10]

Perhaps the most significant intellectual or attitudinal basis for the mode of thought that expresses itself through emblematic forms is the typological exegesis and allegorical habit of mind that the Renaissance inherited from the Middle Ages. From the Middle Ages down to the eighteenth century the view was generally held that God had communicated to humankind through the Bible, Book of the Word, and through creation, the Book of Nature. The medieval allegorist and the Renaissance emblem writer regarded nature as containing objects and creatures that point to meanings beyond themselves, meanings that in the act of creation God had stamped into the qualities, actions, and forms of the things themselves. Nature is thus, as Schöne puts it, "das Seiende als ein zugleich Bedeutendes" (p. 48). Seen from this perspective the relationship of thing to meaning, picture to elucidation, is not necessarily arbitrary, since such relationships are deemed to be inherent. The fact that a twentieth-century reader may discover errors or inconsistencies does not mean that baroque emblem writers and readers regarded this use of nature symbolism as in any sense arbitrary.

An individual creature, such as the eagle, was capable of producing as many discrete and separate meanings as it has attributes and qualities. The high flight of the eagle, its nobility and strength, its relationship to the sun, the testing of its young ones in the nest, its ability to rejuvenate itself by flying into the sun, its uncanny instinct to detect carrion, its protection of the mole—these together with other actions and aspects produce meanings that have been interpreted morally, politically, and spiritually. In each case the equation of concept and eagle is based on an assumed truth. This is still the case where the "fact" is now recognized as a fiction or a superstition. The fabulous stories about unicorns, phoenixes, and basilisks depend for their truth on tradition and authority, rather than on observation. Basically, such emblems are founded on what were earlier regarded as facts of nature.

One example from Alciatus will illustrate this significative, or one might say typological, use of nature in the emblem. The chameleon can connote the flatterer because it feeds on thin air and changes its color according to the environment, taking on every hue except for red and white, the latter being the color of virtue and honesty. We are, therefore, not surprised to find that Alciatus has an emblem "In adulatores" (Paris, 1540, No. 88), that features the chameleon in its *pictura* (see Illustration 3).

The epigram describes the attributes of the animal noted above and applies them to the relationship of the flatterer to his prince. The result is a moral observation with general political implications, couched in the art form of the emblem.

Much of the knowledge upon which such emblems are based is no longer part of our tradition. How many of us would recognize in the crow a highly developed sense of conjugal loyalty? The popular songs may have a special place for doves but hardly for crows! However, the conjugal loyalty of crows was proverbial, and by extension crows were known as a peaceful and united species. This was the basis for an Alciatus emblem on political and social concord. Emblem No. 6 (Paris, 1542) shows two crows supporting a scepter; the epigram makes reference to the "wondrous harmony" of crows and makes the point that the power of the prince stands or falls by popular consent.[11]

Information about such creatures as, for example, the chameleon, crow, and frog, ranges from simple, everyday observations, through "facts of nature" deriving from the Ancients, some of which will not stand empirical test, or even observation, to scientific truth. Knowledge coming from classical writers extends from proverbial commonplaces to esoteric and mysterious information known to the learned few.

Thematically Alciatus's collection is a clever combination of erudition, humanistic morality, practical wisdom, common sense, and a dash of more lighthearted entertainment. "Wer vieles bringt, wird manchem etwas bringen"—and so it was with the little book that started what was to become an avalanche of emblems. How else can we explain its phenomenal success? Some of Alciatus's followers offered a similar mix, but soon a tendency towards greater specialization both in theme and content becomes apparent. As a form the emblem allows for many developments and different uses. Thus with Sambucus and Junius hermetic lore and humanistic tradition predominate, whereas de la Pèrriere's *La Morosophie* (Lyons, 1553) combines *Zeitkritik* and the characteristic concerns of the *Fürstenspiegel*.

Emblem writers seem to have been remarkably slow in using the emblem for religious purposes. The first emblem book completely devoted to a religious subject, *Emblems, ou Devises Chrestiennes*, was

In adulatores. LXXXVIII.

Der Furſten heuchler. LXXXVIII.

Chameleon von lufft ſich nert,
Den er ſtet vacht in offnen ſchlund,
Auch on rot vnd weyß er ſich kert
In alle farb in ainer ſtund:
Alſo hat allzeyt offnen mund
Ein ſchmaychler, friſt die arm gemain,
Vnd lobt dem Furſten all ſein fund
On frumbkeyt, vnd die warheyt rain.

N iij

Semper hiat, ſemper tenuem qua ueſatur auram,
   Reciprocat chamæleon,
Et mutat faciem, uarios ſumitʠ colores,
   Præter rubrum uel candidum:
Sic & adulator populari ueſcitur aura,
   Hiansʠ; uncta deuorat,
Et ſolum mores imitatur prinäpis atros,
   Albi & pudici neſäus.

Illustration 3: Andreas Alciatus, *Emblematum libellus* (Paris, 1540), p. 196.

published in Lyons in 1571 (forty years after the appearance of Alciatus's *Emblematum liber*) by the Huguenot writer Georgette de Montenay.[12] The production of religious emblem books began slowly: Simon Rosarius, *Antithesis Christi et Antichristi* (Geneva, 1578). Julius Hortinus Roscius, *Emblemata sacra* (Rome, 1589), and Augustus Callias, *Emblemata sacra* (Heidelberg, 1591) seem to be the only religious emblem books published in the sixteenth century prior to the somewhat late advent of the Jesuits on the scene. Probably the first Jesuit to publish a religious emblem book was Frans de Costere with his *De Vita . . . Mariae* (Antwerp, 1587). De Costere was followed by Canisius and Spanmüller, but the flood of Jesuit emblem writing really begins only in the seventeenth century with Jan David, Jeremias Drexel, and Hermann Hugo.[13] The Jesuits themselves produced over four hundred emblem books, and as a thematic group religious emblems probably account for one-third of the total book production.

If the sixteenth century is the age of encyclopedic and humanistic emblem books in which moral, philosophical, and political content predominates, then the seventeenth century witnesses a greater specialization and also diversification in the use of this new form. Reference has already been made to the emergence of the religious emblem book that was used for many purposes by writers of various confessions and denominations. The scope is indeed broad, ranging from homely sermonizing and simple Bible illustration, through dogma and catechism, lives of the saints, meditations upon the Virgin Mary, meditation both occasional and thematically organized, to mysticism. In addition to general collections of moral and philosophical emblems that continued to appear, the first Neostoic emblem book appeared in 1607. In this year Otto van Veen published his influential collection *Q. HoratI Flacci Emblemata* (Antwerp); a tremendous success, it was translated into French and German and ran through at least thirty-four editions.

Another important development was the emergence in the Netherlands of love emblems. It started in 1601 with the appearance of an anonymous volume under the title *Quaeris quid sit amor*, with cupid as the central figure. Daniel Heinsius was the author of this extremely successful collection; his lead was taken up by van Veen with a collection in 1608 and by Hooft in 1611. These secular love emblems were very quickly appropriated for religious purposes, and it does, indeed, appear that Dutch love emblems had an almost catalytic influence in the development of the whole tradition of the religious emblem.

Increasing specialization can also be seen in choice of material. Camerarius drew upon the realm of nature for each of the four hundred emblems in his four books of emblems, first published in the later 1590s. One of the most highly specialized emblem books remains the collection by Michael Maier entitled *Atlanta Fugiens* (1617). This work contains mottoes and epigrams in Latin and German and a musical setting for the Latin epigram. A learned Latin commentary is appended to each emblem. Maier's volume may thus be considered a "Gesamtkunstwerk" *in nuce*.

Looking back over representative examples of the emblem books of the sixteenth and seventeenth centuries one recognizes in them a veritable mirror of the manifold interests and concerns of the age. Emblems reflect contemporary thinking on such divergent themes as war and love, social mores and alchemical mysteries, humanist values and Calvinist doctrines, moral philosophy and political wisdom, *vanitas* and death. In a nutshell, the emblem taught people how to live in the widest sense, and also how to die.

In the production of emblem books Germany played a large and decisive role. The very first emblem book ever published, Alciatus's

Emblematum liber, was the work of Augsburg printers. In the following two centuries it is estimated that about a third of all emblem books were "made in Germany."

Modern German theories of the emblem recognize in this combination of picture and text "eine Doppelfunktion des Darstellens und Deutens" (Schöne, p. 21), which may take many forms. The representational function is, of course, largely reserved for the *pictura*, but insofar as the epigram may describe the picture or even extend it verbally, the text also participates in the representation. Since the texts of an emblem can fulfill a representational function — there are also many collections of *emblemata nuda*, i.e., emblems with no pictures at all — we are not surprised to discover that many writers of literary works create through words alone emblematic images and other structures that are reminiscent of the emblem. In short, there is something that may be called emblematic literature; indeed much of the literature of the sixteenth and seventeenth centuries requires reading in the light of the emblem.[14] In the limited space available I can only indicate briefly how an emblematic mode of thought and form of expression helped shape one major genre, German baroque poetry.[15]

The transition from the emblem proper to emblematic poetry can be traced in several ways. The most direct link is the emblematic epigram that re-creates or extends the *pictura* before embarking upon an interpretation. Many an Alciatus epigram neatly divides into a representational or descriptive section followed by an interpretational part of equal length. Thus, in the *Emblematum liber* (Paris, 1542) Wolfgang Hunger begins his translation of Alciatus's crow emblem on unity (No. 6) with a description of the *pictura*:

> Die Krawen halten sonderlich
> Vnder inn frid vnd eynigkeyt,
> Drumb malt man sy nit vnbillich
> Zu dem scepter der herlichkeyt.

The second half of this epigram provides the abstract statement of meaning:

> Dan yedes volcks einhelligkeyt
> Gibt vnd nimbt den herren iren gwalt,
> Wo die zerbricht, kumbt in gleych leyd,
> Drumb furst der deinen lieb erhalt.

Some emblem writers keep the epigram short and then add a fourth component, an emblem poem, that "explains" the emblem more fully.

Recht thun/ist Gott lieb.

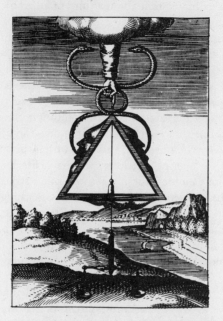

E In fromb Mann brauche seyn Witz vnd Kunst/
Spricht jedem recht/acht auff kein Gunst;
Dieweil er weiß/daß Gott geliebt/
Der gleiche Maaß eim jeden giebt.

Illustration 4: Andreas Friedrich, *Emblemata nova* (Frankfurt, 1617), p. 53.

For instance, Andreas Friedrich's emblem 26 has as the title "Recht thun / ist Gott lieb," which is embodied in a hieroglyphical combination of a hand appearing from a cloud encircled with two snakes which are connected to an equilateral triangle, each side of which bears a face; the triangle is connected to a pair of scales. The four-line epigram speaks in general about the just man, but it does not elucidate the picture closely. This is reserved for the twenty-two-line *Erklärung* (see Illustration 4).

In collections of *emblemata nuda*, which according to Heckscher and Wirth may comprise as much as a tenth of all emblem book production (cf. col. 101), it is evident that words must re-create the visual experience normally special to the *pictura*. Some collections of poetry are also virtually naked emblems. I have suggested elsewhere that Greiffenberg's *Tugend-Übung* should be regarded as naked emblems, a kind of conversation game, and ultimately as a veiled reflection of some very acute personal problems. In this "exercise" seven shepherdesses each choose a symbolic object or motif that functions as the verbalized *pictura*, for which each shepherdess composes a motto and "explanation" in the form of a sonnet. For instance, the first shepherdess names as her heroic emblem "die vom Apollo geliebte und wegen ihrer Ehr' in einen Lorbeer-Baum verwandelte Dafne." The motto reads "Die Sieges-kron / ist Tugend-lohn." Daphne is chosen because she embodies paradigmatically a commitment to virtue, which triumphs over all adversity: "Tugend" is "ein' Allbeherrscherin," "Ehr" remains "das höchste Gut."[16]

Leaving aside the emblem books and collections of *emblemata nuda* in whatever form, we find some poems that are consciously, indeed self-consciously, modeled on emblems. Thus Paul Fleming wrote a color poem "Aus dem Alziat über die Farben," which, as the title tells us, is based on an Alciatus emblem. In the Held edition (Frankfurt am Main, 1566) the unillustrated emblem on colors is numbered 61. Fleming's poem is evidently a translation of Alciatus's twenty-line epigram into a German poem of the same length and deals with each of the nine colors in the same fashion. In every instance a color is associated with its traditional concept. Thus, black "steht zu schwarzen Traurigkeiten," white means "ohne Falschheit sein," green signifies "daß man hofft," and dark red symbolizes "Liebeseifer." Ultimately the poem is a listing of separate colors with no thematic links.

Martin Opitz also played with colors and one wonders whether he, too, did not have the Alciatus emblem in front of him. His poem "Bedeutung der Farben," however, is focused on the subject of love. In this petrarchistic poem Opitz uses no less than eleven different colors, over half of them identical with those in Alciatus's emblem. Optiz's purpose is to describe the state of mind of a lover by reference to colors and their traditional meanings. The colors thus paint a spiritual portrait of the petrarchistic lover.

Since the emblem is a combination of representational picture and textual elucidation, the emblematic image in literature is the verbal analogue, the emblem *in nuce*. Baroque poetry is rich in examples of emblematic imagery. On occasion the poet seems to be describing an actual emblem picture. In his ode entitled simply "Entsagung" (Ode V, 17), Paul Fleming discusses the pleasures and pain of love, an example of which is a little scene in which Cupid is tempted to steal honey from a beehive, only to be stung for his efforts. The moral taught by this "Exempel" is stated in the last line of this passage:

Der süße Saft der gelben Bienen,
Kupido, der verführte dich;
Da du dich wolltst zu tief erkühnen,
So kriegst du einen bittern Stich.
Dies dein Exempel lehret alle:
Wo Honig ist, da ist auch Galle.

What Fleming describes in words, Alciatus features in an emblem.[17]

In "Neujahrsode 1633" Fleming prays for peace, unity, and an end to warfare, at a time when in fact the terrible Thirty Years War was only reaching its midpoint. Following the appeal to Mars to cease his battles, the desire for peace is translated into the emblematic image of martins nesting in a helmet:

Dieser Helm wird nütze sein,
Daß die Schwalben nisten drein,
Daß man, wann der Frühling kömmt,
Junge Vögel da vernimmt.

The description recalls an emblem of Alciatus with the motto "Ex bello pax," showing bees flying towards a helmet in which they have presumably built their hive.[18] Fleming's combination of helmet and nesting martins is striking—visual and rich in significance that is accessible through the emblematic tradition. The overall meaning is clear and could be stated in Alciatus's general phrase "peace from war," but the full implication depends on the reader's recognition of the ideas associated with the martin. As a species this bird is associated in European tradition with notions of prudent trust, security, goodness, procreation, justice, and caring.[19] Martins, or *Hausschwalben*, nest in the eaves of human habitation, where they feel safe in the enjoyment of human protection. They were regarded as a bird of good omen, and the house where they nest was believed to be protected against fire and lightning; they were also supposed to avoid an evil house. In tending their young, martins exhibit an exemplary combination of justice and generosity, treating all their offspring alike. Some of these ideas are relevant in Fleming's emblematic image, which in visual terms suggests the desire that war turn to a peace characterized by security and creativity, justice and generosity.

Emblematic images are frequently used by poets as strategies in argument. In such cases the choice of motif depends on its "truth"; the emblem must possess what has been called "documentary character" if it is to persuade the reader. In his long stoic poem *Trostgedicht Jn*

Widerwertigkeit deß Kriegs Martin Opitz discusses on several occasions
the invulnerability of virtue (the quotations below are from *Geistliche
Poemata*, 1638; ed. E. Trunz, 1975, pp. 348, 368, 372). To demonstrate
the strength of virtue in adversity Opitz cites the instance of saffron,
which only gives off its fragrance when rubbed and bruised:

> . . . Je mehr man Saffron reibet /
> Je stärker schmäckt er auch: Je mehr man Tugend treibet /
> Je höher schlägt sie auß . . .

To express the superiority of the stoic heart over Fortuna, Opitz employs
the ancient notion that the laurel can withstand fire and lightning:

> Deß Donners harte Krafft / wie die Gelehrten sagen /
> Pflegt in den Lorbeerbaum gar nimmer einzuschlagen:
> So ist auch für die Macht deß Glückes jederzeit
> Der Tugend grünes Laub versichert vnd befreit.

Finally, Opitz refers to the oak tree that grows new branches to replace
those cut off as proof of the ability of stoic virtue to prosper in adversity:

> . . . Die Tugend gibt kein Blut;
> Man mag sie / wie man wil / verfolgen / neyden / hassen /
> Sie helt jhr großes Wort: Sich nicht bewegen lassen;
> Jst einer Eichen gleich / je öffter man sie schlägt /
> Je mehr man sie behäwt / je mehr sie äste trägt.

In every instance the poet draws upon a presumed fact of nature—saffron, laurel, and oak—embodying a general truth in order to make a
persuasive statement. The emblematic image is thus neither decoration,
nor mere repetition. A significant meaning, whether stated or simply implied, is associated with an aspect of the *res* (object) that can be depicted
in the emblematic *pictura* or named in the literary text.

In these examples of emblematic imagery, a single visualizable object, or a combination of objects, is regarded as bodying forth certain
abstract notions. Frequently, the poet will create a pattern of visual images, each of which is complete in itself but is not related to its neighbor
in terms of image field. In a sonnet by Greiffenberg celebrating the great
faith of the Canaanite woman who compels Christ to heal her—
"vom unbesiegbaren / trägst du den Sieg davon"—Christ is described
both as a stone concealing "ein Gnaden-fünklein," and a rock, containing "Heiles-safft"; then images of tiger, pelican, Mars, and Venus pass
in quick succession:

das Tiger / wird gar bald ein Pelican dir seyn:
der Mars / ein Venus Stern; Blitz-Donner / Sonnenschein.[20]

Here, as elsewhere, the poet lists a series of motifs: tiger, pelican, Mars, Venus, thunder and lightning, and sunshine, without explicit interpretation. Such patterns of unrelated images, which are associated together by virtue of their relationship to the theme or concept (itself often unstated), have caused modern readers aesthetic and intellectual problems. They have been considered capricious and inappropriately faulted for not satisfying ahistorical aesthetic theories that enshrine organicism and coherence as the ultimate criteria. However, at least superficially, this asyndetic piling up of discrete images finds a parallel in the ideogrammatic poetry of some twentieth-century poets. Ezra Pound and such objectivist poets as Zukofsky and Oppen, and postmodernists such as Olson and Creeley, developed a method of image composition that Pound derived in part from a misreading of Chinese ideograms.[21] In German literature of the twentieth century a certain influence of, or affinity with, the Chinese ideogram and Japanese haiku verse can also be discovered; the names of Klabund and Brecht come to mind.[22] However, both the hieroglyph and certain forms of emblem, as well as modern ideogrammic verse, combine images in a technically similar manner: they use the mode of paratactic juxtaposition. And just as the scholars of the Renaissance had misinterpreted the Egyptian hieroglyphs, because they ignored the phonetic aspects, so also did Pound and his followers overlook the phonetic implications of the Chinese characters. In both cases, the misunderstanding had creative results.

The juxtaposition of emblematic images—indeed, even the accumulation of verbal emblems—often resembles the multiple emblems (*mehrständige Sinnbilder*) of Harsdörffer and the Nürnberg writers. An instance of this is Greiffenberg's sonnet "Über des Creutzes Nutzbarkeit," where we read (p. 82; see note 20):

> Ein schöne Sach / im Leiden Früchte bringen!
> die Edlen Stein / zeugt die gesalzne Flut.
> Es wird das Gold vollkommen in der Glut.
> Aus hartem Felß die süßen Brunnen springen.
> Die Rose muß her durch die Dörner dringen.
> Die Märtyr-Kron / wächst aus vergossnem Blut.

Precious stone, gold, springs of water, rose, and martyr's crown are discrete images, following one upon the other without any explanation

or link; they are, however, related to the theme announced in the title of
the sonnet. We should not expect organic unity among these asyndetic
images. Nor should we demand contiguity of imagery in all poetry. Frequently, the baroque poet is circling a complex subject, illuminating it
from different angles, suggesting a meaning by providing analogies or,
as in the case of the emblem, by juxtaposing a series of visual em-
bodiments of the idea.

From these series of emblematic images, which frequently fill the
octave of a sonnet, it is but a short step to the complete poem, conceived
and executed in an emblematic fashion. The poem that comes closest to
the emblem itself is probably the epigram. Czepko's titles can function as
the *pictura*, which is then elucidated in the couplet that follows:

> Ie reiner Glas
> Ie schöner Bild.

> Mensch, stille deine Seel, alsbald sie klar und rein,
> Entbildet sich in ihr der Höchsten Krafft und Schein.[23]

Some of Silesius's epigrams combine *pictura* and motto, or visual motif
and theme, in the title, which is then treated more fully in the epigram:

> Die geistliche Goldmachung

> Dann wird das Blei zu Gold, dann fällt der Zufall hin,
> Wenn ich mit Gott durch Gott in Gott verwandelt bin.[24]

The basis of the typological emblem is, as indicated above, an assumed "fact of nature," for which the test of truth is neither the litmus
paper nor the slide rule of modern science. Many emblem writers, and
also many emblematic poets, derive visual motifs together with their at-
tendant meanings from myth and fable, which today would be written
off as superstitious or fantastic. However, in reading these texts a certain
humility is never out of place, since the history of the pursuit of knowledge is one in which a proven truth is later discovered to be error, and the
faith of one generation is the superstitition of another. Interestingly
enough, an emblematic poet will occasionally insist on the truth of the
nature motif he employs, as though anticipating a skeptical response on
the part of his reader. Thus Silesius suggests that the story concerning the
birth of the pearl, conceived in the oyster shell from a drop of dew, is
readily proved ("beweist"), in case the reader is not prepared to believe
("Wo dus nicht glauben willst"). The birth of the pearl is then interpreted religiously as demonstrating spiritual regeneration:

Die Perlengeburt

Die Perle wird vom Tau in einer Muschelhöhle
Gezeuget und geborn und dies ist bald beweist,
Wo dus nicht glauben willst: der Tau ist Gottes Geist
Die Perle Jesus Christ, die Muschel meine Seele.[25]

In form the epigram is also perfectly emblematic: the motto like an *inscriptio* identifies the visual subject; it is then described in the first two lines of the epigram, which assume the function of the *pictura;* the meaning of the whole is interpreted in the final two lines in the manner of a *subscriptio*.

Many readers have observed that the sonnet and ode forms lend themselves particularly well to the emblematic mode. Windfuhr[26] and Jöns[27] have discussed some of Gryphius's emblematic sonnets, Anna Kiel[28] sonnets by Rompler von Löwenhalt, and I have drawn attention to several examples in Greiffenberg's oeuvre (see note 16), one of which must suffice by way of illustration.

GOTTes Vorsehungs-Spiegel

DEr Kasten schwebte schon / HErr GOtt / in deinen Sinnen /
als sich der Himmel trübt und sich die Flut anhebt'.
Eh die alt' Erd' ertrank / schon in der neuen lebt
der beeder Welten Held / auf deines Rahts schaubühnen.
Das Feur war schon gekült / als jene Drey darinnen.
Auch David war gekrönt / weil er in Elend schwebt.
das Weib war schon entzuckt / eh ihr der Drach nachstrebt.
GOtt pflegt die Schnur / eh man in Irrgang kommt / zu spinnen.
Die Schlange war entgifft / eh Paulus sie berührt.
der Freuden-Lehre [Evangelium] Liecht brann schon in GOttes wißen /
ehe man ein Füncklein noch in allen Seelen spürt.
Vor Unglücks Schickung / ist der Höchst auf Hülff beflißen.
drum folget ihm / wie fremd und seltsam Er euch führt.
sein' Hand hat aus der Höll / geschweig aus Noht / gerißen.[29]

The title "GOTTes Vorsehungs-Spiegel" names the subject of the poem and already combines the abstract theme *Vorsehung* with a general image *Spiegel* somewhat in the manner of an emblem motto. The octave and first tercet "mirror" the theme in eight different images or concrete instances from the Old and New Testament, carefully spanning the period from the Flood to Christ's message of salvation, "der Freuden-Lehre Liecht." This series of images is the verbal counterpart of the emblem *pictura*, the full meaning of which is then elucidated in the final tercet, which has the function of the interpretative *subscriptio*. The general sense is first stated in the line "Vor Unglücks Schickung / ist der Höchst auf Hülff beflißen" and then elaborated in the concluding lines.

Although much of the literature of the seventeenth century is the creation of the same attitude of mind and mode of composition that produced the emblem book, it is incontestable that the concept "emblem" has been stretched too far and applied indiscriminately. There is a danger that this term, which has received sharper contours in recent years, is almost becoming as fashionable today as "existentialism" was yesterday, and "ambiguity" the day before.

NOTES

1. Mario Praz, *Studies in Seventeenth-Century Imagery*, 2nd ed. (Rome, 1964).
2. John Landwehr, *Dutch Emblem Books: A Bibliography* (Utrecht, 1962); *Emblem Books in the Low Countries, 1554–1949: A Bibliography* (Utrecht, 1970); *German Emblem Books: A Bibliography* (Utrecht, 1972).
3. Wolfgang Harms and Hartmut Freytag, *Außerliterarische Wirkungen barocker Emblembücher: Emblematik in Ludwigsburg, Gaarz und Pommersfelden* (München, 1975).
4. Grete Lesky, *Barocke Embleme in Vorau und anderen Stiften Österreichs* (Graz, [1962]).
5. Henry Green, *Shakespeare and the Emblem Writers* (London, 1870).
6. Cf. Arthur Henkel, "Die geheimnisvolle Welt der Embleme," *Heidelberger Jahrbücher*, 19 (1975), 1-23.
7. Eleanor of Austria, Dowager Queen of France, chose the phoenix and the motto "unica semper avis" to characterize her widowhood.
8. The rules of Paolo Giovio are quoted in Italian and translated into German by Albrecht Schöne, *Emblematik und Drama im Zeitalter des Barock*, 2nd ed. (München, 1968), p. 44; they will be found in English in Praz, p. 63.
9. Cf. Claude Paradin, *Devises Héroïques* (Lyons, 1557), p. 63.
10. Cf. Arthur Henkel and Albrecht Schöne, *Emblemata: Handbuch zur Sinnbildkunst des XVI. und XVII. Jahrhunderts* (Stuttgart, 1967), col. 601.
11. Cf. Peter M. Daly, *Emblem Theory: Recent German Contributions to the Characterization of the Emblem Genre* (Nendeln, 1979), pp. 82-85.
12. De Montenay's is assumed to be the first religious emblem book, if we discount Maraffi's *Figure del Vecchio Testamento* (Geneva, 1554), a collection of Bible figures, which like the hieroglyphic Bibles have been wrongly classified as emblem books.
13. See the surveys of Jesuit emblem books carried out by G. Richard Dimler,

70   PETER M. DALY

S.J., and published in the *Archivum Historicum Societates Iesu*, 1976, 1977, 1978; cf. also H. Breidenbach, "Vanitas und Tod beim Emblematiker J. Drexel," *Europäische Tradition und Deutscher Literaturbarock*, ed. G. Hoffmeister (Bern, 1973), pp. 391-410.

14. See Peter M. Daly, *Literature in the Light of the Emblem: Structural Parallels between the Emblem and Literature in the Sixteenth and Seventeenth Centuries* (Toronto, 1979).

15. Albrecht Schöne has established the various ways in which an emblematic mode shapes baroque drama (see note 8).

16. For a fuller discussion of the *Tugend-Übung*, see Peter M. Daly, *Dichtung und Emblematik bei Catharina Regina von Greiffenberg* (Bonn, 1976), pp. 66-113.

17. Cf. *Emblematum liber* (Augsburg, 1531), No. E4b and 5; Held editions Nos. 101 and 102. See also *Thronus Cupidinis* (1620), D6, and Daniel Heinsius, *Nederduytsche Poemata* (Amsterdam, 1616), p. 42.

18. Cf. Paris editions No. 45. This motif recurs in many variations, e.g., Covarrubias, *Emblemas Morales* (Madrid, 1610), Book I, No. 7, where bees nest in a skull.

19. Cf. Peter M. Daly, "Of Macbeth, Martlets and 'other Fowles of Heauen,' " *Mosaic*, 12 (1978), 23-46.

20. Catharina Regina von Greiffenberg, *Geistliche Sonnette, Lieder und Gedichte* (Nürnberg, 1662), p. 125.

21. Cf. Laszlo Géfin, "Ideogram: The History of a Poetic Method" (diss. McGill University 1979).

22. Cf. Antony Tatlow, *Brechts chinesische Gedichte* (Frankfurt a.M., 1973), and Ingrid Schuster, *China und Japan in der deutschen Literatur, 1890-1925* (München, 1977).

23. Daniel von Czepko, *Sexcenta Monodisticha* (1655), V, 78; in *Geistliche Schriften*, Vol. I, ed. Werner Milch (Breslav, 1930).

24. Angelus Silesius, *Der Cherubinische Wandersmann* (1657 ff.), I, 102; in *Sämtliche poetische Werke*, Vol. III, ed. L. Held (München, 1949).

25. *Der Cherubinische Wandersmann*, III, 248.

26. Manfred Windfuhr, *Die barocke Bildlichkeit und ihre Kritiker* (Stuttgart, 1966), p. 92.

27. Dietrich Walter Jöns, *Das "Sinnen-Bild": Studien zur allegorischen Bildlichkeit bei Andreas Gryphius* (Stuttgart, 1966), pp. 91-102.

28. Anna Kiel, "Jesias Rompler von Löwenhalt: Ein Dichter des Frühbarock," (diss. Amsterdam 1940).

29. *Geistliche Sonnette, Lieder und Gedichte*, p. 17 (see note 20).

SELECTED BIBLIOGRAPHY

Secondary Literature

Clements, Robert J. *Picta Poesis: Literary and Humanistic Theory in Renaissance Emblem Books.* Rome, 1960.

Daly, Peter M. *Emblem Theory: Recent German Contributions to the Characterization of the Emblem Genre.* Nendeln, 1979.

——. *Literature in the Light of the Emblem: Structural Parallels between the Emblem and Literature in the Sixteenth and Seventeenth Centuries.* Toronto, 1979.

Freeman, Rosemary. *English Emblem Books.* London, 1948; rpt. 1967.

Giehlow, Karl. *Die Hieroglyphenkunde des Humanismus in der Allegorie der Renaissance, besonders der Ehrenpforte Kaisers Maximilian I.* Jahrbuch der kunsthistorischen Sammlungen des allerhöchsten Kaiserhauses, 32, Heft 1. Wien and Leipzig, 1915.

Harms, Wolfgang, and Hartmut Freytag. *Außerliterarische Wirkungen barocker Emblembücher: Emblematik in Ludwigsburg, Gaarz und Pommersfelden.* München, 1975.

Heckscher, William S., and Karl-August Wirth. "Emblem, Emblembuch," *Reallexikon zur Deutschen Kunstgeschichte.* Stuttgart, 1959. Vol. V, cols. 85–228.

Henkel, Arthur, and Albrecht Schöne. *Emblemata: Handbuch zur Sinnbildkunst des XVI. und XVII. Jahrhunderts.* Stuttgart, 1967; rev. ed., 1976.

Homann, Holger. *Studien zur Emblematik des 16. Jahrhunderts.* Utrecht, 1971.

Jöns, Dietrich Walter. *Das "Sinnen-Bild": Studien zur allegorischen Bildlichkeit bei Andreas Gryphius.* Stuttgart, 1966.

Landwehr, John. *Dutch Emblem Books: A Bibliography.* Utrecht, 1962.

——. *Emblem Books in the Low Countries, 1554–1949: A Bibliography.* Utrecht, 1970.

——. *German Emblem Books: A Bibliography.* Utrecht, 1972.

Praz, Mario. *Studies in Seventeenth-Century Imagery.* 2nd ed. Rome, 1964.

Schöne, Albrecht. *Emblematik und Drama im Zeitalter des Barock.* 2nd ed. München, 1968.

5

Baroque Philology: The Position of German in the European Family of Languages

Peter Schaeffer

In the investigation of an age in which the ideal of the *poeta doctus*, whose work was intended to exhibit his universal scholarship, still enjoyed an untarnished reputation, it will come as no surprise to find the personal union of poet and scholar far more the rule than the exception it grew to be in later periods. As a consequence, the concerns of creative writing and critical research appear joined in that organic inter-dependence which only late-eighteenth-century aesthetics was radically to repudiate. Accordingly, at least a glance at the manifold activities of baroque philology, rather than a mere pendant to a summary view of the literature of the period, forms an integral part of its consideration.

Selecting among the wealth of topics that occur under the general heading of the German Language, its nature and its antiquities, the present sketch will address the apologetic aspect, i.e., the vindication of German as a vehicle of consummate literary expression in competition with both the classical languages and the rival European vernaculars — a vindication made intrinsically by reason of its native structure as well as historically by the demonstration of its literary achievements in the course of the nearly thousand years of its documented past.

In the larger context of the times this defense of the language was apparently a peculiarly German undertaking, for while in other countries such as England, France, and Spain the rise of the modern literary vernacular accompanied the consolidation of the national state, the territory of the Holy Roman Empire of the German nation was split into over three hundred, often minuscule, sovereignties, and the language remained as the only measure by which anyone could classify oneself as German. Or to reduce the matter to the simplest formula: in the Western countries mentioned, the language and its literature were the emblems of national identity—in Germany, its necessary surrogate. Thus England had Shakespeare, Spain Cervantes, and France its imminent classicism at the time that Opitz was still engaged in formulating the very foundations of contemporary German literary endeavor.

Opitz's pioneering work in German poetics is discussed in the essay by Solomon in this volume. What deserves mention here is his youthful diatribe, entitled *Aristarchus sive De Contemptu Linguae Teutonicae*, of 1618. Like his other contributions, this one, too, for all its originality, had its sources in questions left unanswered in the previous century. The Renaissance had paid little attention to the theoretical justification of German as a literary language. Vadianus in his *De Poetica* of just a century before had ventured a brief encomium of medieval German literature, extolling the German language for its copiousness and its capacity for refined expression.[1] At the same time Erasmus in his *De Ratione Studii* had set as the cornerstone of education the study of Greek and Latin, "since in these two languages there is set forth nearly everything that is worthwhile knowing."[2] The massive progagandistic efforts of Reformation and Counter-Reformation had, of course, generated a vast volume of German writing, some of it even on a recognizably literary level. However, a German and a Latin literature continued to develop side by side with little theoretical reflection on this phenomenon,[3] although the latter part of the sixteenth century saw the appearance of a number of attempts at formulating German grammar, thereby consciously elevating it to the status of an appropriate object of scholarship. For Opitz the problem had become both more complex and more urgent: the one because the value of German had now to be asserted not only against the ancient languages but also against the neighboring vernaculars; the other because he witnessed the contamination of German by waves of unassimilated loan words and a predilection for the use of foreign languages altogether in preference to German. The outbreak of the Thirty Years War, fought out to a great extent by foreign troops on German soil, was only to aggravate this predicament.

Opitz begins his argument in the *Aristarchus* with a contemplation of the glorious German past, again a practice inherited from the previous century, with its rediscovery of Tacitus and its zeal for collecting, publishing, and studying newly found monuments of ancient German literature, history, and law.[4] With genial ahistoricity Opitz contrasts the decline of the classical languages in the Middle Ages, and once again since the heyday of humanism, with the fact that German has come down through the centuries in the pristine purity of its singular expressiveness. But the present is on the point of spelling doom for this language because of the influx of a monstrous vocabulary and structural cancers derived from the indiscriminate import of foreign elements. Travel and other foreign contacts, far from leading to emulation of, say, the French or Italian practice of cultivating their respective tongues, has simply resulted in estrangement from German and the mindless aping of the seemingly exotic. As a consequence the German language has become a sewer to collect the offal of all the others. In reality, however (he continues), the native character of our words and the flow of our sentences is so happily contrived that it need yield nothing to the majesty of Spanish, the niceties of Italian, or the graceful eloquence of French. From the heroic chants mentioned by Tacitus through the remains of the intervening centuries recently published by Goldast,* the corpus of German literature testifies that there has never been a species of poetry in any language with which German could not enter into competition. The brief work concludes with a summons to cherish this heritage on pain of national self-destruction and to defend and develop the inherent powers of the mother tongue. Affectionate pride in the German language generating an urge to explore its achievements, such as Opitz had articulated here with aphoristic hyperbole, were to prove the motivation producing numerous works of philological scholarship throughout the following decades.

The most ambitious of these in scope and volume was to be the treatise *Von der Teutschen HaubtSprache* by the Hanoverian Justus Georg Schottel, or as he always preferred to call himself, Schottelius (1612-76), which appeared in 1663. As the title page indicates, he incorporated into this work several earlier writings of his own in expanded form, adding, however, from his fully mature work a number of significant elements to make it, as it were, his definitive statement on the sub-

---

*Melchior Goldast von Haiminsfeld (15/8-1635), jurist and antiquarian, wrote *Scriptores rerum Suevicarum* (1605), *Scriptores rerum Alamannicarum*, 3 vols. (1606), and *Collectio constitutionum imperialium*, 4 vols. (1607-15).

ject. The whole is divided into five books for a total of over fifteen hundred pages, the first consisting of ten panegyrics (*Lobrede[n] von der Uhralten Teutschen HaubtSprache*), which chart the course of the entire investigation. A preview of the work, its nature and method, is followed by the testimonials of famous men, beginning with Charlemagne, exalting the German language, and as its counterpart a refutation of the adverse criticism from foreign sources. The reader will notice at once, if only from the differentiation of the typeface, that although Schottelius like all his contemporaries is an uncompromising opponent of language contamination, the book is interlaced with Latin terms and phrases, or even with long passages, sometimes extending over several pages. One reason for this is that the book was intended to be accessible to the non-German-speaking scholarly world in order to have an international apologetic effect;[5] the second reason is that the treatment of the subject requires a commensurate technical vocabulary, which either did not exist in German at all or is here introduced for the first time.

Despite his frequent retrospections in this first book, and a predilection for arraying documentary evidence, one must not impute to Schottelius historical thinking in the modern sense, which was quite beyond the possibilities of his time. On the basic contention that the German language has always been substantially the same and true to itself, his often-stated goal is to expound its ultimate intrinsic principles, its *Grundrichtigkeit*. The passage of time—and Schottelius distinguishes five periods (*Denkzeiten*), dating respectively from the origin of German, from Charlemagne, from the restoration of the Empire by Rudolf of Habsburg, from Luther, and from the current endeavors to return German to its original purity and equip it for its future mission—does not imply any radical development of the language but only the elaboration of its immutable principles or the accretion of accidental changes, for better or worse. This basic substance is the sum of the irreducible root words which German possesses in peculiar abundance and upon which the whole language rests as a building does upon its immovable foundations, or music upon its individual notes. Besides its wealth of root words, which also, as a relatively new departure, establishes German as akin to, but not dependent upon nor inferior to Latin, the genius of the language further manifests itself in its unique capacity to aggregate these roots into compounds, which Schottelius calls *Verdopplungen*, although a compound often consists of several more than two elements. Mastery of German and the ability to use it for every manner of refined, especially poetic, diction thus consists of thorough familiarity with all its integral parts and of sovereign skill in assembling these parts according to the innate laws of the language; it is, in a word, an art of combination, comparable to the construction of mosaics from a myriad of pieces.

German thus having been demonstrated to be a suitable, indeed a superior poetic vehicle, Schottelius goes on to show by examples that it has always been cultivated and regarded in this sense. While still assuming an ultimately divine origin of language, Schottelius with an evident partiality for empirical data ventures into the area of comparative philology to note the similarities between German root words and their counterparts in numerous other modern European languages. The underlying assumption is that there was an ancient Teutonic or Celtic (!) language which survives in contemporary German in its purest form, while developing into dialects in the various related languages, e.g., English and the Scandinavian family. The autonomy of German is thus the best argument for restoring it, principally among its native speakers, to its full esteem. Schottelius recognizes that dialects have also arisen within German, and he distinguishes between the Low German dialects (variants of the older form of the language) and the High German dialects (variants of its more refined form). The panegyrics close with an admission that no adequate dictionary of German exists as yet and principles are set down according to which such a dictionary should be compiled, a task that was not accomplished until two centuries later.

The remaining four books of the treatise translate into practical directives what the first book had established in theory, offering a detailed handbook of grammar and syntax, modeled on Latin grammar, which has survived to the present day; a guide to metrics, prosody, and poetic genres; and, finally, a miscellany including annotated listings (of place names and proper names, proverbs and idiomatic expressions), a remarkably inclusive bibliography pertaining to German philology, and an index of some five thousand German root words, with a systematic introduction.

Schottelius's chapter on proper translation into German deserves some attention. Far from being a mere excursus this chapter centers on the final practical test of the principles expressed throughout the treatise. It is cast in the form of a dialogue of the teacher-pupil variety, the point of departure being the observation that generally a translation can be distinguished from a work originally written in German by its less than idiomatic or even cumbersome texture. This results from an inadequate command of the inner workings (*Grundrichtigkeit*) of the German language, and Schottelius with evident delight in the game offers an abundant sampling of the absurdities that result when, in translating from Latin into German and vice versa, a verbatim method instead of a knowledgeable transference of idiom to idiom is attempted and the translator is met with incomprehension, if not outright ridicule. The key to the avoidance of this pitfall is a sovereign command of the peculiar genius of both languages in question, derived from a thorough study of semantic structure as well as untiring perusal of the most renowned authors. Luther's translation of the Bible serves as the ideal illustration of the point at issue.

Still, the interlocutor objects, it may not always be possible to find an adequate expression in the target language, as was the case when early Roman writers attempted to put books written in highly differentiated Greek into their still fairly primitive Latin. In that case, Schottelius's spokesman replies, it is perfectly acceptable to make judicious use of loan words, adequately circumscribed and adopted into the new language as technical vocabulary. This had in fact been done over the centuries, when Greek and Latin supplied the terminology of theology, philosophy, jurisprudence, and other sciences, for which there simply were no German counterparts. The difference between this practice and mere language contamination seems to hinge on the question whether the loan word fills a real need, enriching the language into which it is adopted and eventually assimilated, or whether it is simply borrowed because the translator is ignorant of the propensities of his own language, or, far worse, is alienated from it and modishly inclined to favor foreign words.

This chapter, one might observe in passing, should occupy a particularly important place when the history of the theory and practice of translation in the sixteenth and seventeenth centuries — the period which saw the translation of the Bible, the most important Greco-Roman classics, and a significant amount of literature from other vernaculars into German — comes to be written. Schottelius's treatise as a whole, moreover, is about the most abundant statement of seventeenth-century thought on the German language. As Paul Hankamer so aptly put it, it is a baroque *summa philologica*.[6]

Daniel Georg Morhof (1639-91) is best remembered — and one should perhaps add: to the extent that he is remembered at all — for his monumental *Polyhistor*, an attempt to encompass critically the entire corpus of what was known to have beeen written on literature, philosophy, and the major academic disciplines,[7] but it is his other major work, the *Unterricht von der Teutschen Sprache und Poesie, Deren Ur-*

sprung, Fortgang und Lehr-Sätzen)1682; 2nd ed. 1700; 3rd ed. 1718),
that belongs to the present subject, inasmuch as from the very beginning
of the work its apologetic purpose is in evidence:

Welches [viz., the proof of the excellence of the German language] auch deßhal-
ben nötig ist / weilen sich auch unter gelehrten Leuten / und die von Teutscher
Herkunfft seyn / einige finden / die ihre Mutter-Sprache lästern / und deren
Grobheit und Ungeschicklichkeit zu guten Erfindungen / und zierlicher Ausbildung der Gedancken vorzugeben sich nicht scheuen. (3rd ed., p. 3)

If Schottelius had chosen the integrating method of demonstrating that
the German language possesses all the attributes of refinement and
literary capacity anyone might possibly seek in a general way in any other
language, Morhof adopts for a similar purpose a distinctly comparative
approach, vindicating diachronically the greater antiquity (and hence
the excellence) of German in relation to Latin and Greek, and syn-
chronically the merits of German literature taken as a whole in comparison with the literary corpus of the leading Western vernaculars. This
task comprises the first two sections of his treatise, while the third is
devoted to the orthography, grammar, syntax, and prosody of German,
together with a discussion of selected literary genres.

It is for Morhof's time a perfectly credible supposition that once the
antiquity of German has been demonstrated, its excellence necessarily
follows, since among the undisputed hallmarks of excellence the existence of a long and venerable tradition is of prime importance. The line
of argumentation Morhof follows is sufficiently curious for the modern
reader but all the more illuminating for the scholarly trends of the time.
Granted that German may indeed be primitive and uncouth, as those
denigrators whom he addresses dare to claim, then it is from this very
source that Morhof will prove its antiquity. For as it is evident that a
highly refined language derives from one less refined, so the one less
refined must precede the other in time. The Greeks themselves acknowledged that they had received the rudiments of their language and their
philosophy from barbarian predecessors, namely, the Scythians, whom
Morhof effortlessly identifies with the inhabitants of the ancient Germania. Indeed, a close comparison of the basic vocabulary of Greek and
Latin with that of German shows that German was the source of the classical languages and accordingly the more ancient. The etymologies that
Morhof offers in support of this contention are altogether plausible sets
of Indo-European cognates, even if a relationship is sometimes errone-
ously assumed. But the question of priority in derivation is answered ac-

cording to Morhof's axiom, and this consistently, so long as the words under discussion were conceived as static entities and not as stages in a complex development. In defense of such etymologies he courageously crosses swords with all comers:

Sensus von Sinn / (welches letzte Skinnerus meint von den Lateinern auf die Teutschen gekommen zu seyn / als wann dieselbe nicht eher ihre Sinne zu nennen gewust / oder dieselbe gar gehabt hätten / ehe die Römer sie es gelehret) . . . (3rd ed., p. 77)

Not only is the identification of the word with that which it designates striking, but also the perfect logical reversibility of the argument.

The result of a quantitatively and qualitatively staggering exhibition of such etymologies is the proof that German outdoes the classical languages in antiquity, and that the latter are in fact filiations of German. Similarly the contemporary vernaculars, so far as Morhof is acquainted with them, are shown to be on the Romance side Latin dialects,[8] and on the Germanic, derivative forms of German—the latter a point that Schottelius had made.

Morhof's programmatic exaltation of the German language is not necessarily a radical departure from the classicist standpoint of the Renaissance, in whose ideology Latin and Greek occupied a position of absolute and timeless supremacy.[9] For an ambivalence in the evaluation of Germanic antiquity, either as the corrupter of classical eloquence or the venerable ancestor of contemporary German, existed even in the previous century and found its ultimate basis in the divergent readings of Tacitus. One need but peruse Celtis's preface to his edition of Hrotsvit (tenth century), or Bebel's (1472-1518) introduction to his collection of German proverbs, or the fervent admiration for Old High German poetry occasionally surfacing in the commentaries of Beatus Rhenanus (1485-1547) to see that the national patriotic trend relativized the classicist ideology from the beginning, and to conclude that Morhof rather than overturn the Renaissance standpoint chose to emphasize one element of its ambivalent totality.

Morhof's second approach to the vindication of German is to compare its literary monuments with those of the principal vernaculars, and, of course, to find as a result that German can more than hold its own. This tendency is apparent from the beginning of the work, and the sketches of the various literatures are stylized to the function of a foil for this end. It is also evident from the arrangement of chapters: French, Italian, and Spanish, being more remote from German and hence less estimable, are dealt with first, followed by English, Dutch, and Norse as the more closely related and thus more appealing. As overwhelming as the amount of factual material must be to the reader, and as admirable as Morhof's versatility was at a time when the sources of bibliography flowed as a mere trickle compared with the torrents of information available today, the impression resulting is less that of literary history than of a subjectively annotated and quite sporadically assembled catalog. Although the first mention of Shakespeare in a German book (3rd ed., p. 229), for example, is at least a curiosity, it is a mention and no more:

Und der John Dryden hat gar wohl gelehrt von der Dramaticâ Poesi geschrieben. Die Engelländer / die er hierinnen anführet / sind Shakespeare, Fletcher, Beaumont, von welchen ich nichts gesehen habe. (3rd ed., p. 229)

In any event, the comparative approach serves as a mere preface to set off the excellence of German literature all the more strikingly. For its presentation Morhof devises three periods that are, from his standpoint, not devoid of some intrinsic merit: they date from the largely legendary beginnings to the era of Charlemagne, who is praised for his systematic concern for language and literature; from thence to the end of the sixteenth century; and finally to the contemporary scene, beginning with the Opitzian revival. The principal element of abiding interest in these chapters is the evidence of the extent to which older literature was known at all in the seventeenth century and how it was evaluated. To mention but a single example: the relatively positive evaluation of Hans Sachs (3rd ed., pp. 341 ff.) comes as a surprise in view of the generally presumed disdain of baroque aesthetics for the copious output of the redoubtable Nürnberg shoemaker.

The third part of Morhof's *Unterricht*, leaving the apologetic and descriptive concern with German for a normative treatment of its structure, belongs in a discussion of poetics rather than in the present essay. Suffice it to add that for close to a century after his death Morhof remained a respected authority in the scholarly world.

Although Christian Hofmann von Hofmannswaldau (1617-79) was a consummate master of the German language and author of some of its most exquisite poetry, as even over two centuries of futile critical attempts to consign him to oblivion indirectly attest, his inclusion among contributors to baroque philology may require some explanation. Indeed, while Opitz is remembered almost equally for his theoretical work and his poetry, and Schottelius and Morhof, though principally scholars, also wrote verses of at least commendable craftsmanship, Hofmann devoted himself in literature exclusively to original writing and translation. He is mentioned here because his work to a notable extent fulfills the theoretical imperatives formulated by the others. This is true particularly of his two masterful translations,[10] which can be related to Schottelius's chapter on this subject, and more generally of his work as a whole, which he understood as contributions to world literature, or at least to German literature as an equal among contemporary European literatures.

By a circuitous route, the preface to the 1679 edition of his *Deutsche Übersetzungen und Getichte* eventually makes this point about the equal status of German literature. Hofmann recalls that, following Opitz, he studied Latin, Italian, French, Dutch, and English authors for their stylistic accomplishments, not merely so as to imitate them but also to make their techniques productive for his mother tongue. He justifies his own lifelong occupation with poetry through an excursus into its nature and history, beginning with the familiar concept of the *poeta vates* in antiquity and continuing into German literature up to his own times. The brief panorama of medieval literature, in spite of its jumbled chronology, reveals genuine appreciation, coupled, however, with the expectedly ahistorical assessment that this early literature is often difficult to read because of its deficient orthography, and that it is defective in its as yet unrefined metrics. This is followed by a catalog of the accomplishments of a dozen poets of his own century, from Opitz down to his younger friend and contemporary, Casper von Lohenstein. The conclusion drawn from this survey is a confident assurance that German literature has indeed taken its equal place on the European scene:

Dis werde ich mich noch beyzufügen unterstehen / daß durch gedachter Männer Fleiß und Nachsinnen / die Deutsche Poesie so reine worden / daß sie der Außländischen nichts mehr nachgiebet. (Vorrede)

It is significant that Hofmann arrives at a point similar to that of Morhof, but with a rather different methodological accent. In the first place he is content to claim the equality of German with other literatures, without straining to assert its superiority. In addition, perhaps lacking the encyclopedic bibliographical command of Morhof, the cosmopolitan patrician reveals a decidedly more profound esteem for foreign literatures, to which he gladly confesses himself indebted at the outset of his deliberations, and his gentle side glances at their—by German standards—somewhat imperfect metrics sound a different note from the systematic depreciation for the sake of exalting German.

It is noteworthy that in the major work of his own creation, the *Heldenbriefe*, Hofmann in effect produced an artistic reconciliation between the ambivalent tendencies of Renaissance tradition, classicistic on the one side and nationalistic on the other, which, as previously mentioned, Morhof had theoretically weighted strongly in favor of the latter. Even without the telling phrase appended to his introductory mention of the *Heldenbriefe* — "dazu dann Ovidius mein Anführer gewesen" — this becomes evident from the nature of the work itself. For the genre is clearly of classical origin, but in versification and largely in subject matter it is decidedly German. Steering a middle course between pedantic imitation of the classics and the equally fruitless alternative of developing a wholly autonomous native literature, Hofmann produced a work of genuine emulation, not denying its antecedents in antiquity but in no way limited by obligations to tradition.

Works by four representative authors germane to the subject of this sketch have been examined in necessary brevity to provide at least a cursory insight into the patterns of philological speculation typical for the seventeenth century. The choice of these particular authors was intended to provide an exemplary rather than a comprehensive selection, and this may explain the absence of other, perhaps equally important, contributors to the discussion. A word of explanation for the omission of the towering figure of Leibniz seems especially in order. His thoughts on the subject of language derive their force only from the larger context of his vast philosophical opus, and to the extent that he is one of the few figures of the German baroque to have been given consistent international recognition, the general reader will more readily find avenues of access to his work than to that of the authors discussed here. Besides, coming fairly late in the seventeenth century and directing his visions to an as yet uncharted future, he may be a figure far more influential on the subsequent period of the Enlightenment than immediately upon his own. While observing with interest the endeavors of the language societies which counted Opitz and Schottelius among their guiding lights, he also remained consistently aloof from their sincere but often narrowly tendentious and less than scientific activities.

For the rest, much of the philological theory of the baroque taken by itself now has little more than historical, in some respects antiquarian, interests. But the literature that developed in consequence of the guidelines it provided, although often independent of and even counter to them, has stood the proverbial test of time, proving to be not only an object of keen scholarly interest but also of immediate and profound aesthetic enjoyment.

NOTES

1. Joachim Vadianus, *De Poetica et Carminis Ratione* (Vienna: Alantsee, 1518), p. civ.
2. Desiderius Erasmus, *Omnia Opera*, I (Leyden: Petrus Vander Aa, 1703), 521 (author's translation).
3. Some examples, seemingly to the contrary, are found in Günter Hess, *Deutsch-lateinische Narrenzunft: Studien zum Verhältnis von Volkssprache und Latinität in der satirischen Literatur des 16. Jahrhunderts* (München: Beck, 1971), where the question is usually resolved according to the purpose served by one or the other language, not its own merits.
4. An important phase of this activity is presented in Bernhard Hertenstein, *Joachim von Watt (Vadianus), Bartholomäus Schobinger, Melchior Goldast: Die Beschäftigung mit dem Althochdeutschen von St. Gallen in Humanismus und Frühbarock* (Berlin: de Gruyter, 1975).
5. There is no evidence that the book ever received any attention outside German-speaking countries.
6. Paul Hankamer, *Die Sprache* (Bonn: Cohen, 1927; rpt. Hildesheim: Olms, 1965), p. 124.
7. A brief summary of the *Polyhistor* is given in Liliencron's article in *Allgemeine Deutsche Biographie*, XXII (Leipzig, 1885), 236-42.
8. Nicodemus Frischlin's Latin comedy *Iulius Redivivus* (1584) illustrates the same point humorously in the persons of the French huckster and the Italian chimney sweep.
9. This position is maintained by Henning Boetius in his *Nachwort* (p. 425) to the modern edition of Morhof's *Unterricht* (see bibliography).
10. *Der getreue Schäfer* from the Italian of Giambattista Guarini (1538-1612) and *Der sterbende Socrates* from the French of Théophile de Viau (1590-1626); on the first translation see Elida M. Szarota, "Deutsche Pastor-Fido-Übersetzungen und europäische Tradition," in *Europäische Tradition und deutscher Literaturbarock*, ed. Gerhart Hoffmeister (Bern and München: Francke, 1973), pp. 305-28.

SELECTED BIBLIOGRAPHY

Primary Sources

H[ofmann] v[on] H[ofmannswaldau], C[hristian]. *Deutsche Übersetzungen und Getichte*. Breslau: Fellgibel, 1679.
Morhof, Daniel Georg. *Unterricht von der Teutschen Sprache und Poesie, Deren Ursprung, Fortgang und Lehr-Sätzen*. 3rd ed. Lübeck: Kloßen, 1718.
———. *Unterricht von der Teutschen Sprache und Poesie*. Henning Boetius,

ed. Bad Homburg: Gehlen, 1969. (The basis of this edition is the 2nd ed. of 1700.)

Opitz, Martin. *Aristarchus sive De Contemptu Linguae Teutonicae.* Bethaniae (1618). Facs. rpt. in Martin Opitz, *Jugendschriften vor 1619*, Stuttgart: Metzler, 1970, pp. [65]-[90].

Schottelius, Justus Georg. *Ausführliche Arbeit von der Teutschen Haubt-Sprache.* Braunschweig: Zilliger, 1663. Facs. rpt. Wolfgang Hecht, ed., 2 vols. Tübingen: Niemeyer, 1967.

Secondary Literature

Berns. Jörg Jochen, and Borm, Wolfgang. *Justus Georg Schottelius. Ein Teutscher Gelehrter am Wolfenbütteler Hof.* Wolfenbüttel: Herzog-August-Bibliothek, 1976.

Dünninger, Josef. "Geschichte der deutschen Philologie." In *Deutsche Philologie im Aufriß.* 2nd ed. Berlin: Erich Schmidt, 1957. Vol. I, cols. 83-222.

Erasmus, Desiderius. *Omnia Opera*, I. Leyden: Petrus Vander Aa, 1703.

Hankamer, Paul. *Die Sprache, ihr Begriff und ihre Deutung im sechzehnten und siebzehnten Jahrhundert.* Bonn: Cohen, 1927; rpt. Hildesheim: Olms, 1965.

Hess, Günter. *Deutsch-lateinische Narrenzunft: Studien zum Verhältnis von Volkssprache und Latinität in der satirischen Literatur des 16. Jahrhunderts.* München: Beck, 1971.

Hertenstein, Bernard. *Joachim von Watt (Vadianus), Bartholomäus Schobinger, Melchior Goldast: Die Beschäftigung mit dem Althochdeutschen von St. Gallen in Humanismus und Frühbarock.* Berlin: de Gruyter, 1975.

Lempicki, Sigmund von. *Geschichte der deutschen Literaturwissenschaft bis zum Ende des 18. Jahrhunderts.* 2nd ed. Göttingen: Vandenhoeck, 1968.

Schulenburg, Sigrid von der. *Leibniz als Sprachforscher.* Frankfurt a.M: Klostermann, 1973.

Szarota, Elida M. "Deutsche *Pastor-Fido*-Übersetzungen und europäische Tradition," in *Europäische Tradition und deutscher Literaturbarock*, ed. Gerhart Hoffmeister. Bern and München: Francke, 1973.

Vadianus, Joachim. *De Poetica et Carminis Ratione.* Vienna: Alantsee, 1518. Also: Kritsche Ausgabe mit deutscher Übersetzung und Kommentar von Peter Schäffer, München: Fink, 1973-77.

II

The Comparative View

6

Neo-Latin Tradition and Vernacular Poetry

Leonard Forster

The continuity of Western European literature with the literature of antiquity was assured by the continued use of the Latin language as the normal vehicle of government in church and state, of the liturgy, of learning, of intellectual effort generally, and thus also of literature. For centuries Latin was the universal esperanto of the cultivated, in which Italians and Englishmen, Frenchmen and Poles, Swedes and Hungarians, Germans and Spaniards could and did communicate with one another. What was written in Latin reached an international public, through the medium of the church which conducted its business in Latin, or by students who went from country to country secure in the knowledge that wherever they went lectures would be given in Latin. It was more widely read than any one vernacular until, by the middle of the seventeenth century, French came to rival it and ultimately to displace it, to be displaced in its turn in our century by English. The Latin tradition was a living one, and Latin was an essential tool for the cultivated person, the bulk of whose schooling was in Latin and who learned to write Latin before he learned to write his native tongue. Men of the Middle Ages, the Renaissance, and the baroque lived in conditions of bilingualism, in which Latin and a vernacular existed side by side in the community, with each having a definite role to play.[1]

A man writing in Latin was writing for a public of educated men; he was not addressing the populace in his own country but persons of

87

culture all over Europe. He was likely to be read not only by people of different languages but by people of a different religion. The latter was a far more important division than that by language or nationality. The culture of the ancient world was the common basis of education for Catholic and Protestant alike; within this tradition, using this language, they could—and did—meet.

On the whole, though many Protestant authors were read by liberal Catholics, the *Index librorum prohibitorum* inhibited wide circulation of Protestant books in Catholic countries. There was no such express prohibition in Protestant lands, so that the truly European literature of the seventeenth century may be said to be Latin literature written by Catholics, especially Jesuits. Andreas Gryphius, a deeply religious Protestant, shows extensive acquaintance with Jesuit literature not only in his dramas but also in his lyric poetry; the Polish Jesuit Sarbiewski was widely read in England; the German Jesuits Hieremias Drexel, Jacob Bidermann, and Jacob Balde were read all over Euope, as the various printings of their works indicate; English hymnals still contain translations of the Latin hymns of the French clerics Claude and Jean Baptiste de Santeul and Charles Coffin. On the Protestant side Hugo Grotius, Johannes Secundus, both Dutchmen, and the Welshman John Owen were equally widely known. Owen's epigrams were translated into German in 1651.

The classics of Italian Renaissance literature in Latin of the quattrocento and cinquecento and even earlier continued to be read north of the Alps by Catholic and Protestant alike; one of the most influential was Petrarch's *De remediis utriusque fortunae*, which was often reprinted in Latin and in translation in the seventeenth century in handy pocket editions. The Italian historian Famianus Strada was read in Protestant schools and universities, as were the eclogues of the Italian Carmelite Baptista Mantuanus, and the letters of the Florentine humanist Angelo Poliziano. (Mathias Casimir Sarbiewski even adapted a cycle of poems by the Italian Jesuit Mario Bettini and passed them off as his own.)[2]

By the end of the sixteenth century, Latin literature comprised a wide variety of genres. It had been found particularly suited to the celebration of dynastic and other occasions, and courtly festivities and pageants were performed or recorded in Latin as well as in the vernacular. The genres of Latin literature were secular and religious, amatory and meditative; they reflected the whole range of contemporary culture, from scientific and theological treatises through devotional works to dramas, pageants and operas, epics, and lyric poems. And a new genre becomes discernible, the most important new development in sixteenth-century Latin literature: the emblem.[3] The first edition of Alciati's *Emblemata*, with which the genre began, was published in Augsburg (1531). Latin also afforded a model for satirical episodic and courtly political novels in the works of John Barclay, *Euphormio* (1605) and *Argenis* (1621); the latter was translated into German by Martin Opitz in 1626 and again by August Bohse in 1701. Over and above all this, Latin verses constituted the small change of social intercourse among intellectuals; those who now exchange offprints then exchanged elegiacs, written or printed, and the rapidly executed set of verses took the place occupied in the nineteenth century by the visiting card.

Germany's contribution to this European literature in the sixteenth century had been distinguished, due not least to the example and the educational reforms of Melanchthon. The lyrics and epigrams of Eobanus Hessus and Euricius Cordus, of Conrad Celtis and Petrus Lotichius, were on a level with what was being produced elsewhere in Europe at the time, and in certain spheres the Germans were in the lead. Erasmus spent the greater part of his life in German lands, and most of his works first appeared there. The German literary scene in the six-teenth century is unthinkable without him and the range of literary genres that he cultivated or even inaugurated. In the Reformation German satire was a potent weapon, and here too Erasmus was a model. Beside him the figure of Ulrich von Hutten stands out, not only for his part in the *Epistolae obscurorum virorum** but for his other writings as well. He is in fact an exponential figure: the humanist drawn into the great religious struggle of his time and forsaking Latin in order to reach a wider public—as he thought—by the use of German. But his Latin works were read all over Europe, wherever people were interested in what Luther and his like were thinking; his German writings were read only in Germany.

The task that faced German writers about 1600 was to produce in German a body of literature that could stand up to what Germans had already produced in Latin. In other countries this had already been done or was being done—especially in Italy, France, the Netherlands, and England. Germans were in contact with the avant-garde in these coun-tries who were creating a European literature in the vernaculars. The discussion of these matters between German, French, English, and

---

*See Peter Schaeffer, "Letters of Obscure Men," in *The Renaissance and Refor-mation in Germany*, ed. G. Hoffmeister (New York: Ungar, 1977), pp. 129-40.

Dutch writers was carried on in Latin, as can be seen, for instance, in Alexander Reifferscheidt's great collection of literary correspondence from the decisive early years of the century.[4]

Though on one plane people were conscious of the difference—in quality as well as in language—between the two media, on other planes it was neglected or ignored. Martin Opitz spoke in 1623 of Petrus Lotichius as "der Fürst aller Deutschen Poeten," although we have not a single line of German from his pen. In other words, Opitz and his contemporaries were fully aware of the symbiosis of German and Latin in which they were living and to which they were contributing. And Opitz's mention of the great figure of later sixteenth-century Latin lyric in Germany also makes plain how clearly he realized the continuity between the Latin literature of the sixteenth century and the new struggling German literature of the seventeenth.

This situation has been illuminated in detail by Karl Otto Conrady in what is by now a classic investigation, *Lateinische Dichtungstradition und deutsche Lyrik des 17. Jahrhunderts* (1962). He shows that German baroque literature is the organic continuation of the Latin literature of the preceding century. This was not merely passive assimilation but active continuation. The work of Opitz and his followers took over the categories and the rhetorical figures that the humanists had used; the basic approach to literature was the same—people now wrote German the way they wrote Latin, and applied the same standards of excellence.

The number of German baroque poets who had *not* first learned to write verse in Latin could be counted on the fingers of one hand (Grimmelshausen is one, Johann Beer perhaps another). They could treat the same subject in the two languages, and very often this took the form of autotranslation—translating into German a piece they themselves had first written in Latin; *aus meinem Lateinischen* is a common subtitle. Here the intention is to demonstrate that the same theme can be treated with as much elegance in the vernacular as in Latin. This demonstration, constantly repeated, was important.

The rhetorical and poetic resources of Latin were well known, minutely codified, and intensely studied; they presented no problems and no secrets. In a certain sense, for someone who had gone through the educational mill, Latin virtually wrote itself; German, like the other vernaculars, was untried and had to be constantly tested and exercised—it was quite literally more difficult to write than Latin. So we find much Latin written with an eye to writing in the vernacular. Opitz's *Aristarchus*, in defense of the vernacular, was written in Latin. Had he written it in German he would not have reached the audience he was aiming at.

In the same way, much translation from Latin by Opitz and others was not aimed at a public that could not read Latin but at people like the translators themselves, bilingual and bicultural, who could appreciate the technical and stylistic problems involved and who saw the translation as one more piece of evidence to show that certain themes could be treated equally well in German. This is made particularly clear, for instance, by the circumstance that the title of Opitz's German translation of Hugo Grotius's poem on the capture of La Rochelle, *Hugonis Grotii de Capta Rupella Carmen Heroicum Mart. Opitius versibus Germanicis reddidit* (1620), is in Latin and not in German. The members of the Fruchtbringende Gesellschaft were encouraged to produce translations as a contribution to the refinement of the German language, not as additional reading matter for the German public.[5]

By contrast, many translations from the vernacular into Latin, especially in the field of devotional literature, were intended for an international public that could not read the particular vernacular. Pierre Nicole's translation of Pascal's *Provinciales* (published in Helmstedt) was widely read. The works of St. John of the Cross were translated into Latin by a Polish Carmelite, Father Andreas à Jesu, and published at Cologne in 1639; it was in this form that Quirinus Kuhlmann knew them.[6] Kaspar von Barth's translation of Fernando de Rojas's *Celestina* as *Pornoboscodidascalus* (1624) was similarly aimed at those who could not read Spanish.

In the second half of the seventeenth century many people felt that the main objective had been achieved: German literature could show its face beside the other vernacular literatures and even beside the literatures of antiquity. This feeling tended to be embodied in characteristic overstatement. In 1667 the young Leibniz, then aged twenty-one, gave expression to what young people were then feeling; the destructive wars were over for the time being and the German Muse was showing what she could do:

> Was lobt man viel die Griechen?
> Sie müssen sich verkriechen,
> Wenn sich die teutsche Musa regt.
> Was sonst die Römer gaben,
> Kann man zu Hause haben,
> Nachdem sich Mars bei uns gelegt.[7]

The function of the Neo-Latin component in literature had changed: it was no longer felt as trend-setting and was beginning to be thought old-fashioned. Leibniz's lines show that after the middle of the century the social prestige of German poetry had increased so as to equal or surpass that of Latin. Let us take a hypothetical instance. Suppose you are a well-to-do citizen of, shall we say, Breslau; that you have just become engaged; and that the wedding is to take place in a few months time. Herr Martin Opitz has kindly consented to contribute a poem to the obligatory publication celebrating the occasion. Which would you prefer, which would confer more prestige — a German poem or a Latin one? During the lifetime of Martin Opitz one could reasonably be in some doubt. And how would it be a generation later? A Latin epithalamium (wedding poem) would certainly be well within the powers of Herr von Hofmannswaldau, but would it occur to you to ask him for one? The answer is almost certainly No, for he seems in effect not to have written any.

The state of European Neo-Latin lyric poetry at the beginning of the century can be easily studied in the great series of anthologies edited by Janus Gruter of Heidelberg, the *Delitiae poetarum italorum, gallorum, belgicorum, germanorum*, published at Frankfurt-am-Main under various pseudonyms between 1608 and 1616, comprising eighteen volumes with thousands more lines than the whole corpus of Latin poetry of antiquity put together. They were not the result of a large-scale research project by the scholarly librarian Janus Gruter, but of the business sense of the Frankfurt publisher Jonas Rosa, who wanted a more modern counterpart to the two-volume anthology of Johannes Mathias Toscanus, "editum ante annos triginta ac saepe deinde desideratum" (edited thirty years ago and much in demand since), *Carmina illustrium poetarum italorum* (Paris, 1576). Rosa knew his market, for there were several attempts at much the same time to meet this particular need. Gruter, on the other hand, was interested in modern poetry generally, not only in Latin but also in the vernacular. He had been one of the pioneers of Renaissance poetry in the Netherlands before settling in Heidelberg, where he became the focal point of a circle of poets interested in writing Renaissance poetry in German, and where Martin Opitz found welcome and encouragement. The Neolatin poems Opitz translated in his *Teutsche Poemata* of 1624 (except his own) can be found in Gruter's anthologies. Opitz's models are bilingual too: the Pléiade is unthinkable without the strong humanist element — represented in Germany by Ronsard's friend Paul Schede Melissus — and Opitz's other great source of inspiration, Daniel Heinsius, wrote in Dutch, Latin, and Greek. This was a European pattern at this stage.

Opitz is the exponential case of the man who continues to write

Latin alongside German, but whose German work gradually assumes greater importance as his skill increases. This was not the case with all his contemporaries. His friend Kaspar von Barth (whose adversaria, i.e., marginal comments, in his personal copy of Opitz's *Teutsche Poemata* have proved so enlightening to later scholars) was more productive as a Latin writer. His *Deutscher Phönix* (1626) was largely unaffected by the Opitzian reform, despite his friendship with Opitz: his Latin poetry, however, points forward to the rococo (e.g., *Tarraei Hebii Amphitheatrum Gratiarum*, Hanau, 1613) and he even translated from other languages into Latin.[8]

We need to consider successive stages of the interrelation between writing in Latin and writing in the vernacular. We saw that there were different combinations in Opitz's generation; in all of them literary correspondence and literary discussion was carried on in Latin, even though much of the literary writing was in the vernacular. Alongside there existed the various "Sprachgesellschaften"—first and foremost the Fruchtbringende Gesellschaft, pledged to further the cause of the German language. The only letters we have from Opitz that are written in German are addressed to this society. But this did not mean that members were inhibited from writing or publishing in Latin. Georg Philipp Harsdörffer, a member of the Fruchtbringende and one of the moving spirits of the Pegnitzschäfer, wrote several works in Latin; one, characteristically, dealt with the German language itself—his *Specimen Philologiae Germanicae* (Nürnberg, 1646), a work obviously not aimed at a purely German public but at readers elsewhere in Europe, who needed to be informed about the progress of German literature in the past twenty years.

By contrast, Leibniz's *Unvorgreiffliche Gedanken betreffend die Ausübung und Verbesserung der deutschen Sprache* (written in 1697 but published posthumously) is one of the few works the philosopher wrote in German; the bulk of his production is in Latin and, increasingly, in French. This work was aimed at his fellow countrymen. Its subject matter was by Leibniz's European standards purely parochial; although as a young man he had felt that German could rival or surpass Latin as a vehicle for belles lettres, he was under no illusions about its practical value as a vehicle for the communication of scientific or philosophical ideas to a European public.

In the universities Latin reigned supreme. Apart, of course, from the quite isolated case of Paracelsus a century before, the real breach was not made until 1688, when Christian Thomasius in Leipzig announced

the first public university lecture in German. The subject was characteristic; he lectured on *Gratians Grundregeln, vernünftig, klug und artig
zu leben*. The text he was intending to explain was Balthasar Gracián's
Oráculo manual in the French translation of Amelot de la Houssaye, and
he promised further to speak on the subject of *Welcher Gestalt man
denen Franzosen im gemeinen Leben und Wandel nachahmen solle*.
The increasing importance of French in the practical world could not be
more clearly documented. Even so, at much the same time, the newly
founded ducal academy at Wolfenbüttel for the training of young noblemen still laid stress on Latin as a "hochnotwendige und bei allen Na-
tionen durchgehende Sprache" in the world of politics and diplomacy.[9]

The Latin poet of the sixteenth century had, as we saw, not only the
full gamut of genres as then understood but also a wide range of forms at
his disposal: the lyric meters for odes and songs; the elegiac couplet for
reflective poetry and the epigram; and the hexameter for narrative.
With these forms he could write different kinds of poetry: love lyrics,
epithalamia, epicedia (funeral poems), pastoral elegy, reflective
philosophical or political poetry, the stinging epigram and the sacred
song, *vers de société* and mystical verse. By comparison the range of
forms available in German was extremely restricted: the Meistersinger
had by bureaucratic rigidity imparted to the many lyric metrical and
stanzaic forms they elaborated a woodenness which not even Hans Sachs
managed to overcome. For other themes—dramatic, reflective, or narrative—there was in effect only the Knittelvers, whether strict or free; it
too had a certain woodenness, which has on the positive side a stark
quality often compared with that achieved in contemporary woodcuts,
and on the negative side a dreary monotony, enhanced by formulaic
phrases and formulaic paired rhymes. The analogy with the woodcut is
illuminating; it only holds for the technically rather crude productions of
the fifteenth and early sixteenth centuries. No one handled the Knittel as
Dürer and his followers handled the woodblock; no work in that meter
has the delicacy of Dürer's great series on the life of Mary or the grandeur
of his *Apocalypsis cum figuris*. One sometimes wonders whether people
in the sixteenth century noticed this discrepancy. If they did, they
presumably reckoned that similar effects could be achieved in Latin, and
that that was the correct medium for them.

One of the chief differences between sixteenth- and seventeenth-
century German literature is therefore the great increase in the poetic
forms and genres available to the seventeenth-century poet. Each of

these forms permitted and indeed encouraged the assumption of a series of possible attitudes; they could be taken up with varying degrees of seriousness, but in a century for which "Dasein heißt eine Rolle spielen" (H. O. Burger), their function was well understood, and the way the poet addressed his audience was determined by the role or attitude appropriate to each occasion. The poet struck a different attitude as pastoral poet or writer of holy sonnets or of frivolous erotic verse; the same man could write them all. It has been suggested that this possibility entailed a liberation of the personality, which was now free to act out a wider variety of roles.

In the sixteenth century all these resources were already available to the French and Italians; they were also available to Germans who wrote Latin and who could therefore take advantage of the potentialities for self-expression through self-presentation ("mise-en-scène de soi-même") that the classical and humanist genres offered. It would be tedious to list all these potentialities in detail, but two may be mentioned here: one is the descriptive treatment of landscape, whether ideal or actual; the other is religious or secular meditation.

For the first the Roman poets supplied models, mainly Vergil but also Horace ("O fons Bandusiae splendidior vitro" had many imitators in Latin before Opitz took up the theme in his poem on the Wolfsbrunnen near Heidelberg). Here too the graphic arts were akin; Dürer's landscape watercolors, and the real or fantastic natural scenes in which his figures are set, chime with the sense of natural scenery developed by the humanist poets; Dürer's *Melencolia* is a symbol of one kind of meditation, his saints in the desert are engaged in another. Increasingly, as in the graphic arts, the two themes were treated together: poets meditated in a landscape or in a garden. The characteristically humanist genre of the hodoeporicon, the poem treating of a journey (Horace's *iter Brundusinum* was usually the model here) enabled the poet to describe scenery and to philosophize about it in a way for which literature in German offered neither opportunity nor vehicle.

We can deal with only one sixteenth-century Latin poet here and it seems best to take Petrus Lotichius Secundus, whom Opitz esteemed so highly; a poet, moreover, who was particularly at home in the meditative vein and in the treatment of nature. One of his most successful descriptive pieces was his elegy (El. II. 4) on the siege of Magdeburg in 1550. This was taken up and translated in 1631, not once but three times, because it was then felt to be a prophetic foreboding of the total destruction of the

city by Tilly in that year—an event that shocked Protestant Europe. The
combination of rapid description and meditation can be seen in the lines

> Quaque fuit murus, terras proscindet arator
> Urbsque sub his, dicet, collibus alta fuit,

in which a peasant of the future is shown meditating over the scene of
destruction. In 1631 an anonymous author, rather uncertainly following
Opitz, had rendered them as:

> Und wird der Bauersmann mit seinem Pflug und Pferden
> In dieser Mawren Stadt umbreißen bloß die Erden,
> Und so du etwan fragst, was da gewesen bey,
> Antwort Er, daß alda ein Stadt gestanden sey.[10]

Andreas Gryphius remembered this passage, improved on its melody,
and widened its scope in the Sonnet I.8 (also in the introductory
monologue of *Catharina von Georgien*, lines 26 ff.):

> Du sihst / wohin du sihst nur eitelkeit auf erden.
> Was dieser heute bawt / reist jener morgen ein:
> Wo itzund städte stehn / wird eine wiesen sein
> Auff der ein schäffers kind wird spilen mit den heerden.
> Was itzund prächtig blüht sol bald zutretten werden.

The lines quoted from Lotichius, however, represent only a small
part of a long and carefully articulated poem of 108 lines. It begins in
medieval style with the poet's dream vision of the maiden, the personification of Magdeburg (the city of the maiden), and continues with
her lament. The poet wakes up before she finishes, and in rural seclu-
sion, in a grove at the foot of a mountain beside a rushing stream, he considers the significance of this dream; here too the combination of landscape and meditation is present (lines 75 ff.):

> Montis in accessi radicibus adiacet imis
> 　　lucus, ubi variae consociantur aves.
> Est sacer arbustis vastisque recessibus horror,
> 　　per medium raucae volvitur amnis aquae.
> Hic trepidae speciem repetens in valle quietis,
> 　　ergo quod (aiebam) somnia pondus habent?

> There is a copse at the foot of an inaccessible mountain
> where various kinds of birds come together; the awesome
> and gloomy wood covers a lot of ground;

through the middle of it rushes a noisy stream. In this
valley I sought some sort of quietness of mind: What,
if anything, I asked myself, do dreams mean?

The poem concludes with a description of the battle between an eagle
and a cock—the heraldic emblems of the emperor and the king of
France—and a pious wish for peace. The whole is a poetic and rhetorical
achievement that could not have been attempted in German in 1550.

Lotichius summons up a society of like-minded friends for whom he
writes, and we are told their names; this poem too is addressed to a
friend, the eminent Neolatin poet Joachim Camerarius the elder
(1500-74). There were little circles like this all over Europe, which kept
in touch with one another by correspondence in Latin. What might seem
to be a purely parochial or personal matter acquires in this context
representative value. And so Lotichius's poems about his war service in
Germany and his travels in France and Italy and the reflections he has
there strike an answering chord in readers elsewhere who either have
visited Lyon, Montpellier, Venice, and Rome or who hope some day to
do so, and in readers who have been involved in military operations or
fear they might be. Here too the changing, foreign landscape is personalized by meditation and enlivened by amorous encounters. A
variegated cultured existence is evoked before our eyes, one particular
European way of life; and there is barely a trait in it that is not taken up
by vernacular poets in the following century, who lived in similar circles
of like-minded cultured persons. One of Lotichius's favorite images is the
running water of a river, and water, as Jean Rousset had pointed out, is
one of the typical images in the European poetry of the following century.[11] Although Lotichius was highly thought of, he seems to have been
very little translated, but there was a constant series of editions of his
works until well into the eighteenth century. In 1754 he received the
supreme compliment Latinists could bestow: the great Dutch scholar
Peter Burmann the younger edited his works on the same scale as though
he were a classical author, with the full paraphernalia of textual and
critical notes. Jacob Balde received a similar compliment at the beginning of the nineteenth century, not from a Bavarian Catholic scholar but
from a Swiss Protestant.[12]

The example of Lotichius must serve to exemplify Conrady's thesis
that the Latin poetry of the sixteenth century already contained within
itself the elements of the German poetry of the seventeenth. Lotichius
was a Protestant; our next example must be a later one, from the middle

of the seventeenth century and a Catholic, Jacob Balde (1603-68), an Alsatian who spent most of his life in Bavaria.

Balde, by virtue of his membership of the Society of Jesus, had a European public for his work such as no Protestant poet of the time could have, and he was firmly rooted in a social framework that gave him both confidence and security. He too addresses many of his poems to friends, whose names he gives. They, like Lotichius's friends, mean little to us today, but as fellow Jesuits they too were fellow citizens of a Catholic Europe in which their names were familiar. But Balde goes further than this; his generosity embraced poets from Protestant lands who like him wrote international poetry in Latin, and he addresses odes to the Reformed Dutchmen Caspar Barlaeus and Hugo Grotius, who were among Martin Opitz's models too.

Balde was trained in the *Spiritual Exercises* of the founder of the Society, St. Ignatius Loyola, who enjoins meditation, and meditation and resultant ecstasy—what Balde calls "enthusiasmus"—is a characteristic of his poetry. Another characteristic is one common to many Jesuit poets—the transposition of secular motifs into the religious sphere, the *geistliche Kontrafaktur* or *parodia christiana*. His model and inspiration here was the Polish Jesuit Mathias Casimir Sarbiewski, but a nineteenth-century critic thought he had surpassed him in "ingenio, inventione, vi poetica et majestate lyrica."[13] His work ranged from poetry written to order to meet religious or political occasions; through contemplation of the varying fortunes of the imperial arms in the Thirty Years War, quiet evocations of idyllic peace or meditation, and a great stanzaic *Poema de vanitate mundi*; two humorous pieces and two dramas. Whereas one of Lotichius's traits had been a simple and straightforward style, here the baroque style is in full flood, and Balde's poetry is seen to be akin to that Bavarian baroque architecture and painting which did not come to its full flowering until after Balde's death.

In the Protestant North, with its national and regional church organization, in which Latin was no longer the language of the liturgy, Neo-Latin poetry fulfilled the function, as we saw, of opening the way for a new vernacular poetry in a European style and accompanying it for some distance on that way. In the Catholic South the sense of a universal church with a universal linguistic and literary medium ensured that prestige was on the side of Latin and that the vernacular was restricted to works addressed to the uneducated (who could be courtiers, as addressed by Abraham à Sancta Clara, or peasants listening to their parish priest). Friedrich von Spee, using the form of the "Gesellschaftslied" as elaborated in the preceding century, was able by a remarkable feat of re-creation to transpose this Latin reflection into a highly stylized religious pastoral that had its roots in the German popular tradition.[14] The Opitz-ian reform, which brought German Protestant literature into line with the other literatures of Europe, was not accepted in the South, partly on religious grounds but partly because no one felt the necessity for it. It would, moreover, have had little appeal to those accustomed to the old style; Bavarian readers used to the Knittelvers would have barely been able to scan the Opitzian Alexandrine.

The stylistic difference between the baroque splendor of Balde's Latin odes and the clumsy starkness of his few productions in German verse is striking. The first stanza of his translation of his own *Poema de vanitate mundi* (1636)[15] is by North German, Opitzian, standards hopelessly antiquated, despite the modish alternation of masculine and feminine rhymes:

> Nichts kan ich sehen / das ewig wert /
>   Nichts sichers kann ich finden.
> Zerschlagen wird das Gstreiß [Gesträuch] vom Pferdt /
>   Gantz Wälder von den Winden.
> Thonaw vnd Rhein / reißt Brucken ein /
>   Das Thal versinckt im Nebel:
> ReichsStätt and Märckt / auch hohe Berg /
>   Förcht Donnerklapff vnd Schwebel.

This becomes clear when it is placed side by side with, for instance, Andreas Gryphius's

> Die Herrlichkeit der Erden
> Muß Rauch und Asche werden,
> Kein Fels, kein Erz kann stehn.

Gryphius translated Balde's two meditations on graveyards (Lyr. II. 39 and Silv. VII. 7) into the new Opitzian style with great effect in 1657 in his *Kirchhofsgedanken*. This kind of meditative poetry and the impressive treatment of the *vanitas* theme, so fundamental to the temper of the century, ensured this and similar works wide popularity all over Europe. In Nürnberg and Breslau, both islands of Protestantism in a Catholic ocean, Balde was eagerly read. Gryphius's interest we saw; in Nürnberg Johann Klaj translated one of Balde's odes (Silv. V. 19) on the passage of learning from the Mediterranean to Germany, adapted it discreetly to the praise of Balde himself, and published it in Hars-dörffer's *Gesprächsspiele* in 1646.

The range and variety of Balde's work is seen to be remarkable when one realizes that he was precluded from treating one of the chief themes of the century, secular love. But like other Jesuits, especially Sarbiewski in Latin and Spee in German, he could use petrarchistic topoi in the service of divine love in variations on the Song of Songs.

The Jesuit contribution to the Latin-German symbiosis cannot be underestimated, and it is particularly evident in the drama. Although Balde, too, wrote a drama and comedy, the main figures are Jacob Bidermann and Jacob Masen, beside a whole host of others whose stature is only now being fully recognized, thanks to the work of Jean-Marie Valentin and Elida Maria Szarota.[16] The importance of Jesuit drama for the work of Gryphius has long been recognized, but it still remains a largely neglected field, in common with other works of South-German Catholic literature. In the drama, South and North met, but it was a one-sided relationship, in which the North gained more than the South.

Latin was international, but even more importantly, it was inter-confessional. By contrast the prestige, even the validity, of Opitz's German stopped at the "Pfaffengasse" (the ecclesiastical states on the left bank of the Rhine) and at the frontiers of Bavaria and the Habsburg lands. Jacob Bidermann (1578–1639) therefore must serve as an illustration for the field of the influential Jesuit drama. He illustrates too the transition from the sixteenth to the seventeenth century; his best-known play, *Cenodoxus*, was performed at Munich in 1602. It follows the sixteenth-century tradition in being a school play, written by a schoolmaster for his pupils to perform. This tradition was in fact the soil from which much German seventeenth-century drama also sprang—from the numerous Latin plays written and performed at Jesuit colleges everywhere, through the similar Latin or German productions of Protestant schools (e.g., in Breslau, where Lohenstein was a pupil), to the German comedies of Christian Weise at Zittau.

The second Munich performance of *Cenodoxus* in 1609 illustrates a further development. The stage of the Jesuit college had meanwhile become in effect the court stage of the duchy, and the audience consisted of nobles, courtiers, and prominent citizens of the town. Although the Jesuit drama continued to exist and flourish at school level, it increasingly became a form of court entertainment, reaching its high point at the Viennese court with the plays of Nicolaus Avancini. Bidermann operated at first with a very simple stage, suited to the resources of his school Avancini half a century later in his *Pietas victrix* (1659) could work with the far greater resources at the disposal of the imperial court—hidden choruses, columns of fire, aerial battles, contests on sea and land involving the hosts of heaven and hell. On this level the drama developed rapidly in the direction of the opera, the truly baroque "Gesamtkunstwerk." It is important to remember that it did this precisely because the text was in Latin and the performance therefore had to offer something else to the unlearned.

Bidermann's plays anticipate the themes, roles, and conflicts of later baroque drama in German. In *Belisarius* the theme of fortune is treated in the rise and fall of the general—"quod altum est, altè labitur" (from a great rise a great fall). The theme of life as a dream and the spiritual reality behind it is treated in *Cosmarchia*. The theme of true and false personality—"Sein und Schein" in a different form—is the subject of *Philemon martyr*, like Rotrou's *Saint-Genest* the story of an actor who plays the role of a Christian martyr and is thereby converted into actually becoming one; the complex problem of an actor acting the part of himself is an aspect of the theme of mistaken identity that contemporaries loved. The theme of the statesman presented itself to Bidermann in the story of Barlaam and Josaphat, and the theme of salvation is basic to *Cenodoxus*, the central figure of which incorporated the sin of pride.

After 1620 Bidermann wrote no more plays. His last plays were in prose. In this he was considerably in advance of his time. In some respects, however, he looked back to the medieval drama, e.g., in his extensive use of personified virtues and vices, guardian angels, and devils.

Cenodoxus is Bidermann's best known play nowadays because it was translated into German in his own lifetime by Johann Meichel. This translation, like Balde's version of his own poem, illustrates the gap between German and Latin in south Germany. Meichel's well-intentioned but unsubtle Knittelverse transmit little of the polish and subtlety of Bidermann's Latin senarii (iambics). Bidermann in Latin is akin to Shakespeare or Lope de Vega; Bidermann in Meichel's German is reminiscent of Hans Sachs. Meichel's German version was written for Bavarians; Bidermann was writing in the first place for the youth of Bavaria, both humanistic and courtly, but beyond that he was writing for the learned world. It was in Latin that the learned world, especially the Protestant learned world, read him and his fellow Jesuits.

Balde was a lyric poet who also wrote a couple of dramas. Bidermann was a dramatist who also wrote epigrams, reflective poetry, and a certain amount of narrative prose, including amusing and entertaining anecdotes. His plays, like Shakespeare's, mingle comedy and tragedy, and his classical model was Plautus rather than Seneca. There are those who consider him the best German dramatist before Lessing. It was sad for the German stage that this brilliant, versatile, profound, and humane man could not become the model for the drama of the eighteenth century; but that was one of the consequences of the political and religious fragmentation of Germany.

In Protestant lands serious drama, apart from the productions of the "Wanderbühne," was largely restricted to schools, where the model was Seneca,[17] as understood in Holland by Daniel Heinsius as theorist and Joost van den Vondel as practitioner. Latin drama flourished in the Netherlands, but produced nothing in Protestant Germany to rival the theater of the Jesuits. Bidermann's Protestant Strassburg contemporary Caspar Brülow and his work are of minor interest only.

In the Renaissance the literary genre that carried the most prestige was the epic poem, and Opitz was still of this opinion. It was attempted all over Europe, most successfully in Italy, by Boiardo, Ariosto, and Tasso; less successfully in France with Ronsard's *Franciade*; with distinction in England by Spenser and later Milton; and in Portugal by Camões. In Latin Petrarch had early set the standard with his unfinished *Africa*, and further attempts were made all over Europe. They were most successful on a more modest scale than the full Vergilian model of twelve books, especially when devoted to religious themes like Jacopo Sannazaro's *De partu virginis* (1526) and Marco Girolamo Vida's *Christias* (1535). Bidermann wrote a *Herodias* (1622), a subject suited to baroque taste; it was treated slightly later by Giambattista Marino in *La strage degli innocenti* (1632), and on the Protestant side by Andreas Gryphius (*Herodis furiae et Rachelis lachrymae*, Glogau, 1633, and *Dei vindicis impetus et Herodis interitus*, Danzig, 1635), who was also interested in Bidermann's other works and translated some of his epigrams. Gryphius further treated the end of Christ's life in his *Olivetum* (1646). It is noteworthy that these comparatively large-scale Latin works by Gryphius were written while he was living abroad — in Holland and Italy. The Latin example bore no fruit for German literature; German efforts at a large-scale epic poem proved abortive (Freinsheim, Hohberg). Young Leibniz (see note 7) had felt the same:

> Horaz in Fleming lebet,
> In Opitz Naso schwebet
> In Greiff Senecens Traurigkeit.
> Nur Maro wird gemisset . . .

Paul Fleming is recognized as a major figure in German literature on the strength of his vernacular poems alone, but his writing in Latin is scarcely inferior to it in quantity or in quality. It used to be thought that his Latin poetry was a kind of apprenticeship (as it certainly was for Opitz), which he grew out of as his control of German verse increased. But even the bare dates of composition show this view to be erroneous. Fleming wrote Latin and German verses side by side, to the same people and on similar occasions and about similar topics, throughout his life; he has to be considered as a completely bilingual poet. The love poetry in his Latin *Suavia* can be paralleled in his German verses; the holy sonnets, in which he rivals Gryphius and Donne, have parallels in his Latin epigrams; he produces German adaptations of Latin verses by Sarbiewski and Latin reworkings of German poems by Weckherlin and Opitz. He was fully aware of the work of Neo-Latin poets who had preceded him, and in one poem (*Suavia* 13) he invokes the ladies hymned by twenty-three ancient and modern poets, from Anacreon to Buchanan. His work both in Latin and in German is distinguished by its organic blend of petrarchism, stoicism, and a generous Lutheran piety, which allows him to respect Jesuits such as Sarbiewski as well as liberal Calvinists such as Hugo Grotius and Caspar Barlaeus, who in their turn, as we saw, were admired by Jacob Balde. There is a humanist world here transcending religious divisions, rooted in a common basic Christianity and in the heritage of antiquity, not merely passively received but actively exploited and continued.

Fleming seems not to make any functional distinction between his literary use of German or Latin; he seems equally at home in either, for any purpose. Andreas Gryphius's Latin writing is restricted to his early years; his last book published in Latin was an epithalamium printed in Leszno in 1649, when he was thirty-three years old. His main lyric and dramatic work was yet to come. But Latin as a vehicle of learned discussion and political administration was part of his life, both as a lecturer in a bewildering variety of subjects at the University of Leiden and as Syndikus of Glogau. He was well acquainted, not only with the German and Latin writings of his Lutheran coreligionists, but with those of Catholics too, especially those of the Jesuits Balde, Bidermann, and Sarbiewski, some of whose lyric poems he translated, as well as with the Jesuit drama.[18] It is characteristic of the international character of the Jesuit drama that the plays Gryphius translated were not by German Jesuits but by the Frenchman Nicolaus Caussin and the Englishman Joseph Simon.

In his own dramatic writing, however, Seneca was his model; in this he remained true to the Protestant school tradition he had inherited and which he found flourishing in the vernacular drama of the Netherlands. What attracted him to the work of the Jesuits was the combination of dramatic presentation and existential reflection and meditation, all of which he was able to exploit in his own way.

With Gryphius German baroque literature achieves the independence it had so long striven for. Latin remains an international vehicle in certain contexts, in scholarship and diplomacy, and it adds a decorative cachet to certain festive occasions, but it is no longer a natural and normal vehicle for literature, as it was for Opitz and Fleming throughout their lives and for Gryphius himself until he reached maturity. As Wehrli points out, this is not a case of nationalist "Überwindung der lateinischen Tradition," but of humane, organic assimilation and creative further development.[19]

This process was fully understood in the age of Goethe. Gottlob Nathanael Fischer produced a Latin *Musenalmanach* in 1786; he gave a short survey of Latin writing in Germany and observed of the sixteenth and seventeenth centuries:

vix enim alia via ad linguam partriam perficiendam perveniri potuisse videtur, quam animis hominum linguae cultioris ope ad sensum pulchri et decori conformandi.[20]

It is hard to imagine any way in which our native language could have been brought to perfection other than by molding men's minds to appreciate what is beautiful and worthy by means of a more cultivated language.

He goes on to point to the occasional use of Latin in his own day by Lessing and Klopstock. But, as he realizes, this is now an academic pastime, not mainstream literature any longer.

NOTES

1. Max Wehrli, "Latein und Deutsch in der Barockliteratur," in *Akten des V. Internationalen Germanisten-Kongresses* Cambridge 1975, ed. Leonard Forster and H.-G. Roloff, 1 (Bern, 1976), 134 ff.; Leonard Forster, "Deutsche und europäische Barockliteratur," *Wolfenbütteler Beiträge*, 2 (1975), 64 ff.; rpt. in Leonard Forster, *Kleine Schriften zur deutschen Literatur im 17. Jahrhundert*, Beihefte zu *Daphnis*, 1 (Amsterdam, 1977); Leonard Forster, "Die Bedeutung des Neulateinischen in zer deutschen

Barockliteratur," in *Deutsche Barockliteratur und europäische Kultur*, Dokumente des Internationalen Arbeitskreises für deutsche Barockliteratur, 3, ed. Martin Bircher and Eberhard Mannack (Hamburg, 1977), 55 ff.

2. John Sparrow in *Oxford Slavonic Papers*, 8 and 12 (1958 and 1965).

3. The contribution of the Latin—and later the polyglot—emblem to the spread of Renaissance values, concepts, and imagery is still being investigated and forms the subject of an independent contribution to this volume by Peter M. Daly.

4. Alexander Reifferscheidt, *Quellen zur Geschichte des geistigen Lebens in Deutschland während des siebzehnten Jahrhunderts* (Heilbronn, 1889); see also Jan van Dorsten, *Poets Patrons and Professors* (Leiden and Oxford, 1962), and *The Radical Arts* (Leiden and Oxford, 1973); Leonard Forster, "Charles Utenhove and Germany," in *European Context: Studies in the History and Literature of the Netherlands Presented to Theodoor Weevers*, ed. P. K. King and P. F. Vincent (Leeds, 1971); rpt. in Leonard Forster, *Kleine Schriften*, pp. 81 ff.

5. Leonard Forster, "Deutsche und europäische Barockliteratur," (see note 1).

6. Leonard Forster and A. A. Parker, "Quirinus Kuhlmann and the Poetry of St. John of the Cross," *Bulletin of Hispanic Studies*, 25 (1958); rpt. in Leonard Forster, *Kleine Schriften*, p. 235.

7. G. W. Leibniz, "Verse so ich 1667 zu Frankfurt-am-Main auf Herrn Christian Meische vorhabendes Florilegium gemacht"; quoted by J. M. Lappenberg, *Paul Flemings deutsche Gedichte*, II (Stuttgart, 1865), 635.

8. See the essay in A. Schroeter, *Beiträge zur Geschichte der neulateinischen Poesie Deutschlands und Hollands*, Palaestra, 77 (Berlin, 1909), pp. 267 ff.; J. Hoffmeister, *Kaspar von Barth und sein Deutscher Phönix* (Heidelberg, 1931); Baerbel Becker-Cantarino, "La Celestina en Alemania: el Pornoboscodidascalus 1624 de Kaspar Barth," in *La Celestina y su contorno social*, ed. M. Criado de Val (Barcelona, 1975. Gerhart Hoffmeister, *Die spanische Diana in Deutschland* (Berlin, 1972).

9. Alfred Kuhlenkamp, *Die Ritterakademie Rudolf-Antoniana in Wolfenbüttel 1687–1715* (Braunschweig, 1975), p. 30.

10. Contemporary German translation quoted by Schroeter, p. 50 (see note 8); the original text, with modern rendering into German elegiacs, is conveniently accessible in Harry Schnur, *Lateinische Gedichte deutscher Humanisten, lateinisch und deutsch*, Reclam UB, No. 8739–45 (Stuttgart, 1967), pp. 252 ff.

11. Jean Rousset, *La littérature de l'âge baroque en France* (Paris, 1960), pp. 142 ff., and *L'intérieur et l'extérieur* (Paris, 1968), pp. 199 ff.

12. Petrus Burmannus Secundus, *Petri Lotichii Secundi Solitariensis poemata omnia* (Amsterdam, 1754). For the edition of Balde see note 13.

13. Johann Conrad von Orelli, *Jacobi Balde Carmina selecta, edidit et notis illustravit Johannes Conradus Orellius* (Zürich, 1805), p. xvi. On the importance of Sarbiewski see Maren-Sofie Røstvig, *The Happy Man* (Oslo and Oxford, 1962).

14. Eric Jacobson, *Die Metamorphosen der Liebe und Friedrich Spees Trutznachtigall*, Dan. Hist. Filol. Medd., 34.3 (Copenhagen, 1954).

15. Jacob Balde, *Die deutschen Dichtungen*, ed. Rudolf Berger (Bonn, 1972), p. 43.

16. Elida Maria Szarota, *Künstler, Grübler und Rebellen: Studien zum europäischen Märtyrerdrama des 17. Jahrhunderts* (Bern, 1967) and her later studies still in progress; Willi Flemming, *Das Ordensdrama*, Deutsche Literatur in Entwicklungsreihen, Reihe Barockdrama, 2 (Leipzig, 1930), includes Meichel's translation of *Cenodoxus* and the Latin text of Avancini's *Pietas victrix;* Jean-Marie Valentin, *Le théâtre des Jésuites dans les pays de langue allemande* (1554–1680), 3 vols. (Bern, 1978).

17. Paul Stachel, *Seneca und das deutsche Renaissancedrama*, Palaestra, 46 (Berlin, 1907).

18. See also Hugh Powell, "Observations on the Erudition of Andreas Gryphius," *Orbis Litterarum*, 25 (1970), 115 ff.

19. Wehrli, "Latein und Deutsch," p. 135 (see note 1).

20. Gottlob Nathanael Fischer, *Calendarium musarum latinum* (Leipzig, 1786), p. 37; author's translation.

SELECTED BIBLIOGRAPHY

Neo-Latin Literature in General

Dörrie, Heinrich. *Der heroische Brief*. Berlin, 1968.

Grant, W. Leonard. *Neo-Latin Literature and the Pastoral*. Chapel Hill, N.C., 1965.

IJsewijn, J. *Companion to Neo-Latin Studies*. Amsterdam, 1977.

Laurens, Pierre, and Claudie Balavoine. *Musae reduces, anthologie de la poésie latine dans l'Europe de la renaissance*. 2 vols. Leiden, 1975.

McFarlane, I. D. *Renaissance Latin Poetry*. Manchester & New York, 1980.

Nichols, Fred J. *An Anthology of Neo-Latin Poetry*. New Haven & London, 1979.

Perosa, A., and J. Sparrow. *Renaissance Latin Verse: An Anthology*. London, 1979.

Van Tieghem, P. *La littérature latine de la renaissance*. Paris, 1944; rpt. Geneva, 1966.

Wright, F. A., and T. A. Sinclair. *History of Later Latin Literature from the Middle of the Fourth to the End of the Seventeenth Century*. London, 1931.

German Neo-Latin Literature, Especially in the Seventeenth Century

Conrady, Karl Otto. *Lateinische Dichtungstradition und deutsche Lyrik des 17. Jahrhunderts.* Bonn, 1962.

Ellinger, Georg. *Deutsche Lyriker des 16. Jahrhunderts.* Lateinische Literatur-denkmäler des 15. und 16. Jahrhunderts, 7. Berlin, 1983.

——. *Geschichte der neulateinischen Literatur Deutschlands im sechzehnten Jahrhundert,* I–III.1. Berlin, 1929–33; rpt. 1960.

——, and Brigitte Ristow. "Neulateinische Dichtung Deutschlands im 16. Jahrhundert (mit Ausnahme des Dramas)." In *Reallexikon der deutschen Literaturgeschichte,* P. Merker and W. Stammler, eds., 2nd ed. Berlin, 1965.

IJsewijn, J., and E. Kessler. *Acta Conventus Neo-Latini Lovaniensis.* Leuven and München, 1973.

Schnur, Harry. *Lateinische Gedichte deutscher Humanisten, lateinisch und deutsch.* Reclam UB, No. 8739–45. Stuttgart, 1967.

Schroeter, Adalbert. *Beiträge zur Geschichte der neulateinischen Poesie Deutschlands und Hollands.* Palaestra 77. Berlin, 1909.

Wehrli, Max. "Deutsche und lateinische Dichtung im 16. und 17. Jahrhundert." In *Das Erbe der Antike.* Zürich, 1963.

Individual Authors

Petrus Lotichius Secundus

Coppel, Bernhard. "Bericht über Vorarbeiten zu einer neuen Lotichius-Edition." *Daphnis,* 7 (1978), 55 ff.

——. "Petrus Lotichius Secundus und Catullus." In J. IJsewijn and E. Kessler, *Acta,* p. 159 ff.

Ellinger, G. *Geschichte der neulateinischen Literatur,* II, p. 340 ff.

Ludwig, W. "Petrus Lotichius Secundus and the Roman Elegists, Prolegomena to a Study of Neo-Latin Elegy." In *Classical Influences on European Culture 1500–1700,* R. R. Bolgar, ed. Cambridge, 1976, p. 171 ff.

Schroeter, A. *Beiträge,* p. 361 ff.

Jacob Balde

Galle, J. *Die lateinische Lyrik J. Baldes und die Geschichte ihrer Übertragungen.* Münster, 1973.

Heinrich, Anton. *Die lyrischen Dichtungen J. Baldes.* Quellen und Forschungen, 122. Strassburg, 1915.

Herzog, U. *Divina poesis: Studien zu J. Baldes geistlicher Odendichtung.* Hermaea, 36. Tübingen, 1976.

Müller, B., ed. *Carmina lyrica.* Regensburg, 1844.

Müller, M. H. *Parodia christiana.* Zürich, 1964.

Wehrli, Max, ed. *Dichtungen.* Cologne, 1963.

Jacob Bidermann

Best, T. W. *Jacob Bidermann*. TWA, 314. New York, 1975.
Tarot, R., ed. *Ludi Theatrales*, 1666; rpt. Tübingen, 1967.
Translations of *Philemon martyr* by Max Wehrli, Cologne, 1960, and of *Cenodoxus* by D. G. Dyer and C. Longrigg, Edinburgh, 1975, both with original text *en face*.

*Paul Fleming**

Carpi, Anna Maria. *Paul Fleming de se ipso ad se ipsum*. Milan, 1973. This volume contains some discussion of Fleming's Latin poetry — other than love poems — which still awaits full treatment.
Pyritz, Hans. *Paul Flemings Liebeslyrik*, Palaestra, 234. Göttingen, 1963.

*Andreas Gryphius**

Mannack, Eberhard. *Andreas Gryphius*. Sammlung Metzler, 76. Stuttgart, 1968.

---

*These writers are both dealt with elsewhere in this volume.

7

Spain in German Literature of the Seventeenth Century

Barbara Becker-Cantarino

"Sonsten sein wir alle wohlauf und werden morgen por los años dela reyna ein comedia española halten. . . . es una comedia española y por esto ya es mejor de todas las otras fiestas" (Otherwise we are all well and tomorrow for the queen's birthday a Spanish play will be performed. . . . it's a Spanish play and therefore it is better than all other celebrations),[1] the emperor Leopold I wrote to his ambassador at the Spanish court in 1667. Leopold's letters to Count Pötting in Madrid, in which a curious mixture of German and Spanish is liberally sprinkled with Latin and occasionally with an Italian phrase, attest to the great importance of Spain and its culture for Germany in the seventeenth century. Born of a Spanish mother and married to the infanta Margareta Teresa in his first marriage, Leopold I kept his close relationship to Spain throughout his reign, 1658–1705, continuing the Habsburg tradition of having Spanish *comedias* performed as court spectacles in Vienna and transmitting to Germany all aspects of Spanish culture and literature.

Since the union of Aragón and Castille in 1479 by the Reyes Católicos, Ferdinand and Isabella, Spain gradually developed into a major European power. With Charles I (1516–56), who also ruled the Netherlands and who, as heir to the Habsburg dominions was elected Holy Roman Emperor—Charles V—in 1519, a universal monarchy seemed to have been realized. The poet Acuña expressed the feeling of a Spanish mission:

Ya se acerca Señor, o ya es llegada
La edad dichosa en que promete el cielo
Una grey y un pastor sólo en el suelo,
Por suerte á nuestros tiempos reservada.
Ya tan alto principio en tal jornada
Nos muestra el fin de vuestro santo celo,
Y anuncia al mundo para más consuelo
Un monarca, un imperio y una espada.[2]

The age draws near, my Lord, or has already arrived,
The fortunate age for which Heavens have promised
Only one shepherd and only one flock on earth,
By good fortune reserved for our times.
Already such great beginnings for such a journey
Show us the aim of your holy zeal,
And announce to the world for its greater comfort
One ruler, one empire and one sword.

Under Philip II (1556–98), who succeeded to all his father's dominions (including Naples and the Low Countries, but not Germany), Spain became the greatest power in Europe. It brought Christianity to millions in its colonies, and contained the spread of Protestantism. Spanish monks and mystics, such as St. John of the Cross and St. Teresa de Avila, gave Catholicism a new content, and the theologians and jurists created the basis of international law. The sixteenth and early seventeenth centuries, Spain's *Siglo de Oro*, saw a flowering of literature in all genres, from *romances* (Spanish ballads), poetry, prose writings, mystic literature, to the novel, and to the drama in particular, which culminated in the plays of Calderón (1600–81). His highly intellectualized exposition of Catholic dogma in his *autos sacramentales* made him perhaps the perfect representative of the Counter-Reformation.

Because of its rapid decline of political and economic power in the seventeenth century, especially after 1650, Spain's far-reaching influence during its Golden Age has been overshadowed and is often played down. Its cultural and political hegemony over Europe has been aptly summarized by H. Hatzfeld,[3] who concludes that the influence of Spanish culture, in its spirit and style, supplanted the Italian and classical character in European literature of the sixteenth century.

The influence and reception of Spanish culture and literature in Germany was extensive and varied. It ranged from admiration and emulation to acid criticism and rejection of all things Spanish, from imitation to creative, innovative assimilation of Spanish thought and literature. To understand such contradictory reception, one need only remember the fact that Spain was the dominant figure of the Counter-Reformation, its leadership being espoused in Germany by the Habsburgs. Thus the Catholic parts of Germany, especially through the courts in Vienna and, to a lesser extent, in Munich, turned to Spanish writings early and with enthusiasm; Protestant parts did so later, more cautiously and critically, often through intermediate sources, such as French or Latin translations of Spanish writings.

Moreover, the order of the Jesuits, which since its papal recognition in 1540 led the spiritual renewal of Catholicism, transmitted Spanish ideas and writings through prominent members of its order and through its Latin schools and universities. While the imperial court and the Jesuits were the institutions instrumental in the reception of Spain, it was the highly developed artistic and intellectual nature of Spanish literature in itself that even the Protestant writers such as Moscherosch and Harsdörffer recognized and assimilated. Only in this sense can we accept H. Tiemann's statement: "Doch regt sich in beiden Teilen [Protestant and Catholic] ein gemeinsames allgemein-deutsches Agens [active principle], das sich der spanischen Literatur zuwendet."[4] In its "new" beginnings with Opitz, German literature turned to Spanish writings because they provided sophisticated examples in all areas of literary endeavors, and because direct channels for transmission existed through the Habsburgs, the Catholic courts, and the Jesuits during the Counter-Reformation.

Already during the 1540s the Jesuits had entered Germany; the bishop of Trier chosen in 1546 was a member of this order. By the beginning of the seventeenth century, Jesuit schools and universities extended from Vienna, Ingolstadt, Dillingen, Würzburg, and Freiburg to Trier and Cologne, education having been perceived as the major instrument in the spiritual renewal for Catholicism. Many Spanish Jesuits came to Germany, while the work of the late-scholastic philosopher Francisco Suárez, *Disputationes metaphysicae* (1597), was reprinted already in 1600 in Mainz, and the author became the most influential theological writer not only in Catholic but also in Protestant universities in Germany and in Holland.[5] In their theological disputes Protestant theologians espoused Suárez's metaphysical system, the "disciplina necessaria et utilissima" (a necessary and most helpful discipline), as a practical intellectualism in order to develop their own dogma and to counter the Jesuits.

In the year of Suárez's death (1617), the *Opus Metaphysicum* of the Giessen Professor Christoph Scheibler appeared; it became the most widely used handbook of Protestant scholasticism in the seventeenth century. Scheibler was reverently called by his contemporaries "the Protestant Suárez." Even Protestant university education was so much dominated by scholastic disputation and discipline that the Hamburg pastor and trenchant satirist Johann Balthasar Schupp could write in his *Der Deutsche Lucianus* (1659): "Ich war ein Knabe von 15. Jahren, als ich auff Universitäten kam, und nichts hört als von Darapti und Felapton, von dem Collegio Connembricensi, von dem Ruvio, von dem Suaretz. Es stiegen diese Logische Helden ein wenig über meinen Horizont."[6] After fruitless attempts at mastering the art of disputations, the hero Lucianus consults an older and wiser fellow student, who advises him: "Ich lese den einigen Scheiblerum. . . . der ist perspicuus. Daraus lerne ich mehr, als aus allen Scholasticis . . ." Thus Lucianus sets out to memorize a mere ten pages in octavo from Scheibler each morning, which seems to him better than memorizing ten chapters from the Bible! Schupp's criticism of academic education and the theological disputes of his fellow Protestants at the same time reveals the permeating influence of Spanish Jesuit thinking.

Receptive to religious questions, seventeenth-century Germany opened its gates to an influx of Spanish mystic-ascetic writings, which were published in Latin or in German translations in Catholic parts of Germany—in Munich, Ingolstadt, Dillingen, Würzburg, Mainz, and especially in Cologne.[7] The textbook and bibliographical guide on mysticism, *Pro theologia mystica clavis* (1640), by the Jesuit Maximilianus Sandaeus of Cologne, contains references to a large number of Spanish works. For example, it has been shown that the mystic Angelus Silesius (who converted to Catholicism in 1653 and served as a court physician in Vienna for some years) became acquainted with the Spanish tradition through Sandaeus's *Clavis*.[8]

The religious poetry of Spee, of Johann Khuen and Laurentius von Schnüffis has not been studied in detail in regard to its indebtedness to Spanish mysticism. This would no doubt reveal numerous affinities, since Spanish religious poetry was appreciated even in the Protestant Nürnberg circle. The worldly Harsdörffer rendered into German St. Teresa de Jesús' one hundred maxims in 1650[9] and also translated the "Cántico espiritual" of Juan de la Cruz.[10]

The ever-present influence of the Spanish mystics can best be shown in the sectarian visionary poet Quirinus Kuhlmann (1651–89). His sixty-second "Kühlpsalm" is prefaced "Als er . . . mit Johannes â Cruce den

Berg Carmel durch di dunkle nacht, mit der lebendigen Libes-flamme, . . . aufstig . . . den 26 Julius 1680."[11] A translation from St. John of the Cross, his "companion on the way," forms the first of three parts of this poem, comprising one entire poem from St. John of the Cross ("Llama de amor viva") and portions of two others (three verses from "Noche oscura" and four verses from the "Cántico espiritual"). Kuhlmann used the Latin translation of the words of St. John of the Cross by a Polish Carmelite, Fr. Andreas à Jesu, which appeared in Cologne in 1639.[12] This edition provided Kuhlmann with the Spanish text (which was always prefaced to the Latin translation of each poem) and a literal translation.

A stanza from the sixty-second "Kühlpsalm" juxtaposed with its Spanish model ("Llama de amor viva") and Andreas's Latin inter-mediary shows Kuhlmann's great poetic skill:

> 4. O lebend Libesflamme,
> Di liblichst trifft den tiffsten Seelengrund!
> Nun bäumst du sanfft im stamme!
> Ei liber, mach das ende kund!
> Reiss das geweb im Süssen anlauffsrund![13]

> ¡Oh llama de amor viva,
> que tiernamente hieres
> de mi alma en el más profundo centro!
> Pues ya no eres esquiva,
> acaba ya si quieres,
> rompe la tela de este dulce encuentro.[14]

> O Flamma Amoris viua
> Quae suauiter feris
> Animae meae profundissimum centrum
> Quandoquidem iam non es molesta
> Impone iam si placet finem
> Abrumpe telam dulcis huius occursus.[15]

Kuhlmann has preserved a high degree of fidelity to the Spanish text, which is highly concentrated in expression. Throughout his poem he uses the five-line *lira* stanza—which was originally an Italian invention but had become a distinctively Spanish form—to preserve its unity. Thus he even rendered the six-line stanzas of the "Llama de amor viva" in the form of the *lira*. Harsdörffer, incidentally, used a ten-line stanza in translating St. John's *lira*.

Kuhlmann was able to retain, and to condense further, St. John's remarkably compressive style, while even introducing a great deal of himself. The first section of the sixty-second "Kühlpsalm" is not only an excellent translation in itself, in its selective and composite rendering of St. John it is also an expressive poem in its own right. It shows the strong influence of the Doctor Mysticus of Roman Catholicism on a sectarian "enthusiast" and "revivalist," who met his death at the stake in Russia.

Another important institution through which the ideas and writings of Spain entered Germany was the court, especially in Vienna. With the Spanish-born Ferdinand, who had resided in Vienna since 1522 as the representative of his brother, the Emperor Charles V, the close relationship of the imperial court with Spain began. The emperors Maximilian II (1564-76) and Rudolf II (1576-1612) had spent some time in Spain, and with Leopold I (1640-1705), a last great admirer of this country ascended the throne. Since the days of Ferdinand, Spanish nobles frequently visited or lived in Vienna, bringing with them educated clerics and writers in their entourage. Spanish court ceremony—customs in dress, in polite discourse, and in entertainment—were introduced to Germany. The Spanish language was studied by men associated with the court. Especially notable were theatrical performances and court festivities in Vienna—when, upon the request of the empress, the Spanish princess Margareta Teresa, plays by Calderón,[16] Moreto, and many minor dramatists were performed during the 1660s and 1670s. While the Jesuits had introduced and perfected Latin school drama for the educational purposes of the Counter-Reformation, the German courtly society was entertained by moral and allegorical spectacles that conveyed the ideas of the Spanish courtly society.

Such ideas also entered Germany with the didactic-philosophical writings of Guevara, Saavedra Fajardo, and Gracián. The Franciscan bishop and court preacher of Charles I (Emperor Charles V), Antonio de Guevara (ca. 1480-1545), presented a Christian, courtly world view coupled with humanistic learning in writings such as his *Reloj de principes* (1529), *Menosprecio de corte y alabanza de aldea* (1539), and *Epístolas familiares* (1539-41). Widely read in Europe during the sixteenth century, Guevara was translated into German and popularized by the prolific writer Aegidius Albertinus, a secretary and librarian at Elector Maximilian's court in Munich.[17]

One of the many contemporary reflections of Guevara's ideas as adapted by Albertinus is the protagonist's "Farewell to this World" in Grimmelshausen's *Simplicissimus* (1669):[18]

ADjeu Welt / dann auff dich ist nicht zu trauen / noch von dir nichts zu hoffen / in deinem Hauß ist das vergangene schon verschwunden / das gegenwärtige verschwindet unter den Händen / das zukünfftige hat nie angefangen / das allerbeständigste fällt / das allerstärckste zerbricht / und das aller-ewigste nimmt ein End; also / daß du ein Todter bist unter den Todten / und in hundert Jahren lästu uns nicht eine Stund lebene. Adjeu Welt / denn du nimmst uns gefangen. (Book V, chap. 24)

Simplicissimus's contemplations in this entire chapter have been taken almost verbatim from Aegidius Albertinus's *Missbrauch des Hoff- und Lob des Landlebens* (1623), a German version of Guevara's *Menosprecio de corte y alabanza de aldea*. Only the introductory phrase to this chapter, "Adjeu Welt," which is repeated throughout, differs from Albertinus's "Behüt dich Gott Welt" (for "quédate adiós mundo"). Grimmelshausen accentuates his passage somewhat differently but can be said to have followed the Albertinus-Guevara passage closely, while in other places more deliberately adapting and integrating the source into his own fiction. Guevara's ascetic sermon has provided the concepts and stylistic form for Simplicissimus's final farewell to the vanity of this world.

Diego Saavedra Fajardo (1584-1648), who spent several years in Germany as the Spanish king's ambassador to the Imperial Diet at Regensburg (1640) and the Congress at Munster, published his book of political emblems, *Idea de un príncipe político-cristiano* (1640), in Munster and Munich. This handbook for a Christian ruler also contained timely, rational advice for the courtier in its 101 emblematic pictures complemented by explanatory verses. A German translation appeared in 1655, while a Latin rendition of 1649 was published many times throughout the century. The immense popularity of this work is reflected in Harsdörffer's numerous references to and borrowings from this emblem book in his *Frauenzimmer Gesprächsspiele* (1641-49) and in Lohenstein's state novel *Arminius* (1689-90).[19]

The Jesuit Baltasar Gracián, who formulated the *conceptismo*, the dark allegorical style, in his *Agudeza y arte de ingenio* (1648), became an influential author of pragmatic philosophical treatises on worldly wisdom. Lohenstein adapted Gracián's early work, *El político Don Fernando El Católico* (1640), as *Lorentz Gratians Staats-kluger catholischer Ferdinand* (1672), a handbook for regental wisdom, courting the House of Habsburg. Gracián's *Oráculo manual* (1647), a synthesis of Gracián's thinking in aphoristic form, was the subject of Christian Thomasius's programmatic lecture series in Leipzig in 1687. In Lohenstein's state novel *Arminius*, the German protagonist seems to fulfill the maxims that Gracián formulated for a worldly-wise hero to the point that literal reminiscences abound in the novel.

It was the novel, the "new" genre in seventeenth-century German literature, that was most decisively shaped by influences from the Romance tradition, and chiefly by Spanish prose fiction, which, at times, originated in Italy and was often transmitted to Germany through French translations. This "novel" genre was thus aptly named *Roman* in German. The *Amadis* (1569-94), whose first twelve volumes have been shown to have originated in fifteenth-century Spain, is a monstrously long novel of chivalry and courtly life, love and intrigues. It fascinated German readers throughout the seventeenth century — in spite of attacks against its immorality and lack of erudition by scholars and the clergy — in ever new translations and adaptations from French versions.[20]

Diego de San Pedro's *Cárcel de amor* (1492), a sentimental pastoral novel in epistolary form and with Italian narrative motifs, was first popularized in Germany in the 1624 rendering by the Austrian Hans Ludwig von Kuffstein. Already in 1619 Kuffstein had translated two other Spanish pastoral novels, Jorge de Montemayor's *Diana* and its continuation, the *Diana enamorada*.[21] It was the prolific mediator for the Romance literature in Germany, Harsdörffer, who "modernized" Kuffstein's *Diana* in 1646. The numerous translations and adaptations of the *Diana* novels in all European languages attest to the popularity of pastoral fiction. It seems to have been in the circle of the Nürnberg poets, where the Spanish *Diana*, especially its formal aspects, were used as poetic models.

The picaresque novel (*Schelmenroman*) was the most well known Spanish contribution, which no study of the German baroque novel fails to discuss. In the figure of the picaro (rogue), the unscrupulous, anti-social adventurer, life is depicted in a satirical and realistic fashion. The *Lazarillo de Tormes* (1554) was translated into German in 1614 and 1617;[22] in 1615 Aegidius Albertinus adapted Mateo Aleman's *Guzmán de Alfarache* (1599) in a moralizing, ascetic version. Aleman's novel has rightly been considered the paradigm of the picaresque type. The story is told from the perspective of the hero who visits Italy and Germany in the course of his occupations as a servant, beggar, cardinal's page, cook, teacher, actor, etc., affording the reader a view of many different social classes and a colorful world. It is the parable of the lost son who, in spite of repeated admonitions, falls prey to the enticements of this world, repents (in Albertinus's second part of the novel), and is prepared for his return to God by a hermit. The picaresque novella *Rinconete y Cortadillo* (1613) by Cervantes was translated in 1617, and his *Don Quijote* (1605-15) appeared transformed into a satiric, picaresque knight in the first German version of 1648.[23] Quevedo's *Buscón* (1616) was rendered into German after a French version by an anonymous translator in 1671; Francisco de Ubeda's *La Pícara Justina* (1605) was translated after a free Italian version already during the 1620s — depicting a female picara not unlike Grimmelshausen's *Landstörtzerin Courasche* (1670).

With these ubiquitous models of the picaresque, Grimmelshausen's work assumed a new dimension. A close connection of the picaresque with the Counter-Reformation through *Guzmán de Alfarache* and *Simplicissimus* has been demonstrated,[24] and the question of "originality" within the picaresque tradition blurs individual variations as well as interdependencies. There is no room to attempt a discussion or a review of previous statements on the subject of Grimmelshausen's novels. In his comparative study of the *Lazarillo*, the *Guzmán de Alfarache*, and *Simplicissimus*, G. Rötzer points to Grimmelshausen's eschatological perspective which prevented him from making a realistic description and satiric indictment of the social situation, as the Spanish picaresque novel had done. Rather, war in *Simplicissimus* is a colorful backdrop for the exemplary confrontation of this world and salvation. The theological-dogmatic substance is the higher aim of this novel:

Die Deutung der Welt sub specie aeternitatis zwingt Simplicissimus, der noch keine bürgerliche Weltbejahung kennt, zum Weltverzicht. . . . Die Spanier . . . setzten sich mit einer historischen Situation ihrer nationalen Entwicklung auseinander; Gesellschaftskritik und theologische Aspekte vermischten sich. Albertinus und Grimmelshausen klammerten soziale Implikationen aus: die Welt sei der Ort der Unbeständigkeit schlechthin. Aber Grimmelshausens Versuch, die Welt durch die Natur zu ersetzen, ist ein erster zaghafter Ansatz, auch wenn er ihn wieder zurücknimmt, dem Diesseits einen neuen Wertz zue verleihen.[26]

When Johann Michael Moscherosch adapted Quevedo's *Sueños* (1627) in his satirical prose work *Gesichte Philanders von Sittewald* (1642), he used a French translation and left his model farther behind with each new edition. The protagonist's original guide, Desengaño (disillusionment), an old man in ragged clothes who leads the young man through the world's main street of dissimulation, becomes Expertus Robertus, a rather likable, knowledgeable guide. Moscherosch addresses the "teutsch gesinnte Leser" (preface) and adds many moral maxims and learned quotes criticizing the ways of this world, especially the *wälsch* (French) manners of dishonesty:

Wann ich das Hertz recht erkundschaffete, so kam mir alle mahl dieser vnwider-
sprechliche Schluß vor, daß ich sagte: diese Leute sind warhafftig nicht wie sie
sich vor der Welt stellen, es ist Heucheley dahinter. . . .

> Dannenhero
> Los Spagnoles parescan sabios, y sont locos
> Los Franceses parescan y sont locos
> Los Italianos parescan y sont sabios
> Los Alemanes parescan locos, y sont sabios.[27]

> (The Spaniards appear wise, but are fools;
> The French appear and are fools;
> The Italians appear and are wise;
> The Germans appear to be fools, but are wise.)

The German Protestant Moscherosch added new "visions" and attacked the very ideals of a courtly life, which during the first decades of the century had been transmitted, above all, through Spanish writings.

The Spanish cultural and literary model exerts its foremost influence during the first half of the seventeenth century. During the Counter-Reformation, the imperial court and the Jesuits are its major channels; religious poetry and prose writings, especially the novel, are the main genres to stimulate German literature of the age. Major authors (Cervantes, Lope) figure less prominently than minor ones; Spanish drama (Calderón) exerts relatively little influence upon the development of German drama.

Concurrent with Spain's cultural hegemony, resentment and rejection of this country developed. In his play *Das Friedewünschende Deutschland* (1647), Rist has Don Antonio, clad in fashionable Spanish dress, say:

> Teutschland wil mit Spanien hinken,
> Wenn Kitarra singt und klingt,
> Teutschland will sich mit Grandezzen
> Spanien an die Seite setzen.[28]

Rist is criticizing Germany's hispanophilia. Anti-Spanish sentiment increased with Spanish political and military presence in Germany during the sixteenth century; during the Counter-Reformation it grew virulent, especially in Protestant circles. And while Spain—its literature and culture — was totally rejected in the eighteenth century by, above all, the French Enlighteners in what has been perceived in Spain as the "Black Legend,"[29] its cultural heritage and literature were rediscovered by the German Romantics. Then, once again, Spain inspired German literature.

NOTES

The works by Farinelli, Tiemann, and Schramm (see bibliography) contain detailed surveys of Spanish-German literary relations in the seventeenth century; more secondary literature and an excellent, updated account can best be found in Hoffmeister, *Spanien und Deutschland*, pp. 15–85 (see bibliography).

1. *Privatbriefe Kaiser Leopold I. an den Grafen F. E. Pötting, 1622–1673*, ed. A. F. Pribram and M. Landwehr von Pragenau (Vienna, 1903), Fontes Rerum Austriacarum, 56, p. 344; author's translation. A very readable new biography is John P. Spielman, *Leopold I of Austria* (London: Thames & Hudson, 1977).

2. Acuña's poem is quoted from Farinelli (see bibliography), p. 147; author's translation.

3. H. Hatzfeld, "El predominio del espírito español en la literatura europea en el siglo XVII," *Revista de Filología Hispánica*, 3 (1941), 9–23.

4. Tiemann (see bibliography), p. 41.

5. Karl Eschweiler, "Die Philosophie der spanischen Spätscholastik auf den deutschen Universitäten des siebzehnten Jahrhunderts," *Gesammelte Aufsätze zur Kulturgeschichte Spaniens*, ed. H. Finke, Spanische Forschungen der Görres-Gesellschaft, I (Münster, 1928), pp. 251–325.

6. *Johann Balthasar Schupp: Streitschriften Zweiter Teil*, ed. Carl Vogt, Neudrucke deutscher Literaturwerke des XVI. und XVII. Jahrhunderts, 225–26 (Halle: Niemeyer, 1911), pp. 15–16.

7. No census or bibliography exists; Tiemann (see bibliography), pp. 80–81, estimates about 70 editions and translations of Spanish mystics (Alonso de Orozco, Diego de Estella, Teresa de Jesús, Juan de la Cruz, etc.) and about 170 of Spanish ascetic works, especially those by Luis de Granada. There is no comprehensive study of the interrelationship of Spanish and German religious writings in the sixteenth and seventeenth centuries.

8. Jaime Tarracó, *A. Silesius y la mística española*, Analecta sacra Tarraconensia, 39 (Barcelona, 1957); German version in Spanische Forschungen der Görres-Gesellschaft, ser. I, vol. 15 (1960).

9. Georg Philipp Harsdörffer, *Nathan und Jotham: Das ist geistliche und weltliche Lehrgedichte* . . . (Nürnberg, 1650). The appendix to part I contains "Teresa's geistreiche Denk-Sprüche."

10. Harsdörffer's translation of the "Cántico espiritual" is contained in Johann Michael Dilherr, *Göttliche Liebesflamme* (Nürnberg, 1654).

11. Quirinus Kuhlmann, *Der Kühlpsalter*, ed. Robert L. Beare, p. 10.

12. Leonard Forster and A. A. Parker, "Quirinus Kuhlmann and the Poetry of St. John of the Cross," *Bulletin of Hispanic Studies*, 35 (1958), 1-23, is the only in-depth, comparative study of a German and Spanish religious poem; rpt. in *Daphnis*, 6 (1977), 235-62.

13. *Kühlpsalter*, p. 11.

14. The Spanish and Latin versions of "Llama de amor viva" are quoted from Forster and Parker, p. 4 (see note 12 above).

15. Ibid., p. 7.

16. Franzbach (see bibliography) presents exhaustive research on Calderón in Germany, while other dramatists and Spanish performances in Austria and Germany have received relatively little attention.

17. Christoph Schweitzer, "Antonio de Guevara in Deutschland," *Roma-nistisches Jahrbuch*, 11 (1960), 328-75, and 28 (1977), 322-25; Carlton L. Iiams, "Aegidius Albertinus and Antonio de Guevara" (diss. University of California, Berkeley, 1956).

18. Günther Weydt, "Adjeu Welt: Weltklage und Lebensrückblick bei Guevara, Albertinus und Grimmelshausen," *Neophilologus*, 46 (1962), 105-25.

19. Valuable references in Mulagk (see bibliography), pp. 324-32.

20. Weddige's investigation (see bibliography) has thrown new light on this corpus of fiction; it is also a model for reception studies.

21. Hoffmeister, *Die spanische Diana* (see bibliography), carefully analyzes Kuffstein's renditions and demonstrates its importance for the German novel in the seventeenth century. Harsdörffer's numerous adaptations from Spanish literature have not been studied in detail; there is a chapter "Harsdörffer und die spanische Literatur" in Christoph Schweitzer, "Spanien in der deutschen Literatur des 17. Jahrhunderts" (diss. Yale University 1954), pp. 171-210.

22. The 1614 translation of *Lazarillo de Tormes* was published only in 1951 by H. Tiemann (see bibliography) in a bibliophile edition; the 1617 translation was published anonymously and reprinted repeatedly; another translation followed in 1656. Cf. Rötzer (bibliography), pp. 1-54.

23. See R. Alewyn, "Die ersten deutschen Übersetzer des 'Don Quijote' und des 'Lazarillo de Tormes,'" *Zeitschrift für deutsche Philologie*, 54 (1929), 203-16; see also G. Colon, *Die ersten romanischen und germanischen Übersetzungen des Don Quijote* (Bern and München: Francke, 1974).

24. Parker (see bibliography), pp. 75-94.

25. For a review of research, see Gerhart Hoffmeister, "Grimmelshausens 'Simplicissimus' und der spanisch-deutsche Schelmenroman: Beobachtungen zum Forschungsstand," *Daphnis*, 5 (1976), 275-94.

26. Rötzer (see bibliography), pp. 145-46.
27. Moscherosch (see bibliography), p. 10.
28. Rist, *Sämtliche Werke*, ed. Eberhard Mannack (Berlin: de Gruyter, 1971), XI, 83.
29. Julian Juderías, *La Leyenda negra: Estudios acerca del concepto de España en el extranjero* (Barcelona, 1917); B. Becker-Cantarino, "Die 'Schwarze Legende': Zum Spanienbild in der deutschen Literatur des 18. Jahrhunderts," *Zeitschrift für deutsche Philologie*, 94 (1975), 183-203.

SELECTED BIBLIOGRAPHY

Primary Sources

Albertinus, Aegidius. *Antonii de Guevara . . . Opera Omnia Historico-Politica. 1. Güldene Sendschreiben. 2. Fürstliche Weckuhr und Lustgarten. 3. Miszbrauch desz-Hoffs undd Lob desz Landts-Leben. 4. Der wolgezierte Hoffman, oder Hofschul. 5. Von Gastereyen und Zutrincken. . . .* Frankfurt, 1644-45. (Faber du Faur, no. 901.)

———. *Der Landstörtzer Gusman von Alfarache oder Picaro genannt . . . ausz dem Spanischen verteutscht* (1615). Rpt. Hildesheim: Olms, 1975.

———. *Hofschul.* Erika and Michael Metzger, eds. Nachdrucke deutscher Literatur des 17. Jahrhunderts, 22; Bern and Frankfurt: Lang, 1979.

———. *Von Beschwerligkeit des Hofflebens.* Rpt. Christoph Schweitzer, ed. Nachdrucke deutscher Literatur des 17. Jahrhunderts, 25, forthcoming.

Amadis. Erstes Buch. Nach der ältesten deutschen Bearbeitung (1569-94), Adalbert von Keller, ed. Bibliothek des Literarischen Vereins Stuttgart, 40, 1857. Rpt. Darmstadt: Wissenschaftliche Buchgesellschaft, 1963.

Caesar, Joachim. *Don Kichote de la Mantzscha, das ist: Juncker Harnisch auss Fleckenland* (1648). Hermann Tiemann, ed. Hamburg: de Gruyter, 1928.

Harsdörffer, Georg Philipp. *Diana von H. J. De Monte-Major, in zweyen Theilen Spanisch beschrieben . . . Mit dess Herrn C. G. Polo zuvor nie-gedolmetschtem dritten Theil . . .* (1646). Rpt. Darmstadt: Wissenschaftliche Buchgesellschaft, 1969.

Kuffstein, Hans Ludwig von. *Diana. Erster vnnd anderer Theil der newen ver-teutschten Schäfferey, von der schönen verliebten Diana.* Linz, 1619. (Faber du Faur, no. 798.)

———. *Gefängnüss der Lieb oder Carcel de Amor* (1625). Gerhart Hoffmeister, ed. Nachdrucke deutscher Literatur des 17. Jahrhunderts, 7. Bern and Frankfurt: Lang, 1976.

Kuhlmann, Quirinus. *Der Kühlpsalter.* Robert L. Beare, ed. Neudrucke deutscher Literaturwerke, N.S. 4-5. Tübingen: Niemeyer, 1971.

Leben und Wandel Lazaril von Tormes und Beschreibung . . . Verdeutzscht

1614. Hermann Tiemann, ed. Hamburg: Maximilian-Gesellschaft, 1951.

Moscherosch, Johann Michael. *Gesichte Philanders von Sittewald*, Felix Bobertag, ed. 1883. Rpt. Darmstadt: Wissenschaftliche Buchgesellschaft, 1964.

Ulenhart, Niklas. *Sonderlich-curieuse Historia von Isaac Winckelfelder und Jobst von der Schneid [1617] . . . von neuem wiederum auffgelegt* (1724). Rpt. (private), Prague: Haase, 1923. Veröffentlichungen der Gesellschaft deutscher Bücherfreunde in Böhmen, 5. (Based upon Cervantes's *Novela de Riconete y Cortadillo*.)

——. *Historia von Isaac Winckelfelder*. Rpt. Gerhart Hoffmeister, ed. Paderborn: Schöningh, 1982-83, (forthcoming).

Secondary Literature

Alewyn, Richard. "Der Lazarillo de Tormes und Niklas Ulenhart." *Zeitschrift für deutsche Philologie*, 54 (1929), 212-16.

Brüggemann, Werner. *Cervantes und die Figur des Don Quijote in Kunstanschauung und Dichtung der deutschen Romantik*. Spanische Forschungen der Görres-Gesellschaft, N.S. 7. Münster: Aschendorff, 1958.

Farinelli, Artur. "Spanien und die spanische Literatur im Lichte der deutschen Kritik und Poesie." *Zeitschrift für vergleichende Literaturgeschichte*, N.S. 5 (1892), 135-276; 8 (1895), 318-407.

Franzbach, Martin. *Untersuchungen zum Theater Calderóns in der europäischen Literatur vor der Romantik*. München: Fink, 1974.

Hoffmeister, Gerhart. *Die spanische Diana in Deutschland: Vergleichende Untersuchungen zu Stilwandel und Weltbild des Schäferromans im 17. Jahrhundert*. Philologische Studien und Quellen, 68. Berlin: Erich Schmidt, 1972.

——. *Spanien und Deutschland: Geschichte und Dokumentation der literarischen Beziehungen*. Grundlagen der Romanistik, 9 Berlin: Erich Schmidt, 1976; *y Alemania*.

Mulagk, Karl-Heinz. *Phänomene des politischen Menschen im 17. Jahrhundert: Propedeutische Studien zum Werk Lohensteins unter besonderer Berücksichtigung Diego Saavedra Fajardos und Baltasar Graciáns*. Philologische Studien und Quellen, 66. Berlin: Erich Schmidt, 1973.

Parker, Alexander A. *Literature and the Delinquent: The Picaresque Novel in Spain and Europe 1599-1753*. Edinburgh: University Press, 1967.

Reichardt, Dieter. *Von Quevedos "Buscón" zum deutschen "Avanturier."* Studien zur Germanistik, Anglistik und Komparatistik, 7. Bonn: Bouvier, 1970.

Rötzer, Hans-Gerd. *Picaro—Landtstörtzer—Simplicius: Studien zum niederen Roman in Spanien und Deutschland*. Impulse der Forschung, 4. Darmstadt: Wissenschaftliche Buchgesellschaft, 1972.

Schramm, Edmund. "Die Einwirkung der spanischen Literatur auf die deutsche." *Deutsche Philologie im Aufriß*. W. Stammler, ed. Berlin, 1957. III, 261-306.

Stadler, Ulrich. "Parodistisches in der Justina Dietzin Picara: Über die Entstehungsbedingungen und zur Wirkungsgeschichte von Ubedas Schelmenroman in Deutschland." *Arcadia*, 7 (1972), 158-70.

Tiemann, Hermann. *Das spanische Schrifttum in Deutschland von der Renaissance zur Romantik*. 1937. Rpt. Hildesheim and New York: Olms, 1971.

Varas Reyes, F. P. "Notas a dos novelas de J. Beer." *Filología moderna*, 3 (1962), 101-35.

Weddige, Hilkert. *Die "Historien vom Amadis aus Frankreich": Dokumentarische Grundlegung zur Entstehung und Rezeption*. Beiträge zur Literatur des XV. bis XVIII. Jahrhunderts, 2. Wiesbaden: Steiner, 1975.

8

The French Model

Janis L. Solomon

Despite the plethora of publications on the German baroque during the past sixty years, there is a surprising lack of basic information upon which to base an appraisal of the degree to which the style and content of German baroque poetry was determined by French, as opposed to Italian, Dutch, or Neolatin models. To a certain extent this is due to the nature of the poetics of *imitatio* prevalent in the European Renaissance and baroque as a whole,[1] and to the all-pervading phenomenon of petrarchism, the effects of which are a near universality of subject matter, style, and form in the European literatures during the sixteenth and seventeenth centuries. The role of France as transmitter and transformer of Italian, Spanish, Neo-Latin, and classical texts and traditions, however, is generally recognized to have been a central one, especially for Germany and the Netherlands. Nevertheless, it has so far been inadequately documented, far too much attention having been wasted on laments over the "servile" importation of alien verse forms, principles, and poetic content.

In a recent publication of the Internationaler Arbeitskreis für deutsche Barockliteratur, a bibliography of seventeenth-century translations from Romance languages and studies of the reception of such translations are listed among the desiderata for the field by the referee for the section on the reception of Romance literatures in Germany.[2] It is perhaps symptomatic that of the nine reports held in that section when the Arbeitskreis met in 1976 only one dealt with a French text, although the direct influence of French literature in the German baroque was

probably greater than that of Italian, and certainly than Spanish,
literature. However, the very breadth of its impact hinders its ready
identification or definition. A further problem lies in the scarcity of
texts, as well as reliable and easily accessible data, and detailed special
studies. The most recent study of the relationship between French and
Germany poetry in the seventeenth century on a larger scale is that of
Adelheid Beckmann (see bibliography), which deals with parallels in
themes and stylistic devices in the two literatures. Detailed analyses of individual translations and imitations are necessary, however, in order to
determine whether a particular poem was used, since these parallels for
the most part have counterparts in other European literatures of the sixteenth and seventeenth centuries as well, as the author herself points out
in her introductory chapter. Even in the case of Opitz, whose relationship to French and Dutch poetry has long been the subject of intense investigation, new material concerning his sources and the use he made of
them has recently been brought to light,[3] and undoubtedly much more
remains to be done regarding other baroque authors, including studies
of the specifically French elements taken over from the work of Opitz.

When referring in the following pages to the French model for German baroque poetry, we are speaking first of all of a program of emulation and imitation with patriotically motivated cultural goals, along with
its corresponding humanistic poetics concerned exclusively with verse,
and predominantly with the lyric genres. Further, we are speaking
primarily of the group of French poets known as the Pléiade and, above
all, of Joachim du Bellay (1522-60), who furnished the model for Opitz's
call for a refined vernacular poetry *Buch von der deutschen Poeterey*
(1624) and of Pierre de Ronsard (1524-85), from whose work a number
of the poetic examples and most of the prosodic rules offered in the
Poeterey are drawn. Many of the best and most imitated sonnets and
odes in Opitz's own edition of his works the following year (*Deutsche
Poemata*, 1625) are translated from or based on Ronsard also.

One of the peculiarities of the influence of the Pléiade in Germany is
the degree to which its effective reception is associated with a single verse
form, the Alexandrine, and flows through the work of a single poet,
Martin Opitz (1597-1639), through whom it exercised an enormous
secondary influence, since virtually every poet of the German baroque
succeeding Opitz imitates the forms, content, or techniques of his poetry,
and in most cases all three. However, Opitz is by no means the first German poet to take note of and imitate the achievements of the French
Renaissance. There had been sporadic attempts at Alexandrine verse in

German for over half a century preceding the appearance of Opitz's *Poeterey*. The Alexandrine version of the eighty-ninth Psalm by Théodore de Bèze for the Huguenot Psalter was translated in 1573 by Ambrosius Lobwasser.[4] The anonymous translator of *Das Buch Extasis* (1573)[5] by Jan van der Noot, a Flemish imitator of Ronsard, manages passable *vers communs* and Alexandrines in German versions of sonnets inserted into this work. Paul Schede-Melissus, who had translated the first fifty Psalms of the Huguenot Psalter one year before Lobwasser (1572), was personally connected with the Pléiade circle and imitated their poetry in at least one German sonnet written in "French" Alexandrines around 1579.[6] The remarks on versification that Opitz attributes to Ernst Schwabe von der Heyde in *Aristarchus* (1618) most probably derive from Ronsard's *Abbrégé* (1565)[7] and Schwabe's translation of the first sonnet of Petrarch's *Canzoniere* (also in *Aristarchus*) shows the influence not of the Italian, but the French sonnet form (Alexandrines with alternating masculine and feminine rhymes, and the rhyme scheme *ccd eed* in the sestet). Weckherlin's *Oden und Gesänge* (1618) contain numerous translations and imitations of Pléiade poems and verse and strophic forms.[8] Tobias Hübner's Alexandrine translation of du Bartas's biblical epic, *La Sepmaine*, began to appear in 1619, not to mention the Alexandrines of Zincgref, Kirchner, and others in the "Anhang mehr auserleßener geticht anderer Teutscher Poëten" appended to Zincgref's edition of Opitz's works, *Martin Opicii Teutsche Poëmata* (1624). Finally, there appear to have been numerous multilingual Dutch broadsheets in the first quarter of the seventeenth century containing German Alexandrines of varying quality.[9]

Schede, Schwabe, Hübner, and Weckherlin all construct their Alexandrines according to the rules of French versification, with fixed accents only at the caesura and rhyme, so that one could say that these poets imitate their French models even more closely than did Opitz. Georg Rudolf Weckherlin (1584-1653), in particular, had seemed motivated to create a new courtly German poetry after the example of the Pléiade, to which end he had translated and imitated both encomiastic odes and songlike odelettes by Ronsard and several poems by du Bellay and Belleau as well as their successors Desportes and Malherbe.[10] Weckherlin's work, generally favorably contrasted with that of Opitz, especially in older literature, nevertheless had little effect upon German baroque poetry.

Despite his many precursors, it was only with Opitz's clear statement of the rules of Alexandrine versification according to the usage of the

Pléiade (caesura, elision of unaccented "e," avoidance of hiatus within the verse, alternation of masculine and feminine rhyme endings), together with the requirement that all German verse be constructed with regular alternation of accented and unaccented syllables according to the natural word accent (following the Dutch precedent), that the Alexandrine achieved its unique status in German baroque poetry. Above all, it was Opitz's examples of the new verse and the relative elegance of his poetic transmission of the Pléiade's synthesis of petrarchism and the sensuality of classical love poetry[11] that assured the success of his ambitious venture to create a new German poetry.

It is not clear whether Opitz recognized the extent to which his Alexandrine marked a major departure from its French form.[13] The French Alexandrine demands an absolute coincidence of word and metrical accent only at the caesura (sixth syllable, which must also mark the end of a word and a phrase) and in the rhyme (twelfth syllable, usually the end of a sentence as well as a line), and maintains a great rhythmic freedom within the line otherwise.[14] In any case, Opitz's strictly alternating[15] adaptation of the French Alexandrine proved irresistible, to the chagrin of countless nineteenth- and some twentieth-century Germanists, who considered the verse foreign to the spirit of Germanic poetry.[16]

For the German baroque, Opitz's *Buch von der deutschen Poeterey*[17] had much the same significance as du Bellay's *Deffence et Illustration de la Langue française* (1549) had for the French Renaissance; in its attention to specific technical matters it resembles more Ronsard's *Abbrégé de l'art poétique français* (1565). Opitz draws heavily upon both authors, but primarily Ronsard, as well as Horace, Scaliger, and Vida for content; indeed, he presumes his reader's acquaintance with these and other sources shared also by Ronsard and du Bellay. Both Opitz and du Bellay write with enthusiasm and a pressing sense that national pride demands the creation of a vernacular literature to match that of other nations. For France, the envied model is Italy; for Germany, it is primarily France, then the Netherlands, and as the model for both of these, Italy also. The Pléiade are more ambitious in their intention to rival the poetry of the ancients and outspoken in rejecting the humanists' attempt to do this in Latin.[18] To be sure, Opitz recommends the most thorough study of the classical authors in order for the aspiring poet to learn how to write properly,[19] but he erects no ideal of re-creating the classical works in his own language by the process of assimilating and "digesting" the ancients, as does du Bellay. Theoretically, the Pléiade reject translation as poetry in its own right. In practice, however, their translations and borrowings are legion. Du Bellay in particular translated with varying degrees of freedom many sonnets from Petrarch and the Italian petrarchists, while Ronsard's borrowings are generally more a form of imitation. Opitz follows their practice rather than their theoretical position in recommending translation as an artistic exercise, and in offering free translations as his own work. As is well known, he chose as subjects for translation and imitation some of the most famous sonnets and odes by the leading poet of the Pléiade, Pierre de Ronsard. Since several of these poems are used as models for the genres sonnet and ode, and as justification for amatory and Anacreontic verse in the *Poeterey*, their influence was even greater than their number[20] might otherwise suggest.

The circumstances that moved both du Bellay and Opitz to the hurried writing and publication of their respective literary manifestoes bear comparison. The year 1548 had seen the publication of Thomas Sebillet's *Art poétique français*, which codified the practice of Clément Marot's (ca. 1495–1544) school, still too much linked with the tradition of the Rhétoriqueurs to suit du Bellay, Ronsard, and their friends. They rapidly sought to counter what they considered a conservative force through the *Deffence* and the publication of their own works:[21] du Bellay's first collection of sonnets, *L'Olive*, appeared in 1549, while Ronsard's *Odes* appeared in 1550 and his *Amours* in 1552. In Opitz's case, the impetus for the *Poeterey* was given by the appearance of his own early poems and youthful manifesto *Aristarchus* in Zincgref's edition (1624), along with three works published separately by Opitz since leaving Heidelberg: his praise of rural life, *Zlatna* (1623), and two translations of long didactic poems by Heinsius, *Lobgesang Jesu Christi* (1621) and *Lobgesang Bacchi* (1622); the *Anhang* contained poems by Zincgref, Weckherlin, Melissus, and others. The appearance of this edition, complete with a preface written by Opitz before fleeing Heidelberg early in 1620, did not please him in 1624. Both the "disorderly" arrangement of the edition (i.e., the lack of a systematic organization by genre or any other obvious formal criterion) and the occasional lapses in alternating meter in his own poems, not to mention those in the *Anhang*, caused Opitz embarrassment. He had since recognized clearly the accentual and alternating principle that he had generally, but not strictly, observed in the Heidelberg poems; the earliest Silesian poems, especially those in the *Aristarchus*, contained many more such instances. Also, he had, perhaps from the editions of Ronsard's works that he had studied in the meantime, evolved the concept of an edition arranged not only according to a division between secular and religious works, but within the former, according to subject matter, social hierarchy, and genre.[22] Opitz's own augmented and purged edition of his works was published the following year (1625).[23]

Opitz is selective in his borrowings in the *Poeterey*. He does not condemn the writing of Neolatin poetry as an exercise in futility; he does not recommend adopting archaisms, dialect, and technical vocabulary, as does Ronsard, nor does he dwell at such length upon enriching the poetic vocabulary of the vernacular with neologisms. In contrast to Ronsard, he warmly recommends enjambment (contributing thereby to the totally different impression created by the German as opposed to the French Alexandrine). He includes a lengthy apology of the poet (chapter 3); his French sources evidently had no need for that. Opitz follows the practice of the Pléiade and subsequent generations in France in recommending the Alexandrine as a heroic meter despite Ronsard's recommendation of the *vers commun* for this purpose (in the prefaces to the *Franciade*). Further, he issues no such wholesale condemnation of older poetry, medieval fixed-form genres, and the popular song as the Pléiade, which demanded a radical break with the national past. In his search for earlier examples of venerable German poetry, Opitz parallels attitudes prevalent in France following the Pléiade. In his own poetic practice, and even in his translations from Ronsard, Opitz is much more moderate in his use of mythological allusions — perhaps partly for religious reasons,[24] but also out of a quest for clarity rather than learned obscurity (the occasionally deserved criticism leveled at Ronsard by Malherbe).

Apart from the enthusiasm for the vernacular, the spirit of which is more fervently patriotic in the *Deffence* than in the *Poeterey*, and various technical points concerning purity of rhyme, prohibition of inversion and omission of articles, elision rules for unaccented "e," and the definitions of *vers commun* and Alexandrine, the most significant aspect of the Pléiade model transmitted by the *Poeterey* lies in the examples, particularly the sonnets and odes based on Ronsard and the two Pindaric odes written after his example. These models set the character and form of their genres for the rest of the century.

The Pléiade had made the sonnet the most important lyric genre in France, as it was to become in the German baroque. Ronsard's early sonnets are written in *vers communs*, the later collections primarily in Alexandrines, but Opitz rarely uses the ten-syllable verse, even when the original is in that verse form. Here again, Opitz parallels the practice of his contemporaries in France, where the Alexandrine enjoyed almost exclusive use as a longer verse.[25] Both in the use of the Alexandrine with alternation of masculine and feminine rhymes and in the preference for the rhyme scheme *abba abba ccd eed*, Opitz's translations and imitations of Ronsard establish the French sonnet as model in Germany rather than the Italian *endecasillabo* form with its greater variety of rhyme schemes, including Weckherlin's favorite, *abab abab cdc dcd*. It has been remarked that the French rhyme scheme favors a sharper division between octet and sestet and the use of *pointe* as conclusion;[26] this tendency toward the epigrammatic is shared by the German baroque sonnet as well. The Pléiade sonnet is typically structured strictly in accordance with its strophic divisions and maintains an essential identity of syntactic unit and line, with very sparing use of enjambment. Opitz, on the other hand, runs over both lines and strophic divisions regularly, with varying degrees of artistic gain. That his contemporaries were acutely aware of the choices and possibilities inherent in the overrunning of the strophic divisions of the sonnet is indicated by Phillip von Zesen's taking particular note of this feature of Opitz's sonnet practice, quoting an example by Petrarch and Marot in addition to two by Opitz (and listing others of this type in his works) in his own poetics.[27] The essentially classicistic and static Renaissance sonnet of the Pléiade becomes much more "baroque" in the transition from French to German, whether at the hands of Weckherlin[28] or Opitz.[29]

Ronsard himself was proud of his introduction of the ode as a high art form in the classical tradition in contrast to the popular chanson of Marot. In fact, however, he also wrote many "odelettes" in an Anacreontic or Horatian vein that tended toward the chanson in spirit and form.[30] Weckherlin translated and imitated both odes addressed to persons of nobility in Alexandrines and lighter amatory or Anacreontic songs in shorter verses. Both types of poem show the influence of the material, style, and strophic forms of his French models.[31] Opitz uses the term "Ode" interchangeably with "Gesang," under which he understands a strophic form suitable for singing, while the elevated Alexandrine poem of praise is not entitled ode at all, and is grouped separately with other occasional poems in all editions of his works. His odes incorporate elements of the popular song elevated to the level of the art song. They were modeled after the lighter songs of Ronsard and contain many of the same themes and motifs, such as the Horatian *carpe diem*, reflections on the ephemeral nature of life, love's pleasures and pains, etc.[32]

Ronsard's attempt to transplant the Pindaric ode was basically unsuccessful. He wrote only fourteen such poems and then abandoned the form. Opitz followed his example in including two of these exotic and prestigious poems with their sequences of strophe, antistrophe, and epode in the *Poeterey*. One of these, an epithalamium for his friend Nüssler, is one of the most pronouncedly Platonic pieces he wrote, reflecting perhaps the strong current of Platonism in the Pléiade, although one certainly need not look for "sources" of such widely disseminated ideas as the Platonic cosmogony. Opitz wrote only these two Pindaric odes, the second of which is an epicedium. Gryphius later used the form for a series of Psalm paraphrases.[33]

Ronsard attempted Sapphic odes as well. Opitz quotes him regarding the necessity of music for this genre, and quotes three of his Sapphic strophes, but gives no examples of his own. He did, however, later translate three Psalms in the modified Sapphic strophes of the Huguenot Psalter and one poem of the *Arcadia* translation in a related form.[34] This "Sapphic" strophe was not frequent in Germany, but a number of attempts were made, more likely as imitations of the Psalm strophe[35] than on the strength of Ronsard's examples in the *Poeterey*.

The eclogues of the Pléiade were, like those of Marot, largely an allegorical genre within which both personal and political topics could be sounded under the guise of pastoral dialogue. Weckherlin imitates this form quite closely. Opitz wrote several "Hirtenlieder" during the Heidelberg period, but is not greatly attracted to the pastoral verse dialogue. His *Schäfferey von der Nimfen Hercinie* (1630) combines narrative and prose dialogue with lyric pieces and passages of verse dialogue, a form suggested perhaps in part by Rémy Belleau's (1528-77) *La Bergerie* (1565), which consists primarily of poems loosely connected with prose narrative.

A further aspect of the Pléiade influence on Opitz and his successors involves the choice of classical models to emulate. Opitz shares with Ronsard and his circle a high esteem for Horace and Anacreon. The Hellenism of the Pléiade is reflected in Opitz's introduction of the Pindaric ode in German and perhaps also in his choice of Sophocles' *Antigone* to translate (1636) as a model for tragedy. Seneca, whose *Troerinnen* he had translated in 1625, is recognizable in the *Antigone* as well. Seneca also informed the Pléiade's concept of tragedy, despite the usual reference to Aristotle.

In choosing models for the moral epigram and religious lyric, Opitz turned to a poet allied with the Pléiade for the popular "Quatrains moraux" (1576) of Guy du Faure, Sieur de Pibrac (1529-84), which he translated in 1634,[36] and to a foe of the Pléiade in selecting Antoine de

Chandieu's "Octonaires sur la vanité du monde" (1583). The French
original of the verses "Von der Welt Eitelkeit. Auß dem Frantzösischen"
(1629), which rank among Opitz's best religious poetry, was only recently
discovered.[37] In both cases Opitz's choice was dictated by the religious or
moral content of the works of these Huguenot poets rather than their
literary allegiances.

Although the influence of the generations preceding and following
the Pléiade in France—Marot on the one hand and du Bartas,
Desportes, Malherbe, and the Précieux*on the other—is less visible in
German baroque poetry than that of the Pléiade itself, it is far from
negligible. A strong formal influence is exercised upon both religious
and secular lyric through the much admired and copied strophic forms
used in Clément Marot's versification of the Psalms, completed by
Théodore de Bèze, known as the Huguenot or Geneva Psalter (complete,
1562). The translations of the Psalter into German by Paul Schede-
Melissus (the first fifty, 1572) and Ambrosius Lobwasser (complete,
1573) were intended to be sung to the melodies composed by Goudimel
and others for the French texts, so that an exact duplication of the
strophic forms by syllable count was necessary. Lobwasser's Psalter was
widely used, but it is difficult to assess precisely its literary influence outside the church song, as some strophes similar to Marot's were used by
Ronsard and his circle as well. Lobwasser's poetic style is decidedly
plainer than the original texts, or those of Melissus, whose ambitions included matching the formal artistry of the original.[38] This was also the
aim of Weckherlin and Opitz, who both composed verse translations or
paraphrases of the Psalms to these same melodies and used their strophic
forms in other poems. Here again, Opitz appears to mark their effective
entrance into German literary practice, as opposed to church usage.
There were numerous other poetic versions of the entire Psalter or parts
thereof in the German baroque, including some in Alexandrines. This
enthusiasm for poetic paraphrases of the Psalms and other books of the
Old Testament, particularly the Song of Solomon and the Lamentations
of Jeremiah (both represented in Opitz's work), and for religious poetry
in general, is a phenomenon common to both France[39] and Germany
during the seventeenth century.

As for the generation following the Pléiade, one might say that
Opitz's concern with the purification and elevation of the German

---

*A group of writers centered in the Hôtel de Rambouillet, ca. 1618–50.

language is closer to the spirit of Malherbe than to the enthusiastic demand for enrichment made by Ronsard and du Bellay. Nonetheless, it was a shock and disappointment to Opitz to learn during his sojourn in Paris in 1630 that in the wake of Malherbe's reign as critical authority, Ronsard was no longer considered the epitome of good style. The later French poets were translated and imitated by Weckherlin, Ernst Christoph Homburg, and others, but little is known of the German reception of *précieux* poetry in comparison to Marinism. Beckmann suggests a *précieux* poem by I. de Benserade (1612–91) as model for at least one of the poems of Christian Hofmann von Hofmannswaldau,[40] although it might also be merely a parallel. Hofmannswaldau did spend several months in Paris in 1640 and doubtless came in contact with literary circles, but the question of his relationship to the Hôtel de Rambouillet is unsettled.[41]

The younger contemporary of Ronsard, Guillaume de Salluste, Sieur du Bartas (1544–90), exercised much influence upon the religious and didactic epic of the German baroque through his biblical epic, *La Semaine* (1579 and 1584 ff.). Hübner's translation of this work (1622 and 1631) is one source of its influence, but perhaps of less importance than Opitz's translations of the scholarly mythological and religious didactic poems of the Dutch poet Daniel Heinsius, modeled after du Bartas and the *Hymnes* of Ronsard. Du Bartas in particular was imitated in his departures from the ideal of classical balance in style exemplified by Ronsard, especially in his didactic digressions and overuse of composita in imitation of the Greek manner of word formation.[42] Opitz quotes a clustered example of such expressions from Heinsius's *Lofsanck Bacchi* in the *Poeterey*, where he correctly refers to Ronsard as source for parts of Heinsius's passage and as ultimate advocate of this type of neologism.

Whereas in Ronsard Opitz unquestionably chose the greatest French poet of the preceding century as his model, no such agreeable equation between influence and quality obtains for the French seventeenth century as reflected in the German baroque. Among contemporary French poets there was no figure of a stature comparable to Ronsard, and the German baroque was evidently unable to make a similarly productive use of the great French essayists and dramatists of the "classical age." Generally it may be said that with few exceptions the contemporary French works imitated and translated in German in the seventeenth century are of secondary importance or entirely ephemeral, although they may have been famous in their day.

The great genre of the French baroque—the drama of Corneille,

Racine, and Molière — bore no fruit in Germany until the following century, despite a 1650 translation of the *Cid* by Greflinger and Velten's
stagings of Molière and Corneille late in the century.[43] It is generally supposed that Andreas Gryphius profited as a dramatist from his acquaintance with the drama of Pierre Corneille,[44] but his real inspiration comes
from the Jesuit theater. Gryphius did translate a contemporary comedy
by the tragedian's immensely successful younger brother, Thomas, entitled *Le berger extravagant: Schwermender Schäffer* (1663),[45] which is
a theatrical adaptation of Charles Sorel's novel of the same name satiriz-
ing the current pastoral vogue *à l'Astrée*. The relationship between
Gryphius's comedy *Verlibtes Gespenst* (1660) and Philippe Quinault's *Le
Fantôme amoureux* (1658) is, despite the identical titles, quite loose.[46]

Neither the classical French drama nor the moralists left significant
imprints upon German baroque literature, but the pastoral volumes of
Honoré d'Urfé, whose *Astrée* (1607-27) was soon translated into German
(1619-35),[47] and the heroic-galant continuation of the genre by the *pré-
cieuse* Madeleine de Scudéry and others had an incalculable influence
upon the manners and self-image of cultivated circles in seventeenth-
century Germany and found many German imitators. Two translations
from the French preceded Philip von Zesen's (1619-89) first independent
novel, *Die adriatische Rosemund* (1645): *Lysander und Kaliste* (1644) by
d'Audiguier and *Ibrahims und der Beständigen Isabellen Wunder-
Geschichte* (1645) by Mlle. de Scudéry. The last book of *Ibrahim* and
Zesen's later translation of de Gerzan's *Afrikanische Sofonisbe* (1647)
also furnished Daniel Casper von Lohenstein (1635-83) with dramatic
material.[48]

In terms of quantity, the religious lyric, devotional literature, the
lyric of the *précieux*, collections of novella and stories,[49] burlesque and
satiric literature, in addition to the more important genres already mentioned, all flourished in seventeenth-century France. These phenomena
appear to have been readily incorporated into the literary production of
the German baroque, although the relationships are seldom so direct
and well documented as those between the Pléiade and the work of Opitz
and Weckherlin.

Opitz's translation (*Die süßen Todesgedanken*, 1632) of the prose
Les douces pensées de la mort (1627) by his Catholic contemporary Jean
Puget de la Serre, a favorite of Richelieu, introduced an example of the
highly rhetorical devotional literature popular in France at the time of
his journey to Paris in 1630.[50] La Serre was subsequently often translated
into German. Religious lyric in France included prayers in sonnet form[51]

and formal experimentation with mixed verses.[52] Both of these phenomena are to be found in Germany as well. Opitz wrote one "prayer sonnet"[53] and is followed in this genre by many others such as Gryphius and Catharina von Greiffenberg (1633–94). It is not clear whether Gryphius's formal experiments have any relation to the parallel French phenomenon, but Gryphius, like Hofmannswaldau, did spend several months in Paris early in his life.

The abundant satiric literature of sixteenth- and seventeenth-century France doubtless exercised considerable influence on its German neighbors. Hans Jakob Christoffel von Grimmelshausen, whose *Simplicissimus Teutsch* counts Charles Sorel's *La vraie histoire comique de Francion* (1623), in translation, among its many sources,[54] makes good use of the beginnings of the realistic French novel. Gryphius's translation of Th. Corneille's dramatization of Sorel's *Berger extravagant* stands more directly in the burlesque tradition, as does his *Horribilicribrifax*, which is not directly dependent on a French source, although the influence of P. Corneille's *L'Illusion comique* is probable.[55] Parody and satire were common in the German baroque lyric as well.[56] One wonders whether Opitz's "Fieberliedlein" (only in Zincgref's edition) and comparable pieces by the later Silesians might not have been inspired by contemporary French burlesque poetry. Opitz's sonnet "Du schöne Tyndaris," which is related to the contre-blason, or parody of the petrarchistic praise of the physical features of the beloved, appears in the *Poeterey* as the first of four examples of the sonnet form. The petrarchistic blason was popularized by Marot, in whose work the contre-blason also appears.[57] In other words, anti-petrarchism, which appears in the Pléiade itself as early as 1553 with du Bellay's "A une dame" (later titled "Contre les pétrarquistes"),[58] was transferred to Germany along with petrarchism in the work of Opitz.

This survey of French influence in the German baroque has not attempted to list the known translations or imitations of literary significance, but only to sketch in a few outlines around the relatively defined focal point of lyric poetry and around the role of Martin Opitz in presenting as a model for German emulation the Pléiade synthesis of petrarchism, Neolatin, and classical poetry and the repertoire of forms and techniques developed by Ronsard from these traditions. It is to be hoped that as more seventeenth-century documents are reprinted and more research of a bibliographical and positivistic nature is undertaken, the French role in the German baroque may eventually be more precisely assessed on a broader basis.

NOTES

1. Cf. August Buck, "Dichtungslehren der Renaissance und des Barocks," in *Renaissance und Barock*, ed. A. Buck et al. (Frankfurt a.M.: Athenaion, 1972), I, 32-36.

2. J.-U. Fechner, in *Deutsche Barockkultur und europäische Kultur*, ed. Martin Bircher (Hamburg: Hauswedell, 1977), pp. 205-7.

3. Cf. Gellinek, Gülich, Rener, and Schulz-Behrend (see bibliography). In regard to the influence of the Pléiade, specific parallels to du Bellay, Ronsard, and other sources are listed by George Schulz-Behrend (ed.) in Opitz, *Gesammelte Werke*, II, 1 (Stuttgart: Hiersemann, 1968, 1978), 331-416.

4. E. Trunz, "Die Entwicklung des deutschen Langverses," *Euphorion*, 39 (1938), 431.

5. L. Forster and J.-U. Fechner, "Das deutsche Sonett des Melissus," in *Rezeption und Produktion zwischen 1570 und 1730: Festschrift für Günther Weydt*, ed. W. Rasch et al. (Bern and München: Francke, 1972), p. 37.

6. It was included by Zincgref in the collection of poems by other German poets appended to Opitz's *Teutsche Poemata* (*Gesammelte Werke*, II, 1, 218-90). For a detailed analysis of the poem and its metrics, see Forster and Fechner, pp. 33-51.

7. R. Schlösser, "Ronsard und Schwabe von der Heide," *Euphorion*, 6 (1899), 271-76.

8. See G. R. Weckherlin, *G. R. Weckherlins Gedichte*, II, ed. H. Fischer (1895; rpt. Hildesheim: Olms, 1968), 473 ff., 508 ff.

9. L. Forster, "German Alexandrines on Dutch Broadsheets before Opitz," in *The German Baroque*, ed. G. Schulz-Behrend (Austin: University of Texas Press, 1972), pp. 11-64.

10. Almost all of Weckherlin's translations from these authors (excepting a few sonnets) appear in the *Oden und Gesänge* (1618), comprising twenty of sixty-eight poems.

11. W. Th. Elwert, "Die Lyrik der Renaissance und des Barocks in den romanischen Ländern," in *Renaissance und Barock* (see note 1), I, 106.

12. A recent article by Wolfram Mauser attempts to link the success of Opitz's poetic reform to its realization of an aristocratic cultural ideal shared also by the bourgeoisie insofar as it based its self-image on the values of the court: "Opitz und der Beginn der Barockliteratur," in *Filologia e critica: Studi in onore di Vittorio Santoli* (Rome: Bulzoni, 1976), II, 281-314.

13. Cf. his remark in the *Poeterey*: "Wiewol die Frantzosen und andere / in den eigentlichen namen sonderlich / die accente so genawe nicht in acht nemen" (*Neudrucke*, N.F. 8, 38). See also W. Mohr, "Romanische Versmaße," *Reallexicon der deutschen Literaturgeschichte*, III, 567.

14. The controversy among Romanists (and Germanists) over the assumption of underlying alternating meter in French syllabic verse has never been com-

pletely resolved. Mohr (note 13, above) appears to follow W. Suchier, *Französische Verslehre*, 2nd ed. (Tübingen: Niemeyer, 1963) in assuming basic alternation with hovering accent for this period, while Baehr (see bibliography) and W. Theodor Elwert, *Französische Metrik*, 2nd ed. (München: Hueber, 1970) speak of metrical freedom except at the rhyme and the caesura (*vers commun* and Alexandrine).

15. Opitz actually does concede the occasional use of words with dactylic rhythm — "denn er [the dactyl] gleichwol auch kan geduldet werden / wenn er mit unterscheide gesatzt wird" (*Neudrucke*, N.F. 8, 38) — but does not consider dactylic meter suited to the natural rhythm of the German language.

16. As Beissner notes, it requires a good deal of arrogance to suppose that whole generations of poets were so misguided as to adopt a verse truly unsuited to their language and poetic intent; see his "Deutsche Barocklyrik," in *Formkräfte der deutschen Dichtung vom Barock bis zur Gegenwart* (Göttingen: Vandenhoeck und Ruprecht, 1963), p. 40.

17. Like the first part of du Bellay's work, Opitz's *Aristarchus* too had dealt with the "defense" of the mother tongue and its poetic potential, but in Latin!

18. Neo-Latin poetry was far too firmly entrenched in Germany to be attacked in like fashion. See L. Forster's essay in this volume.

19. Both the Pléiade and Opitz ascribe to the concept of the *poeta doctus*, demanding learning as well as inborn qualities in the poet.

20. A. Gülich lists twenty; "Opitz' Übersetzungen aus dem Französischen" (diss. Kiel, 1972), p. 50 ff.

21. W. F. Patterson, *French Critical Theory*, I (Ann Arbor: University of Michigan Press, 1935), 296 ff.

22. J. L. Gellinek, *Die weltliche Lyrik des Martin Opitz* (Bern: Francke, 1973), pp. 11-19, esp. p. 15.

23. The most significant changes in comparison to the 1624 edition are the addition of the Ronsard translations and the division of the poems into eight "books" consisting of religious poetry, didactic poetry, mixed occasional poetry, epithalamia, amatoria (*Alexandrinerelegien*), songs, sonnets, and epigrams.

24. Gülich, (note 20, above), p. 52.

25. R. Baehr estimates that the Alexandrine accounts for three-quarters of all the verse written in France from the seventeenth through the nineteenth centuries; see his *Einführung in die französische Verslehre* (München: Beck, 1970), p. 64.

26. Mohr (note 13, above), III, 577.

27. *Hochdeutscher Helikon*, quoted by J.-U. Fechner, *Das deutsche Sonett* (München: Fink, 1969), pp. 293-95.

28. See Beissner (note 16, above), pp. 48 ff.

29. J. L. Gellinek, "Opitz' Liebessonette nach Ronsard," *Europäische Tradition und deutscher Literaturbarock*, ed. G. Hoffmeister (Bern and München: Francke, 1972), pp. 85-116.

30. Patterson (note 21, above), I, 583 ff.

31. K. Viëtor, *Geschichte der deutschen Ode* (München: Drei Masken, 1923), pp. 48-57.

32. Ibid., pp. 58-60. Also Gellinek (note 22, above), pp. 82-98, 123-140.

33. Viëtor, pp. 78-82.

34. Paul Dierks, "Die sapphische Ode in der deutschen Dichtung des 17. Jahrhunderts" (diss. Münster 1969), pp. 23-28.

35. See Dierks's (pp. 43-47) analysis of the role of Crüger's music for Joh. Heermann's "Herzliebster Jesu" in the spread and further modification of the form.

36. Pibrac's *Les Plaisirs de la Vie Rustique* appears to have been one of the models for Opitz's *Zlatna*. See G. Schulz-Behrend, "Opitz' 'Zlatna,' " *Modern Language Notes*, 77 (1962), 408.

37. Gülich (note 20, above), pp. 83-119.

38. Trunz (note 4, above), pp. 431-33. Cf. also E. Trunz, "Die deutschen Übersetzungen des Hugenottenpsalters," *Euphorion*, 29 (1928), pp. 578-617.

39. Elwert (note 11, above), p. 108.

40. The poem is "Auff den mund"; see A. Beckmann, *Motive und Formen der deutschen Lyrik . . .* (Tübingen: Niemeyer, 1960), pp. 109 ff.

41. E. Rotermund, *Chr. Hofmann von Hofmannswaldau* (Stuttgart: Metzler, 1963), p. 8.

42. Elwert (note 11, above), p. 107; Patterson (note 21, above), p. 551.

43. R. Newald, *Die deutsche Literatur vom Späthumanismus zur Empfindsamkeit*, 3rd ed. (München: Beck, 1960), p. 339.

44. E. Mannack, *Andreas Gryphius* (Stuttgart: Metzler, 1968), p. 14. Lehmeyer (see bibliography) has ascertained that Duke Anton Ulrich of Braunschweig used Corneille's *Andromède* as the basis for his Singspiel *Andromeda*, translating some passages literally.

45. Mannack, ibid., p. 64.

46. See E. Lunding, "Assimilierung und Eigenschöpfung in den Lustspielen des Andreas Gryphius," in *Stoffe, Formen, Strukturen: Studien zur deutschen Literatur*, Borcherdt Festschrift, ed. A. Fuchs (München: Hueber, 1962), pp. 80-96, esp. 86 ff. Also E. Mannack, "Andreas Gryphius' Lustspiele—ihre Herkunft, ihre Motive und ihre Entwicklung," *Euphorion*, 58 (1964), 1-40, esp. 28-32.

47. The German translation of Nic. de Montreux's *Les bergeries de Juliette* (1585-98) appeared beginning 159°; Newald (note 43, above), p. 166.

48. Lohenstein's monumental figures, preoccupation with the passions, and choice of material show an awareness of the classicistic French drama of his time. Cf. Newald (note 43, above), pp. 326 ff.

49. Harsdörffer's compendiums appear to have been the prime purveyor of narrative material from France. Cf. G. Weydt, *Nachahmung und Schöpfung im Barock* (Bern and München: Francke, 1968), pp. 61 ff.

50. Passages containing specifically Catholic dogma or referring to the veneration of saints were either omitted or changed by Opitz. For a characterization of translation and original, see Gülich (note 20, above), pp. 120-74.

51. Elwert (note 11, above), p. 108.

52. Elwert, p. 120.

53. "Ihr Himmel trieffet doch . . . ," first in the edition of 1629. See J. L. Solomon, "Martin Opitz: 'Ihr Himmel trieffet doch'," in the special Opitz issue of *Daphnis*, to appear in 1982.

54. G. Weydt, *H. J. Chr. von Grimmelshausen* (Stuttgart: Metzler, 1971), pp. 51 ff.

55. Mannack (note 46, above), p. 15.

56. G. Hoffmeister, *Petrarkistische Lyrik* (Stuttgart: Metzler, 1973), pp. 64, 68, 72, provides information on parodistic tendencies in the tradition of antipetrarchism in Germany.

57. Elwert (note 11, above), p. 103.

58. Hoffmeister, p. 41.

SELECTED BIBLIOGRAPHY

Primary Sources

Bellay, Joachim du. *La Deffence et Illustration de la Langue francoyse*, Émile Person, ed. Paris: Librairie Léopold Cerf, 1892.

Opitz, Martin. *Buch von der deutschen Poeterey* (1624). Richard Alewyn, ed. Neudrucke deutscher Literatur, N.F. 8. Tübingen: Niemeyer, 1963.

———. *Gesammelte Werke*, Bd.I; II, 1, 2, George Schulz-Behrend, ed. Bibliothek des literarischen Vereins in Stuttgart, 295, 300, 301. Stuttgart: Hiersemann, 1968, 1978, 1979. (These volumes contain *Aristarchus*, separata, poems appearing only in the 1624 edition, *Poeterey*, the 1625 edition and other works through 1626.)

———. *Martini Opitii Acht Bücher Deutscher Poematum* . . . Breslau, 1625.

———. *Teutsche Poemata* (1624). Georg Witkowski, ed. Neudrucke deutscher Literatur, 189-92. Halle: Niemeyer, 1902.

Ronsard, Pierre de. *Oeuvres complètes*. Paul Laumonier, ed. 18 vols. Paris, 1914-21.

Weckherlin, Georg Rudolf. *G. R. Weckherlins Gedichte*. 3 vols. Hermann Fischer, ed. Bibliothek des literarischen Vereins in Stuttgart, 199, 200, 245. 2nd ed., 1894-1907; rpt. Hildesheim: Olms, 1968.

(For more extensive bibliography of primary sources, see Beckmann's bibliography.)

Secondary Literature

Baehr, Rudolf. *Einführung in die französische Verslehre*. München: Beck, 1970.

Beckmann, Adelheid. *Motive und Formen der deutschen Lyrik des 17. Jahrhunderts und ihre Entsprechungen in der französischen Lyrik seit Ronsard: Ein Beitrag zur vergleichenden Literaturgeschichte*. Hermaea, N.F. 5. Tübingen: Niemeyer, 1960.

Beissner, Friedrich. "Deutsche Barocklyrik." In *Formkräfte der deutschen Dichtung vom Barock bis zur Gegenwart*. Göttingen: Vandenhoeck und Ruprecht, 1963, pp. 35-55.

Buck, August. "Dichtungslehren der Renaissance und des Barocks." In *Renaissance und Barock*. A. Buck et al., eds. Neues Handbuch der Literaturwissenschaft, 9-10. Frankfurt a.M.: Athenaion, 1972. I, 28-60.

Daly, Peter M. "Catharina Regina von Greiffenberg und Honoré d'Urfé. Einige Bemerkungen zur Frage von Catharinas Rezeption der Schäferdichtung." *Dokumente des Internationalen Arbeitskreises für deutsche Barockliteratur*, 4 (1977), pp. 67-84.

Dierks, Paul. "Die sapphische Ode in der deutschen Dichtung des 17. Jahrhunderts," pp. 23-28. Diss., Münster 1969.

Elwert, W. Theodor. *Französische Metrik*, 2nd ed. München: Hueber, 1970.

———. "Die Lyrik der Renaissance und des Barocks in den romanischen Ländern." In *Renaissance und Barock*. A. Buck et al., eds. I, 82-127. Frankfurt A. M.: Athenaion, 1972.

Fechner, J.-U. In *Deutsche Barockkultur und europäische Kultur*, Martin Bircher, ed. pp. 205-7. Hamburg: Hauswedell, 1977.

———. *Das deutsche Sonett*, pp. 293-95. München: Fink, 1969.

Forster; Leonard. "German Alexandrines on Dutch Broadsheets before Opitz." In *The German Baroque*, G. Schulz-Behrend, ed. pp. 11-64. Austin: University of Texas Press, 1972.

——— and Jörg-Ulrich Fechner. "Das deutsche Sonett des Melissus." In *Rezeption und Produktion zwischen 1570 und 1730: Festschrift für Günther Weydt*. Wolfdietrich Rasch et al., eds. Bern and München: Francke, 1972, pp. 33-51.

Garber, Klaus, ed. *Europäische Bukolik und Georgik*. Darmstadt: Wissenschaftliche Buchgesellschaft, 1976.

Gellinek, Janis Little. "Further Dutch Sources Used by Martin Opitz." *Neophilologus*, 53 (1969), 157-75.

———. "Opitz' Liebessonette nach Ronsard." In *Europäische Tradition und deutscher Literaturbarock: Internationale Beiträge zum Problem von Überlieferung und Umgestaltung*. Gerhart Hoffmeister, ed. Bern and München: Francke, 1973, pp. 85-116.

———. *Die Weltliche Lyrik des Martin Opitz*. Bern and München: Francke, 1973.

Gülich, Anne. "Opitz' Übersetzungen aus dem Französischen." Diss. Kiel 1972.

Hoffmeister, G. *Petrarkistische Lyrik*, pp. 64, 68, 72. Stuttgart: Metzler, 1973.

Lehmeyer, F. Robert. "Anton Ulrichs *Andromeda* und ihre Quellen." In *Europäische Tradition und deutscher Literaturbarock*. G. Hoffmeister, ed. Bern and München: Francke, 1973, pp. 259-74.

Lunding, E. "Assimilierung und Eigenschöpfung in den Lustspielen des Andreas Gryphius." In *Stoffe, Formen, Strukturen: Studien zur deutschen Literatur*, Borcherdt Festschrift, A. Fuchs, ed., pp. 80-96. München: Hueber, 1962.

Mannack, E. *Andreas Gryphius*, p. 14. Stuttgart: Metzler, 1968.

——. "Andreas Gryphius' Lustspiele—ihre Herkunft, ihre Motive und ihre Entwicklung." *Euphorion*, 58 (1964), 1-40.

Mauser, Wolfram. "Opitz und der Beginn der Barockliteratur," in *Filologia e critica: Studi in onore di Vittorio Santoli*, II, 281-314. Rome: Bulzoni, 1976.

Mohr, W. "Romanische Versmaße," *Reallexicon der deutschen Literaturgeschichte*, III, 567.

Newald, R. *Die deutsche Literatur vom Späthumanismus zur Empfindsamkeit*, 3rd ed., p. 339. München: Beck, 1960.

Patterson, Warren Forrest. *French Critical Theory*, I, pp. 296 ff. Ann Arbor: University of Michigan Press, 1935.

——. *Three Centuries of French Poetic Theory: A Critical History of the Chief Arts of Poetry in France (1328-1630)*, 2 vols. Ann Arbor: University of Michigan Press, 1935.

Rener, Frederick M. "Opitz' Sonett an die Bienen." In *Europäische Tradition und deutscher Literaturbarock*. Gerhart Hoffmeister, ed. Bern and München: Francke, 1973. pp. 67-84.

Rotermund, E. *Chr. Hofmann von Hofmannswaldau*, p. 8. Stuttgart: Metzler, 1963.

Schlösser, R. "Ronsard und Schwabe von der Heide," *Euphorion*, 6 (1899) 271-76.

Schulz-Behrend, George. "Opitz' Gedichte 'Auf die Melodey . . .' " *Akten des VI. Internationalen Germanisten-Kongresses Basel 1980*, 3, pp. 24-32.

Springer-Strand, Ingeborg. "*Von der schönen Ariana: Eine sehr anmüthige Historj* (1643)—zur ersten deutschen Übersetzung von Desmarets' 'Ariane'." *Daphnis*, 8, (1979), pp. 339-49.

Suchier, W. *Französische Verslehre*, 2nd ed. Tübingen: Niemeyer, 1963.

Tonnelat, Ernest. "Deux Imitateurs Allemands de Ronsard." *Revue de Littérature Comparée*, 4 (1924), 557-89.

Trunz, E. "Die Entwicklung des deutschen Langverses," *Euphorion*, 39 (1938), 431.

Viëtor, K. *Geschichte der deutschen Ode*, pp. 48-57. München: Drei Masken, 1923.

Weydt, G. *H. J. Chr. von Grimmelshausen*, pp. 51 ff. Stuttgart: Metzler, 1971.

——. *Nachahmung und Schöpfung im Barock*, pp. 61 ff. Bern and München: Francke, 1968.

9

The English Comedians in Germany

Gerhart Hoffmeister

England's contribution to the foundation and development of German literature in the 1600s falls far behind the impact of the French, Spanish, and Italian contributions — with the exception of the theatrical activities and influence of the English actors who played on the continent. Although Opitz included Sidney's pastoral novel *Arcadia* and John Barclay's courtly *Argenis* in his translation program, thus allowing them to exert some influence on the rise of the German novel,[1] German men of letters in general were oriented toward Romance models. Around 1570, German vernacular literature was stagnating. Fresh impulses and ideas were needed to revive it after long decades of propagandizing for or against the Reformation in satirical broadsheets or plays. German drama especially was in a state of general decline: the old types of the Reformation period — the religious play, the Shrovetide farce, and the humanist school drama — were still recited by students or artisans in a didactic spirit without any effort at dramatization; audiences declined, permanent theaters had not yet been established.

A two-pronged invasion by foreign acting companies occurred in Germany in the late 1500s; the Italian commedia dell'arte improvisers performed chiefly in the southern region (e.g., the *comici gelosi* since 1568 in Austria), the English Comedians preferring to stay on the northern plains and only sometimes competing with the Italians for the profitable markets in the south. Whether these English troupes were a disaster or a benefit to German literature at the time will be discussed in this essay.

At the entertainement of the Cardinall Alphonsus and the infant of Spaine in the Low-countryes, they were presented at Antwerpe with sundry pageants and plays: the King of Denmarke, father to him that now reigneth, entertained into his service a company of English comedians, commended unto him by the honourable the Earle of Leicester: The Duke of Brunswicke and the Landgrave of Hessen retaine in their courts certaine of ours of the same quality.

In this manner, according to Thomas Heywood,[2] the first troupe of actors reached the mainland: in the retinue of the Earl of Leicester, who in 1585 crossed the Channel to fight the Spanish in the Netherlands[3] and recommended his players to Frederick II of Denmark, from where they continued on to Brunswick, Hesse, and Saxony.[4] In their contract with Christian I, Duke of Saxony, in 1586 (Dresden), they are called *Geyger vnd Instrumentisten* (Cohn, p.xxv), a designation that indicates the character of their performances as being mainly musical and acrobatic at least in their early days, since they are also referred to as *Springer*, or dancers. "From 1556 to 1584 the names of English musicians are constantly met with in the accounts of the Margravine Court in Prussia" (Cohn, p. xxi).

Dividing the activities of the English actors into several phases, as Anna Baesecke did in 1935,[5] we can easily describe the characteristic traits of their beginnings (1585-1600) as a period when, to win an audience, the language barrier had to be overcome by gestures, mimicry, and music. Simultaneously, it was a phase of transition from individual performers to team work for the purpose of producing a play. At first, because of the language problem, only "pieces and patches" of Elizabethan plays could be transmitted — as an Englishman traveling in Germany observed.[6] An actual report about one of the early performances read as follows:

Den. 26. Novembris sindt alhir angekommen elven Engellender, so alle jungi und rasche Gesellen waren, ausgenommen einer, so tzemlichen althers war, der alle dinge regerede. Dieselben agerden vif taghe uf den rädthuse achter-einandern vif verscheiden comœdien in ihrer engelscher sprache. Sie hetten bie sich vielle verschieden instrumente, dar sie uf spieleten, als luten, zitteren, fiolen, pipen und dergelichen; sie dantzeden vielle neuwe und frömmede dentze (so hier zu lande nicht gepruechlich) in anfang und Ende der comedien. Sie hetten bei sich einen schalkes naren, so in duescher sprache vielle bötze und geckerie machede under den ageren, wenn sie einen neuen actum wollten anfangen und sich umbkledden, darmidt ehr das volck lachent machede. Sie waren von den rade vergeliedet nich lenger als ses taghe. Do die umb waren, mosten sie wedder wichen. Sie kregen in den vif taghen von den, so es hören und sehen wolten, vielle geldes.

(On the 26th of November [1599] there arrived here eleven Englishmen, all young and lively fellows, with the exception of one, a rather elderly man, who had everything under his management. They acted on five successive days five different comedies in their own English tongue. They carried with them various musical instruments, such as lutes, cithern, fiddles, fifes, and such like; they danced many new and foreign dances (not usual in this country) at the beginning and at the end of their comedies. They were accompanied by a clown, who, when a new act had to commence and when they had to change their costume, made many antics and pranks in German during the performance, by which he amused the audience. They were licensed by the Town-Council for six days only, after which time they had to depart. During those five days they took a great deal of money from those who wished to hear and see them.)[7]

Who were these Englishmen, why did they come over, and what compelled them to keep moving on? They were musicians and actors who left England because of unemployment, poverty, and increasing competition among themselves. In 1592, the following passport was made out by Lord Howard:

Messieurs, comme les présents porteurs, Robert Browne, Jehan Bradstriet, Thomas Saxfield, Richard Jones, ont deliberé de faire un voyage en Allemagne, avec intention de passer par le païs de Zelande, Hollande et Frise, et allantz en leur dict voyage d'exercer leurs qualitez en faict de musique, agilitez et joeuz de commedies, tragedies et histoires, pour s'entretenir et fournir à leurs despenses en leur dict voyage . . . (Cohn, p. xxxviii).

(Gentlemen, as the passport-owners present, R. B., J. B. Th. S., R. J. have thought of making a trip through Germany, planning to pass through the Netherlands and going to practice, on the said voyage, their ability as musicians, actors and players of comedies, tragedies and histories, in order to sustain themselves and meet their expenses on their said trip . . .)

Browne and Sackville performed Marlowe in Frankfurt, traveled to several other cities, then split into two troupes, Browne entering the service of Landgraf Moritz of Hesse-Kassel (himself an artist and patron of the arts), his clown Sackville joining Duke Heinrich Julius of Brunswick at Wolfenbüttel and later on settling down as a successful textile merchant. Browne was intermittently in England (1594-96, 1608-18), leaving his ensemble to Green (1608) and later to Reinold (1630 ff.), keeping in touch with splinter groups through the exchange of members.

An essential feature of this troupe life was its constant itinerancy between towns and courts. The latter were needed for patronage, advertisement, winter quarters, and good pay. The court provided glamorous titles such as *Chur-Sächsische Hofkomödianten* and sometimes a permanent stage (Kassel, Brunswick, Wolfenbüttel). If the repertory was exhausted, even the courts would dismiss the strolling actors for a time, while municipal councils permitted only a couple of weeks of performance for fear of disorders and threat to morals and church life. This satirical verse of 1615 characterizes the situation:

Die englische Comoedianten
Haben mehr Leuth denn Predikanten
Da lieber vier stund stehen hören zu
Dann in der Kirch, da sie mit Ruh
Flux einschlaffen auf ein hart bank
Dieweil ein stund ja felt zu lang.[8]

The actors were of the lowest social standing and continuously had to move on to comply with city orders, sometimes to avoid the onslaught of war, but also to satisfy their ever-present eagerness and need to earn their livelihood. "On the move" remained their fate and their curse (Flemming, p. 12). In a way, they became victims of their own lack of cultural roots—Flemming calls this *geistige Kulturlosigkeit*—although they developed their own style, repertory, and histrionic tradition.

The second period (1600–1620) brought about the important switch from English to German, along with a sweeping array of Elizabethan plays[9] which underwent a considerable mutation through emphasis on those aspects that the actors could produce best: action, mimicry, clownishness in an as yet crude German picked up in the streets or in the court stables. The changeover to German had, in fact, started almost upon the arrival of the first troupe in Germany and continued until the second half of the century, when a complete *Durchdeutschung der Truppen*[10] was achieved. The first attempt at a German-language production was by Sackville in Wolfenbüttel around 1592, about the same time as Browne's players received their contract from Landgraf Moritz expressly requiring them "Jederzeit, wan wir ihme ein Argument oder Inhaldt einer neuen comoedien oder Historien sagenn werdenn, schuldig sein, dieselbig in seiner Sprach zu transponiren, undt zu einer Comoedien oder Spill zuzurichten."[11] The fool—with his Low German impromptus—took an early lead in advancing the cause of German, but gradually German actors were included in the ensemble to fill vacancies (Green praised his *hüppenden und spillenden Germans* in an advertise-

ment of 1626; Kindermann, p. 360). German principals finally
established themselves alongside their English rivals, examples being
Eichlin in Nördlingen in 1604 and Schneider with his German students
in the 1640s. For "market" purposes, however, the Germans continued
to use the catchy label "English Comedians" as late as the eighteenth
century.

The third stage (1626-48) constitutes a time of consolidation in
spite of the war. It is the period in which John Green's troupe flourished.
Green had taken over from Browne in 1608; between 1620 and 1626 he
had been back in England, but now he established his headquarters in
Dresden, leading the *Chursächsische Truppe*, apparently the only one
able to secure the patronage of a court during the Thirty Years War.
Green — and since the 1630s his successor Reinold — was more successful
than his rivals because he was more experienced and also able to use acting copies of Elizabethan plays while other principals before him had
had to rely on their memory. Thus, he could do more than his colleagues
to preserve the English theater tradition.

When the war was over, the fourth phase of decline and dissolution
began (1648-1700).[12] Joris Joliphus was the last English principal to
come to Germany employing High German actors (and actresses!) and
offering a new program in keeping with the taste of the baroque age:
Pastorellen und Singspiele nach italienischer Manier (Baesecke, p. 115),
which he may have been exposed to in southern Germany and Austria
(1653-54), and German *Kunstdrama* (Gryphius). These were the last
traces of a direct English influence; now German-led troupes took over,
and German as well as Romance plays filled the gap. Compared with the
meager beginnings without any knowledge of German, a decided emphasis was placed on the word of the text, which allowed for the presentation of lofty dialogues about matters of courtly love and government in
a style partly modeled on Romance originals, partly on German
chancery language. Among German principals of note were Michael D.
Treu, who in 1666 went from Denmark to Munich with a repertory of
English and Spanish plays; Carl A. Paulsen from Hamburg (since 1650),
whose son-in-law Magister Velten (1640-92) took over the *Chur-
Sächsische Komödianten-Gesellschaft* in Dresden; and Andreas Elensen
from Vienna and his successor Hoffmann, who employed the famous
Neuber couple. Hoffmann — under the guidance of Gottsched — was
responsible for reforming the theater of the itinerant players by banning
the fool (1737).

In many respects the fool must be considered the incarnation of the
stage productions by the English Comedians.[13] Very often the principal

of the ensemble, the fool was also the first player to introduce German into the performance, though he needed little to get his clownish acts across. The audience could easily identify with him, since it was accustomed to this crude peasant figure from the Shrovetide plays and because he addressed the spectators directly and served as a link of unity in the patchwork design of the scenes. Within the clown's "play-within-the-play," he had the function of trivializing the courtly culture and ethics by "alles was gutt ist, in argst verkehren, auch aus GOttes Wort ein lauter gespött machen, es vbel ausdeuten, vnd anderst als es gemeint worden, verstehen wöllen."[14] Why he did not strive to imitate the Shakespearean melancholy "wise fool" is obvious: the language barrier, the style of the performance, and the nature of audiences all contributed to prevent this. Instead, the clown was usually named after a common local dish indicating the animal aspect of his existence. Sackville created Jan Posset (Bouset, Boushet, etc.) according to the English spiced alcoholic drink; Reinold founded the *bickelherings compagnie* (1618); Spencer played the Stockfisch part (1617–18). Other popular names were Hans Knappkäse, Jack Pudding, Johan Banser, and Hans Wurst, who actually appeared alongside Jan Bossen in Sackville's performances in Frankfurt in 1596–97.[15]

To cope with the completely different circumstances facing them on the continent, the English actors were compelled to recast their Elizabethan plays considerably. They did retain some of their essential features, however, e.g., their eventful plots and emotional extremism, but, as Gundolf has pointed out:

Sie gingen den umgekehrten Weg wie das englische Drama. Ihre Hauptwirkungen sind: 1. Loslösung des Theaters von der Literatur und dem Pathos der Zeit, Ausbildung eines selbstherrlichen Apparats, 2. Vermehrung des Bühnenrohstoffs und der sinnlichen Unterhaltungsmittel, 3. Zersetzung der Sprache, Ersatz des Verses durch die Prosa in der Theaterproduktion.[16]

In particular, the abandonment of blank verse gave rise to a wide range of improvisations, which turned actual plays stressing word, meaning, content, and organic unity into theater pieces emphasizing the sensational aspect of a given plot, its crude appeal to the senses through mimicry, clownishness, music, and mere noise of battle and screams of bloody murder. For critics like Gundolf, who judge from a Goethean perspective, the "soul" vanishes from a piece mechanically put together like a patchwork design of eventful actions. This is the negative side, supplying easy ammunition to critics who, in recent times, underestimated the overall importance of the English Comedians to the development of the German theater.

In point of fact, adaptations from Shakespeare seemed to prove that "ein verstofflichtes Geschlecht konnte den echten Shakespeare nicht ertragen" (Gundolf, p. 21), because, as *Der bestrafte Brudermord oder Prinz Hamlet aus Dänemark* demonstrates, only the external plot of revenge, the ghost scenes, the shudder, the exaggerated clownish parts remain.[17] All in all, about ten different plays of Shakespeare were adapted, among them *Romeo and Juliet* (production Nördlingen, 1604) and above all *Titus Andronicus* (printed in 1620), a tragedy of 1594 attributed to Shakespeare, bristling with love, murder, and revenge. Alongside these Elizabethan plays humorous Pickelhering pieces and biblical plays were performed.

A portion of this early repertory was published in *Engelische Comedien vnd / Tragedien* in 1620.[18] During the second half of the century the program was broadened considerably to include more German plays (Lohenstein, Gryphius, Rist) and a large number of French (Molière), Spanish (Lope and Calderón), as well as Italian and Dutch works. The title of a later collection—*Schaubühne Englischer vnd Französischer Comödianten* (1670)—makes this evident. Apart from *Der Liebeskampff oder ander Theil der Engelischen Comoedien und Tragoedien* (1630),[19] which presents eight dramas based on Italian novella material and modeled by a German author after the English Comedians, no other printed versions seem to have come down to us, since printing their repertory ran counter to the interests of the principal and his actors. We should also keep in mind that the *Schaubühne* collections of 1620 and 1670 were not necessarily identical with the acting copies of the comedians, since the text often served merely as a starting point for improvisation.

The English Comedians generally took advantage of fairs and Church holidays, such as Easter or Lent, to win big audiences in the towns, announcing their performances through drums, acrobatic hors d'oeuvres, or posters such as this one from Nürnberg (ca. 1628):

Zuwissen sey jederman daß allhier ankommen eine gantz newe Compagni Comoedianten / so niemals zuvor hier zu Land gesehen / mit einem sehr lustigen Pickelhering / welche taeglich agirn werden / schoene Comoedien / Tragoedien / Pastorellen / (Schaeffereyen) vnd Historien / vermengt mit lieblichen vnd lustigen interludien / vnd zwar heut Mittwochs den 21. Aprilis werden sie praesentirn eine sehr lustige Comoedi / genant. Die Liebes Suessigkeit veraendert sich in Todes Bitterkeit. Nach der Comoedi soll praesentirt werden ein schoen Ballet / vnd laecherliches Possenspiel. Die Liebhaber solcher Schauspiele wollen sich nach Mittags Glock 2. einstellen vffm Fechthauß / allda vmb die bestimbte Zeit praezise soll angefangen wereden. (Creizenach, p. xxiv a-b)

A troupe usually consisted of at least six men, but generally not more than two dozen, about half of them being actors, the other half musicians. They staged the show in inns or, if available, in the town hall, school, sports ring, etc. An exception was the construction of the *Ottonium*, the first permanent theater in Kassel (1605) by Moritz after he had returned from a visit to London.

Essentially, the English Comedians used a variation of the Shakespearean stage and further developed the German stage of the sixteenth century: the humanist school theater consisted of a bare (sceneless) front stage and a back stage decorated with hangings that represented houses or interior rooms (Terence stage). In Elizabethan times, companies played mainly in inn yards, then in regular theaters on stages projecting into the audience; they also had an upper stage or balcony, beneath it an inner stage often covered with a curtain. Although the Dutch *Rederijkers* had employed curtains since the 1550s, the English Comedians seem to have introduced them independently to Germany, thereby providing the necessary means for a quick change of scenes or alternation between the front and back stage. Very little decoration was used apart from the hangings (*tepichbreter*) and the movable properties in the rear area such as a throne, an altar, a chair, and a table. The English upper stage, if available, was the seat for the band, and a trapdoor served for special effects (ghosts, etc.). Only during the last phase of development after the end of the war were movable scenes (*Kulissen*) and a front curtain used under the influence of the Italian opera. Simply diagrammed (Flemming, p. 47):

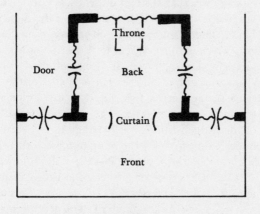

Audience

It was on this kind of stage that the English Comedians played their "main actions" (*Hauptaktionen*), interspersed with musical intermezzi such as dances or *Singspiele*, or rounded off by a comic epilogue.

The literary significance of these eventful pieces, often set in courtly circles and exploiting the discrepancy between their ideal world and the boorish low life, tended, since Gottsched, to be totally discredited. In recent times, however, a more detached view of the whole phenomenon has resulted in a surprising reevaluation—a recognition of the unique dramatic type (*Formtypus*) that came into being through the English Comedians, its contribution to the culture of the baroque age, and its literary impact on writers such as Duke Heinrich Julius of Brunswick, Jakob Ayrer, Gryphius, and Weise. A transitional figure in this process of reevaluation was undoubtedly Willi Flemming. In 1931, he claimed on the one hand: "Dem wandernden Mimen fehlt . . . jeder Zusammenhang mit einer Kulturtradition. Er kann daher auch nicht Träger des Zeitgeistes werden. Ferne steht er aller Literatur" (p. 11). On the other hand, he was clearly able to appreciate the *eigene Formtypus* (p. 22), which the English Comedians had developed, and concluded his introduction with the perceptive remark: "Es geht nicht an, sie beiseitezuschieben, als vegetiere auf ihren Brettern 'abgesunkenes Kulturgut' " (p. 69). Apparently this was stated in response to Gundolf's tenet that these plays were the result of a *Zersetzungsprozeß* (1911, p. 39). Reading some of the plays in the *Schaubühne* one cannot but conclude that the English Comedians' achievement lies in shaping a collective style of putting together pieces for the stage and in presenting them in a new way—a way that stressed theatrical effects, the entertainment of the audience above and beyond any specific didactic purpose. Obviously, they could do a much better job on stage than the German lay actors who merely recited the text; they were the first professional players in Central Europe and as such were able to teach the Germans many a lesson. They brought with them the rich repertory of the Elizabethan stage, which gave their collective style the added dimension of a new content: "Es gibt in der gesamten Theatergeschichte Europas nur wenige Beispiele einer derartigen Kollektiv-Übertragung von einer Nation zur anderen" (Kindermann, p. 366). Common to most of their productions was the appearance of the fool, or Pickelhering, who appropriately enough gave the subtitle to the first printed collection of plays (1620) and the nickname to Reinold's *bickelherings compagnie*. This figure was so successful that it quickly became a standard element of German comedies.

In 1592 Sackville's troupe played at Brunswick and inspired Duke

Heinrich Julius to write ten prose plays in which he exploited the English style of acting and its exaggerated effects. One of them was his *Von einem ungeratenen Sohn* (1594), perhaps written under the influence of *Titus Andronicus*, as is suggested by a comparison of stage directions such as these:

Titus Andronicus (Act VII):
[The emperor's two sons who wanted to murder Titus have been caught. Titus takes revenge.] Jetzt kömpt einer, bringt ihm ein scharfes Scheermesser vnd Schlacht Tuch, er macht das Tuch vmb, gleich als wenn er schlachten will [. . . a bowl is brought]. Der elteste Bruder wird erstlich herüber gehalten, er will reden, aber sie halten jhm das Maul zu. Titus schneidet jhm die Gurgel halb abe. Das Blut rennet in das Gefäß, legen jhn, da das Blut außgerennet, todt an die Erden. [. . . the younger brother comes in.] Helt jhn eben so die Gurgel herüber, etc. (Creizenach, p. 48).

Von einem ungeratenen Sohn (IV, 6)
[Nero slaughters his own son], setzet jhme das Knye auff den Hals, das er nicht mehr ruffen kan, der Knabe aber grunselt gleichwol. . . . Streifet die Ermeln auff, nimbt ein Messer, und schneidet seinen Leib auff, und schepffet mit einem Schälichen jhme das Bluth aus seinem Leibe, und setzt es bey sich. Darnach nimpt er das Hertze jhme aus dem Leibe, und wirfft den Cörper in ein Loch. Nimbt darnach das Gläsichen, und vermischet das Bluth mit Wein und trinckts aus. Das Hertze legt er auf die Kohlen, bratet das, und frißts auff. (Holland, p. 368).

In Duke Heinrich's *Von einem Weibe* (1593) Johan Bousett appears as a merchant's servant who seeing through everything comments in a Low German dialect on the main plot. It seems that this part was specially written for Sackville, and therefore Johan Bousett has a role in the succeeding plays, too, sometimes as the representative of good sense, sometimes as a buffoon, but generally "linguistically differentiated from the rest."[20] In one instance, Johan calls himself, in keeping with the English actors' procedure, *Director des gantzen Werckes*. This occurs in *Vincentius Ladislaus* (1594; VI, 5), where Duke Heinrich creates a *style mêlé* between the English comedy tradition and the Italian one: Johan is well integrated into the plot, also linguistically, by becoming subservient to the principal character, the "capitano" Vincentius. At the same time, his function is raised from that of a mere clown to a Shakespearean court fool.[21]

Shortly after Jakob Ayrer had seen Sackville perform in Nürnberg (1596–97), he also introduced a clown similar in costume, name, and action into his Shrovetide plays written in the Hans Sachs Knittelvers. The result is a peculiar blend between the German and the English tradition, e.g., in *Fassnachtsspil von dem engelländischen Jann Posset, wie er sich in seinem Dienst verhalten*.[22] *Der Engellendisch Narr* (No. 38) usually appears as a servant who tries to get the better of his master and his own wife but fails dismally. He turns out as *der grobe Bauernknecht*, as a clown in the original sense of the word who has something in common with the German medieval *gouch* (No. 24), with Till Eulenspiegel as well as with Sackville's Jahn Posset when he misunderstands words on purpose to achieve a comic effect (No. 51). In Ayrer's plays he is often the leading figure who speaks the prologue and unites the various scenes as a messenger (No. 24).

Both Duke Heinrich and Ayrer created mainly in the traditional spirit and manner, but they learned many tricks of the trade from the English Comedians: they took over the fool, they imitated their stage directions, they learned how a scene was to be put together effectively. In this way, the English Comedians contributed to laying the foundations of the fledgling German drama in the age of the baroque. This is especially true of *Vincentius Ladislaus*, a play about one of the predominant themes of the century, that of reality and illusion, essence and appearance, as contrasted in the simple Johan and Vincentius the pompous braggart.

The longevity of the English Pickelhering is demonstrated at least twice more in the course of the seventeenth century; first a Pickelhering steps on stage called up by Peter Squentz in Gryphius's *Absurda Comica* (1657-58), a play reminiscent of the Bottom-Quince scenes in Shakespeare's *A Midsummer Night's Dream*. In his preface, Gryphius mentioned Daniel Schwenter as his source, but he may also have seen a performance of Grambergen's play in Amsterdam in 1650, and he may have been acquainted with productions of the Pyramus and Thisbe story enacted by the English Comedians.[23]

Twenty years later Christian Weise also took up the Pickelhering in his early comedy *Die triumphierende Keuschheit* (1678), a "Joseph's play," in which the fool is split into father and son in order to lead the secondary action among the servants. Pickelhering appears in slapstick scenes as the boorish clown commenting on his superiors in a satirical vein, pretending to be wiser than they are, but in the end outwitted by them, cowardly when he is supposed to be brave, talkative when he should hold his tongue.[24]

After Weise's time the Pickelhering remained alive, in spite of Gottsched's attack, well beyond the first decades of the eighteenth century.

The extemporized clown comedy (*Hanswurstspiel*) delighted many audiences after the first *Hauptaktion* ended on stage. Interestingly enough, Hanswurst was a clownish character welded together from several sources: the German-Austrian medieval tradition of the Shrovetide farce—the name itself first occurs in a Low German version of Brant's *Ship of Fools* in 1519—the English actors' Pickelhering, and the Italian *arlecchino*. On this basis, the Viennese Hanswurst was re-created by Stranitzky around 1710 and, after being defended by Möser (*Harlekin oder die Verteidigung des Grotesk Komischen*, 1761) and Goethe (*Hanswursts Hochzeit oder der Lauf der Welt*, 1773-75) against Gottsched's ban, was further developed by Raimund and Nestroy in the nineteenth century. Hanswurst, indeed, still lingers on in some of today's puppet shows.

Josef A. Stranitzky was registered as a medical practitioner, and this leads us to a similar case which Christian Thomasius commented on in his *Juristische Händel* (part III, 1724) under the marginal gloss: "Der andere Casus von einem Gauckler / Seiltäntzer und Pickelhering / der Doctor Medicinae werden wollen / Frage an die Facultät" (p. 177). He decides the question by recommending that the man should not be considered "infamous" because of his lowly social standing, but also that because of his lack of Latin, he should not be promoted to M.D. (cf. p. 184). Apart from this special case Thomasius took the following view:

So ferne ich aber als ein Juriste davon schreiben soll, kan ich die Comödianten überhaupt nicht für unehrlich halten, nachdem in Teutschland auch unter denen Evangelischen Fürsten durch eine allgemeine Gewohnheit das Gegentheil eingeführet ist, und die Comödianten zuweilen mit dem Ehren-Titul Fürstlicher Kammerdiener, Hoff-Comödianten u.s.w. begnadigt werden. (p. 170)[25]

Looking back on the activities of the English Comedians as they evolved from 1585 to 1737, and particularly observing their use of the clown as a principal and key character, their contribution to the flourishing of a specifically baroque spirit becomes apparent. It consists above all in the art of producing effective *spielnahe* (Baesecke) performances emancipated from the former dominance of the text—several scholars speak of the rift between theater and literature[26]—in favor of productions with lavish costumes, pompous music, and the raging of exaggerated passions, as for instance in George Peele's *The Turkish Mahomet and Hyrin the Fair Greek*, a gala performance given by Spencer's troupe in 1612 in the presence of the emperor in Regensburg. Similar productions support the view that these actors could not belong to the "periphery" of the baroque, as Flemming claimed (1933, p. 16), but were an essential part of it. This refers to their developing of the stage, to their acting, and to their subject matter, as well as to their style. Content and style were an expression of the European *theatrum mundi* tradition in that these actors transplanted the repertory of an entire period, the Elizabethan one, to the continent. They took up Italian Renaissance motifs, Spanish baroque plays, French, Dutch, and German dramas and traveled with them from northern to southern Germany, from the west to the east, from Danzig to Warsaw and Prague. In this sense the English Comedians and their German successors were "ein sehr wesentliches Element einer gemeinsam-europäischen Theaterkultur der Barockzeit" (Kindermann, p. 359). During the second half of the century Romance influences seem to have gained the upper hand over the English imports, in keeping with the general cultural trend of the age: *Hauptaktionen* turned into pompous *Haupt- und Staatsaktionen*, crude style into generally more refined gallant language, Hanswurst into Harlekin; clownish intermezzi were replaced more and more by *Singspiele* in Joliphus's troupe, whose principal preferred pastoral operettas of Italian inspiration with impressive costumes and decoration.[27]

Although the English Comedians cannot compare with the Jesuit theater, the last *Schaubühne* collection shows that they were at least striving toward a similarly high baroque *Senecastil* (Baesecke, p. 149), consciously endeavoring to shape their products stylistically and literarily in the light of the baroque demands on rhetorical-representative art.[28]

NOTES

1. See Volker Meid, *Der deutsche Barockroman*, Sammlung Metzler (Stuttgart: Metzler, 1974), pp. 13 ff.; he discusses John Owen's popularity with Zesen, Titz, Rist, Logau, and others.

2. Thomas Heywood, *Apology for Actors* (1612; rpt. London: Shakespeare Society, 1841), p. 40.

3. Apparently the itinerant actors enjoyed belonging to the retinue of a prince; Robert Browne spent the winter of 1619 at the court of Frederick V, the "Winter King," in Prague; John Green accompanied Archduke Ferdinand from Graz to Passau (1607–8).

4. See the correspondence between the dukes in Albert Cohn, *Shakespeare in Germany in the Sixteenth and Seventeenth Centuries* (London, 1865; rpt. Wiesbaden: Sändig, 1967), pp. xxiii–xxv.

5. Anna Baesecke, *Das Schauspiel der englischen Komödianten in Deutschland: Seine dramatische Form und seine Entwicklung* (Halle: Niemeyer,

1935), pp. 70 ff.; cf. Heinz Kindermann, *Theatergeschichte Europas*, III (Salzburg: Otto Müller, 1959), 368 ff.

6. *Shakespeare-Jahrbuch*, 40 (1904), 229 ff. (Fynes Moryson).

7. According to Röchell's *Chronik der Stadt Münster*, quoted and translated by Cohn, pp. cxxxiv ff.; cf. Marx Mangoldt's "Schilderung der Sacke-villeschen Truppe" (1597), rpt. in Heinrich Julius von Braunschweig, *Von einem Weibe; Von Vincentio Ladislao*. Reclam 8776 (Stuttgart, 1967), p. 102.

8. Quoted from Willi Flemming, ed., *Das Schauspiel der Wanderbühne*, vol. III of *Barockdrama*, Deutsche Literatur in Entwicklungsreihen (Leipzig, 1931; rpt. Hildesheim: Olms, 1965), p. 13.

9. See Wilhelm Creizenach, ed., *Die Schauspiele der englischen Komö-dianten*, Deutsche Nationalliteratur, 23 (Berlin and Stuttgart, 1888; rpt. Darmstadt: Wissenschaftliche Buchgesellschaft, 1967), p. xxvii ff.

10. Friedrich Gundolf, *Shakespeare und der deutsche Geist* (Bad Godesberg: Küpper, 1947), p. 17.

11. Quoted in Kindermann (note 5, above), p. 354.

12. Somewhat arbitrarily, at least in my judgment, Duvan Ludvik distinguishes between three "waves" of English Comedians, the one of 1586, 1592, and 1642, the third period coinciding with the Puritan Interregnum of 1642-60, when theaters were closed by the Cromwell Parliament. In addition he divides the actors into the "old" companies (1586 and 1642-48) and the "late" ones (1642-48 and 1660-71). His theory is based mainly on the assumption that the Dutch actors were actually English ones. See his "Zur Chronologie und Topographie der 'Alten' und 'Späten' englischen Komö-dianten in Deutschland," *Acta Neophilologica*, 8 (1975), 47-65.

13. See A. Baesecke's expression "Symbol des Theaters" (note 5, above), p. 68.

14. W. L. Holland, ed., *Die Schauspiele des Herzogs Heinrich Julius von Braunschweig*, Bibliothek des litterarischen Vereins Stuttgart, 36 (Stuttgart, 1855; rpt. Amsterdam: Rodopi, 1967), p. 168.

15. See Marx Mangoldt (note 7, above).

16. See Gundolf (note 10, above), p. 43.

17. Produced in Dresden, 1626, manuscript from Paulsen's repertory printed in 1781; rpt. in Creizenach, pp. 147-186. See R. Freudenstein, *Der bestrafte Brudermord* (Hamburg: Cram, de Gruyter, 1958).

18. For a detailed description see Creizenach (note 9, above), pp. lxviii ff.

19. See Werner Richter, *Liebeskampf 1630 und Schaubühne 1670*, Palaestra, 78 (Berlin: Mayer & Müller, 1910).

20. A. H. J. Knight, *Heinrich Julius, Duke of Brunswick* (Oxford: Basil Blackwell, 1948), p. 119; see the clown's statement "Ick bin een Engelsmann" in *Von einer Ehebrecherin* (1594), Act II, 3.

21. Eckehard Catholy, *Das deutsche Lustspiel: Vom Mittelalter bis zum Ende der Barockzeit* (Darmstadt: Wissenschaftliche Buchgesellschaft, 1968), p. 137.

22. No. 51 in Jakob Ayrer, *Dramen*, 5 vols., ed. A. von Keller, Bibliothek des literarischen Vereins Stuttgart, 80 (Stuttgart, 1865; rpt. Hildesheim: Olms, 1973).

23. See Hugh Powell, ed., Andreas Gryphius, *Herr Peter Squentz* (Leicester: Leicester University Press, 1969), pp. xlii ff.

24. See the text in Christian Weise, *Der grünenden Jugend überflüssige Gedanken*, ed. Max von Waldberg, Neudrucke deutscher Literaturwerke, 242–45 (Halle: Niemeyer, 1914).

25. Christian Thomasius, *Juristische Händel*, part III, 2nd ed. (Halle, 1724), pp. 169 ff.: "Insonderheit von Comödien und Possenspielern," rpt. in Gertrud Schubart-Fikentscher, *Zur Stellung der Komödianten im 17. und 18. Jahrhundert* (Berlin-Ost: Akademie-Verlag, 1963), appendix.

26. Among them E. Catholy, p. 123; Gundolf, pp. 43 ff.; Horst Oppel, *Englisch-deutsche Literaturbeziehungen*, I (Berlin: Erich Schmidt, 1971), 48.

27. On Ayrer's Singspiele around 1600, see E. Catholy, pp. 138–47; also Hans-Albrecht Koch, *Das deutsche Singspiel*, Sammlung Metzler, 133 (Stuttgart: Metzler, 1974); H. Oppel, pp. 49 ff.; on Romance influences, see my article "Kuffstein und die Komödianten," *Daphnis* 1982 (in press).

28. A. Baesecke investigates "Symmetrie und Parallelismus" as stylistic devices, pp. 141 ff.; for a detailed bibliography on the English Comedians, see Gernot Gabel, *Drama und Theater des deutschen Barock: Eine Handbibliographie der Sekundärliteratur* (Hamburg: Selbstverlag, 1974), pp. 67–76.

SELECTED BIBLIOGRAPHY

Primary Sources

Ayrer, Jakob. *Dramen*. Adelbert von Keller, ed. 5 vols. Bibliothek des literarischen Vereins Stuttgart, 80. Stuttgart, 1865. Rpt. Hildesheim: Olms, 1973.

Braunschweig, Heinrich Julius von. *Von einem Weibe; von Vincentio Ladislao*. Reclam 8776. Stuttgart, 1967, p. 102.

Brennecke, Ernest, ed. *Shakespeare in Germany, 1590–1700: With Translations of Five Early Plays*. Chicago: University of Chicago Press, 1965.

Creizenach, Wilhelm ed. *Die Schauspiele der englischen Komödianten*. Deutsche Nationalliteratur, 23. Berlin and Stuttgart, 1888. Rpt. Darmstadt: Wissenschaftliche Buchgesellschaft, 1967.

Flemming, Willi, ed. *Das Schauspiel der Wanderbühne*. Vol. III of *Barockdrama*. Deutsche Literatur in Entwicklungsreihen. Leipzig, 1931. Rpt. Hildesheim: Olms, 1965.

Gryphius, Andreas. *Herr Peter Squentz*. Hugh Powell, ed. Leicester: Leicester University Press, 1969.

Holland, W. L., ed. *Die Schauspiele des Herzogs Heinrich Julius von Braunschweig*. Bibliothek des litterarischen Vereins Stuttgart, 36, 1855. Rpt. Amsterdam: Rodopi, 1967.

Thomasius, Christian. *Juristische Händel*. 2nd ed. Halle, 1724.

Weise, Christian. *Der grünenden Jugend überflüssige Gedanken*. Max von Waldberg, ed. Neudrucke deutscher Literaturwerke, 242-45. Halle: Niemeyer, 1914.

Secondary Literature

Alexander, Robert J. "George Jolly (Joris Joliphus), der wandernde Player und Manager: Neues zu seiner Tätigkeit in Deutschland (1648-68)." In *Kleine Schriften der Gesellschaft für Theatergeschichte*, 29-30 (1978), 31-48.

Baesecke, Anna. *Das Schauspiel der englischen Komödianten in Deutschland: Seine dramatische Form und seine Entwicklung*. Halle: Niemeyer, 1935.

Casey, P. F. "The Fool in the Dramas of Herzog Heinrich Julius von Braunschweig." *Colloquia Germanica*, 10 (1976-77), 121-27.

Catholy, Eckehard. *Das deutsche Lustspiel: Vom Mittelalter bis zum Ende der Barockzeit*. Darmstadt: Wissenschaftliche Buchgesellschaft, 1968.

Cohn, Albert. *Shakespeare in Germany in the Sixteenth and Seventeenth Centuries*. London, 1865. Rpt. Wiesbaden: Sändig, 1967.

Freudenstein, R. *Der bestrafte Brudermord*. Hamburg: Cram, de Gruyter, 1958.

Gabel, Gernot. *Drama und Theater des deutschen Barock: Eine Handbibliographie der Sekundärliteratur*. Hamburg: Selbstverlag, 1974, pp. 67-76.

Gundolf, Friedrich. *Shakespeare und der deutsche Geist*. Bad Godesberg: Küpper, 1947.

Heywood, Thomas. *Apology for Actors* (1612). Rpt. London: Shakespeare Society, 1841, p. 40.

Hoffmeister, Gerhart. "Kuffstein und die Komödianten." *Daphnis* 1982 (in press).

Kindermann, Heinz. *Theatergeschichte Europas*. Vol. III. Salzburg: Otto Müller, 1959.

Knight, A. H. J. *Heinrich Julius, Duke of Brunswick*. Oxford: Basil Blackwell, 1948.

Koch, Albrecht. *Das deutsche Singspiel*, Sammlung Metzler, 133. Stuttgart: Metzler, 1974.

Ludvik, Dusan. "Zur Chronologie und Topographie der 'Alten' und 'Späten' englischen Komödianten in Deutschland." *Acta Neophilologica*, 8 (1975), 47-65.

Meid, Volker. *Der deutsche Barockroman*, Sammlung Metzler. Stuttgart: Metzler, 1974, p. 13 ff.

Murad, Orlene. "The 'Theatre Letter' of Archduchess Maria Magdalena: A Report on the Activities of the English Comedians in Graz, Austria, in 1608." *Mosaic*, 10 (1977), 119-31.

———. *The English Comedians at the Habsburg Court in Graz, 1607–1608.* Salzburg: Institut für englische Sprache und Literatur, 1978.

Oppel, Horst. *Englisch-deutsche Literaturbeziehungen.* Vol. I. Berlin: Erich Schmidt, 1971.

Richter, Werner. *Liebeskampf 1630 und Schaubühne 1670.* Palaestra, 78. Berlin: Mayer & Müller, 1910.

Schubart-Fikentscher, Gertrud. *Zur Stellung der Komödianten im 17. und 18. Jahrhundert.* Berlin-Ost: Akademie-Verlag, 1963.

Shakespeare-Jahrbuch, 40 (1904), 229 ff.

10

The Dutch Example

Robert R. Heitner

What in Germany was the period of baroque—a time of relatively minor authors hardly known outside their homeland and not widely appreciated even there—was in neighboring Holland the *Gouden Eeuw*, the Golden Age. While "baroque" to cultivated Germans, unless they happen to be literary specialists, is today still a term primarily for architecture and music, the modern Dutch are keenly aware of their Golden Age poets and dramatists Hooft, Bredero, and Vondel, and their popular moralist Cats. Main streets and parks bear these men's names. It is still the custom to play Vondel's drama *Gijsbreght van Aemstel* every New Year's at the Amsterdam Schouwburg. This above all others was the great classical epoch.

The relationship of Germany to Holland was that of a poor cousin to a new millionaire. The bloodline was there, and for Low German speakers the language was readily understandable; but the status was decidedly different. The hundreds of German students who streamed to Holland, and the aristocrats on their cavalier tours, found themselves in a brisk, self-confident, and quite foreign atmosphere. The Netherlanders of both north and south had always been comfortable, well fed, and relatively free and independent. But in the sixteenth century they achieved things that the Germans would still be striving for in the eighteenth: a sense of national unity, a strong middle class, considerable liberty of thought and conscience, and an upsurge of literature and art.

This mighty cultural blossoming was grafted onto a strong root, the artistic tradition of the people. Whereas in Germany the earnest, yet

159

faintly ridiculous, Meistersinger guilds were composed only of trades-
men, the tradesmen-members of the prestigious *Rederijkerkamers*
(Chambers of Rhetoricians) of the Netherlands sat side by side with
scholarly and aristocratic members, even William of Orange himself;
and women were members, too. The Chambers supported public char-
ities, and their great common meetings, the *landjuwelen*, were festivals
at which spectators from every part of the country could enjoy poetry and
drama contests. When the Spanish tyranny put the Flemish south into
eclipse, the cultural, as well as political and economic, leadership went
at once to the north. After the Union of Utrecht in 1579, the conglomer-
ate of seven provinces known collectively as Holland developed with
astonishing speed despite continuing warfare against the Spanish.
Worldwide trade from the ports of Amsterdam and Rotterdam brought
unprecedented economic gains, while independence, patriotism, and
religious fervor provided spirit. Together these promoted a great pros-
pering of Dutch painting and literature in the late sixteenth and the first
half of the seventeenth century. Exiled southerners, especially those from
Brabant and its formerly flourishing city of Antwerp, contributed a very
significant share to this thriving culture.

The first important move was the foundation in 1575 of the University of Leiden, the Protestant successor to Louvain. It was a typically
courageous and confident Dutch gesture to inaugurate this university
just one year after the siege of the city had been lifted and before William
of Orange could be certain of uniting the provinces. The success of the
new university, heralding the success of its nation, was swift: by attract-
ing or training a number of great scholars it became the most illustrious
seat of learning in Europe. First came Justus Lipsius (1547-1606), whose
book *De Constantia* bred the Stoic thought which prevailed in the seventeenth century; then came Joseph Scaliger (1540-1609), famous son of
the (perhaps less justly[1]) famous Julius Caesar Scaliger. Daniel Heinsius
(1580-1655) studied and then taught there, reigning alone until
Claudius Salmasius came from France in 1631 to rival his success.
Another who studied and then became a famous professor at Leiden was
the theologian Gerhard Vossius (1577-1649), known also as a theorist of
drama. The academic excellence of these men attracted not only
students but royal patronage. They belonged to a small elite that made
up the Republic of Letters. When one of them, Daniel Heinsius, published verses in the vernacular, Dutch was given its credentials as a
literary language.

Considerable groundwork for this recognition of the language had been laid in the sixteenth century by the *Rederijker*, particularly those of the south, who wished to eliminate dialectical peculiarities and foreign words. Thus they anticipated the efforts of the "Sprachgesellschaften" in behalf of German.[2] A milestone in the struggle for language purity, in 1584, was the *Twe-spraack van de Nederduitsche Letterkunde* (Dialogue on Dutch Literature) by the rhetorician Hendrik Laurenszoon Spieghel (1549-1612). However, it was not until 1650 that Vondel was moved to state that the language was at last rid of its nonnative elements.[3]

In respect to the adoption of classical prosody, the minor poet Jan van Hout (1542-1609) is credited with introducing the Alexandrine into Dutch literature about 1575, and with it the principle that word accent must coincide with the stress of the metric foot. Although the Chambers, like the Meistersinger guilds in Germany, clung to the old irregular *knuppelrijm* (*Knüttelvers*), they, too, were using Alexandrines frequently by the end of the sixteenth century. Metric regularity was gradually popularized in a series of songbooks that began to appear in 1589. The best known is *Den Bloem-hof van de Nederlantsche Ieught*, 1608 (Garden of Dutch Youth). The mildly amorous content of these songs and their approximation of Renaissance verse forms were eagerly accepted by the fashionable circles that had begun to assemble, particularly in Amsterdam, independently of the Chambers but filled with their members. The most brilliant one met in the house of the wealthy merchant Roemer Visscher (1547-1620). Conservatively Catholic and continuing to use irregular meters in his own verse, this man was nevertheless interested in the study of ancient and Renaissance literature. Thanks to his two talented and beautiful daughters Anna (1584-1651) and Maria Tesselschade (1594-1649), a veritable salon, comparable to those in France, developed at Roemer Visscher's house. To its gatherings came the most gifted and appreciative persons in Amsterdam and Leiden. Its successor was at the castle of Muiden, near Amsterdam, presided over by Pieter Corneliszoon Hooft (1581-1647), who was a lyric poet, Holland's first classical dramatist, and also its first great historian. For such audiences Heinsius published his epoch-making collection 1616, the *Nederduytsche Poemata*.

It was the combination of Amsterdam and Leiden, town and gown, that made the Holland of the Golden Age so attractive to young Germans. It is easier to name the few German authors who neither studied at Leiden nor visited Amsterdam (e.g., Klaj, Dach, Gerhardt, Grimmelshausen, Christian Weise) than the many who did one or both. For the most part, they were deeply impressed. Schottel, who was in Leiden from 1633 to 1636, may have been stimulated by the Dutch example to his own efforts at purifying German. Only two, however, Opitz and Gryphius, were the real conductors of the Dutch energy to German literature.

Even before he arrived in Leiden himself in the fall of 1620, Opitz was acquainted with the *Bloem-hof* miscellany and the Dutch poems of Heinsius. In 1619 he had translated Heinsius's long poem *Lofsanck van Bacchus*. Although his stay in Holland was short, Opitz met Heinsius, Vossius, and Petrus Scriverius (1576–1660), the editor of the *Neder-duytsche Poemata*. Opitz's youthful works stand under the sign of contemporary Dutch poetry, however much they may also owe to Ronsard and the Pléiade. The first volume of his *Teutsche Poemata* (1624) has numerous borrowings and imitations of poems by Heinsius, Bredero, Roemer Visscher, and some anonymous authors found in the *Bloem-hof*. Sometimes he translated literally, only improving the rhythms, when necessary, in accordance with the strict rules formulated by Abraham van der Myl in his *Lingua Belgica* (1612) and followed by Heinsius.

Thanks to Opitz, Heinsius's verses became well known in Germany. But Heinsius also influenced Opitz's original works. Thus the *Lofsanck van Bacchus* became the model for *Das Lob des Krieges-Gottes* (1628), and Heinsius's poem "Pastorael" inspired Opitz's "Galathee," which in turn became the model for the "Corydon" songs written in Germany about 1625–50.[4] In respect to theory, nothing could be more important than that Opitz was influenced by Dutch poetry (and especially by Heinsius, who was among the first to carry the practice through in his works), to demand in *Das Buch von der deutschen Poeterey* that accented and unaccented syllables should follow in regular alternation and that word and metric stress should coincide. It was also from Heinsius that Opitz learned to insist on native words, to require placing of the adjective before substantives, and to relegate the verbal noun to second place when forming compounds. In sum, although Ronsard's *Abrégé de l'art poétique français* was the theoretical basis for Opitz's prescriptions, it was Heinsius's lyrics on which he tested these rules and if necessary changed them to conform to a Germanic language.[5]

In the homely, moralizing poetry of Jacob Cats (1577–1660), the Dutch received a treasure of popular literature that can best be compared to Gellert's fables in eighteenth-century Germany. No writer was read or cherished more than he, and his fame extended into Germany, where he was translated by a long series of admirers, including Titz,

Neumark, Dedekind, and Greflinger. However, although Cats employed Alexandrines and the pastoral mode, he had no more influence on the course of German baroque poetry than on Amsterdam poets, from whom he remained aloof in his strict Calvinism, remote on a country estate. For something like his prosaic moralizing and realistic country scenes one must wait, as far as German literature is concerned, for Johann Heinrich Voss's idylls. It is unlikely that Gellert or Voss were at all affected by Cats.

The far more distinguished poet Constantyn Huygens (1596–1687), a member of Hooft's "Muiderkring" (Muiden circle) and father of the eminent scientist Christian Huygens, was likewise of little discernible importance for Germany, despite his prominence in Dutch literary history. As a highly placed public servant—for sixty-two years he was private secretary to the princes of Orange—his interests were turned abroad. He translated John Donne and corresponded with Corneille about prosody. As a strict Calvinist, however, he felt closer to Cats, and like Cats, he wrote on some homely subjects, e.g., his marriage, in *Dagwercks*; his new house near The Hague, in *Hofwijck*; and a blind friend, in *Oogentroost*. At the same time, he inclined toward preciosity of style. It does not seem that this grand seigneur came into contact with German students of poetic talent.

No German writer spent as much time in Holland as Philipp von Zesen, all in all some twenty-seven years of his life between 1642 and 1684. Vossius became his mentor. Too late for Roemer Visscher and Hooft, he frequented the salon of a learned woman with a special interest in theology, Anna Maria Schuurmans (1607–78). Some thirty-three of Zesen's works were printed in Amsterdam, among which was his splendid description of the city (1664). Yet Zesen did not take Dutch literature as his model. German lyric poetry at his time probably needed no further inspiration from Heinsius and the others. He could not have found models for his prose works in Dutch literature, and he was not a dramatist who could have learned from Hooft and Vondel. It has often been suggested that Amsterdam's still prestigious Chamber "De Eglantier" (The Eglantine), which since the early sixteenth century had been the leading one in the whole north, was in his mind when he founded his Deutschgesinnte Genossenschaft in Hamburg in 1643. A flower, the rose, was the symbol of Zesen's "Sprachgesellschaft," and its four "Zünfte" were each named after a flower, like most of the Dutch and Flemish Chambers. In addition, Zesen followed Dutch practice in immediately granting membership to women. Vondel himself became a member in 1671, but this is the only evidence of a connection between him and Zesen.

Germany hardly needed to look to Holland where emblem books were concerned. The progenitor of all these enormously popular works, the *Emblemata* of Andreas Alciati, had been published in Augsburg in 1531, and in the later sixteenth century Holtzwart and Fischart had assembled their own emblem books, as did Rollenhagen in 1611. Yet the Germans must have noticed the great activity in Holland, where the most famous authors avidly compiled such books. Dirck Coornhert (1522-90), a Dutch rhetorician who was a poet, dramatist, and translator of Seneca and Cicero, began the series by translating the Latin *De rerum usu et abusu* (Concerning the Use and Abuse of Things) in 1585. In 1601 the young Heinsius published the first original Dutch emblem book. Innovatively he devoted it to the theme of love and gave it the romantic title, *Quaeris quid sit amor* (You Ask What Love May Be). He followed this with a second in 1613; both were published under a pseudonym. Bredero did the poems for an emblem book in 1607, and Hooft published a book of love emblems in 1611. Vondel published two emblem books, in 1613 and 1617; Anna Visscher, with some help from Roemer, published one in 1614. Finally Cats fell in line, publishing an emblem book in his own dry, realistic style in 1618. Investigation of the possible relationships of these emblems to Dutch literature has just begun.[6]

The Fleming Jan van der Noot (ca. 1539-ca. 1595), while a refugee in Cologne, wrote an epic in Renaissance style, but it was published in full only in German, under the title *Das Buch Extasis* (1576), and exerted virtually no effect. Otherwise the literature of the Netherlands was wanting in the genres of epic and novel. Its drama made up handsomely for this. There was a long tradition of writing and performing plays; in fact, this was the chief activity of the Chambers. There were farces, often very crude, called *kluchten*; morality plays called *spelen van sinnen* (plays of meaning); heroic plays with biblical or mythological subjects, pointing clear contemporary morals; and a small body of unique fourteenth-century chivalric plays called *abele spelen* (artistic plays). The moralities made extensive use of allegorical figures, called *sinnekens*, and they eventually drew criticism because of their excessive and often incongruous didacticism. Through them, however, the people grew accustomed to a stage given over to the discussion of serious historical, political, and religious matters. This was quite different from Germany. Theatricals were such an integral part of life in the Netherlands that the Calvinist theologians after the Reformation had very limited success in opposing them. Amsterdam especially was a theater-loving town. Numerous dramatists (part-time, amateur ones, to be sure) lived there around the turn of the seventeenth century, and their works were played, if not always printed, e.g., Abraham de Koning (ca. 1586-1618) and Theodore Rodenburgh (ca. 1578-1644).

Those dramatists who studied the classics and were favorably impressed by the Neolatin plays of Hugo Grotius—*Adamus exul*, 1601 (Adam in Exile), and *Christus patiens*, 1608 (Passion of Christ)—as well as of Heinsius—*Auriacus*, 1601 (William of Orange)—could not long remain satisfied with the conservatism of the Chambers. One of them was Dr. Samuel Coster (1579-1665), an Amsterdam physician and former Leiden student who began writing comedy and then turned to plays in the Senecan manner. He stayed within the Dutch tradition of didacticism, nevertheless: his *Ithys* (1615) was directed against the vanity of court life; his *Iphigenie* (1617) and *Polyxena* (1619) were transparent antique masks for an attack on theological controversies, particularly those then going on at the Council of Dort. All three works were full of sound and fury and offered bloody sights in plenty. When the Chamber "De Eglantier" would not bend to new ways, Dr. Coster founded a so-called Academy, which was actually a theater, in the city. In 1632 "De Eglantier" became reconciled with the Academy, and the success of the joint enterprise was eventually so great that, with the city magistrates' assistance, a large, impressive, and well-equipped theater—the Schouwburg—was constructed. This opened in January 1638. It was the first true municipal standing theater on the Continent—130 years before the modest and short-lived "national theater" in Hamburg.

With the conscious turn from the *Rederijker* style to a new classicism, the influence of Senecan tragedy became paramount. This meant ghost and magic scenes, dream sequences, and detailed description—sometimes depiction—of bloody horrors. But, more importantly, it meant long, pompous speeches, rodomontades, and disquisitions full of antitheses, rhetorical figures, and Homeric similes—in a word, a new emphasis on language. It meant division into five acts with choruses after the first four, and ever-increasing punctiliousness about the unities. Under Senecan influence serious Dutch drama became monumental and static. Like the old moralities, it was written to edify and educate. One must imagine a first act composed of a long, elaborate monologue giving the exposition. In the second, third, and fourth acts various personages hold a kind of dialogue, that is, one personage utters a long speech while another may warn or reprimand the speaker; or there may be long stretches of wearisome stichomythy.[7] The fifth act is composed of a lengthy lament and a prediction of future weal or woe, and has no dramatic value whatever. It is reported that audiences in Amsterdam generally walked out after the fourth act.

Admittedly there is a great difference between reading and actually seeing such a play. The Schouwburg had elaborate permanent scenery and its actors, who were professionals, wore opulent costumes. There was music: the choruses filled out the entr'actes with their songs. And there was the Amsterdam specialty of *vertoningen*, or living pictures. These were grandiose tableaux comprised of many actors frozen in startling attitudes (e.g., being crowned, murdered, executed), depicting a part of the story narrated in the dialogue but not acted out. Rembrandt's imposing "Night Watch" is thought to represent a *vertoning* in Vondel's *Gijsbreght van Aemstel*. There were also moving dumb shows, as when in *Gijsbreght* the gaily dressed nobles proceed to church on Christmas Eve and in *Joseph in Dothan* a caravan of Arab merchants crosses the stage. The broad but shallow stage of the Schouwburg was better suited to tableaux and declamation than to action. The impression made by such a classical play must have been that of a sonorous recitation, sumptuously mounted, illustrated with brilliant displays, and punctuated with a few actions, e.g., the appearance of an angel, demon, or allegorical personage, an entrance, an exit, or a sudden act of violence cutting off a long-winded speaker in mid speech.

When Hooft wrote his first two plays, *Achilles en Polyxena* (1598) and *Theseus ende Ariadne* (1601), both unpublished until 1614, he was on his long sojourn in Italy, where he is supposed to have learned much about the fashionable Renaissance forms. Yet they are still very similar to the old heroic plays of the Chambers, in which the classical material is unconsciously travestied. It was not until Hooft studied law in Leiden (1606–9) and presumably saw and read the Latin dramas of Grotius and Heinsius that he wrote his *Geeraerdt van Velzen* (1612, printed 1613), in accordance with his understanding of the classical rules. The story was medieval but well known to the Dutch through the popular ballad "Graaf Floris V." To be sure, in this work of new style Hooft did not abandon the Dutch tradition of pointing a specific moral. He had previously done this in *Achilles en Polyxena*, in which it is demonstrated that citizens must sacrifice their personal desires to the good of the government; the same political lesson is taught in *Theseus ende Ariadne*. In *Geeraerdt van Velzen*, the moral is not very different: although Floris is a villainous tyrant who has raped Geeraerdt's wife and slain his brother, putting him to death without due process of law is a wrongful act of personal vengeance; the sentence of the States-General should have been awaited.

In all these plays by Hooft, the Stoic virtue of passivity is preached, but nowhere as strikingly as in his last drama, *Baeto oft Oorsprong der Hollanderen*, 1617 (Baeto, or the Origin of the Dutch), printed in 1626. The mythical subject matter harks back to early Germanic times, thus anticipating the German Hermann-dramas of the eighteenth century. In a curious way, passivity is meant to enhance national pride. Baeto, heir to the throne of the Chatti, is hated by his stepmother, who turns his royal father against him. Baeto prefers exile to struggle and bloodshed and becomes, as a result, the Aeneas of Holland. Grotius's ideas underlay Hooft's Stoicism: the Dutch should promote peace, unity, and freedom by suppressing their individual wishes. Hooft's main purpose was to promulgate his political philosophy; not surprisingly, his dramas, having neither plot nor character development, show all too plainly the weaknesses of the classical form. They are replete, however, with ghosts, magicians, oracles, and allegorical personages.

The foremost comic dramatist of the Golden Age was Gerbrand Adriaanszoon Bredero (1585-1618). Like many other Dutch writers he was the son of a tradesman, a shoemaker, and like a number of others he combined a talent for painting with one for writing lyrics and dramas. His accomplishments admitted him to the socially elevated circles of Hooft and the Visschers—nothing unusual in Holland. Although not university trained, he set about learning Latin. Through his study of Plautus and Terence he was able to improve the old *klucht* into something approaching character comedy. His *Klucht van de koe*, 1612 (Farce of the Cow), and *Klucht van de molenaar*, 1613 (Farce of the Miller), were followed by a reworking of Terence's *Eunuchus* in modern dress entitled *Het moortje*, 1615 (The Moorish Girl). He also made use of subjects from Italian and Spanish literature in serious plays with comic intermezzi, as in *Rodderich ende Alphonsus* (1611), *Griane* (1612), and *Lucelle* (1616). In 1618, the year of his untimely death, came his masterpiece, *De Spaansche Brabander* (The Spanish-Mannered Brabantine). In this comedy he transformed material from the Spanish novel *Lazarillo de Tormes* into an amusing satire on the presumptuous airs and actual poverty of refugees in Amsterdam, the central theme being a typically baroque one, the contrast between *Schein* and *Sein*. There is little action and far too much narrative revealing the epic source; the charm of the play lies in its realistic street scenes. Dutch comedies were written in verse, this one in Alexandrines that do not hold up well in the dialectical passages. No one surpassed Bredero, however, in combining native Dutch humor with classical influences.

Overshadowing everyone else, Joost van der Vondel (1587-1679) was the supreme genius of the Dutch theater. With just a year of university training he, like Bredero, acquired Latin—and, later, Greek as well—in order to read the classics. Like Hans Sachs, he was a tradesman, if not himself a craftsman. He successfully managed a silk business inherited from his father. His literary activity, as might be expected, began in a *Rederijkerkamer* in Amsterdam, the Flemish "Wit Lavendel" (White Lavender), to which he, as member of a refugee family, was naturally drawn. Helped by de Koning, who was also in this Chamber, he set himself at first to writing poems on commission. However, as early as 1610 his first drama, *Het Pascha* (The Passover), was presented on the Chamber's stage, and in 1612 it was published. It is regarded as an old-fashioned *Rederijker* drama, with naive, straightforward dialogue that is rather charming. But Vondel was already progressive enough to restrict the cast of characters, to narrate the plagues instead of depicting them, and to omit the traditional *sinnekens*. Was he already aware of the Latin dramas of Grotius and Heinsius? His intelligence and innate desire to follow good models might justify such an assumption. In any case, *Het Pascha*, the fifth act of which is simply an undramatic oration, adumbrates what was to come later from Vondel's pen: it is more like a long poem than a play.

Not until 1620, after becoming a member of the Hooft circle, did Vondel write his second play, *Hierusalem verwoest* (Jerusalem Destroyed). From Hooft he had learned something about the unity of place, and kept the various locales to one general area. Also, he did not end his play with a fifth-act chorus as before. Senecan influence has now made the dialogue erudite and declamatory, and correspondingly artificial. There is no action: the play merely describes and agonizes over the terrible situation. In 1625, Vondel had Hooft assist him to translate Seneca's *Troades* under the title *De Amsteldamsche Hecuba*. It was the year in which Opitz translated the same play into German, no doubt motivated—as was Vondel—by his admiration for the scholarly opinions and poetic accomplishments of Heinsius and Grotius. In 1628, Vondel translated Seneca's *Hippolytus*. This marked the zenith of Seneca's theoretical influence on Vondel, which then abated, while the practical influence continued. Meanwhile, in 1625-26 Vondel wrote his third original drama, *Palamedes of Vermoorde onnozelheid* (Palamedes, or

Murdered Innocence), which was inspired by the poet's long-nurtured outrage over the execution in 1619 of the freedom hero Olden-barneveldt, who was on the losing side in the Council of Dort. Everyone could see that Palamedes, put by the calumny of crafty priests into disfavor with Agamemnon (Prince Mauritz of Orange), was the unfortunate liberal Calvinist or "Remonstrant" Oldenbarneveldt. As a result, the authorities made Vondel pay a fine, but the play continued to be printed and read.

Vondel met Grotius in 1631, and Grotius, having left Seneca behind, introduced his profoundly respectful new acquaintance to the tragedies of Greece. Henceforward Vondel would regard Sophocles and Euripides as his masters (in theory), while the Roman tragedies would be considered somewhat tasteless. In 1634 Grotius (1583-1645) wrote a third Latin drama, *Sophompaneas*,[8] modeling it on Euripides, and the next year Vondel translated this weak treatment of the story of Joseph's revelation of himself to his amazed father and brothers as *Joseph in t'hof* (Joseph at Court). The exercise did not affect his next original piece, which has the usual Senecan verbosity and stasis: it was the national drama *Gijsbreght van Aemstel*, which turned out to be his greatest and most lasting popular success. Commissioned for the opening of the new Schouwburg, it was presented on January 3, 1638, and then again some 120 times during the author's lifetime. Like Hooft's *Geeraerdt*, with which its material is closely allied, and even more like *Baeto*, the strangely passive patriotism of the play consists of Stoic acceptance of misfortune, sweetened by the promise of later reward. The titular hero is an ally of Geeraerdt van Velzen, and his town of Amsterdam is being besieged by adherents of the murdered Count Floris. These foes gain entry through Gijsbreght's gullible reception into town of a supposedly empty ship which is actually full of soldiers, like the Trojan horse. (The dependence of the story on the description of the fall of Troy in the *Aeneid* has been demonstrated, step by step.)[9] Instead of fighting to the last in his beleaguered castle, Gijsbreght lets himself be persuaded by his wife Badeloch and the archangel Raphael to escape. The sense of defeat is mitigated by Raphael's prediction that Amsterdam destroyed will rise again as great and flourishing Amsterdam (just as ruined Troy gave birth to imperial Rome). In spite of the exciting events, speeches are substituted for action. There is a dream scene, as Badeloch gets a warning of impending disaster, and a grisly tableau shows some nuns being slaughtered in their cloister. The main beauty of the work is in its poetic diction, particularly in the choruses, which became popular in their

musical settings. Municipal pride and affectionate tradition explain why
Gijsbreght is still played. Even though the best directors like to under-
take its production, any comparison with the constant playing of
Shakespeare's historical dramas can hardly be made.

In 1639 Vondel translated Sophocles' *Electra*.[10] Some of the Greek
play's simple unity and certainly its division of the choral songs into the
customary Greek tripartite arrangement of strophe, antistrophe, and
epode are mirrored in Vondel's original *De Maeghden* (The Maidens) of
the same year. The subject matter is the massacre of St. Ursula and her
eleven thousand virgins at Cologne; it shows both Vondel's sentiment for
the city in which he had been born to refugee parents from Antwerp and
his progress from the Mennonite faith to Catholicism. Under Jesuit
guidance he was converted in 1641. There is a certain dramatic tension
in *De Maeghden*: barbarous Attila falls in love with the captive saint,
and she rejects him so steadfastly that love turns to hatred. But the play's
possibilities are crushed under lengthy speeches dealing with matters of
doctrine. Its simplicity degenerates into poverty, and the characters
become orating lay figures. There is also some Senecan horror: Attila
slays Ursula with a javelin, the chorus describes the martyrdom of the
virgins, and in the fifth act (which is no more than an epilogue) the warning ghost of Ursula appears holding a blood-dripping head.

Vondel called *De Gebroeders*, 1640 (The Brothers) his favorite
play. Its dismal Old Testament subject, the sacrifice of seven sons of Saul
to appease the offended Gibeonites, gave little room for action. The judgment is heard, is resisted, is carried out. The lamenting of the princes'
mothers struck the same chord as that of the mothers of the Bethlehem
massacre in Heinsius's *Herodes infanticida* (1635). A tableau of the seven
hanged men is shown at the end of the fourth act. The choral songs have
the tripartite arrangement, now the rule with Vondel. The lesson of the
work is passive acceptance. Two further plays in 1640 rounded off the
Joseph trilogy begun with the translation of *Sophompaneas*, and this
trilogy found much favor with the public. *Joseph in Dothan* is an illustrated epic. *Joseph in Egypten* is the expansion into five acts of a single
dramatic incident, the attempted seduction of the hero by Potiphar's
wife. In 1641, Vondel's colorless martyr tragedy *Peter en Pauwels* (Peter
and Paul) signaled the end of the vogue he had rather briefly enjoyed. It
was never played.

In the same year Jan Vos (ca. 1615–67) burst onto the stage with his
sensational *Aran en Titus*, an adaptation of the Titus Andronicus

material brought over to the Continent by the English Comedians. Jan Vos was not a scholar but a man of the theater. His *Aran en Titus* offered a string of lively, if crude, actions and twelve gruesome murders; emphasis was decidedly removed from the word and placed on crass theatricality. Surprisingly, even the esteemed scholar Caspar Barlaeus (1584–1648) commended *Aran en Titus*. In 1647 Vos was named director of the Schouwburg, which prospered mightily. In 1665 a thorough renovation of the building was completed. Vos had it equipped with the latest inventions of Italian stagecraft. His last work, *Medea* (1665), showed what this new theater — and Vos's taste — were capable of: the play calls for a series of metamorphoses so astounding that they would task a modern stage.

Vondel, shunned by many friends after his conversion and weighed down by heart-breaking family troubles, wrote on. His *Maria Stuart of gemartelde majesteit*, 1646 (Mary Stuart, or Martyred Majesty), was not staged because of its pro-Catholic and anti-Queen Elizabeth bias; again Vondel had to pay a fine for his political indiscretion. Mary appears only in Acts II and IV, at first refuting all accusations and then passively preparing for death. What is in the other three acts? In Act I, Mary's confessor speaks with the tutor Melvin and the exposition is given; in Act III there is a long stretch of stichomythy as Melvin reviews the whole case with Mary's judges; in Act V there is a detailed report of the execution and a tableau showing the corpse. The preface mentions Aristotle's rule that the hero may not be perfect — and yet Mary, like all of Vondel's heroes before this, is! Vondel explains that all the accusations against her introduce enough imperfection. This is typical of his naive approach to the classics he so much admired.

In 1647 Vondel was again commissioned to write a play, this one in celebration of the end to hostilities with Spain and official recognition of Dutch independence. Vondel's only comedy, or rather pastorale, *De Leeuwendalers* (The People of Liondale), therefore allegorizes the reunion of the North and South in peaceful coexistence. Leeuwendaal (The Netherlands) is a formerly harmonious community divided by a sudden quarrel which leads two gods to demand from the people the annual sacrifice of a youth. Aside from this framework there is the central plot of a country Romeo and Juliet separated by their feuding parents. Only when the young man saves the girl from an attacker is a happy ending possible. Despite the Alexandrines, we see realistic situations among the peasants and hear their earthy dialogue.

It was Vondel's last popular success. He had lost touch with the times, although he had yet to produce his greatest work, *Lucifer* (1654). Advancing age paradoxically stimulated his creative activity. Between 1648 and 1668 he wrote twelve original plays and translated four more Greek tragedies. Of them all, only *Salomon* (1648) still enjoyed any kind of popularity; the others were rarely performed or not at all. Vondel was practically writing for himself. While he reached new heights of baroque tension in *Lucifer* and outdid himself in lyricism in *Adam in ballingschap*, 1664 (Adam in Exile), he never really changed his style. Moreover, his continuing predilection for biblical drama[11] was enough to insure his passing from the scene. Having been crowded from the stage by Vos, he was next entirely superseded by the taste for French classical drama introduced by Lodewijck Meijer's literary society "Nil volentibus arduum" (Nothing Too Much for the Strong-willed), dating from 1669. This inevitable change occurred more than half a century earlier in Holland than in Germany.

The achievements of Dutch dramatists before 1650, however, dominated the German baroque *Kunstdrama* throughout the seventeenth century.[12] When Johann Klaj in 1645 adapted Grotius's *Christus* and Heinsius's *Herodes* into German dramatic recitations, he was following in the footsteps of the popularizers of *Auriacus* and *Herodes*[13] in Holland, except that circumstances dictated a mere one-person performance instead of a regular staging. To be sure, the actual German *Kunstdrama* was conceived during Gryphius's six-year stay in Holland (1638–44), when the newly opened Amsterdam theater and the works of Hooft, Bredero, and Vondel definitively shaped the young man's taste. As a preliminary exercise he faithfully translated *De Gebroeders* ca. 1640.[14] Superficial evidence of imitation in his own later plays include his use of Vondel's term "Reyhen" for the choruses; his frequent division of the choral passages into strophe, antistrophe, and epode; his not marking off (except in *Leo Armenius*) entrances and exits as numbered scenes; his flexible handling of the unity of place; his adoption of Hooft's and Vondel's practice of narrating in advance the content of the play; and his use (like Hooft's) of allegorical personages. Closer inspection reveals that various lines in Gryphius's texts were inspired by or directly taken over from Vondel and Hooft. Further consideration reveals the common theme of *Leo Armenius* and *Geeraerdt van Velzen*: is it right to dispatch a tyrant? In both, a magician is asked to foretell the outcome of the venture, and in both, the hero's wife is against violence. *Leo Armenius*, like Vondel's *Gijsbreght*, has the wife's dream of warning and a strongly antithetical Christmas mood. In their conjugal tenderness, Leo and Theodosia reflect Gijsbreght and Badeloch.

Gryphius's *Catharina von Georgien* probably owes its central motif of the love-smitten tyrant to *De Maeghden*, for the historical Shah Abbas only had political reasons for executing the captive queen. Both female martyrs appear in spirit to their murderers, predicting doom. Like Vondel's Mary Stuart, Catharina gives a detailed account of the events preceding her imprisonment and turns from hope of deliverance to contemplation of death with equanimity. Especially in its second version (1663), Gryphius's *Carolus Stuardus* shows similarity to *Maria Stuart*: talk of last-minute rescue, scenes of stichomythy in which an advocate pleads for the sovereign's life, strong criticism of England, and living pictures (Gryphius has three to Vondel's one). Gryphius's *Papinianus* seems clearly indebted to Vondel's *Palamedes*, for in each a venerable man is unjustly persecuted, and both heroes stoically accept their fates, convinced that their civil martyrdom serves the cause of moral law. The relationship between *De Leuuwendalers* and *Die geliebte Dornrose* is quite obvious: Gryphius's Dornrose and Kornblume find the same solution to their dilemma as Vondel's Hageroos (cf, Dornrose) and Adelaert. Gryphius's peasants quarrel over a cock with practically the same words as Vondel's Warner and Govert. In Gryphius's *Horribilicribrifax* the braggart officers recall the main character of Bredero's *De Spaansche Brabander*. The play's comic use of foreign languages is prefigured in a number of Dutch comedies.

More important by far than such details is Gryphius's essentially Dutch concept of tragedy and comedy as literary forms. According to this fairly primitive concept, drama was a series of pictures illustrating a story, and study of the ancients had succeeded only in replacing the pictures with verbal descriptions, the tragic poet's interest being in the elegance of his language. Transferred from Holland to Germany, that is, from a well-equipped standing theater with professional actors (and, after 1650, even actresses) to a schoolboy stage, tragedy in this form—less so comedy—could only bore and bewilder its captive audience of loyal parents and honored sovereigns. At most, such plays could interest a reading audience, who could absorb their inordinate length in easy stages (one example: the incredibly tedious historical speech in Act III of *Catharina von Georgien*). German texts tended to be longer than Dutch ones: when *Leo Armenius* was performed at the Schouwburg on January 6, 1659, it had to be shortened. Small wonder that *Papinianus*, enlivened at least with absorbing scenes of horror, was the one Gryphius drama firmly on the repertory of the wandering troupes. Small wonder, too, that Lohenstein resorted to every shocking and amazing theatrical tactic he could seize upon to lend the form greater viability. As was the case with Vos's innovations in Holland, Lohenstein's efforts were ultimately in vain. Not until Gottsched, viewing the wreckage, adopted the form of French tragedy and comedy did the history of German drama really begin.

Besides Gryphius, there are some scattered instances of direct contact with Dutch drama. In 1662, David Elias Heidenreich of Weissenfels made a prose adaptation of *De Gebroeders*, while in the same year Hieronymus Thomae imitated Vos's *Aran en Titus* in his *Titus und Tomyris oder die Rachbegierigen*. Christoph Kormart, who may also have adapted Vondel's *Palamedes, Lucifer*, and *David in ballingschap* (but if so, these versions are lost), translated *Maria Stuart* into prose in 1672 for some Leipzig students who liked to put on plays. However, he increased the original fifteen scenes to thirty-one and brought in Queen Elizabeth! Finally, Konstantin Christian Dedekind reworked Vondel's *Samson* with music in 1676.

After 1648, troupes of professional Dutch actors made forays into Germany, particularly the Low German sections, and continued to do so until the mid-eighteenth century. Mainly, they presented adaptations of romantic Spanish plays, but one also hears of a performance in Hamburg in the 1740s by the Spatsier troupe of Vondel's *Gijsbreght*, the Joseph-trilogy, and even the early *Hierusalem verwoest*. The reported facts that the troupe of Michael Daniel Treu gave the Joseph-trilogy in 1666, and that Johannes Velten presented Vos's *Medea* in 1678 and in 1688 both the Joseph-trilogy and *Die Rache der Gibeoniter* (presumably Heidenreich's translation of *De Gebroeders*, since Gryphius's translation was not published until 1698) suggest that these Germans were imitating the Dutch and trying, particularly in Hamburg, to compete with them. The Dutch troupes familiarized the German ones with their living pictures, their middle curtain, and their employment of actresses. On the other hand, they came too late and showed too few of their classics for these to have had any significant effect. The most telling contribution they could have made — the exclusion of Hanswurst from serious works and the use of verse dialogue — was not accepted by the German popular theater. They did give the earliest German troupes a model of professionalism. Thus for the last time Holland's historic role was played: that of being a step ahead of its poor but potentially great cousin.

NOTES

1. See Edith Kern, *The Influence of Heinsius and Vossius upon French Dramatic Theory*, The Johns Hopkins Studies in Romance Literatures and Languages, extra vol. 26 (Baltimore: The Johns Hopkins Press, 1949), pp. 48, 142.

2. On the other hand, the Germans had their Luther Bible, that most effective propagator of literary language, a century before the Dutch finally got their *Statenbijbel* (1626-37).

3. "Onze spraack is sedert weinige jaren herwaart van bastaard-woorden en onduitsch allengs geschuimt" (our language has gradually been cleansed during the last few years of bastard words and un-Dutchness), writes Vondel in *Poëzy of verscheide Gedichten* (Leewarden: Gybert Sybes, 1651), p. 5.

4. Th. Weevers, "The Influence of Heinsius on Two Genres of the German Baroque," *Journal of English and Germanic Philology*, 37 (1938), 524, 531.

5. Julius Bernhard Muth, "Über das Verhältnis von Martin Opitz zu Daniel Heinsius" (diss. Leipzig 1872), pp. 13-15.

6. See W. A. P. Smit and P. Brachin, *Vondel (1587-1679): Contribution à l'histoire de la tragédie au XVIIᵉ siècle* (Paris: Didier, 1964), pp. 41-42, 49. See also Myra Scholz-Heerspink, "Vondel's *Gijsbreght van Aemstel* as Emblematic and Figural Drama," *Spektator*, 4 (1975), 570-81.

7. Stichomythy is an extended exchange of one-line speeches, a technique originating with Greek drama.

8. "Sophompaneas" is supposedly the Egyptian word for "savior of the world."

9. See Alfred Hermann, "Joost van den Vondels *Gijsbrecht van Aemstel* in seinem Verhältnis zum zweiten Buch von Vergils *Aeneis*" (diss. Leipzig 1928).

10. Compare Opitz's translation of Sophocles' *Antigone* in 1636.

11. Of Vondel's twelve plays, only *Batavische Gebroeders* (1663), *Phaëton* (1663), and the exotic *Zungchin* (1667) were on nonbiblical subjects.

12. For a contrary opinion, see Erik Lunding, *Das schlesische Kunstdrama: Eine Darstellung und Deutung* (Copenhagen: Haace, 1940), esp. pp. 44-51; and Edward Verhofstadt, "Vondel und Gryphius: Versuch einer literarischen Topographie," *Neophilologus*, 53 (1969), 290-99.

13. Dominicus van der Stichel adapted Heinsius's *Herodes infanticida* in a Dutch version entitled *De Moord der onnoozelen*, 1639 (The Murder of the Innocents).

14. Gryphius also translated the French Jesuit Nicolas Caussin's Latin martyr tragedy *Felicitas*, perhaps as early as 1634. He could hardly have found its form widely different from that of Vondel's plays.

SELECTED BIBLIOGRAPHY

Secondary Literature

Haerten, Heinz. *Vondel und der deutsche Barock*. Disquisitiones Carolinae, 6. Nymegen: Zentrale Druckerei, 1934.

Hermann, Alfred, "Joost van den Vondels *Gijsbrecht van Aemstel* in seinem Verhältnis zum zweiten Buch von Vergils *Aeneis*. Diss. Leipzig 1928.

Kern, Edith. *The Influence of Heinsius and Vossius upon French Dramatic Theory*, The Johns Hopkins Studies in Romance Literatures and Languages, extra vol. 26. Baltimore: The Johns Hopkins Press, 1949, pp. 48, 142.

Lunding, Erik. *Das schlesische Kunstdrama: Eine Darstellung und Deutung*. Copenhagen: Haace, 1940.

Muth, Julius Bernhard. "Über das Verhältnis von Martin Opitz zu Daniel Heinsius." Diss. Leipzig 1872.

Pott, Clarence K. "Holland-German Literary Relations in the Seventeenth Century: Vondel and Gryphius." *Journal of English and Germanic Philology*, 47 (1948), 127–38.

Schneppen, Heinz. *Niederländische Universitäten und deutsches Geistesleben: Von der Gründung der Universität Leiden bis ins späte 18. Jahrhundert*. Neue Münstersche Beiträge zur Geschichtsforschung, 6. Münster: Aschendorffsche Verlagsbuchhandlung, 1960.

Schöffler, Herbert. *Deutsches Geistesleben zwischen Reformation und Aufklärung: Von M. Opitz zu Chr. Wolff*. 2nd ed. Frankfurt: Klostermann, 1956.

Scholz-Heerspink, Myra, "Vondel's *Gijsbreght van Aemstel* as Emblematic and Figural Drama," *Spektator*, 4 (1975), 570–81.

Schönle, Gustav. *Deutsch-niederländische Beziehungen in der Literatur des 17. Jahrhunderts*. Leidse Germanistische en Anglistische Reeks, 7. Leiden: Universitaire Pers, 1968.

Smit, W. A. P. "The Dutch Theatre in the Renaissance—A Problem and a Task for the Literary Historian." *Dutch Studies*, 1 (1974), 44–69.

—— and P. Brachin. *Vondel (1587–1679): Contribution à l'histoire de la tragédie au XVIIᵉ siècle*. Paris: Didier, 1964.

Stachel, Paul. *Seneca und das deutsche Renaissancedrama*. Studien zur Literatur- und Stilgeschichte des 16. und 17. Jahrhunderts. Palaestra, 46. Berlin: Mayer und Müller, 1907.

Trunz, Erich. *Dichtung und Volkstum in den Niederlanden im 17. Jahrhundert: Ein Vergleich mit Deutschland und ein Überblick über die niederländisch-deutschen Beziehungen in diesem Jahrhundert*. Schriften zur Deutschen Akademie in München, 2. München: Ernst Reinhardt, 1937.

Van Ingen, Ferdinand. "Do ut des: Holländisch-deutsche Wechselbeziehungen im 17. Jahrhundert." *Deutsche Barockliteratur und europäische Kultur*. Zweites Jahrestreffen des Internationalen Arbeitskreises für deutsche

Barockliteratur in der Herzog August Bibliothek Wolfenbüttel 28. bis 31. August 1976. Vorträge und Referate. Martin Bircher and Eberhard Mannack, eds. Hamburg: Hauswedell, 1977, pp. 72-115.

———. "Die Übersetzung als Rezeptionsdokument: Vondel in Deutschland— Gryphius in Holland." *Michigan Germanic Studies*, 4 (1978), 131-64.

Verhofstadt, Edward. "Vondel und Gryphius: Versuch einer literarischen Topographie," *Neophilologus*, 53 (1969), 290-99.

Vondel. *Poëzy of verscheide Gedichten*. Leewarden: Gybert Sybes, 1651, p. 5.

Weevers, Th. "The Influence of Heinsius on Two Genres of the German Baroque," *Journal of English and Germanic Philology*, 37 (1938), 524, 531.

11

Excursus:
German Baroque Literature
in Colonial America

Christoph E. Schweitzer

Any sketch of baroque aspects in German literary works produced in Colonial America is necessarily preliminary, since relatively few literary scholars have devoted their attention to these works. We have no reliable editions of any of the writings, some of which exist in manuscript form only. In the case of published works we must rely on the very rare originals or on their copies made available through the Readex Microprint edition of Early American Imprints published by the American Antiquarian Society. Only some of the poetry has been reprinted in anthologies. Since few readers will have the material readily at hand, the sources will be quoted here somewhat more extensively than would normally be the case.

The majority of studies dealing with early German-American authors approach them as being important from a religious, historical, sociological, or musicological—but not from a literary—point of view. This is not surprising. The various documents from these authors furnish valuable insights into the life and concerns of the large and active German-speaking community of Colonial America. Nor is it surprising that the religious aspect has been stressed at the expense of the literary: early German-American authors, as we shall see, wrote primarily for a religious purpose; at the same time, though, they intended to persuade others and thus used literary devices. These devices justify the present study of early German-American works.

It seems best to concentrate on a few names and focus on those aspects of literature that belong to the baroque tradition. However, it cannot be stressed enough that the number of persons, male and female, publishing in German during the Colonial period was very high. In John J. Stoudt's representative anthology there are some seventy authors, most of whom expressed themselves in hymns.[1] A few typical examples from the large number produced will be discussed.

It is only proper to begin with Francis Daniel Pastorius (1651–1719), the son of Melchior Adam Pastorius. Father and son were respected jurists with wide-ranging interests, including that of literature. Francis Daniel, who had come under the influence of the great pietist Philipp Jakob Spener, heard of the plans of the so-called German (or Frankfurt) Company to purchase land in Pennsylvania. These plans were the result of William Penn's missionary activities in Germany, where he impressed many with his humanitarian views. Pastorius was made agent of the company and arrived in Philadelphia in 1683, where he was greeted by Penn, with whom he remained on good terms. In the same year German-town — which since 1854 has been part of the city of Philadelphia — was founded, and Pastorius became the natural leader of the rapidly increasing number of Germans who settled here. With minor exceptions, Philadelphia, Germantown, and, a little later, Ephrata, Pennsylvania, were the places where books and pamphlets in German were published up until the War of Independence and from which they were distributed after the war — in addition to those imported from Germany — over the ever-widening territory settled by successive waves of immigrants.

Pastorius, like so many emigrants after him, left his native country, as he said, "to lead a quiet, godly & honest life in a howling wilderness, (which J observed to be a heavy Task for any to perform among the bad examples & numberless Vanitates Vanitatum in Europe)."[2] In contrast to many of his fellow emigrants, however, he did not belong to any of the many radical pietistic sects. In America Pastorius was attracted to the Society of Friends.

The part of his work that is of interest to us has been published only in very fragmentary form. Pastorius amassed voluminous excerpts from authors in many languages from antiquity on. He then grouped these excerpts thematically, added, if appropriate, a translation-adaptation of his own (into German and English primarily), and left the most important encyclopedic manuscript (called the *Bee-Hive*) to his two sons, who, as he realized, would not have the benefit of his continental education. However, he also made other collections, such as the *Deliciae Hortenses*, in which we find the following verse:

> Füglich und klüglich hat's Jener bedacht
> Und alles nach Unserer Meynung gemacht,
> Der seinen Lustgarten dermassen auffputzte,
> Das solcher ergetzte, und ebenfalls nutzte.[3]

Here we have the well-known Horatian formula, encountered so frequently in baroque literature, applied by Pastorius to God's creation, which is called both beautiful and useful. It is in keeping with his other work that Pastorius sees God in rather human terms and that the garden is the place where His benevolence manifests itself. If the transcription is correct, the basic dactylic meter shows an unstressed first syllable in all but the first line. Such verses remind one, of course, of the epigrammatic art of a Logau. The similarity between the two authors will also be clearly seen in the following poem by Pastorius:

> Zur Zeit der Anno 1692 in Pennsilvanien entstandenen Trennung
>
> Iedes schonet seiner Art,
> Tÿger, Wolf u. Leopard
> Eÿ wie komts dañ dasz ein Christ /
> Wider seines Gleichen ist?
> Da ihm doch sein Herr gebeüt
> Liebe, Fried u. Einigkeit. Joh. 13:34. /[4]

As Logau addressed himself to the unseemly religious strife among supposed Christians during and after the Thirty Years War, so also did Pastorius when there was religious division in his adopted country. To drive home his point, Pastorius here contrasts war between humans and the tolerance shown to members of the same species in nature, even among the most ferocious animals. The pithiness of the epigram, however, is lessened by the addition of the two last lines referring to Christ's command, which convey a similar message.

Pastorius's most famous literary product is his poem against slavery, probably written in 1688:

> Allermaßen ungebührlich
> Ist der Handel dieser Zeit,
> Daß ein Mensch so unnatürlich
> Andre drückt mit Dienstbarkeit.
> Ich möcht einen solchen fragen,

Ob er wohl ein Sklav möcht sein?
Ohne Zweifel wird er sagen:
Ach bewahr mich Gott! Nein, Nein![5]

The epigrammatic tradition and Pastorius's humanitarian attitude are felicitously combined in the plea. Like many of his fellow immigrants, Pastorius seems to have been especially sensitive to the basic injustice of slavery. After all, he belonged to a minority, too.

Only a small part of Pastorius's poetry has yet been published; thus, an evaluation must be tentative. His strength lies in an epigrammatic quality reminiscent of Logau, whom he resembles also in training and career as well as in anticourtly tendencies. Pastorius goes beyond the baroque in his poems on flowers and apiary matters, poems that, with their inclusion of accurate detail, point forward to Brockes rather than to any of Pastorius's sources. Such attention to detail is in keeping with his regret for having wasted "precious time, spent in learning Sperling's Physic, Metaphysic and other unnecessary sophistical argumentations," rather than in "engineering and printing."[6] Clearly, the urgent daily demands of the struggling Germantown community are reflected in these remarks.

Many of Pastorius's literary efforts are obviously not in final form for publication. The epigrams, for instance, in contrast to those of Logau and other baroque practitioners of the genre, usually lack a title, which shows that Pastorius stopped short of giving many of his verses the polish required for artistic perfection. He might also have felt unsure about the poetry's fate among his fellow immigrants in the New World: their orientation was strictly religious when it came to books, and thus they would have had little appreciation for verses other than hymns. Pastorius was ahead of his time as far as the German-Americans were concerned.

Johannes Kelpius (1673–1708), who was born in Siebenbürgen (Transylvania), and had studied theology at various universities, joined a group of about forty people who decided to await the millennium and the Second Coming of Christ in the New World. They arrived in America in 1694 after a stay in London, where they had established contacts with members of the Philadelphian Society. For a very brief time Kelpius was an agent of the German Company, but nothing could have been further from his mind than business affairs. He became a hermit on the banks of the Wissahickon, between Philadelphia and Germantown, where he meditated, prayed, studied, taught, and wrote. From this period he left in manuscript form a journal, a beautiful introduction to prayer, and, most important to our present study, a number of hymns. The hymn manuscript contains twelve compositions, their tunes, and an English translation.[7] Only a few of the hymns have ever been published.

The explanatory notes, title, summary, and first stanza of one of the hymns will best illustrate the nature of Kelpius's art:

1706 im maÿ

Als ich in Christian   Ein Verliebtes Girren der   *oder:*
Warners Hauße in einem   Trostlosen Seele   *von des Willens*
Engen Bette einem   Jn der Morgen Demmerung   *auff und absteig*
Sarg nicht ungleich   *und stille*
geschwächet darnieder   *stehen.*
lag.

[Melody]

Jnnhalt:
Die Seele begehret die Früchte der Eh
Doch da sie Sich kehret zu frühe zur Höh'
Entweichet der Bräutigam und läst sie allein
Sie wünschet vollkommen gelaßen zu sein
So findet man endlich das Seelige ein—
1.
Hier lieg ich geschmieget
erkränket im Schrein
fast gäntzlich besieget
von süßester Pein
Jch denke des blühenden lieblichen Maÿn
allwo mich der schönste wird Ewig erfreu'n
Und diese zerbrechliche Hütte verneu'n.[8]

The exact indication of the origin of the hymn—from a time when the Warners had taken the sick Kelpius into their home in German-town—suggests that the manuscript was not meant for publication. The title is reminiscent of those found in the poetry of Friedrich Spee, Johann Scheffler (Angelus Silesius), and Christian Knorr von Rosenroth among others.[9] The tradition of the soul's longing for the friend, the bride-groom, goes back to the Song of Songs. It is well known that biblical language and imagery was often taken over by hymnists, especially those inclined toward pietism and mysticism. Since these are tendencies that brought many religious dissidents to America, the frequent use of erotic language found in the German-American hymns comes as no surprise.

In Kelpius's hymn, the friend of the Song of Songs is interpreted as Christ, the bridegroom whom—according to the *Jnnhalt* above—the soul has desired too anxiously. As a consequence, Christ leaves the soul until it has found perfect peace and blessed oneness, two key concepts found in all mystical literature. Because of this abandonment by the beloved, the sick "I" of the hymn goes back and forth between the awareness of pain and disconsolation, on the one hand, and the love of Christ and the anticipation of a union with Him, on the other. Coupled with the effusion of these sentiments—there are twenty-five stanzas[10]— there is the realization that only through the death of one's own volition, and the simultaneous surrendering of that volition to Christ's, can the rebirth, the new existence, occur. The four short initial lines, with their alternating feminine and masculine rhymes, serve the urgency of the questioning and pleading voice of the speaker. The three longer, con- cluding dactylic lines, connected by masculine rhymes, give something like an answer to the pleading voice by referring to the joys of the new life to come.

The last hymn in Kelpius's manuscript has no title in the German version, but "The Best Choice" is the title found in the English trans- lation. It begins "Ich liebe Jesus nur allein / Den Bräut'gam deiner / meiner Seelen" ("deiner" and "meiner" are juxtaposed vertically). The final stanzas read:

6.

Die Magnet-Nadel irre geht
Wenn sie vom Pol verrücket
auch gar nicht ehe stille stehet
biß der sie zu sich zücket
  und weil mein Herz
  dein Liebes Kertz
berührt mit ihren Flammen
drum eilen sie zusammen.

7.

Und ob du schon gleich dem Nord-Stern
Jm Himmel wohnest droben
und ich auff Erden walle fern
Folg' ich doch unverschoben
  dir meinem licht
  mein angesicht
Will sich nur zu dir wenden
an allen Orth und Enden.

8.

Abwesend hör ich deine Stimm
wenn mein hertz zu dir fähret
und ich hinwiederum vernim̃
waß mich dein Mund da lehret.
   drum ob du schon
   Jns himmels thron
So weit bist abgelegen
bistu mir doch zugegen.

9.

Die Nadel ihre Krafft verliehrt
So daß sie stille stehet
wenn sie mit Fetten wird beschmirt
und dem Stern nicht nachgehet
   drum Soll mich nicht
   Kein ander Licht
Nach Liebe mehr berühren
Nur deine Soll mich führen.[11]

Again, the number of stresses varies from line to line, as do the rhyme patterns, to give the hymn a dynamic quality that agrees with the urgency of the longing. Concepts such as that of the distant Christ who is nevertheless accessible to the speaker's heart and terms like *zu sich zücket*, *Liebes Kertz*, and *Flammen* are all familiar to students of pietistic and mystical writing. Of special interest is the comparison of the soul to the compass needle and Christ to the North Star, an analogy also found in European emblematic literature.[12] Kelpius effectively relates the initial wavering of the needle to a person's restless erring, and the constant orientation of the needle toward the distant North Star to the speaker's vow to turn toward Christ's light. Passing over the weak eighth stanza, we see a reaffirmation of the vow in the last stanza: as the needle covered with grease will stop searching for the North Star, so will earthly love prostrate the human being, impeding the pursuit of Christ's love.

The theme of condemning matrimony and, at the same time, longing for Sophia, from whom humans were separated by the Fall, is common to Kelpius and to the most important and prolific German-American literary figure of Colonial time, Conrad Beissel (1691–1768).[13] As a matter of fact, Beissel had originally hoped to join Kelpius in his monastic retreat on the Wissahickon, but finding upon his arrival in Germantown that Kelpius had died and the remainder of the group had dispersed, Beissel ultimately set out to found his own Christian commune of celibates.

In contrast to Pastorius and Kelpius, Beissel came from a poor family (in Eberbach on the Neckar). As a young man he liked to play the fiddle and was apprenticed to become a baker, a trade he excelled in. However, while still young he was "awakened" to devote himself to God and to search unceasingly for a pure Christian life. He was persecuted for his interest in a variety of radical pietistic sects and emigrated to Germantown in 1720, where he joined the Dunkers. Insistence on his own interpretation of various religious tenets made him seek the solitary life in what he called Ephrata, about sixty miles west of the City of Brotherly Love. Soon other Germans joined him to form a community that reached about three hundred persons at its peak. When Beissel died the community rapidly declined and finally dissolved.

The fascinating story of Ephrata, where Beissel tried to inspire his followers to imitate the life of the early Christians, can only be touched on here. The brothers and sisters were remarkably industrious: they built their own dwellings, some of which are still standing, raised crops, and printed books with their own paper. Equally impressive are the many beautifully illuminated manuscripts, the music Beissel composed and had performed with the help of various choirs, and the religious treatises and hymns he and other members of the community wrote. These are truly outstanding achievements, especially when one considers that the community received no outside help and had to start from scratch. Although the remarks here are limited to Beissel's literary efforts and their baroque roots, it must be stressed that the writings of other members of the Ephrata experiment share similar qualities and also merit attention. However, Beissel clearly set the tone and was the most productive of the group.

One of Beissel's earliest publications contains prose sayings that cry out for versification, as can be seen in the following example:

> Weit ist der gereisst, der nahe bey ihm selber ist,
> hoch ist der gestiegen, der allezeit in der tiefen wandelt.[14]

From this use of two representative baroque devices — antithesis and paradox — it is but a small step to the Alexandrine couplet in the manner of Angelus Silesius. It is instructive to compare a couplet from Silesius's *Cherubinischer Wandersmann* with one by Beissel, taken from the section entitled "Poetische Gedichte" in his next publication; both couplets are based on Matthew 18, 3:

> Du must zum Kinde werden.

> Mensch wirstu nicht ein Kind, so gehstu nimmer ein,
> Wo GOttes Kinder seynd: die Thür ist gar zu klein.[15]

Beissel, using similar metaphorical language, writes:

> Die Himmels thür ist klein, wilt du dardurch eingehen
> Must du ein kindlein sein, sonst bleibst du drausen stehen.[16]

Angelus Silesius gives the solution, which is the reason for making his assertion, in the last half of the second line and thus brings the couplet to a satisfactory conclusion. Beissel, less felicitously, ends with the negative consequence for the person who is not childlike. Otherwise both poets effectively use smallness as the common denominator for the child and the gate to heaven.

There are definite similarities also between the following two couplets. In the *Cherubinische Wandersmann* we read:

> Die Babel.

> Du bist die Babel selbst: gehst du nicht auß dir auß,
> So bleibstu ewiglich deß Teufels Polter-Hauß.[17]

And in the "Poetische Gedichte":

> Wer Gott geniesen will, geh von sich selber aus,
> So wird das hertz bereit, zu Gottes Tempel-Hauss.[18]

Here Beissel stresses the good that results from the loss of personal identity, while Angelus Silesius dwells on the negative consequences of self-centered existence. Whereas the latter ends the couplet with the vivid expression "deß Teufels Polter-Hauß," Beissel resorts to the somewhat redundant "Gottes Tempel-Hauss."

Many other strikingly similar couplets could be cited from the two collections. Beissel belongs to the long mystical tradition that found such a seminal spokesman in Jakob Böhme and such perfect artistic expression in the *Cherubinische Wandersmann*. In the following verses, from the middle of a prose passage of a later date, Beissel tries to describe the miracle of *unio mystica*:

> O Wunder! was ist das? GOtt hat verlassen Sich,
> Geht selber von Sich aus, und ziehet ein in mich:
> Halt ich nun gleichen Preiß, und thu verlassen mich,
> So geb ich Jhm so vil, als Er mir gibt aus Sich.[19]

The mystic union is described here in terms of correspondences between the actions of God and the speaker. The repetitive rhyme scheme felicitously reinforces the statement by making the first and last rhyme words refer to God, who holds man in an "embrace." Most astonishing, though, are the two lines that are separated from the ones just quoted by three dots placed at the two sides and in the middle:

> Die Lib hats schwerst Gewicht, sie ziehet mich in GOtt
> Und was noch groeser ist, sie reisset GOtt in Tod.

These lines are identical with couplet II, 2 of the *Cherubinische Wandersmann*, omitting only Silesius's title and the beginning (both "Die Lieb ist ein Magnet"). One can only conclude that Beissel must have known the famous work by Angelus Silesius, a work that has had such an impressive history in many parts of the world.

Beissel's mystical sayings were published only once during his lifetime. His hymns, on the other hand, were reprinted from collection to collection and obviously were used extensively in the many and long daily services at Ephrata. Hymns have to respond to the sentiments of a group of people; since they are sung, the individual word often carries less weight than in a poem. Hymns also tend to be repetitive: the community of believers wants to be led into a given emotional state which they are ready to maintain—through the music and the words—for a period of time. Extreme in this respect are the *Bruder-Lied* and the *Schwester-Lied* of over two hundred stanzas each in the 1766 *Paradisisches Wunder-Spiel*. Clearly, such compositions have only marginal literary value, yet German religious writings, especially in the form of hymns and spanning the period from Luther to the late baroque, exerted considerable influence all over the world in German-speaking communities and—through translations—beyond these boundaries. They deserve our attention.

Ephrata hymnals follow tradition in usually not identifying authorship. The strong-willed Beissel, however, is identified as the author more often than any of the other contributors to the many collections. He is caught here in the dilemma, typical for many baroque authors, of a desire for anonymity and pride of individual accomplishment. One of his many hymns takes up the *Adjeu Welt* theme that can be found in a variety of baroque works:

> [1.] GUTe nacht, O welt!
> Du bist mir verstellt,
> Meine lust u. mein Vergnügen,
> Kan mit dir sich nicht mehr fügen,
> Bleib mir nur verstellt,
> Ich habs so erwählt.[20]

The condemnation of the world as one of appearance and deceit in the following stanzas repeats what has been said by other authors before, but Beissel usually does not end his hymns on a negative note; here, too, he turns from the deceptive world to the joys of a life with God. His quietist and mystic tendencies, his goal of divesting himself of the I and of absorbing the divine come out clearly in the last two stanzas:

> 15. Ich will sonst nichts thun,
> Als alleine ruh'n,
> Herr! in deinem raht und willen,
> Daß du selber kanst erfüllen,
> Was noch ist zu thun,
> Las mich in dir ruhn.

> 16. So werd ich wohl dein,
> Und du bleiben mein,
> Wenn nichts mehr in mir von allen,
> Als was Dir nur kan gefallen:
> Werde ich wol dein,
> Und du bleiben mein.

The proximity of the thoughts expressed here to Angelus Silesius, Gottfried Arnold, Gerhard Tersteegen, and similar authors is evident. The hymn is, however, of special interest because of its peculiar structure. While lines 3 and 4 regularly end with feminine rhymes, the remaining four lines are always masculine and often repeat the same rhyme words. Lines 1 and 2 contain an assertion that is elaborated in the following two; the ending brings the triumphant conclusion. Such an intricate pattern of rhymes, rhythm, and thought—carried out over sixteen stanzas—is ample proof that Beissel was an author who was well aware of the importance of form.

Many of the sects had their own hymn writers, each following subject matters for which European parallels can be found. While the Moravian settlers wrote hymns that differed little from what was written on the continent, Nikolaus Ludwig von Zinzendorf's extempore creations from Indian campsites use various native geographical and tribal names with curious effect. Here is the first stanza of one of his lengthy narratives:

> Wajomik im Nov. 1742.

> WIr dachten an den hirten-treu /
>   des Jesuah Jehovah
> in der betrübten wüsteney.
>   mit namen Skehantowa.[21]

From what we could gather, there is not much of additional literary interest in the various collections of hymns and some occasional poetry of the period. One exception should be noted. In 1739 Hans Lucas Falckeisen, a Schwenkfelder from Basel, wrote the following poem in Pennsylvania:

Das zehnde Lied welches er in pennsÿlvanien erst gemachet. auf eine englische Melodie.

Höchstes Guth, ewiges wesen erschein,
O laß dein wunder-Krafft und macht gantz aus,

allgenugsamer Gott, $\begin{Bmatrix} \text{schenck} \\ \text{schütt} \end{Bmatrix}$ aus, dein wein,

Tisch auf und öffne dein Herrlichkeits Haus,
Ach komm, ja koe doch, es ist höchst zeit,
O eile doch mein Gott, ich bin bereit
dich schleunigst einzuholen in dem Schmuck,
und im Geleit, derer, so mit mir im Druck.

Krieg, Hunger, Pestilentz, Todt, Höll, verschling,
das schalckhafft, wiederstehend, trotzig Heer.

Donner, Blitz, Hagel, Feür, $\begin{Bmatrix} \text{freß} \\ \text{reis} \end{Bmatrix}$ auß bezwing,

all gifft und gifft: fähigs im gschöpff, Erd, meer.
Öffne die Tieffe! und zerspreng den Pfull!*
Stürtzs Thier und d'Hur hinnein! saͤbts Trachen Stuhl,**
Ihr Element zerschmeltzt Himmel vergeh!
Daß kein alte Spuhr sich jemahls mehr seh!

Allgegenwärtiges Wesen! O! Geist!
der Aug, Ohr, Hertz, Seel, Sinn, durchprüfft und kennt!
Überall zugleich ist, = sieht = würckt = alls weist!
ja alle Geister selbst mit nahmen nennt!
Entdeck wo was und wer du bist! durchs Sein!
O! offenbahr allso dich eins allein!

Da alls zu $\begin{Bmatrix} \text{Licht} \\ \text{geist} \end{Bmatrix}$ und $\begin{Bmatrix} \text{Recht} \\ \text{gott} \end{Bmatrix}$ gebohren ist.

selbst sieht, fühlt, kennt wo was und wer du bist.[22]

Almost all the hymns we have seen have shown a melodious flow of words and thoughts. In fact, the syntax of these hymns followed melodic pat-

---

*Cesspool
**Dragon's perch

terns and repetitive phrasing that tended to deemphasize the importance of the individual word. Falckeisen's verses are completely different. Their difficult, even awkward rhythm — basically iambic pentameter, with masculine rhymes throughout — make the reference to an "English melody" seem rather farfetched. Each word is given emphasis; some of the lines resemble the heaping of nouns found in a Gryphius poem.

The structure of Falckeisen's *Lied* is clear: the speaker begins with an urgent call for God's coming. In the second stanza he pleads with God to destroy completely all negative forces of this world. Falckeisen has a most impressive list of both God's powerful means and the incarnations of evil that are to be annihilated by those means. In the concluding stanza God's omniscience is affirmed, and again, intensifying the initial plea, God is asked to reveal Himself as the one and only to human eyes, feeling, and knowledge as to His location, essence, and identity. Too little is known about Falckeisen to assess his significance accurately; the above poem is certainly a unique product within the corpus of Colonial German-American literature.

The New World not only made it possible for the various sects to establish their ideal communities where one could live a life of complete religious commitment, it also offered opportunities that proved too strong an enticement for many to lead such a life. There was no longer governmental persecution that had united the faithful in their homeland. Religious concerns became less and less important and religious writing less interesting. The political issues connected with the War of Independence pressed themselves onto the German population, too. With that the baroque theme of a Christian utopia no longer inspired craftsmen or authors in the same all-encompassing manner it had some of the early German-American immigrants.

NOTES

1. *Pennsylvania German Poetry, 1685–1830*, ed. John Joseph Stoudt (Allentown, Pa.: Schlechter's, 1956).

2. Marion Dexter Learned, *The Life of Francis Daniel Pastorius, the Founder of Germantown* (Philadelphia: Campbell, 1908), p. 110.

3. Heinrich Arnim Rattermann, ed., *Deutsch-Amerikanische Dichter und Dichtungen des 17ten und 18ten Jahrhunderts* (German-American Historical Society of Illinois, 1915), p. 13.

4. Marion Dexter Learned, "From Pastorius' Bee-Hive or Bee-Stock,"

Americana Germanica, 1, No. 4 (1897), 107. Pastorius's English version is found on p. 109 of the article.

5. Rattermann, p. 18.

6. Learned, *The Life of Francis Daniel Pastorius*, p. 187.

7. Kelpius's manuscript has been reproduced in *Church Music and Musical Life in Pennsylvania in the Eighteenth Century*, I (Philadelphia: Pennsylvania Society of the Colonial Dames of America, 1926), 19–165.

8. *Church Music*, pp. 138 ff. Both Rattermann, pp. 24 ff., and Stoudt, pp. 7 ff., print Kelpius's hymn; however, both transcriptions are rather inaccurate. The matter of capitalization is, among other problems, a difficult one to solve.

9. It has been pointed out that there is a close resemblance between the hymns of Kelpius and those found in Christian Knorr von Rosenroth's *Neuer Helicon* (1684); see, for instance, Julius Friedrich Sachse, *The German Pietists of Provincial Pennsylvania, 1694–1708* (Philadelphia, 1895), p. 235. The initial four lines of the first stanza of aria 18 in the *Neue Helicon*, as well as the meter and rhyme scheme of the entire stanza, seem indeed to have served as the model for Kelpius's hymn of May 1706. Many other specific parallels between the poetry of the two men exist.

10. One hymn in the manuscript has 136 stanzas of four rhymed Alexandrines each.

11. *Church Music*, pp. 160 ff. See also Rattermann, pp. 28 ff., and Stoudt, pp. 12 f.

12. See Arthur Henkel and Albrecht Schöne, eds., *Emblemata: Handbuch zur Sinnbildkunst des XVI. und XVII. Jahrhunderts* (Stuttgart: Metzler, 1967), pp. 82 f. and 1471 ff.

13. On Beissel see Guy T. Hollyday and Christoph E. Schweitzer, "The Present Status of Conrad Beissel/Ephrata Research," *Monatshefte*, 68 (1976), 171–78. To this should be added Dennis McCort, "Johann Conrad Beissel, Colonial Mystic Poet," *German-American Studies*, 8 (1974), 1–26. McCord also points to the parallels between the *Cherubinische Wandersmann* and verses by Beissel, without, however, noticing the identical wording to which I refer below. It should be noted that Beissel shares with Gottfried Arnold not only the cult of Sophia but also his admiration for Angelus Silesius. It is difficult, if not impossible, to sort out exact relationships here.

14. Conrad Beissel, *Mystische Und sehr geheyme Sprueche* (Philadelphia: Benjamin Franklin, 1730), p. 6. These prose sayings were first printed in 1728, but no copy of the book has been found. In 1730 a section entitled "Poetische Gedichte" was added.

15. Angelus Silesius, *Cherubinischer Wandersmann*, ed. Georg Ellinger (Halle: Niemeyer, 1895), I, 153.

16. *Mystische Und sehr geheyme Sprueche*, p. 19.

17. Angelus Silesius, I, 226.

18. *Mystische Und sehr geheyme Sprueche*, p. 15.
19. Conrad Beissel, *Urstaendliche und Erfahrungs-volle Hohe Zeugnuesse* (Ephrata, 1745), p. 51.
20. Beissel's hymn is found first in *JACOBS Kampff- und Ritter-Platz* (Philadelphia: Benjamin Franklin, 1736), pp. 38 f. In the original there is no line separation.
21. Zinzendorf's poem is in *Das Gesang-Buch der Gemeine in Herrn-Huth* [Supplement to the *Gesang-Buch*] XI–XII [1742], p. 1766 (Faber du Faur, no. 1481); also Stoudt, p. 100. In the original there is no line separation.
22. The manuscript is entitled "Hanß Lucas Falckeißen von Basel seine Lieder" and is at the Schwenkfelder Library, Pennsburg, Pennsylvania. I am grateful to the Library for permission to publish the poem. In the original there is no line separation; again, capitalization is a problem that cannot be resolved completely. Stoudt's transcription, p. 92, is very inaccurate.

SELECTED BIBLIOGRAPHY

Primary Sources

Angelus Silesius. *Cherubinischer Wandersmann* (1657; Book VI according to the 2nd ed. of 1675). Georg Ellinger, ed. Neudrucke der deutschen Literatur des 16. und 17. Jahrhunderts, 135–138. Halle: Niemeyer, 1895.
[Beissel, Conrad.] *Mystische Und sehr geheyme Sprueche*. Philadelphia: Benjamin Franklin, 1730. (Early American Imprints, No. 3252.)
[——.] *Urstaendliche und Erfahrungs-volle Hohe Zeugnuesse*. Ephrata, 1745. (Early American Imprints, No. 5538).
Church Music and Musical Life in Pennsylvania in the Eighteenth Century. Vol. I. Publications of the Pennsylvania Society of the Colonial Dames of America, 4. Philadelphia: Printed for the Society, 1926.
[Ephrata Publication.] *JACOBS Kampff- und Ritter-Platz*. Philadelphia: Benjamin Franklin, 1736. (Early American Imprints, No. 3986).
Falckeisen, Hans Lucas von. Manuscript of his poems at the Schwenkfelder Library, Pennsburg, Pennsylvania.
Das Gesang-Buch der Gemeine in Herrn-Huth (Supplement to the *Gesang-Buch*) XI-XII, 1742, p. 1766 (Faber du Faur, No. 1481).
Rattermann, Heinrich Arnim, ed. *Deutsch-Amerikanische Dichter und Dichtungen des 17ten und 18ten Jahrhunderts: Eine Anthologie*. Sonderabdruck aus dem *Jahrbuch der Deutsch-Amerikanischen Historischen Gesellschaft von Illinois*, Jahrgang 1914, Copyright 1915: German-American Historical Society of Illinois.
Stoudt, John Joseph, ed. *Pennsylvania German Poetry, 1685–1830*. The Pennsylvania German Folklore Society, 20 (1955). Allentown, Pa.: Schlechter's, 1956.

Secondary Literature

Henkel, Arthur, and Albrecht Schöne, eds. *Emblemata: Handbuch zur Sinn-bildkunst des XVI. und XVII. Jahrhunderts.* Stuttgart: Metzler, 1967, pp. 82 f and 1471 ff.

Hollyday, Guy T., and Christoph E. Schweitzer. "The Present Status of Conrad Beissel/Ephrata Research." *Monatshefte*, 68 (1976), 171-78.

Lashlee, Ernest L. "Johannes Kelpius and His Woman in the Wilderness: A Chapter in the History of Colonial Pennsylvania Religious Thought." In *Glaube, Geist, Geschichte: Festschrift für Ernst Benz zum 60. Geburstage am 17. November 1967*, Gerhard Müller and Wienfried Zeller, eds. Leiden: Brill, 1967, pp. 327-38.

Learned, Marion Dexter. "From Pastorius' Bee-Hive or Bee-Stock." *Americana Germanica*, 1, No. 4 (1897), 67-110; continued in 2 (1898), No. 1, 33-42; No. 2, 59-70; No. 4, 65-79.

——. *The Life of Francis Daniel Pastorius, the Founder of Germantown; Illustrated with Ninety Photographic Reproductions; With an Appreciation of Pastorius by Samuel Whitaker Pennypacker.* Philadelphia: Campbell, 1908.

McCort, Dennis. "Johann Conrad Beissel, Colonial Mystic Poet." *German-American Studies*, 8 (1974), 1-26; rpt. in *German-American Literature*, Don Heinrich Tolzmann, ed., pp. 108-27. (see below).

Sachse, Julius Friedrich. *The German Pietists of Provincial Pennsylvania, 1694-1708.* Philadelphia, 1895; rpt. New York: AMS Press, 1970.

——. *The German Sectarians of Pennsylvania, 1708-1742: A Critical and Legendary History of the Ephrata Cloister and the Dunkers.* 2 vols. Philadelphia, 1899 and 1900; rpt. New York: AMS Press, 1971.

Seidensticker, Oswald. *Bilder aus der Deutsch-pennsylvanischen Geschichte.* Vol. II of *Geschichtsblätter: Bilder and Mittheilungen aus dem Leben der Deutschen in Amerika*, Carl Schurz, ed. New York: Steiger, 1885.

Stoeffler, F. Ernest, ed. *Continental Pietism and Early American Christianity.* Grand Rapids, Mich.: William B. Eerdmans, 1976.

Stoudt, John Joseph. "Pennsylvania German Poetry Until 1816: A Survey." *German Life and Letters*, 13 (1960), 145-53; rpt. in *German-American Literature*, Don Heinrich Tolzmann, ed., pp. 8-17.

Tolzmann, Don Heinrich, ed. *German-American Literature.* Metuchen, N.J. The Scarecrow Press, 1977.

III

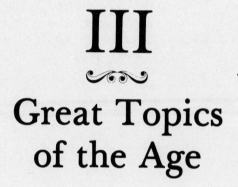

Great Topics
of the Age

12

Love: From Petrarchism to Eroticism

Hans Wagener

In chapter 3 of his *Buch von der Deutschen Poeterey* Martin Opitz scorns all those poets of classical antiquity, "die jhre reine sprache mit garstigen epicurischen schrifften besudelt / vnd sich an jhrer eigenen schande erlustiget haben. Mit denen wir aber vmbgehen mußen wie die bienen / welche jhr honig auß den gesunden blumen saugen / vnd die gifftigen Kraeuter stehen lassen." And he continues:

Doch wie ehrliche / auffrichtige / keusche gemüter (welche von den auch keuschen Musen erfodert werden) derer die jhre geschickligkeit mit vblen sitten vertunckeln nicht entgelten können / so sind auch nicht alle Poeten die von Liebessachen schreiben zue meiden; denn viel vnter jhnen so züchtig reden / das sie ein jegliches ehrbares frawenzimmer vngeschewet lesen möchte. Man kan jhnen auch deßentwegen wol jhre einbildungen lassen / vnd ein wenig vberse-hen / weil die liebe gleichsam der wetzstein ist an dem sie jhren subtilen Verstand scherffen / vnd niemals mehr sinnreiche gedancken vnd einfälle haben / als wann sie von jhrer Buhlschafften Himlischen schöne / jugend / freundligkeit / haß vnnd gunst reden.[1]

Two things are important in this statement by the legislator of German baroque literature. First, the sanctioning of love as a legitimate topic for serious poets; secondly, the demand of a chaste tone, i.e., the require-ment to treat the delicate subject in such a way that even well-bred women would find it to be suitable reading. There is no doubt that Opitz is extremely defensive and cautious in this statement, since the subject of love had been treated with a great lack of discernment and decency dur-

197

ing the preceding late-medieval and Reformation period. What is not clear in Opitz's words is the discrimination between various kinds of love, which had formed the basis of Renaissance theory and which would easily have solved his dilemma.

In the love theory of the Renaissance, classical and Christian elements are fused,[2] with a clear preponderance of classical views, particularly with reference to Plato. In his commentary on Benivieni's *Canzone de amore* (1485–86), Pico della Mirandola, for example, even goes beyond the traditional differentiation between spiritual and lustful love and discriminates between:

1. celestial love, or love of the angels — which is directed towards spiritual beauty (*bellezza intelligibile*);
2. human or reasonable love (*amore volgare*) — which he defines as a desire for love of the senses through the sense of sight, as a mirror of celestial love; and
3. animalistic love, or sexual desire — which sees beauty only in the body.

This same tripartition is found in Marsilio Ficino's tract on love (published in 1544), which he presents as a commentary on Plato's *Symposion*.

Theories of this kind were not only readily adopted and assimilated by seventeenth-century French society, but also by German theoreticians such as Georg Philipp Harsdörffer, who drew not only on Italian, but particularly on French models of social behavior, which he introduced to Germany. He, too, distinguishes between three kinds of love:

1. angelic love — which is only directed towards the mind of the other person;
2. animalistic love — which is concerned with the other's body only; and
3. human love — which holds the balance between angelic and animalistic desires.[3] This kind of love is consciously controlled by the human will and mind.

Love tempered and controlled by reason (the French called it *l'amour raisonnable*) was the concept which would gain even greater popularity during the second half of the seventeenth century, underlying the forms of polite behavior and moderation.

A tripartition of categories of love such as Harsdörffer's is also found in Balthasar Kindermann's *Deutscher Wohlredner* (1680), testimony not only to the effect of Harsdörffer's success as an importer of Italian and

French ideas, but also to the widespread validity of these ideas in the German-speaking areas.

Recognizing the fact that not all theoreticians and writers of the German baroque were quite as keenly aware of these distinctions as Harsdörffer was, it is yet interesting to note how poets in many cases subscribed to similar categories. These may, therefore, rightfully serve as a guide to characterize and categorize the variegated descriptions of love in the lyric, drama, and prose of the German baroque.

While Opitz's *Buch von der Deutschen Poeterey* (1624) was the theoretical basis of all new poetry, the second edition of his *Teutsche Poemata* (1625) gave the practical examples, mostly in the form of translations. In these translations as well as in his own poetic inventions, Opitz introduced Germany to a kind of love lyric that had dominated European love poetry for three hundred years: petrarchistic poetry, or petrarchism.[4] Petrarchism may be defined as a poetic style that directly or indirectly imitates the poetry of Petrarch. Poetic style here does not only refer to the form of the sonnet; it includes a whole repertoire of typical motifs, metaphors, and rhetorical devices. It also comprises certain relations between the lover and his adored woman, their attitudes and patterns of behavior. Like most other forms of German seventeenth-century literature, petrarchism had flourished in Italy, France, Spain, England, and the Netherlands long before it was introduced to Germany. Before Opitz made it popular, it had in part been adopted by the Neo-Latin poets of the sixteenth century; it had found access to the *Gesellschaftslied* of Regnart and Schallenberg; and it was echoed in Theobald Höck's *Schönes Blumenfeld* (1601) as well as in Georg Rudolf Weckherlin's early poetry.

If abstracted, the erotic situation in petrarchism appears generally as fixed:[5] Man and woman are not on the same level, but so far apart that they cannot possibly be united in love. A consummation of love is not part of petrarchistic poetry. The man is a devoted slave of love, eaten up by fervor, tormented, close to death: he is thus described as lovesick. Having lost his self, his very soul, he is torn between fear and hope, deep melancholy and optimism. He is sighing, crying, and thinking about death as a result of being rejected by the woman. The woman is a gruesome tyrant, who is unpermeable to love. Love is suffering and joy at the same time, with an emphasis on elegiac tones. It is bittersweet, a word that already points to an antithetic, hyperbolic style. In contrast to Petrarch himself, women and love are described in fixed formulae behind which true feeling seems to have been lost. The woman is praised as an incarnation of virtue and of beauty, which is described in ever recurrent metaphors and similes taken from the inanimate world of precious stones and the universe. Mythological elements (particularly references to Cupid and Venus) often provide an appropriate setting. The influence of the French troubadours on Petrarch accounts for the obvious similarities to medieval *Minnesang*.

Opitz as well as his friends and successors subscribed to the literary fashion of petrarchism. According to Hans Pyritz, Paul Fleming in his German love poetry was Germany's foremost seventeenth-century petrarchist.[6] But he has also shown that Fleming went above and beyond this kind of formalized poetry. It is debatable whether or not the young Fleming was a strict petrarchist and whether only the older poet in his more mature work, undertaken under the influence of his journey to Persia, found a new mode of expression; but it is evident that much of his poetry is confessional in character rather than stylized. (Of course, his "confessions" are different from those of young Goethe in that they established types and norms of their own.) It is directed to and fulfills real functions in his correspondence with the sisters Elsabe and (later) Anna Niehus in Reval. More and more personal experience intruded into his poetry. Poems in which he expressed his longing for and in which he woos the beloved girl give reign to the unpetrarchan hope for a positive outcome. Also the motif of faithfulness (*Treue*) becomes important. It gives the poems an intimacy and simple, truly emotional style that goes far beyond the conventions of petrarchism.

It was not until Johann Christian Günther, the late-baroque Silesian individualist, cried out his deeply felt sorrow, disappointment, and hope that such a personal tone was heard again in German lyrical poetry. That Günther, too, still drew heavily on traditional Petrarchan and also petrarchistic forms of expression, must not be forgotten.

Set apart from petrarchism is also Simon Dach, the poet from Königsberg, a city that because of its distance from the cultural centers of the time offered an opportunity for a different kind of poetry. Dach's (and his friends') *Gelegenheitsdichtung* (casual poetry), intended for weddings, funerals, etc., was written in a much simpler, honest folksonglike tone than the poetry of most Silesians.[7]

Following the introduction of petrarchism in Germany by Opitz, there was also a strong current of antipetrarchism,[8] which in a satirical manner poked fun at the conventional style, in poems often written by the petrarchists, such as Opitz and Fleming, themselves. The most in-

teresting poet in this connection is Christian Hofmann von Hofmannswaldau, who used all the traditional petrarchistic means of expression,
but did so in order to describe love *and* its sexual consummation in
mystical terms. Eroticism and sensuality as part of a carpe diem
philosophy have turned petrarchism upside down in poems such as
"Albanie gebrauche deiner zeit." Other Silesian poets of the time, for example, Daniel Casper von Lohenstein, wrote poetry of a similar kind.
The next step to outright tastelessness as found in the poetry of some of
the *gallant* poets was but a small one (see Johann von Besser's poem
"Nicht schäme dich / du saubere Melinde"). Was it escapism from an
overly restrained culture into sexual fantasies? Most likely so.

The role of love in baroque drama can best be exemplified by referring to some plays by the most prominent German dramatists of the age,
Andreas Gryphius and Daniel Casper von Lohenstein. Love is the main
theme in Gryphius's tragedy *Cardenio und Celinde* (published 1657), as
he himself points out in his preface: "Mein Vorsatz ist zweyerley Liebe.
Eine keusche / sitsame vnd doch inbrünstige in *Olympien*: Eine rasende /
tolle vnd verzweifflende in *Celinden*, abzubilden."[9] Cardenio, the title
hero, is blinded by his physical attraction to Celinde and by his desire for
Olympia, whose husband Lysander he plans to murder. Celinde is
desperately trying to keep Cardenio's love; this drives her to follow the
advice of the sorceress Tyche to cut out the heart of her dead former
lover Marcellus in order to regain Cardenio's favor by magical means.
Olympia's love for her husband Lysander is a less passionate one, but it
has grown in time out of mutual respect. Cardenio's love for Olympia
easily turns into hate because of her marrying Lysander, but quickly
reverts to passionate desire when he believes that she is the veiled lady he
is meeting in the street. When the latter reveals herself as the allegorical
counterpart to Amor (a skeleton with bow and arrow), the vanity of his
desires becomes obvious to him.

Certainly, vanity is one of the themes of *Cardenio und Celinde*, as it
is so often in Gryphius's works, but here it is connected with the theme
that people are subject to their drives, their desires, their lust—in short:
their affects. The drama is a defense of reason controlling the affects, an
idea that Gryphius might have adopted from Descartes's *Traité des passions*.[10] Passion can be controlled by reason; love based on physical attraction alone is wrong and cannot last. True love and affection on the
basis of mutual esteem of the other person's qualities is the ideal, a belief
much in line with Harsdörffer's theories.

Gryphius's play, which is based on Italian sources, is set among the
city patriciate. That the same principles apply to both the high society of
the cities and the rural society of peasants he demonstrated in his double
comedy *Verlibtes Gespenste* and *Die Gelibte Dornrose*. Here a similar
situation is given among both societies. In *Verlibtes Gespenste*, Sulpicius
loves Chloris, but her mother Cornelia wants to win him over to herself
with the aid of an aphrodisiac. In *Gelibte Dornrose*, Dornrose loves
Kornblume, but the crude Matz Aschewedel wants to gain her favors
with magical means and finally by force.[11] Again, just as in *Cardenio
und Celinde*, Gryphius presents two kinds of love, love based on mutual
understanding and esteem, and love on the basis of physical desire.

Love and reason — or, more pointedly formulated, eroticism and
politics — are the main theme in Lohenstein's tragedies. His *Sophonisbe*
(1666; first published 1680) may serve as an example, particularly since
the theme was extremely popular among European seventeenth-century
dramatists such as Jean Mairet and Pierre Corneille. The historical
material, as reported by the Roman historian Livy, is an episode from
the Second Punic War (between Rome and Carthage). For Lohenstein
Sophonisbe is the incarnation of sexual energies, whereas Scipio is the
representative of pure reason and political necessity. The hot, passionate
inhabitants of Africa are confronted with the cool, thinking representa-
tives of an expanding world power, Rome. Masanissa is placed in the
middle between Scipio and Sophonisbe. He has to decide between love,
sex, passion, and political reason, and he finally does opt for the latter.

Already in his dedicatory prologue, Lohenstein states:

Die Lust / die man mit Fug auch Marter nennen kan /
Verrücket die Vernunft / verstellet das Gemütte.
Man stellt kein Schauspiel auf / daß nicht die Raserey /
Der Liebe Meisterin / im gantzen Spiele sey.[12]

Ehrsucht (ambition) is added to the negative affects which account for
the downfall of the seemingly powerful. Virtue is the ability to master
one's drives. Says Scipio:

Nun diese Tugend muß auch Masanissa lernen /
Wil er mir ehnlich sein / sein Name bey den Sternen
Im Sinnen-Zirckel stehn. Wer Wollust übermannt /
Thut mehr / als der den Feind an Sieges-Wagen spannt /
Ja zwey drey Syphax zwingt. (IV, 285-89)[13]

Lohenstein sees this virtue of self-control incorporated in the Rome of
this time. In *Agrippina* he shows Nero's downfall in his becoming prey to

his sexual desires. In this drama sex is not just a matter of a personal nature but an instrument of gaining personal political power.[14]

Something that unites Gryphius and Lohenstein is the fact that they both see erotic forces as negative and mastery of oneself with the aid of reason as positive. They both subscribe to the Stoic teachings about the affects, the passions that man has to learn to master by using reason. But whereas Gryphius is also concerned about love in the private world, Lohenstein concentrates on the great political scenes in history in which reason and self-control, in his view, gain the victory over those who are their passions' slaves.

As is generally known, most German discussions of literature in the seventeenth century did not include remarks about the novel. Thus Opitz, for example, just talks about "ein Heroisch getichte," referring to a verse epic, but not a novel.[15] Novels were written about mostly in polemical tracts attacking them. A good example is Gotthard Heidegger's *Mythoscopia Romantica* (1698), a book that, significantly, did not appear until the end of the century. Here novels are attacked for dealing with the theme of love, a topic considered dangerous reading for young women.

Love indeed was considered the most necessary ingredient of a novel. Let us take a look, for example, at Pierre Daniel Huet's *Traité de l'origine des romans* (Paris, 1670), a German translation of which was provided by Eberhard Werner Happel, inserted into his novel *Der Insulanische Mandorell* (Hamburg, 1682). Huet defines novels as "des fictions d'aventures amoureuses, écrites en Prose avec art, pour le plaisir & l'instruction des Lecteurs. Ie dis des fictions, pour les distinguer des Histoires veritables. I'ajouste, d'aventures amoureuses, parce que l'amour doit estre le principal sujet du Roman." And later he adds: "Enfin les Poëmes [epics] ont pur sujet une action militaire ou politique, & ne traittent l'amour que par occasion: les Romans au contraire ont l'amour pour sujet principal, & ne traittent la politique & la guerre que par incident."[16] (. . . fictions of amorous adventures, written in prose with art, for the pleasure and instruction of the readers. I am saying fictions, in order to distinguish them from true stories. I am adding amorous adventures, because love must be the main subject of the novel. . . . Finally the poems [epics] have as their subject matter a military or political action, and they treat love only occasionally: the novels, on the contrary, deal with love as their main subject and they deal with politics and war only incidentally.) Huet, of course, is talking about one kind of novel only, the courtly-historical one, which developed during the first half of the seventeenth century in France with authors such as Marin de Gomberville (*Polexandre*, 1637, and *Carithée*, 1662), Mlle. de Scudéry (*Le Grand Cyre*, 10 vols., 1649-53, and *Clélie*, 10 vols., 1654-60), and the Seigneur de La Calprenède (*Cléopatre*, 12 vols, 1647-58, and *Cassandre*, 10 vols., 1642-50).[17] The novel of amorous adventure became the great fashion during the 1640s and 1650s. German translations and redactions of these and other French novels appeared in rapid succession, soon spurring imitations. Andreas Heinrich Buchholtz's *Herkules und Valiska* (1659-60) and *Herkuliskus und Herkuladisla* (1665), Duke Anton Ulrich of Braunschweig-Wolfenbüttel's *Aramena* (5 vols., 1669-73) and *Octavia* (6 vols., 1677-1707), Daniel Casper von Lohenstein's *Arminius* (1689-90), and Heinrich Anshelm von Zigler und Kliphausen's *Asiatische Banise* (1689) were the most famous and widely read German examples.

Love and politics are closely intertwined in the action of these novels; indeed, love seems to be the ruling force behind politics. Alliances are concluded and wars are made supposedly in the service of the beloved woman rather than as a result of power politics. The plot is patterned after the structural model of the late-Greek *Ethiopiea* by Heliodorus, the basic structural principle being that of unification, separation, and reunification of the lovers. At the beginning of the novel a princely hero falls in love with a heroine of equally high social standing, but their ultimate union is delayed by numerous obstacles. War breaks out or the heroine is abducted and separated from her hero. The hero has to carry his search for her through many countries, but finally succeeds in finding her. In the course of the story she has to defend her chastity and he has to prove his faithfulness many times over. The novel ends in a great celebration, the couple — or, more often, many couples — are united in wedlock.

The way love is depicted in these novels follows from the characters' high social standing and from their model role for contemporary high society. The hero is handsome, strong, and courageous; the heroine has an almost superhuman, angelic beauty, intelligence, and amiability. Noble-mindedness and a kind of behavior which is dictated through accepted rules of good manners are expected traits. Next to magnanimity (i.e., open-mindedness and generosity), constancy is the second great virtue (i.e., equanimity in the face of all dangers and all possible temptations). Love between hero and heroine is not sensual or lustful, but is based solely on mutual worship of the other's supreme qualities of character. Chastity is the ruling force of this kind of love; a kiss is con-

sidered almost sinful. The lovers shower one another with elaborate compliments; compose arias about the depth of their affection; write poems
and love letters, continually assuring one another of their constancy.
Love is merely a touchstone of virtuous behavior. It is not a sexual, erotic
experience, but an ethical element. In the feeling of love, the courtly-
historical novel offers a field for the realization of virtue and thus of
perfection within its world.

This kind of love, no doubt, comes close to Harsdörffer's angelic
love, since the characters are just as unreal and typefied. Reason is
holding all feelings of passion in check. Self-restraint prevents any viola-
tion of the social rules of good behavior. The description of love is not actually the main theme in the novels, but rather the proof of constancy
and genuineness of this love. Having to be superhumanly chaste, the
women are cool or at least reserved. The consummation of love is only
possible in marriage. The social norm determines the lovers' behavior to
such an extent that they can only be presented as types acting in formal
artificiality. Love here is a constructed, contrived game, mirroring the
age's interest in formalized playfulness rather than in individual experiences.[18] The seventeenth century is submitting everything to form
and norm, even love, for which the courtly-historical novel is the best
example.

The picaresque novel is in many respects the opposite of the courtly-
historical one, particularly in its treatment of the theme of love. Just as
the courtly-historical novel paints an ideal picture of the nobility and
escapes into a historical dreamworld, the picaresque novel affords a picture of life among the lower social classes of the present or the recent
past; it does not mirror the entire spectrum of society but rather reveals
its seamy side. From its Spanish origins on, survival was its main theme,
and in order to survive the picaro had to lie, steal, and generally rely on
his wits. Hunger and starvation constantly threatened his physical existence. Therefore, survival, not love, is in the center of attention. Just as
at the end of *Lazarillo de Tormes* the hero's marriage is rather dubious
because of rumors about his wife's past, love in Grimmelshausen's
Simplicissimus and *Courasche* is seldom more than a physical activity.

In short, love in the picaresque novel corresponds closely to
Harsdörffer's second category, which he calls "auf die Schoenheit deß
Leibes absehend / Viehisch." Simplicius, who observes the activities of
young people in Hanau, experiences this kind of love. He practices it
himself as a rich prisoner of war in L., the only exception being his feelings for the girl he is forced to marry at gunpoint. His later enterprises as

a gentleman farmer again conform to the pattern. His escapades as a "prisoner" in the "mountain of Venus" in Paris add a variant insofar as Simplicius now serves as a prostitute to rich ladies. Now love is not only lustful but a means to an end, namely, to make money the easy way. The nature of love remains the same, and this is not different in *Courasche*, where the title heroine is merely using her erotic abilities to climb up or down the social ladder of military charges. Johann Beer's novels by and large do not differ very much from this pattern, at least not in their truly picaresque parts.

The characteristic consequence of the emphasis on physical love in the picaresque novel is the fact that the characters merely report facts. Love is not a subject for discussion; tender feelings do not have to be analyzed because they rarely exist. Lust does not require or call for verbalization, confessions, or compliments. The physical act of love does not necessitate the observance of the rules of social behavior.

The third type of novel that enjoyed great popularity during the seventeenth century is the pastoral novel. It is characterized by a mixture of prose and lyric and by the pastoral mask behind which very often real-life persons, including the poet, were disguised. For the baroque, the pastoral world represented a society free from class divisions, a reborn Arcadia, the idealized Golden Age.

The German examples were again stimulated by earlier foreign models. The Italian Renaissance had already displayed a tremendous interest in pastoral literature, drawing on Vergil's *Eclogues* and Longus's *Daphnis and Chloë*. Boccaccio's *Ninfale d'Ameto* (1341) and Jacopo Sannazaro's *Arcadia* (1502) were soon followed by Jorge de Montemayor's *Diana* (1559) in Spain. Cervantes' *Galatea* (1585) and Lope de Vega's *Arcadia* (1598) followed suit. Sir Philip Sidney's *Arcadia* (1590-93), translated and edited by Martin Opitz in 1638, was, next to Montemayor, probably the most influential foreign model, closely followed by Honoré d'Urfé's *Astrée* (1607-27).

Since the pastoral world was considered an ideal one, "pure" love, often described with a lot of mythological references, was its main theme. It is a love that seems to be totally removed from reality and its problems and vicissitudes, but, in fact, is not. This is the case because in the pastoral novels the poets merely translate their own and their environment's love relations and affairs. Thus, for example, even Martin Opitz's prose eclogue *Schäfferey von der Nimfen Hercinie* (1630) on the one hand creates an idyllic world in the Riesengebirge which contrasts with the actual rage and destruction of the Thirty Years War. On the other hand, the poet tries to come to terms with a personal problem: should he remain at home with a girl he loves or should he undertake a trip to Paris? The conclusion he finally reaches after lengthy discussions with his friends is that whereas sensual love is bound to external beauty, spiritual love is free from time and place. Therefore, it is possible for him to make the trip, particularly since he is undertaking it in the service of the fatherland. Thus, the pastoral merely solves a love problem in a sophistical manner.

In other works the author's love itself constitutes the plot, and it is interesting to note that in most cases the ending is a negative one. Philipp von Zesen's novel *Die Adriatische Rosemund* (1645) is a case in point. At the home of friends in Holland, the young German, Markhold, makes the acquaintance of the beautiful Rosemund from Venice. They want to get married, but Markhold is a Protestant and Rosemund's family is Catholic. Since Markhold insists that prospective offspring be raised as Protestants, the two lovers cannot be united. Rosemund becomes ill and slowly wastes away.

Whether or not Zesen used *Die Adriatische Rosemund* merely to glorify himself as an independent bourgeois poet, or whether Rosemund is merely a symbol of Zesen's faithfulness to his "Deutschgesinnte Genossenschaft," is immaterial in this context. Important is the negative outcome and the fact that Rosemund, realizing the impossibility of being united with Markhold, becomes a shepherdess. Her shepherd's cottage in its symbolic, ideal description becomes a temple of her glorification of Markhold: the shepherd's life becomes an ideal for the complete realization of a love that cannot be realized in the real world. Such a love requires the creation of a world, appropriate to the "celestial Rosemund," of whom Markhold more than once declares himself unworthy. Again we have an angel who is loving, but this time the hero is not in every respect her equal, but instead is an indecisive young man who venerates her, yet does not really love her.

Passion is usually not to be found in the pastoral novels. Love is again tempered by reason. In his *Schäfferey* Opitz had already demanded that reason and love be united, and in some of these pastoral works Harsdörffer's ideal of human love is realized. Perhaps the best example for this kind of love is Johann Thomas's *Damon und Lisille* (1663), a novel that treats, in pastoral disguise, the love, courtship, engagement, wedding, and marriage of Damon and Lisille. Although the novel is told in the third person, the title characters obviously represent the author himself and his wife Elisabeth, who died in childbed after three years of marriage. The style is simple and unpretentious, genuinely felt, cordial, and graceful, without preciosity and bucolic oversweetness. What is new in this novel is the fact that marriage itself, even its everyday routine and problems, is treated. *Damon und Lisille* does not merely idealize love, the beauty of a girl, and her wedding to a handsome shepherd; it deals with the trials this love encounters in daily life and with the difficulties of marriage as well as with its idealized joys. Love has become an individual experience that is more important than social conventions and other recognized standards of the time. It has become part of the bourgeois life, which here is introduced into literature under a very thin pastoral layer.

Trying to write about love in German baroque literature can easily develop into an undertaking equal to writing a history of German seventeenth-century literature. On the other hand, it is easy to see from the examples chosen how, following different foreign influences and traditions, the three main genres have realized similar yet intrinsically different ways of dealing with the theme of love.

NOTES

1. Martin Opitz, *Buch von der Deutschen Poeterey* (1624), ed. Richard Alewyn (Tübingen: Max Niemeyer, 1963), p. 13.

2. See Paul Kluckhohn, *Die Auffassung der Liebe in der Literatur des 18. Jahrhunderts und in der deutschen Romantik* (1922; rpt. Tübingen: Max Niemeyer, 1966), p. 14; Gerhard Wilhelm Stern, *Die Liebe im deutschen Roman des siebzehnten Jahrhunderts*, Germanische Studien, 120 (Berlin: Dr. Emil Ebering, 1932), pp. 34 ff.

3. Georg Philipp Harsdörffer, *Frauenzimmer Gesprächspiele*, ed. Irmgard Böttcher, III, (1643; rpt. Tübingen: Niemeyer, 1968), 127: "V. Ich verstehe die Liebe ins gemein: wie denn wissend / daß selben / den Verstand allein belangend / fŭr Englisch / auf die Schönheit deß Leibes absehend / Viehisch / beedes aber verlangend / Menschlich ist."

4. On petrarchism see Hans Pyritz, *Paul Flemings deutsche Liebeslyrik*, Palaestra, 180 (Leipzig: Mayer & Müller, 1932); Gerhart Hoffmeister, "Barocker Petrarkismus: Wandlungen und Möglichkeiten der Liebessprache in der Lyrik des 17. Jahrhunderts," in *Europäische Tradition und deutscher Literaturbarock*, ed. Gerhart Hoffmeister (Bern and München: Francke, 1973), pp. 37-53; and Gerhart Hoffmeister, *Petrarkistische Lyrik*, Sammlung Metzler, 119 (Stuttgart: Metzler, 1973).

5. See Pyritz, p. 37.
6. Ibid.
7. For a more complete treatment of the variations of and deviations from petrarchism see Hoffmeister, *Petrarkistische Lyrik*, pp. 65 ff.
8. See Jörg-Ulrich Fechner, *Der Antipetrarkismus: Studien zur Liebessatire in barocker Lyrik*, Beiträge zur neueren Literaturgeschichte, Dritte Folge, 2 (Heidelberg: Carl Winter, 1966).
9. Andreas Gryphius, *Gesamtausgabe der deutschsprachigen Werke*, ed. Marian Szyrocki and Hugh Powell, vol. V: *Trauerspiele II*, ed. Hugh Powell (Tübingen: Max Niemeyer, 1965), 100.
10. See Herbert Schöffler, *Deutsches Geistesleben zwischen Reformation und Aufklärung: Von Martin Opitz zu Christian Wolff* (Frankfurt a.M.: Vittorio Klostermann, 1956), pp. 156 f.
11. It is amazing to see that Gryphius has characterized the rural world more vividly and with more warmth and sympathy than he has the educated burghers.
12. Daniel Casper von Lohenstein, *Afrikanische Trauerspiele*, ed. Klaus Günther Just, Bibliothek des Literarischen Vereins in Stuttgart, 294 (Stuttgart: Anton Hiersemann, 1957), p. 247.
13. Ibid., p. 231.
14. Gryphius's Chach Abas in *Catharina von Georgien* could be interpreted along these lines, too.
15. Opitz, p. 17.
16. Pierre Daniel Huet, *Traité de l'origine des romans (1670)*, Sammlung Metzler, 54 (Stuttgart: Metzler, 1966), pp. 4 f. and 7.
17. For the following see Hans Wagener, *The German Baroque Novel*, Twayne's World Authors Series, 229 (New York: Twayne, 1973), pp. 98 ff., 105 f., and 13 ff.
18. See Stern, pp. 153 f.

SELECTED BIBLIOGRAPHY

Secondary Literature

Beckmann, Adelheid. *Motive und Formen der deutschen Lyrik des 17. Jahrhunderts und ihre Entsprechungen in der französischen Lyrik seit Ronsard.* Hermaea, Germanistische Forschungen, N.F., 5. Tübingen: Max Niemeyer, 1960.
Cohn, Egon. *Gesellschaftsideale und Gesellschaftsroman des 17. Jahrhunderts: Studien zur deutschen Bildungsgeschichte.* Germanische Studien, 13. Berlin: Emil Ebering, 1921.
Fechner, Jörg-Ulrich. *Der Antipetrarkismus: Studien zur Liebessatire in*

barocker Lyrik. Beiträge zur neueren Literaturgeschichte, Dritte Folge, 2. Heidelberg: Carl Winter, 1966.

Forster, Leonard W. *The Icy Fire: Five Studies in European Petrarchism.* London: Cambridge University Press, 1969.

Hoffmeister, Gerhart. *Petrarkistische Lyrik.* Sammlung Metzler, 119. Stuttgart: Metzler, 1973.

——. "Barocker Petrarkismus: Wandlungen und Möglichkeiten der Liebessprache in der Lyrik des 17. Jahrhunderts." In *Europäische Tradition und deutscher Literaturbarock: Internationale Beiträge zum Problem von Überlieferung und Umgestaltung.* Gerhart Hoffmeister, ed. Bern and München: Francke, 1973.

Kluckhohn, Paul. *Die Auffassung der Liebe in der Literatur des 18. Jahrhunderts und in der deutschen Romantik,* 1922. Rpt. Tübingen: Max Niemeyer, 1966.

Pyritz, Hans. *Paul Flemings deutsche Liebeslyrik.* Palaestra, 180. Leipzig: Mayer & Müller, 1932.

Rener, Frederick M. "Sweet Imagery in German Baroque Poetry." *South Atlantic Bulletin,* 34, No. 3 (1971), 14-22.

Stern, Wilhelm Gerhard. *Die Liebe im deutschen Roman des siebzehnten Jahrhunderts.* Germanische Studien, 120. Berlin: Dr. Emil Ebering, 1932.

van Ingen, Ferdinand. "Philipp von Zesens 'Adriatische Rosemund': Kunst und Leben." In *Philipp von Zesen, 1619-1689.* F. van Ingen, ed. Wiesbaden: Franz Steiner, 1972, pp. 47-122.

Wagener, Hans. *The German Baroque Novel.* Twayne's World Authors Series, 229. New York: Twayne, 1973.

13

Vanity and Constancy

Giles R. Hoyt

The themes of *vanitas* and *constantia* are without doubt as ancient as man's reflection on himself and his existence, but they became preeminent in seventeenth-century European thought and art when several traditions stressing these themes merged in a climate of religious and social unrest. Renaissance humanism provided the catalyst for the combining of Judeo-Christian and Stoic thought, both of which, although starting from different points of view, find constancy to be the natural antedote to the agonizing conclusion that nothing, no man or nation, is more than a function of a certain time and place.

The biblical tradition is manifest in the words of the Preacher, "Vanity of vanities, . . . vanity of vanities; all is vanity" (Ecclesiastes 1: 2). There is no guarantee that anything lasting will come of man's labors (1: 14), no guarantee that future generations will carry on one's work or even that it will be remembered (1: 11). Man seems no different from beasts and, in spite of his apparent greatness of spirit, may simply perish in unconsciousness as do beasts (3: 19-21). Wisdom and folly, justice and injustice, happiness and sadness all amount to the same thing (1: 16-18; 2: 1-11). It does not appear that any principles or guidelines exist which lead to spiritual contentment, because even great learning, wealth, and power are really vanity and do not alter the fact of dissolution and death. Man remains vexed by his ultimate transitoriness and inability to perfect life. Vanity means, then, that all returns to dust (3: 20) and has no final effect beyond itself or even on itself.

Such a seemingly nihilistic view of life should lead to utter desolation and despair, but the Preacher proceeds in his rather meandering way, down two ameliorating paths—acceptance of the situation by gathering as much good as one can (9: 7-10) and higher realization that a great Deity planned it to be so. God does have a plan for man, who must keep certain rules, though he may not understand them. This ultimately sets man apart from beasts, requires him to reflect on his behavior, and to remain constant to the bitter lessons learned in life: "Sorrow is better than laughter; for by the sadness of the countenance the heart is made better" (7: 3). In fact, everything is measured according to God's plan: "To every thing there is a season, and a time to every purpose under heaven" (3: 1). Man will be judged according to his ability to remain constant to God's requirements (12: 13-14), though the results of this judgment are not discussed.

The Christian tradition upholds this view while negating the carpe diem viewpoint inherent in the Preacher's words and stressing the necessity for "correct" belief. The fallen state of man, a result of disobedience to God, is seen as the ultimate reason for his confusion, since the inconstancy of the original parents, Adam and Eve, is compounded in all subsequent generations. Unlike Old Testament tradition, Christianity speaks more to the individual who may be redeemed and aided by the Holy Spirit through Christ. Constant belief and constant good works lead to permanence of spiritual values. In spite of factional struggles, conflict of doctrines, and wars of religion, Christians have retained unaltered the basic tenet that the world of man is vanity, and only constancy in right belief can provide man with the hope that God provides *ordo* (structure and meaning) in the universe.

The Stoic tradition, emerging at the beginning of the Hellenistic Age (ca. 300 B.C.) and remaining influential through the Roman era (to ca. A.D. 300), also treated vanity and constancy as central themes. Stoicism existed apart from religious precepts per se as a means of looking at the world reasonably and acting according to reason's dictates. It thus provides a mechanism that can be combined with almost any compatible religious system. Of greatest importance for Europe up through the seventeenth century are the works of Epictetus (ca. A.D. 55-135) and especially Seneca (ca. 4 B.C.-A.D. 65). The overlapping of much of Seneca's thought with that of the Preacher, as well as with Christian ethics in general, proved to Christian thinkers and poets that he was one of the divinely inspired pagan ancients whose works were worthy of consideration and even of imitation. They agreed when Seneca noted the vanity present in all things: "let us remember that all things are equally unimportant, presenting a different appearance on the outside, but equally empty within."[1] This extends even to those things held most dear, including oneself: the wise man "considers not only slaves, property and positions of honor, but also his body, his eyes, his hands—everything which can make life dearer, even his very self, as among things uncertain" (p. 71). Just as the Preacher had done (8: 14), Seneca noted that justice is uneven and evil men prosper (p. 77). The end result of human life for both the good and the evil is dust and dissolution.[2]

As in the biblical tradition, however, the *vanitas* setting provides for Stoics the ground out of which the wisdom of *constantia* arises, the difference being that in the biblical tradition the essence of God's creation is completely meaningful, but appearances blind us to the inherent meaning.[3] It is imperative in the continually changing world of appearances to find the essential quality of things and to live in accordance with God's law, the center of all things in the biblical tradition, or with nature's law, the ultimate force in the Stoic tradition. In both it is the responsibility of the individual to assume the correct posture by submitting himself to the necessity of law; this is the only path seen to freedom from care or sin.[4] Thus, man, subject to *fortuna* (i.e., the unforeseeable shifting of events in time), is strengthened by insight into *providentia* (i.e., the overriding order).[5]

Because of the many parallels between Christianity and Stoic thought, Renaissance writers in their fascination with classical works did not feel that they were swerving from their faith when they made full use of the vocabulary and underlying principles of Epictetus or Seneca. Indeed, Boethius in his *Consolatio philosophiae* (A.D. 525) had already extensively combined Stoic thought and language in a Christian meditative frame. But as Bonamy Dobrée points out, a "thematic idea" cannot be merely cross-fertilized; rather "it has to be borne up on the wave of some other deep feeling, or some newly sensed assumption, which can become a basis for living."[6]

The Belgian humanist Justus Lipsius (1547–1606) provided the impetus for a reevaluation of Stoic thought that became influential throughout Europe, but especially in Germany. His *De Constantia* (1584), a work in dialogue form between a distraught young exile and his older friend, was translated from Latin into German as *Von der Bestendigkeit* (1599).[7] Lipsius provides in a clear, curt style the practical conclusions to be drawn from the combined wisdom of Christianity and Stoicism, with references also to the latter's rival movement, Epicurianism. Epicureanism, though stressing external, materialistic involvement in life, is always on the fringe of even the most dedicated Stoic thinking, since its origins are in the same way basically concerned with dressing the imbalance between insignificant man and an overwhelming world. Lipsius incorporated materialistic concerns where it was useful, for he was above all a practical thinker who stressed an active live.[8] In fact, Lipsius came under attack from Protestants and Catholics alike for his concern with wordly matters to the exclusion of much orthodox Christian doctrine accepted by both churches. It is significant that his basic approach to the institutional church was, like that of Martin Opitz, practical; he moved between denominations as the need dictated.

Lipsius provided, however, a welcome reformulation of Christian as well as of Stoic thought, and was very well received by such fervent Christian poets as Andreas Gryphius (1616-64) and Catharina Regina von Greiffenberg (1633-94). Lipsius states that "Gottes Gemüt ist ohn allen Wandel," and that disorder and inconstancy exist only in the human perspective, for if there is a God, then there is providence; and if providence, then there is order.[9] There are distinct limits to human knowledge beyond which only constant faith is valid (p. 44v). Using the military vocabulary so common in baroque imagery, man is seen as a soldier of God who is to do His will. Nonetheless, Lipsius directs his concern to the individual in the knowledge that everyone is really concerned about his own fate (p. 22r). As we see in the martyr dramas of Pierre Corneille (1606-84) and of Gryphius, God's will is carried out by individuals who are constant in their duties. Lipsius defines *constantia* as "eine rechtmessige und unbewegliche stercke des gemüts / die von keinem eusserlichen oder zufelligen dinge erlebt oder untergedruckt wird" (p. 10r). The origins of constancy are in humility and patience, the balance of which lead to "gesunde Vernunfft" between disorderly arrogance or sniveling passivity (p. 10v).

As one sees in Ecclesiastes, Boethius, and the literature of the Middle Ages, the concept of divine *ordo* is translated into an ethical imperative. For Lipsius, as it was for the Stoics and the church fathers, especially St. Augustine, *providentia* ("Versehung") is a metaphysical order that is reflected in *fatum*: "ein unbeweglicher schlus der versehung / welcher an den beweglichen dingen hengt" (p. 56v). *Fortuna* ("Glück") is the apparent disordered shifting of things and events in the physical world. Thus, one has a platonic tripartite system, *providentia, fatum*, and *fortuna*, which structures the world view in much of seventeenth-century European literature.

The key to overcoming *fortuna* is *constantia;* it is the ethical and intellectual link between a human mind and the divine plan. Lipsius states that "Creutz und Unglück" lead to manhood and strength. The historical figure Papinianus, later used by Gryphius as a tragic dramatic character, is cited as an example of how misfortune can uncover one's purpose in the scheme of things; Papinianus remained constant to his principles even when faced with the loss of his property, family, and finally his life (p. 95r). As in the Christian martyr tradition, Papinianus engages an external fate that he internally wills to happen. One finds in his example the exemplary Christian attitude of accepting misfortune in order to be part of God's higher order. It reflects also the Stoic way to tranquility, as expressed by Epictetus: "Seek not that the things which happen should happen as you wish; but wish the things which happen to be as they are, and you will have a tranquil flow of life."[10] Or as Lipsius says in reference to the immediate tumultuous situation in Europe: "wir . . . sollen wissen / das aller schaden / welchen wir leiden / einem andern dinge etwa worzu in dieser Welt diene" (p. 103r). The latter is not spoken by a naive apologist, but by the character Carolus Langius, who also relates to his younger friend many examples of the cruelty of both nature and man.

It is also within the context of great social, political, and religious unrest that both the fictitious dialogue and the actual writing of *De Constantia* took place, although the violence that would make Germany a battleground for thirty years between 1618 and 1648, and that would involve virtually all of Europe, had not yet reached its peak. The reaction of late feudalism to the strong middle class and the new order of absolutism with its centralization of power combined to provide a fertile sociopolitical background for the intellectual and theological struggles mentioned earlier. The cultural and historical origins and implications of these movements have been the topic of many studies utilizing many different points of view. One may easily conclude, however, that in such an environment the thematic constellation of *vanitas-constantia* could become primary in thought and art.[11]

Within the European context, *vanitas* and *constantia* appear in many variations when they are applied by various literary artists and combined with different supporting themes. They also dominate for a shorter period of time in France and England, for example, than in Germany. The literature of these two countries tends towards greater interest in the Epicurean direction than does Germany's. Comparisons show, nonetheless, that vanity and constancy appear together as mutually dependent themes and function in similar ways throughout European literatures. It is not without reason that the baroque period is described as the last which reflects a unified cultural movement.

The emblem provides a basic structural means for the presentation of themes. It has the function of revealing to man's intellect the inner qualities and design of natural phenomena. It does so by focusing on the hidden meanings of objects in the world which contain messages about the moral nature of life and its ultimate design.[12] For example, one of the most common emblems for *fortitudo*, constancy in the face of adversity, is a palm tree supporting a great weight in its crown, but yet growing straight and tall in spite of this burden.[13] This image, showing how strength comes to constancy through confrontation with negative forces, appears in European emblem literature, poetry, art, and drama throughout the period.

A meditative sonnet, "Das beglückende Unglück," one of several on that theme by the Austrian Protestant poet Catharina Regina von Greiffenberg, who suffered considerable religious persecution, combines the emblems of the palm tree and the mirror with light and dark imagery. The poem ends in a conceit which explains the necessity for both constancy and adversity:

> Es dunken uns zwar schwer die Creutz und Trübsal-Zeiten:
> Jedoch sie / nach dem Geist / sehr nutzlich seynd und gut:
> dieweil / den Palmen gleich / der Christlich Heldenmuht
> sich schwinget hock empor in Widerwärtigkeiten.
>
> . . .
>
> Es muß das Spiegelglaß sehr wol geschliffen seyn /
> sonst ist es nicht gerecht und wirffet falschen Schein.
> der Mensch / in dem sich Gott bespiegelt / soll er leuchten /
> so muß durch Creutzes-Stahl er werden zugericht.
> Allein in Unglücks-Nacht / siht man das Liecht im Liecht.
> uns nutzt das Creutz / als wie dem Feld das Thau-befeuchten.[14]

The interplay of constancy with evil times permits the Christian to develop *fortitudo*, to prove himself not only to God, but also to himself. The argument is developed by a series of emblematic images, e.g., the polishing of a mirror so that it reflects the light correctly, as man must reflect the light of Christ. The *pointe* of the poem returns to the cross introduced in the first line, but with a new awareness of its significance. The emblematic exposition has enabled the poet to expose the inner, true qualities of appearances which initially seem onerous.

The commonplace of life as dream is used by both Protestant and Catholic poets, and this reflects the Stoic-humanist tradition common to both. Compare the following sonnets by Andreas Gryphius with the French Catholic poet Jacques Des Barreaux (1599–1673):

> Was sind wir menschen doch? ein wohnhaus grimmer schmertzen.
> Ein ball des falschen glücks / ein irrlicht dieser zeit.
>
> . . .
>
> Dis leben fleucht davon wie ein geschwätz und schertzen.
> Die vor uns abgelegt des schwachen leibes kleidt
> Und in das todten buch der grossen sterblichkeit
> Längst eingeschrieben sind / sind uns aus sinn und hertzen.
> Gleich wie ein eitel traum leicht aus der acht hinfält
>
> . . .
>
> So mus auch unser nahm / lob ehr und ruhm verschwinden.
>
> . . .
>
> Was sag ich? wir vergehn gleich als ein rauch von winden.[15]

> Tout n'est plein icy-bas que de vaine apparence,
> Ce qu'on donne à sagesse est conduit par le sort,
> L'on monte et l'on descend avec pareil effort,
> Sans jamais rencontrer l'estat de consistance.
>
> . . .
>
> Comme on resve en son lict, resver en la maison,
> Espérer sans succes, et craindre sans raison,
>
> . . .
>
> Travailler avec peine et travailler sans fruit,
> Le dirai-je, Mortels, qu'est-ce que cette vie?
> C'est un songe qui dure un peu plus qu'une nuit.[16]

> (Everything in the world is full of vain illusion,
> What we attribute to wisdom, is really the result of chance,
> One rises and falls with equal effort
> Without ever achieving a state of balance.
>
> . . .
>
> As one dreams in one's bed, or in one's home,
> Hoping without success, fearing without reason,
>
> . . .
>
> Working painfully but unsuccessfully,
> Shall I say it, Mortals, What is this life?
> It is a dream which lasts but little longer
> than a night.)

Both sonnets treat life as a concatenation of constantly shifting appearances, the achievement of which leaves nothing of consequence for the human spirit, since time will prove the frailty of the world and human action in the world to be consequential. Life is not static; it is seen as a movement up and down between levels, but even the higher levels of human existence, those hardest to obtain and most sought after, will be reduced to nothing and forgotten. Indeed, man cannot really claim credit for attainment of the higher social and economic levels, because they are more a function of a given time and place than of individual effort. Man himself, in a sense, becomes an emblem of inconstancy and vanity as he attempts to achieve the very opposite. As the Preacher, Seneca, and Marcus Aurelius remind us, one's good fortune may change overnight.

While Gryphius's argument makes greater use of metaphor than does Des Barreaux's more analytic exposition, the message is essentially the same — a somewhat personalized (by the interjection of the poets' "I" in the conclusions) view that experiential reality is chimeric. Closely connected with the *vanitas* theme in these poems and in general is the theme of death, most often in the Christian form of *memento mori*. It strongly colors such meditative poems as Gryphius's oft-treated sonnet "Es ist alles eitel":

> Du sihst / wohin du sihst nur eitelkeit auff erden.
> > Was dieser heute bawt / reist jener morgen ein:
> > Wo itzund städte stehn / wird eine wiesen sein
> Auff der ein schäffers kind wird spilen mitt den heerden.
> Was itzund prächtig blüht sol bald zutretten werden.
> > Was itzt so pocht undt trotzt ist morgen asch und bein.
> > Nichts ist das ewig sey / kein ertz kein marmorstein.
> Itz lacht das gluck uns an / bald donnern die beschwerden.
> > Der hohen thaten ruhm mus wie ein traum vergehn.
> > Soll den das spiell der zeitt / der leichte mensche bestehn.
>
> Ach! was ist alles dis was wir für köstlich achten /
> > Als schlechte nichtikeitt / als schaten staub und windt.
> > Als eine wiesen blum / die man nicht wieder findt.
> Noch wil was ewig ist kein einig mensch betrachten.[17]

Such dynamic imagery indicates the violence of worldly vanity—it is more than mere decay, it is also a process of being ripped asunder. In the sixth line, the *vanitas* theme is combined with the theme of *memento mori*, the admonition that all will be reduced, possibly with violence, to ashes and bone. The interplay of *vanitas* and *memento mori* is joined by a third supporting theme, that of *fortuna* in the eighth line, thus underscoring the continuous, unpredictable shifting of man's physical and emotional condition.

The technique of intensification is applied when the commonplace motifs of vanity (dream, game, shadow, dust, wind, and flower) are combined in a crescendo that permits the introduction of the unnamed but obvious fourth theme that could counteract even the seemingly overwhelming effect of the negative themes and motifs previously introduced. The fourth theme is unnamed because each individual must name it independently; but the conclusion of Gryphius's cycle of poems *Kirch-Hof Gedancken*, as just one example, leaves little doubt as to what the fourth illuminating theme is:

> Ach Todten! Ach! was lern ich hier!
> Was war ich vor! was werd ich werden!
> Was ewig; bleibt uns für und für!
> Und ich bekümmer mich umb Erden!
> O lehrt mich / die ihr lieget / stehn!
> Daß / wenn ich Jahr und Zeiten schlisse /
> Wenn ich die Welt zum Abschied grüsse /
> Mög auß dem Tod ins Leben gehn.[18]

The conceit based on the word *stehn* implies the extended meaning *stare* (in Stoic terminology: to remain constant). Paradoxically, those who are now "lying" are best able to point the way to constancy in the face of death. The paradox is extended to its fullest meaning when the hope of life is attained by accepting death as part of God's providence.

This is, of course, the basic Christian thesis found in one form or another throughout European literature. The tragedies of Pierre Corneille and Andreas Gryphius all show the Christian heroes and heroines achieving deliverance from life's vanity through constancy in faith, the latter being the primary Christian variation on the *constantia* theme. The shared themes make the content of these as well as other works readily understandable to virtually any contemporary with a basic education, despite often strong individual variations. Polyeucte in Corneille's martyr drama of that name is a young nobleman who must prove his faith to himself by attacking the altar of his people's gods and thus sacrificing himself to achieve identity through death.[19] In the final act, his pronouncement "Je suis chrétien" (I am Christian; Act V, line 1674), brings a death sentence, but it also brings the only sure remedy to his fear of inconstancy. To his beloved he comments "Toute votre félicité / Sujette à l'instabilité" (All your joys are subject to instability; IV, 1105), and compares her earthly loyalty to glass, which shatters too easily. Only of heaven he says "Vos biens ne sont point inconstants" (Your wealth is not at all inconstant; IV, 1150). Rightly or wrongly, he cuts himself off from all human connections.

Although Gryphius is much concerned with the secular workings of
Christian salvation, Catharina von Georgien, in the martyr tragedy
named after her and subtitled *Bewährte Beständigkeit*, agrees with
Polyeucte when, before her execution, she says "Die Erden stinckt uns
an / wir gehen in den Himmel ein" (IV, 428).[20] Her motivations are less
personal, more concerned with her country and the upholding of Christian virtue. The basic theme, however, remains the same as it does in the
plays of the Dutch Joost van den Vondel, particularly *Gebroeders* (1640),
which was translated into German by Gryphius, or in Calderón's plays,
particularly *El príncipe constante* (1629).[21]

Parallel to the literature stressing Christian faith as the highest form
of *constantia*, another body of literature exists that stands much closer to
the secular interests of the Renaissance humanists who studied and absorbed the classical Stoics. Particularly in England, the Stoic themes are
applied to secular situations with more of a pantheist than a Christian
bias. It would seem that Gryphius could agree with the following words
spoken by Clermont d'Ambois in George Chapman's play *Revenge of
Bussy d'Ambois* (1611):[22] "God hath the whole world perfect made and
free" (Act III, scene 4, line 57). But the code of Stoic self-reliance and
human freedom that Clermont postulates based on the divine example is
antithematic to Gryphius or Corneille:

> But he, that knowing how divine a frame
> The whole world is; and of it all, can name
> (Without self-flattery) no part so divine
> As he himself, and therefore will confine
> Freely his whole powers in his proper part,
> Goes on most God-like. He that strives t'invert
> The Universal's course with his poor way,
> Not only dust-like shivers with the sway,
> But crossing God in his great work, all earth
> Bears not so cursed and so damn'd a birth.   (III, 4, 66 ff.)

It is the strength of the individual, not transcendent faith, that
establishes the "Senecal man":

> Chance what can chance me, well or ill is equal
> In my acceptance, since I joy in neither,
> But go with sway of all the world together.
> In all successes Fortune and the day
> To me alike are; I am fix'd, be she
> Never so fickle; and will there repose,
> Far past the reach of any die she throws.   (III, 4, 159 ff.)

Ultimately, Clermont commits suicide to achieve final freedom. He is the opposite of Polyeucte, although like Polyeucte he distrusts his own ability to remain constant and he disdains women for fear of entrapment. His motivations are self-centered. In Polyeucte, the theme of constancy is developed into transcendent faith. Although excessive, Polyeucte's zeal will earn him a martyr's crown, as does Catharina's, whose zeal is more subdued, controlled, and historically directed. Like the Stoics of antiquity, Clermont desires as little dependence on anything outside himself as possible—so much so that the tragic nature of Chapman's plays, like Corneille's later dramas, has been called into question, since tragedy depends on fateful entanglements of emotion and interdependence.[23] Shakespeare, as Dobrée points out, effectively fused Stoic themes with intuition, for example in *King Lear*, when the commonplace, "Men must endure their going hence even as their coming hither," receives the answer: "Ripeness is all."[24] Thus the theme is illuminated from several levels of human experience. Particularly striking is the passage in *Richard II* where the banished Bolingbroke's father, Gaunt, tells him to accept necessity and to bear it lightly:

> There is no virtue like necessity.
> Think not the King did banish thee,
> But thou the King.
> . . .
> For gnarling sorrow hath less power to bite
> The man that mocks at it and sets it light.

To which Bolingbroke replies:

> Oh, who can hold a fire in his hand
> By thinking on the frosty Caucasus?   (I, 3)[25]

There are limits to man's ability to achieve on his own an attitude of detachment and independence from emotional needs; hence, the difficulty in arriving at the Stoic ideal, which for Clermont was possible only in death. Shakespeare's plays do not contain the Christian emphasis on constancy through faith in God's divine plan, which would relieve the agony of the human position. One sees in Shakespeare a use of the themes of constancy and vanity, but they do not necessarily dominate and are thoroughly interwoven with the many other themes of the plays.

The use of themes in seventeenty-century German literature is also not determined by the Christian point of view alone. The humanistic tradition with its more secular orientation is found especially in Martin

Opitz, who particularly in the *Trost-Getichte in Widerwertigkeit des Krieges* (1633) utilizes the *vanitas-constantia* themes.[26] Indeed, it may be said that he fixes these themes as basic for subsequent German poets. He is deeply concerned about the function of poetic art. In the Stoic tradition, things of the world are seen as lacking true value for the individual, and Opitz agrees especially in the case of the poet:

> So ist ja also klar daß nichts von diesen dingen
> Mir rechte Sicherheit und Ruh vermag zu bringen;
> Sie haben nicht Bestand / sind uber unser Recht /
> Und welcher sie beherrscht der ist des Glückes Knecht.
>
> (Book II, 310 ff.)

The long poem *Trost-Getichte* forms a programmatic response to transitoriness and the related impotence of the individual to control the determining factors of his life. Opitz, following Lipsius, whom he studied, calls this impotence *Verhängnis* (necessity): "es muß so gehn nachdem es ist bestimmt" (II, 412). This includes the violence and horror of war. Opitz is against suicide as a way out (II, 525), and stresses an active role in life; he advises flight only into *der Mannheit Burg* (II, 590). In the martial imagery typical of the time (typical partly because he introduced it), he urges a firm individual and public posture. In a variation on the palm tree emblem, he refers to the oak: "Je mehr man sie behaut / je mehr sie äste trägt" (II, 60). The oak is possibly used as an emblem to which Germans might relate more readily. Indeed, he stresses the national character: "Bewahrt . . . / Daß wir von Deutscher Art und Alle Männer seyn" (III, 555). His plea against war is based on the Christian doctrine of love (III, 69 ff.), but active defense is necessary: "Wer soll nicht willig stehn für Herdt und für Altar" (III, 100). The word *stehn* relates, as seen above, to *stare*, with the Stoic meaning to stand firm, to be constant.

Thus the Stoic themes are brought into a public, political context. It is the poet whose duty it is to speak for the public conscience from his individual conscience, the primary Stoic measure of behavior.[27] But Opitz's humanistic message supports individual freedom of conscience: "Laßt Ketzer Ketzer bleiben / Und gleubet ihr für euch" (I, 469 f.). Matters of confession are of less concern to Opitz than matters of poetry and style. In any event poetry is for him *verborgene Theologie*. The poet, however, expresses his conscience publicly and speaks as directly as possible to his audience in order to admonish them to constancy. Opitz criticizes poetry that is full of flourish and esoteric allusions:

O weg mit solcher Kunst / weg / weg mit solchen Sachen
So die Gemüther nur verzagt und weibisch machen
  Die leichtlich wie man wird durch der Getichte Schein
  Und eusserlichen Glantz zu uberreden seyn.
Ich lasse dieses mal die Zuckerworte bleiben /
Wil auff mein Deutsches hier von Deutscher Tugend schreiben /
  Von Mannheit welche steht; und machen offenbar
  Wie keiner unter uns in Nöthen und Gefahr
Die jetzt für Augen schwebt / so gäntzlich sey verlassen /
Daß er nicht wiederumb ein Hertze solle fassen.   (II, 25 ff.)

Poetry should not reflect the vanity of external *Glantz*, but rather the true value of constancy. Form and content must be in balance, in poetry as in life, to achieve the order that transcends time. For Opitz, *virtus* ("Tugend"), *forma*, and *gloria* are synonymous (see Stalder, p. 34). The poet with his *edle Wissenschaft* shows "den rechten Weg bestendig außzuhalten" (IV, 63 ff.). Certainly tragic drama is for him a "Schule der Beständigkeit."[28]

It is apparent that the use of the themes *constantia* and *vanitas* are, as Welzig states regarding *constantia*, "ein in sich vielschichtiges Phänomen."[29] The application of these themes reflects the broad spectrum of seventeenth-century literature from the secularized, rationalistic Chapman to the highly meditative poetry of Greiffenberg. In reference to the latter type of poetry, it is necessary to mention the mystic poets, who take their meditation to a level of complete inwardness and ecstasy. Since they have an inner certainty, they are not concerned with the comfort of constant faith or Stoic *virtus*. Johannes Scheffler (Angelus Silesius, 1624–77), one of the most audacious mystics, tacitly denies the need for the scriptures: "Die Schrifft ist Schrifft sonst nichts. Mein Trost ist Wesenheit / Und daß Gott in mir spricht das Wort der Ewigkeit."[30] The mystic transcends the need for striving towards constancy, which implies an individual will apart from the totality of God, because the mystic's will is completely absorbed in God's: "Auch Christus / wär in ihn ein kleiner eigner Wille / Wie seelig er auch ist / Mensch glaube mir er fiele" (p. 174). *Vanitas* exists only apart from God, since, as in Augustinian thought, He is his own reason and purpose. Because this world, though His creation, is less than He, sin and human folly are integral to it. By permitting the individual will to cease functioning, one can be a part of God, as Daniel von Czepko (1605–60) states in the epigrammatic form so often used by seventeenth-century mystics: "Was ausser der Natur das höchste Wesen ist / das bist du, wenn du dich ohn

Leib und Sinnen siehst" (p. 166). The vanity of temporal existence is overcome, in theory at least, already in this world.

Certainly the mystics constitute a very small minority. Constancy in the secular sphere is the concern of the majority, including those poets, dramatists, and novelists who belong to the nobility. Anton Ulrich von Braunschweig-Lüneburg and one of his models, Mme de Scudéry in France, wrote long novels in which their noble characters' constancy was tested through thousands of pages.[31] Anton Ulrich's novels, especially *Octavia*, contain an incredibly complex interlocking of story lines, further confused by the limited knowledge of the characters in a narrative world based on dissimulation. The heroine's greatest task is passive constancy to her religious faith, while the hero struggles in active constancy to rescue her and establish and preserve the state. The world of court politics appears as an ever shifting quicksand where only faith in a higher order preserves the individual as well as the state, although martyrdom in the name of faith is required of some. Anton Ulrich's novels are both a tract on constancy directed at the nobility and a literary treatment of the historical implications of Christian salvation. The author combines a theological with a secular point of view firmly based on gradualism. As a nobleman he stresses perhaps less the vanity of life than its chaotic nature, since this world is the theater in which God's plan is carried out. Steadfast noblemen function as the prime movers in this plan.

Hans Jakob Christoffel von Grimmelshausen (1622?–76) views the world of political action quite differently in his novel *Simplicissimus*.[32] The upheavals of the Thirty Years War are seen through their effect on the development of one man from naive boyhood through worldly maturity to withdrawal into a life of contemplation. As must be in the largely picaresque form, the concern is with the individual and how he fares in a world basically indifferent or hostile and certainly ruled by *fortuna*. Where Anton Ulrich's idealized heroes are fixed by their constancy to externalized religion and state, Simplex seeks identity, both spirtual and worldly, on an individualized basis. His truth must be internalized — he must learn to be constant to God's providence through a tortuous struggle with himself even more than with the world. The vanity of worldly greatness becomes clear in the fact that Simplex's highest stature in the world comes at a time of greatest spiritual confusion. Although it appears at first that *fortuna* has become constant in her positive treatment of Simplex, in fact it is a matter of "constant inconstancy," for constancy in the world of man can only be illusory, and Simplex's fall is swift. However, Simplex undergoes a process of illumination through strife by which he learns constant faith.

The themes of vanity and constancy appear in contexts other than religious and philosophical ones, although a relationship may exist between a secular or ironic use of the themes and the more serious counterpart. The vanity of the world is often personified as a woman. One recalls the famous Shakespeare quotation "Vanity thy name is woman." In the Stoic tradition one is often admonished to shun *Weiber-Sinn* and have *Mannes Mut* because "ein Mann steht für und für."[33] On the other hand, Catharina von Georgien and Octavia provide the men around them with a model to follow. Philipp von Zesen's Rosemund in his novel *Die Adriatische Rosemund* (1645) is true to her beloved in spite of irreconcilable religious differences that keep them apart and cause her to perish of unrequited love. This is again quite unlike man's unfulfilled longings in the petrarchistic poems of, for example, Paul Fleming (1609-40).[34] Also Opitz, who otherwise would desire the Stoic's calm *virtus*, recognizes the need for the poet's suffering in love in order to achieve greatness in art:

> Doch lieb' ich gleichwol nicht / so bin ich wie ein Scheit /
> Ein Stock / und raues Bley . . .
> . . . das tröstliche Beschweren /
> Ermuntert meinen Geist / daß er sich höher schwingt
> . . .
> Drumb ge' es wie es wil / und muß ich gleich darvon /
> So uberschreit' ich doch des Lebens enge Schranken;
> Der Nahme der mir folgt is meiner Sorgen Lohn.[35]

Opitz maintains seriously that his poetic art will help him overcome the transitoriness of life by permitting his name to live on. Stalder indicates that Opitz felt poetic language could transcend *res futiles et fluxae* (things futile and in flux) by its *forma* (beauty), and thereby could the poet achieve *gloria*.[36] Erotic sufferings are thus in the service of art, and inconstancy in love necessary for the poet.

Gryphius and Greiffenberg, who stress the religious, meditative function of poetry over *forma*, nonetheless recognize in literary art a means to combat *vanitas*; Greiffenberg states this in the sonnet "Auf die unverhinderliche Art der Edlen Dicht-Kunst":

> Trutz / daß man mir verwehr / des Himmels milde Gaben /
> den unsichtbaren Strahl / die schallend' Heimligkeit /
> das Englisch Menschenwerk; das in und nach der Zeit /
> wann alles aus wird seyn / allein bestand wird haben /
> das mit der Ewigkeit / wird in die wette traben /
> die Geistreich wunder'Lust / der Dunkelung befreyt . . .

Poetry transcends because it is used to praise God, not because of innate qualities:

> Es will auch hier mein Geist / in dieser Freyheit zeigen /
> was ich beginnen wurd / im fall ich mein allein:
> daß ich / O Gott / dein' Ehr vor alles würd erheben.
> Gieb Freyheit mir / so will ich Ewigs Lob dir geben.[37]

Where Opitz stresses the classical tradition, Greiffenberg combines the themes of art and freedom from a Christian point of view. Both view poetry as a means of providing individual freedom from the common vanity of life. In fact, in the three traditions developing Stoic thought, the Christian, classical, and humanistic, freedom of the individual through mental preparation and proper attitude is one, if not the main, goal. As Paul Fleming writes:

> Sey in allen Handel
> ohn Wandel.
> Steh feste /
> Was Gott beschleust /
> das ist und heist /
> das beste.[38]

This posture assumes a certain impotence in man to direct events, and it assumes a providential *ordo* by which all is directed, usually to man's ultimate good, if he believes and acts accordingly. As with the mystics, one must submit completely to God's will.

Already noted above is at least implied criticism of such a position in Shakespeare, who views man's postures from all sides and finds them lacking. He does not criticize, overtly anyway, the Christian view of life, but his own is distinctly secular. Of course, that is a characteristic of the Elizabethan theater in general. It is less characteristic, however, of continental theater, except for the English acting troops. The secularization of the German theater came with Daniel Casper von Lohenstein (1635-83) whose counterpart in France is Jean Racine (1639-99). Lohenstein's *Sophonisbe* (1666) treats individuals caught in historical processes. The stance taken by Papinianus, which allows no compromise to virtue, is not at home in the political arena of Lohenstein's works.[39] Sophonisbe tells her husband, whom she is rescuing from prison in spite of her decision to pursue the new Roman ruler of her African homeland, that one must adapt:

> Die Liebe / liebstes Haupt / ist aus des Proteus Orden /

Die sich zu allen macht / nimbt jede Farb an sich
Wie ein Chamaeleon.[40]

As ruler, her personal life is one with the political-historical developments in her land. She remains constant, but it seems less a matter of choice than of her innate predisposition and the necessity of external events. Dido's spirit informs her that it is *Verhängnüs* that causes her demise, and not without *rechtes Recht* (V, 112-3). *Verhängnüs* is seen, however, from the perspective of historical events in which the eschatological order is not stressed. Therefore, the world cannot be the theater only of *vanitas*, which acquires meaning only through constancy to a transcendent reality. The Roman Scipio shows his superiority in the serious game of history not by relying on constancy to ideals, but by strength of reason and discipline. The baroque concern with *vanitas* and *constantia* are now giving way to the themes of historical process and reason, themes that characterize the emerging Enlightenment.

NOTES

1. Seneca, *On Tranquility*, in *Essential Works of Stoicism*, ed. M. Hadas (New York: Bantam, 1961), p. 70. Evidence for the relationship felt to exist between Christian doctrine and Stoic thought is the apocryphal correspondence between St. Paul and Seneca in *New Testament Apocrypha*, ed. E. Henneke (Philadelphia: Westminister, 1965), II, 133 ff.

2. *On Tranquility*, p. 72; Eccles. 12: 12; also Marcus Aurelius, *To Himself*, in *Essential Works of Stoicism*, ed. M. Hadas (New York: Bantam, 1961), p. 114.

3. Wisdom is distinct from "excessive" or ostentatious book learning, which is only "vexation of spirit" (Eccles. 12: 12). "A great number of books overwhelms the learner instead of instructing him" (*On Tranquility*, p. 69).

4. *On Tranquility*, p. 75; Epictetus, *The Manual*, in *Essential Works of Stoicism*, p. 85; also James 1: 25, "the perfect law of liberty."

5. Marcus Aurelius states: "All that is from the gods is full of providence. That which is from fortune is not separated from nature or without an interweaving and involution with the things that are ordered by providence" (*To Himself*, p. 112). Compare this with Boethius, who says "Providence is the very Divine reason itself, seated in the highest Prince, which disposeth of all things. But Fate is a disposition inherent in changeable things, by which providence connecteth all things in their due order." *The Consolation of Philosophy*, in *The Age of Belief*, ed. A. Freemantle (New York: Houghton Mifflin, 1963), p. 56.

6. B. Dobrée, *The Broken Cistern: The Clark Lectures 1952–3* (Bloomington: Indiana University Press, 1955), p. 33.

7. Justus Lipsius, *Von der Bestendigkeit Zwey Bücher, Darinnen das höchste Stück Menschlicher Weisheit gehandelt wird*, trans. Andreas Viritius (Leipzig, 1601), photomechanical rpt. based on 2nd ed., 1601, with variants from 1st ed., 1599, ed. L. W. Forster (Stuttgart: Metzler, 1965).

8. See L. W. Forster's "Nachwort" in *Von der Bestendigkeit*, p. 25. Lipsius belongs very much in the tradition of Dutch ethical humanism founded by Rudolf Agricola and Erasmus, which itself harks back to the *devotio moderna* of the later Middle Ages, a tradition that stressed the *vita activa* and *caritas* as the way to salvation.

9. *Von der Bestendigkeit*, p. 50r.

10. *The Manual*, in *Essential Works of Stoicism*, p. 87.

11. In the seventeenth century the two themes become inextricably combined against the background of belief in a transcendent purpose to the apparent vanity of life. Life's uncertainties could be intellectualized and observed with detachment. See Lipsius, p. 44r; M. Szyrocki, *Die deutsche Literatur des Barock: Eine Einführung* (Hamburg: Rowohlt, 1968), p. 13; W. Mauser, *Dichtung, Religion und Gesellschaft im 17. Jahrhundert: Die Sonette des Andreas Gryphius* (München: Fink, 1976), p. 157.

12. G. Kirchner, *Fortuna in Dichtung und Emblematik des Barock: Tradition und Bedeutungswandel eines Motifs* (Stuttgart: Metzler, 1970), pp. 136 ff. Kirchner discusses also many motifs and themes related to *vanitas* and *constantia*, H.-J. Schings discusses in detail the allegorical way of viewing the world in *Die patristische und stoische Tradition bei Gryphius* (Köln: Böhlau, 1966), pp. 110 ff.

13. A. Schöne, *Emblematik und Drama im Zeitalter des Barock* (München: Beck, 1964), p. 68.

14. C. R. v. Greiffenberg, *Geistliche Sonette, Lieder und Gedichte* (Nürnberg, 1662), photomechanical rpt., ed. H. O. Burger (Darmstadt: Wissenschaftliche Buchgesellschaft, 1967), p. 43.

15. Andreas Gryphius, *Sonette*, ed. M. Szyrocki, in *Gesamtausgabe der deutschsprachigen Werke*, vol. I, ed. M. Szyrocki and H. Powell (Tübingen: Niemeyer, 1963), p. 35.

16. *Anthologie de la poésie baroque française*, vol. II, ed. J. Rousset (Paris: Colin, 1961), p. 94; author's translation.

17. *Sonette*, p. 33. F. Wentzlaff-Eggebert calls the *vanitas* theme in Gryphius's works "nichts anderes als ein gesteigertes *memento mori*"; see *Der triumphierende und der besiegte Tod in der Wort- und Bildkunst des Barock* (Berlin: de Gruyter, 1975), p. 74. For a review of scholarly opinion on the poem see Mauser, pp. 126 f.

18. Gryphius, *Vermischte Gedichte*, ed. M. Szyrocki (*Gesamtausgabe*, vol. III), p. 18.

19. *Théâtre choisi de Corneille*, ed. M. Rat (Paris: Garnier, 1961), pp. 207-79.

20. Gryphius, *Catharina von Georgien*, in *Trauerspiele (Gesamtausgabe*, vol. III).

21. W. Kayser treats the strong reception *El príncipe constante* received in Germany in "Zur Struktur des *Standhafften Prinzen* von Calderón"; see *Gestaltprobleme der Dichtung*, ed. R. Alewyn (Bonn: Bouvier, 1957). See also E. Szarota's excellent treatment of these and other plays in *Künstler, Grübler und Rebellen, Studien zum europäischen Märtyrerdrama des 17. Jahrhunderts* (Bern: Francke, 1967).

22. *The Plays of George Chapman*, vol. I, ed. T. M. Parrott (New York: Russell & Russell, 1961).

23. J. Wieler, *George Chapman: The Effect of Stoicism upon His Tragedies* (New York: King's Crown Press, 1949), p. 17: "too close an adaptation of Stoicism for dramatic purpose must lead to the negation of tragedy."

24. Dobrée, p. 19.

25. W. Shakespeare, *Richard II*, in *The Complete Works*, ed. G. Harrison (New York: Harcourt, 1948), p. 441.

26. M. Opitz, *Gesammelte Werke*, vol. I, ed. G. Schulz-Behrend (Stuttgart: Hiersemann, 1968).

27. X. Stalder points out that Opitz relied on poetry to achieve Stoic *virtus*; see *Formen des barocken Stoizismus: Der Einfluß der Stoa auf die deutsche Barockdichtung, Martin Opitz, Andreas Gryphius und Catharina Regina von Greiffenberg* (Bonn: Bouvier, 1976), p. 34.

28. M. Szyrocki, p. 198, quotes Opitz's preface to his translation of Seneca's *Trojanerinnen* that tragedy is "ein Spiegel derer / die in allem ihrem thun und lassen auf das blosse Glück fassen. wir lernen aber darneben auch durch stetige Besichtigung so vielen Creutzes und Übels / das andern begegnet ist / das unsrige / welches uns begegnen möchte / weniger fürchten und besser erdulden." Szyrocki comments: "Opitz legt also Nachdruck nicht auf das Erregen von Mitleid, wie später Lessing, sondern vor allem auf die Stärkung der Constantia, die einzig den Menschen gegen das Schauspiel der Vergänglichkeit wappnet."

29. Werner Welzig, "Constantia und barocke Beständigkeit," *Deutsche Vierteljahrsschrift für Geistesgeschichte und Literaturwissenschaft*, 35 (1961), p. 418.

30. *Barocklyrik*, vol. III, ed. H. Cysarz (Hildesheim: Olms, 1961), p. 175.

31. Madeleine de Scudéry, *Ibrahim, ou l'Illustre Bassa*, 4 vols. (Paris, 1641-44); *Artamène, ou le Grand Cyrus*, 20 vols. (Paris, 1650-53); *Clélie, histoire romaine*, 10 vols. (Paris, 1654-60). Anton Ulrich von Braunschweig-Lüneburg, *Die Durchleuchtige Syrerin Aramena* (Nürnberg, 1669-73); *Octavia, Römische Geschichte* (Nürnberg, 1677-1707).

32. Grimmelshausen, *Der Abentheuerliche Simplicissimus Teutsch* (Nürnberg, 1669), ed. R. Tarot (Tübingen: Niemeyer, 1967).

33. Opitz, *Trost-Getichte*, II, 364.
34. The reception of the petrarchistic mode in Germany is treated by G. Hoff-meister, *Petrarkistische Lyrik* (Stuttgart: Metzler, 1973).
35. Cysarz, II, 155.
36. Stalder, p. 34.
37. Greiffenberg, p. 88.
38. Cysarz, II, 5.
39. See W. Voßkamp's illuminating comparison of Gryphius and Lohenstein in *Zeit- und Geschichtsauffassung im 17. Jahrhundert bei Gryphius und Lohenstein* (Bonn: Bouvier, 1967). Also G. Spellerberg's *Verhängnis und Geschichte. Untersuchungen zu den Trauerspielen und zu dem Arminius-Roman Daniel Casper von Lohensteins* (Bad Hamburg: Gehlen, 1970).
40. Lohenstein's *Sophonisbe*, in *Barockdrama*, vol. I, ed. W. Flemming (Hildesheim: Olms, 1965), p. 251.

SELECTED BIBLIOGRAPHY

Primary Sources

Anthologie de la poésie baroque française. J. Rousset, ed. Paris: Colin, 1961.

Anton Ulrich von Braunschweig-Lüneburg. *Die Durchleuchtige Syrerin Aramena*. Nürnberg, 1669-73.

──. *Octavia, Römische Geschichte*. Nürnberg, 1677-1707.

Barocklyrik, H. Cysarz, ed. 2nd rev. ed. Hildesheim: Olms, 1961.

Boethius, *The Consolation of Philosophy*. In *The Age of Belief*. A. Freemantle, ed. New York: Houghton Mifflin, 1963.

Chapman, George. *The Plays of George Chapman*. T. M. Parrott, ed. New York: Russell & Russell, 1961.

Corneille, Pierre. *Polyeucte*. In *Théâtre choisi de Corneille*. M. Rat, ed. Paris: Garnier, 1961.

Epictetus, *The Manual*. In *Essential Works of Stoicism*. M. Hadas, ed. New York: Bantam, 1961.

Greiffenberg, Catharina Regina von. *Geistliche Sonette, Lieder und Gedichte*. Nürnberg 1662. Photomechanical rpt., H.-O. Burger, ed. Darmstadt: Wissenschaftliche Buchgesellschaft, 1967.

Grimmelshausen, Hans Jakob Christoffel von. *Der Abentheuerliche Simplicissimus Teutsch*. R. Tarot, ed. Tübingen: Niemeyer, 1967.

Gryphius, Andreas. *Gesamtausgabe der deutschsprachigen Werke*. M. Szyrocki and H. Powell, eds. Tübingen: Niemeyer, 1963.

Letters of Seneca to Paul and Paul to Seneca. In *New Testament Apocrypha*. II, 133 ff. E. Hennecke, ed. Philadelphia: Westminister, 1965.

Lipsius, Justus. *Von der Bestendigkeit Zwey Bücher, Darinnen das höchste*

Stück Menschlicher Weisheit gehandelt wird. Andreas Viritius, trans. Leipzig, 1601. Photomechanical rpt. based on 2nd ed. 1601, with variants from 1st ed. 1599, L. W. Forster, ed. Stuttgart: Metzler, 1965.

Lohenstein, Daniel Casper von. *Sophonisbe.* In *Barockdrama.* Vol. I. W. Flemming, ed. Hildesheim: Olms, 1965.

Marcus Aurelius. *To Himself.* In *Essential Works of Stoicism.* M. Hadas, ed. New York: Bantam, 1961.

Opitz, Martin. *Gesammelte Werke.* Vol. I. G. Schulz-Behrend, ed. Stuttgart: Hiersemann, 1968.

———. *Trost-Getichte,* II, 364.

Scudéry, Madeleine de. *Artamène, ou le Grand Cyrus.* 20 vols. Paris, 1650-53.

———. *Clélie, histoire romaine.* 10 vols. Paris, 1654-60.

———. *Ibrahim, ou l'Illustre Bassa.* 4 vols. Paris, 1641-44.

Seneca, *On Tranquility.* In *Essential Works of Stoicism.* M. Hadas, ed. New York: Bantam, 1961.

Shakespeare, William. *Richard II.* In *The Complete Works.* G. Harrison, ed. New York: Harcourt, 1948.

Secondary Literature

Daly, Peter. *Literature in the Light of the Emblem: Structural Parallels between the Emblem and Literature in the Sixteenth and Seventeenth Centuries.* Toronto: University of Toronto Press, 1979.

Dobrée, Bonamy. *The Broken Cistern: The Clark Lectures 1952-3.* Bloomington: Indiana University Press, 1955.

Kayser, Wolfgang. "Zur Struktur des *Standhafften Prinzen* von Calderon." In *Gestaltprobleme der Dichtung.* R. Alewyn, ed. Bonn: Bouvier, 1957.

Kirchner, Gottfried. *Fortuna in Dichtung und Emblematik des Barock: Tradition und Bedeutungswandel eines Motifs.* Stuttgart: Metzler, 1970.

Mauser, Wolfram. *Dichtung, Religion und Gesellschaft im 17. Jahrhundert: Die Sonette des Andreas Gryphius.* München: Fink, 1976.

Schings, Hans-Jürgen. *Die patristische und stoische Tradition bei Gryphius.* Köln: Böhlau, 1966.

Spellerberg, Gerhard. *Verhängnis und Geschichte: Untersuchungen zu den Trauerspielen und zu dem Arminius-Roman Daniel Casper von Lohensteins.* Bad Homburg: Gehlen, 1970.

Stalder, Xavier. *Formen des barocken Stoizismus: Der Einfluß der Stoa auf die deutsche Barockdichtung, Martin Opitz, Andreas Gryphius und Catharina Regina von Greiffenberg.* Bonn: Bouvier, 1976.

Szarota, Elida. *Künstler, Grübler und Rebellen: Studien zum europäischen Märtyrerdrama des 17. Jahrhunderts.* Bern: Francke, 1967.

Szyrocki, Marian. *Die deutsche Literatur des Barock: Eine Einführung.* Hamburg: Rowohlt, 1968.

Voßkamp, Wilhelm. *Zeit- und Geschichtsauffassung im 17. Jahrhundert bei Gryphius und Lohenstein*. Bonn: Bouvier, 1967.

Welzig, Werner. "Constantia und barocke Beständigkeit," *Deutsche Vierteljahrsschrift für Geistesgeschichte und Literaturwissenschaft*, 35 (1961), 416–32.

Wentzlaff-Eggebert, Friedrich. *Der triumphierende und der besiegte Tod in der Wort- und Bildkunst des Barock*. Berlin: de Gruyter, 1975.

Wieler, John. *George Chapman: The Effect of Stoicism upon His Tragedies*. New York: King's Crown Press, 1949.

14

Illusion and Reality

Peter Skrine

"Stay, illusion!" Horatio adjures the ghost of Hamlet's father. The very words convey a paradox that brings to mind the obsessive dualities of the baroque era. Permanence and transience, false vanity and truth, reality and illusion: their various formulations are familiar to modern baroque scholars, but their manifestations were as yet largely undreamt of in the philosophy of Shakespeare's scholar newly come from Lutheran Wittenberg as the seventeenth century opened.

At first sight it would indeed appear that the theme of illusion and reality in German baroque writing might best be viewed from a philosophical angle. But although German baroque works are often heavy with erudition, they are philosophically lightweight, the products of an age that supplied the lack of ordered abstract thinking by a system of moral attitudes and poses. The sensible world and its contingent and particular phenomena were less the object of the writer's interest than was the spiritual world of abstract being. The coherent truths of faith and revelation went by and large unchallenged; there was no need as yet, in Germany, to save them from the mechanistic and empirical explanations of materialism and its potential reversal of the two key terms reality and illusion.

The old established boundaries between "truth" and "fiction" were still upheld by all the major writers, though Lohenstein may well have harbored doubts. But whatever the philosophies they had studied or were drawn to, whether Platonic, Neo-Platonic or, with Suárez and the Jesuits, Neo-Scholastic, the ontological conception of reality and illusion

233

gave overall precedence to essentially moral viewpoints. The baroque ethic was a matter of attitudes and poses: the pose that gave the greatest opportunity for effect exerted the most powerful appeal on serious writers. In Germany this was the man's attitude to death. Its omnipresence in art and literature can scarcely be overstated.[1] It transcended the barriers of social rank and religious denomination. Moreover, it was a preoccupation common both to the subject matter of fiction and the real lives of ordinary people.

Contemporary researchers now assume that on a conservative estimate there may be as many as two hundred thousand *Leichenpredigten* extant in Germany,[2] the vast majority of them composed by Lutheran pastors. Lutheranism had not yet fully acquired that note of soulful self-deprecation that was to characterize it after the rise of Pietism in the early eighteenth century; nevertheless its tendency to stress the unworthiness of the individual human being in relation to the sublime omnipotence of the Almighty gave rise to an inevitable dialectic as soon as the life and achievements of some defunct notable were passed in funerary review. The demands of social life, the desire to conform to the conventions of a social group and abide by the traditions of the community were understandably real motives behind the funeral sermons, which are the somber counterparts of the equally popular *Hochzeitsgedichte*.

But this proliferation of funeral sermons in seventeenth-century Germany reflects more than just the social importance attached by a certain percentage of its population—the worthier citizens and persons of rank and station—to a particular type of strictly occasional writing. In their blend of homiletics and panegyric they may rightly be said to represent a characteristically German fusion of post-Reformation Christian values with certain aspects of the classical tradition especially favored by post-Renaissance Europe. Their popularity, however, was primarily a compensation for the fact that the burial rites of the Reformed and Evangelical churches were severe simplifications of the medieval liturgical pattern. Some of the more extreme Reformers had actually regarded the act of burial as being no more than a convenient way of disposing of a body and had attached no particular religious significance to it; but such views were obviously out of keeping with baroque feeling.

Lutheran revisions of the burial rites were by no means so radical, but in place of the elaborate medieval structure they, too, prescribed a simpler order characterized by two significantly special features: the substitution of an often lengthy homily for the earlier multiplicity of psalms and antiphons, and the regular inclusion of the *Media vita* hymn.[3] The sermon as an obligatory part of the burial order was an innovation that clearly gave Lutheran divines a welcome opportunity to demonstrate their homiletic skills and oratory in the graver mood appropriate to the occasion, and it accounts for the wide distribution of such writings, especially in the Lutheran areas of Germany.

The introduction of the *Media vita* into the *Kirchenordnungen* of Lutheran churches had subtler effects and calls for closer attention. The first verse of this Latin hymn is traditionally ascribed to Notker of St. Gall: first found in an eleventh-century manuscript, it acquired a reputation for its close association with warfare and battle, thereby incurring ecclesiastical disapproval. Already a vernacular hymn, it must have been a favorite of Luther's, and it was his version and elaboration of it that came to play so prominent and influential a part in Lutheran burial orders. Moreover, from its use in them it came to be included in Cranmer's Prayer Book of 1549 and the 1662 Book of Common Prayer, as a result of which it has become an integral part of the unconscious heritage of the English-speaking peoples.

It is not for nothing that the initial words of Luther's hymn appear in chapter 7 of Opitz's *Buch von der Deutschen Poeterey*, where they are quoted in order to establish the basic alternating trochaic rhythm or mood of seventeenth-century German poetry alongside the iambic. They were familiar to every reader. After all, "Mitten wir im Leben sind / mit dem Tod umbfangen" were the words that time and again proclaimed a stark reality to the survivors as they stood at the graveside of the departed, words that in their blend of spiritual confidence and ominous caution insistently drew attention to the vulnerability of humans and their utter dependence on divine and saving grace.

"In the midst of life we are in death: of whom may we seek for succour but of thee, O Lord, who for our sins art justly displeased?" were words that succinctly conveyed the basic Augustinian message of a "rigorous theological pessimism, tempered by somewhat pallid rays of hope."[4] Was there any man or woman in the Reformed areas of baroque Germany who had not heard them, and very probably on more than one occasion? We would do well to remind ourselves that at that time they had a more immediate relevance than mercifully they do now for most of us.

Plague and pestilence ravaged towns and cities with remorseless regularity, and so, too often, did armies. Primitive living conditions; overcrowding; inadequate sewerage and lack of sanitation; rats, lice, and fleas and other vermin; malnutrition; infected water supplies and contaminated foodstuffs: these were not seen empirically as primary causes, but were experienced by all classes and accepted often with wry humor as realities of life. And death was never very far away.[5] Typhus, smallpox, plague, and venereal diseases threatened such adults as had managed to survive the perils of birth and childhood.

"And why stand we in jeopardy every hour?—Und was stehen wir alle Stund in Gefahr?" asked St. Paul in a passage from 1 Corinthians 15 familiar to Lutherans and Anglicans alike because it was customarily read at funerals. In it the Apostle deals with a question that had a much more vital urgency about it in a period when average expectation of life was so very much more limited. "If there be no resurrection of the dead, then is Christ not risen. And if Christ be not risen, then is our preaching vain, and your faith is also vain. . . . Then they also which are fallen asleep in Christ are perished" (verses 16–18). The Apostle's argument is lucid, and it exerted a profound effect on baroque thinking, especially in the northern, Protestant parts of Europe: "If in this life only we have hope in Christ, we are of all men most miserable" (verse 19); therefore "what advantageth it me, if the dead rise not? Let us eat and drink, for tomorrow we die" (verse 32). Nowhere is there a more explicit statement of the tension between this world and the hereafter, the *Diesseits* and the *Jenseits*, as it was experienced by the vast majority of God-fearing Christian believers in post-Reformation pre-materialistic Europe. And to cap it all, St. Paul saw fit to include what must have seemed an overt allusion to the life-enhancing Epicureanism or hedonism that lay at the heart of Renaissance classical culture—an earthbound alternative only viable if the central Christian reality of resurrection to a heavenly hereafter is rejected as an illusion.

Besides the *Media vita* and chapter 15 of St. Paul's First Epistle to the Corinthians, the burial offices of the Lutheran churches included other texts that were to play significant parts in shaping the outlook of the baroque in Germany and suggest some of its favorite themes. Popular, for instance (though absent from the Book of Common Prayer), was the latter half of chapter 4 of the First Epistle to the Thessalonians, with its consolatory emphasis on "sleeping with Jesus," a notion congenial to Lutheran thinking because of its rejection of purgatorial doctrine. Even more influential was the inclusion of two major penitential psalms, the *De Profundis* (Psalm 130) and *Domine refugium* (Psalm 90), both of which must surely be regarded as primary sources for recurrent images and themes in German poetry, Psalm 90 deserving in particular to be more widely known to modern literary critics for its solemn reminders of the transience of all things and its timely caution, "Lehre uns bedenken, daß wir sterben müssen, auf daß wir klug werden" (verse 12).

It was on the German hymn writers that these texts and readings had their most immediate influence, and not surprisingly when one considers that most of them were Lutheran clergymen who were accustomed to preaching that this world is a vale of misery and paradise an eternal garden, and that death should be regarded as an illusion not touching the real man, who is a spiritual being. Thus Johann Georg Albinus the Elder (1624-79) of Weißenfels and Naumburg:

> Alle Menschen müssen sterben;
> Alles Fleisch vergeht wie Heu.

Or, later, that prolific but underrated Silesian hymn writer Benjamin Schmolck (1672-1737), the teacher of Johann Christian Günther (1695-1723), and a decisive influence on his personal, heartfelt style:

> Je größer Kreuz, je näher Himmel;
> Wer ohne Kreuz, ist ohne Gott.
> Bei Sündenlust und Weltgetümmel
> Vergißt man Hölle, Fluch und Tod.

And, of course, the great Paul Gerhardt (1607-76):

> Ich bin ein Gast auf Erden
> Und hab hier keinen Stand;
> Der Himmel soll mir werden,
> Da ist mein Vaterland.

Or, finest of all, Joachim Neander's (1650-80) great hymnic ode "Wie fleucht dahin der Menschen Zeit," which ought only to be quoted in full.

Seen in the broader perspective of European literature and culture, the resonance of these seventeenth-century hymn writers and their principal forerunners, Johannes Hermann (1585-1647) and Luther, was extraordinarily lasting and far-reaching. Though largely neglected by modern literary historians, there is ample justification for regarding their achievement as Germany's main contribution to the period and, via translated versions, to the cultural heritage of Scandinavia and the English-speaking countries. For in them the new Protestant ethos found a lyric voice at once vernacular and corporate, unmistakably personal and intimate, yet at the same time generalized enough for individuals to be able to express vicariously through it their hopes and fears, longings and sadness, in the knowledge that they could be heard and understood by all brought up to share the same tradition.[6] Although stereotyped in expressive range and language, it radiated that particular sincerity and inwardness which, in retrospect, has been the hallmark of Lutheran spirituality ever since the publication in 1520 of *Von der Freiheit eines Christenmenschen*.

Like translation, music, too, played a leading part in carrying this Protestant baroque tradition beyond the confines of the German-speaking countries; indeed, the Passions and cantatas of J. S. Bach, arising directly out of this tradition and deeply imbued with it, raised it to a level of aesthetic distinction equaled only by the poetry of Gryphius, and actually preserved it for a wider international public. Moreover, the qualities this ethos upheld — God-trusting composure, fortitude in the face of adversity and affliction, humility, self-abasement, and disdain for this present life in the sure hope of a better life hereafter — were all of them qualities that could smoothly coalesce with the moral virtues espoused by Christian Neostoicism, that cast of thought which spread all over Europe as the sixteenth century was closing.

The Stoic position was most notably set forth in the moral writings of Seneca the philosopher, which were widely read and commonplace throughout the period; as the Queen aptly if tritely observes to Hamlet:

> Thou know'st 'tis common; all that live must die,
> Passing through nature to eternity.[7]

The view that life, brief and often bitter, is but a prelude to eternity, and that death may bring about extinction for all except those who have risen above it, was expounded most persuasively in those haunting lines from chapter 26 of the *Consolatio ad Marciam*, in which the philosopher tells the bereaved mother that only the base, imperfect image of her son has perished and that he is now his true, real self, in his eternal state: the vesture of the body, bones, sinews, covering skin, face, hands, and other outward wrappings are but chains and darkness to our eternal souls, suffocating them, hiding them from the truth, imprisoning them in error and illusion.

It is but a step from here to the gloomy splendor of Chassignet or, rather, to that last sonnet of Ronsard, most learned and life-loving of poets:

> Je n'ai plus que les os, un squelette je semble,
> Décharné, dénervé, démusclé, dépulpé,
> Que le trait de la mort sans pardon a frappé,

which Opitz took up and translated as an embellishment for his Senecan *Trostschrift an Herrn David Müllern* (1628), designed no doubt to illustrate the virtues of this typically Stoic prose form in German.[8]

But the most impressive lyrical expression of Stoicism's darkest insights occurs in the second-act chorus of Seneca's *Troades*, that most admired and plundered of classical tragedies, and the one which Opitz had chosen to translate and issue at Wittenberg in 1625 in order to demonstrate the feasibility of regular tragedy in German, in much the same way as Jasper Heywood had used it in 1559 to inaugurate the Elizabethan tradition. In his German version what is remarkable is that Opitz chooses to render the Latin chorus

> Verum est an timidos fabula decipit,
> Umbras corporibus vivere conditis?

as an iambic ode or strophic hymn in alternating rhyme:

> Ob es dann war ist / oder nicht /
> Und lassen wir uns nur betriegen /
> Daß unser Geist lebt wie man spricht /
> Wann gleich die Cörper todt da liegen?

Not only is this similar in style and spirit to his illustration of the genre in the *Buch von der Deutschen Poeterey*, where his model had been Ronsard ("Celuy qui est mort aujourdhuy"), it is of course also akin to the metrical schemes already established among the Protestant hymn writers and reinforced by the later-sixteenth-century convention of the metrical psalm.

It is against this background that Andreas Gryphius (1616–64) should be seen. Staunchly Lutheran, well traveled and cosmopolitan in his intellectual equipment, a competent Latinist, yet firmly rooted in vernacular traditions, Gryphius exhibits more clearly than any of his contemporaries the German position as regards the baroque theme of illusion and reality.[9] His ode "Vanitas! Vanitatum Vanitas!" (Book I; 1643) found its way into the Lutheran hymnbooks, and understandably so: the images are bold and biblical, the tone of voice no more, apparently, than a variation on the mainstream of Lutheran devotion, yet unmistakably the poet's own. Every line, however, is permeated with the themes and images, indeed the vocabulary, of Senecan Stoicism, from disdain for the world and somber laments on the brevity of life and the illusory nature of all things:

> Es hilfft kein weises wissen /
> Wir werden hingerissen /
> Ohn einen unterscheidt /

to the opening statements and rhetorical questions, with their reminiscences of Ecclesiastes and Isaiah, and finally to an emphasis on the theme of false illusion as opposed to true spiritual reality, which dominates the end. It is, however, interesting to note that in Gryphius's ode the key words carrying the illusion-and-reality theme—"leichter *Traum*" and "falscher *Wahn*"—seldom if ever figure in this sense or context in the German Bible, while the word *Phantasie*, as in

> Was ist der Menschen leben /
> Der immer umb mus schweben /
> Als eine phantasie der zeit

is completely absent from the Bible. Indeed, the poem's language comes much closer to that of Gryphius's first great tragic hero, Leo Armenius, after he has been visited by the ghost or apparition announcing his impending downfall:

> Was bilden wir uns ein?
> Soll unß ein leerer wahn / ein falscher dunst bewegen?
> Sol dises zittern sich auß Phantasie erregen?

In fact, what the ode covers in its sixteen six-line stanzas was in multiple ways and senses to become the subject of his most personal and anguished tragedy, *Cardenio und Celinde* (published 1657), which therefore can be said to mark the transposition of this great German baroque theme from the predominantly religious, lyric sphere to the explicitly dramatic.[10]

Cardenio und Celinde is the outstanding German treatment of illusion and reality, and thus a counterpart of Calderón's dramatizations of the theme, or indeed of *Hamlet*. It occupies a special place in the Gryphius tragic canon between the two royal martyr plays, *Catharina von Georgien* and *Carolus Stuardus*, both of which had demonstrated the total contrast between life and eternity by focusing on the process of transition from one plane of being to the other. Within the apparently restricting frame of high-flown pseudoclassical tragedy, both royal protagonists go to meet their death in solemn triumph, a death graciously, even willingly accepted because it offers their crowned but care-worn heads premature relief from mortal misery and the sure prospect of an "immarcescible [imperishable] crown of glory."

Both Catharina and Charles embrace their doom with the same patience saints do martyrdom; Cardenio, however, is neither royal nor a martyr, but an impetuous and passionate young human being caught up in the complexity of life itself. Unsure of where he stands, he has to make his way as best he can through life's ambiguous pressures and navigate a searing personal crisis while we spectators watch him play his part. It is fitting that Gryphius specifies "Das Trauer-Spill beginnet wenig Stunden vor Abends / wehrt durch die Nacht / und endet sich mit dem Anfang des folgenden Tages," for, like other great European baroque works, this is a drama with a marked symbolical dimension and a concern for fictions, shadows, and ghastly dreams of passion. It is a kind of waking dream, from which the characters involved at last awaken to the realization, expressed in the final couplet by that protagonist, that

> Wer hier recht leben wil und jene Kron ererben /
> Die uns das Leben gibt: denck jede Stund ans Sterben.

A crown eternal is therefore as much the ultimate objective of this work, a *comedia* in the Spanish sense, as it is in the more dignified tragedies of state and martyrdom with their closer affinities to Senecan, Dutch, or even contemporary Jesuit Neo-Latin drama.

The spirit and metaphysical content of Gryphius's plays has been much written about, and their intellectual caliber is generally recognized, at least by German scholars. But there is room for some redirection of attention towards their imagery, vocabulary, and action, and towards Gryphius's use of these essential factors to hammer home the fundamental themes of all his writing, not least the problem of reality and illusion, or, rather, of *Schein und Sein*.

As Dryden's Neander knew, " 'Tis true, there is both care and art required to write in verse. A good poet never concludes upon the first line till he has sought out such a rhyme as may fit the sense, already prepared to heighten the second."[11] To follow Gryphius at work in the light of this expert seventeenth-century view is illuminating. Let us just take the key word *Schein*.

In Cardenio's lengthy narration in Act I, he regrets his parents' well-meaning intention to send him to Italy to study:

> Ach freylich wol gemeynet!
> Doch / wie wenn uns zu Nacht ein falsches Irrlicht scheinet;
> Man offt den Weg verläst und in die Täuffen fällt /
> In welchen man versinckt. So ists mit mir bestellt.

At this point the key rhyme is not only feminine, it is also apparently no more than a perfunctory accompaniment to the image of the "falsche Irrlicht," itself subordinate to the similes of the straight and narrow path and of straying, falling, sinking, which dominate the play in both their literal and figurative senses and with the full force of their scriptural associations. The chorus to the act takes up the key word *Schein* in the sense of outward guise or semblance and in a context of mounting turbulence and passion, of lurid flames erupting out of darkness: disguised as constant love, lust has the infernal power to disturb the noblest spirits and jeopardize their hopes of Paradise.

Certainly love leads Celinde to desperate undertakings in Act II, and to involvement with the shadowy, glinting aberrations of black magic, whereas in Act III, as the fateful night draws on, Cardenio in the loneliness of his chamber and prey to passionate despair attempts to burn the portrait of the virtuous Olympia, while as he does so his words reflect the poet's awareness of the action's implications:

> Was hilffts? Ach must du denn / du gar zu wahrer Schein
> Von meiner Seelen Sonn' vergehn und Aschen seyn!

The cumulative effect reaches it climax in Act IV with its extraordinary sequence of scene changes from dark street corner to pleasure garden, then, in a flash, to an awful wilderness and, finally, to a church set in a nocturnal, ghost-haunted graveyard.

The build-up, pace, and effective use of technical resources make Act IV the finest piece of German baroque drama in purely theatrical terms, and the moment when Olympia's beautiful specter turns into a menacing skeleton is a *coup de théâtre* of an intensely baroque kind, probably unrivaled on the seventeenth-century European stage. Empirically though mistakenly perceived as real, the apparition reveals itself as Death, whose realness brooks no contradiction; thus allegory triumphs over verisimilitude, and demonstrates that on the stage it is just an illusion achieved by the use of stage effects and lighting.

What is less evident to the spectator is that these thrilling dramatizations of change and transformation are counterpointed by insistent references to the key words *Schein* and *scheinen*, which now exploit their full potential meaning thanks to baroque delight in conceits and double meanings: they rhyme (no longer just "um des Reimes willen") with *allein* and *weinen*, as if to reinforce the overall conception of two lost souls tragically benighted by their sinful earthly passions until, within the church and at the very graveside, their moment of truth is reached, the spell is broken, and soul-saving mutual recognition flashes upon them:

> Dafern er mit mir armen
> Mitleiden tragen mag / so woll' er sich erbarmen /
> Und führe mich von hier!

Celinde entreats Cardenio from the tomb, while he, perplexed, exclaims:

> Ists! oder ists ein Schein!
> Soll sie *Celinde* denn in lauter Warheit seyn!

The situation, the almost Claderónian manner, stands comparison with the best of Spanish baroque drama. But the flavor is distinctly Lutheran.[12]

The fusion of these two European traditions is one of the salient features of the baroque in Germany when viewed in the wider context of seventeenth-century culture. *Cardenio und Celinde* is the least stylized of the serious German baroque dramas, the one whose movement and internal structure come closest to the Spanish pattern; and in general the Spanish influence or manner is most in evidence in literature of the lighter, more entertaining, less elevated kind, especially where it has a satirical bias.[13] Here, thanks to the prodigious efforts and popular appeal of adaptors and translators such as Aegidius Albertinus (ca. 1560-1620) and Moscherosch (1601-69), a fertile source was channeled into the indigenous vernacular tradition of German storytelling, bringing with it a host of congenial themes and literary motifs, not least a taste for Iberian disenchantment (*desengaño*), seen at its most fully assimilated in the last two chapters of Book V of *Simplicissimus* (1669).

To the majority of its mainly German readers Grimmelshausen's novel is quite simply the most immediate literary product of Germany's uniquely searing experiences during the Thirty Years War, and its protagonist must often seem to be the embodiment of a specifically German makeup. Yet when Simplicissimus comes to contemplate himself in the light of that experience in chapter 25, and sums the whole perplexing phenomenon up by saying "Dein Leben ist kein Leben gewesen / sondern ein Todt; deine Tage ein schwerer Schatten, deine Jahr ein schwerer Traum / deine Wollüst schwere Sünden / deine Jugend eine Phantasey . . ." he is in fact quoting almost verbatim not from the Book of Job but from one of the most seminal of Spanish Renaissance works, the once internationally famous *Menosprecio de corte y alabanza de aldea* by Charles V's companion and court preacher, the Franciscan Antonio de Guevara.

Guevara is also author of the *Golden Book of the Emperor Marcus Aurelius* (1529), or *The Diall of Princes*, which not only anticipated the rediscovery of the emperor's Stoic *Meditations* by some thirty years and played a major part in disseminating the Neostoic outlook, but also represents the prototype of all those baroque courtly novels—or at least of many of their characteristic features, such as their fondness for curious erudition and for the moral and political education of princes in a make-believe imperial Roman setting. Indeed, Guevara seems to have been unusually successful in linking medieval elements and classical motifs with forward-looking, fashionable topics in a manner congenial to German readers of a century later, when Germany, too, had at last entered an analogous phase of cultural stock-taking and reassessment.[14] For instance, one of his favorite subjects, the allied themes of contempt for court life and praise of simple rural living (as in the *Menosprecio*), was to become one of the established corollaries to the basic theme of illusion and reality in German baroque writing, from Opitz's attractively Virgilian or, rather, Horatian *Lob des Feldlebens* of 1623 with its characteristic conclusion:

> Es stehe wer da wil hoch an deß Glückes spitzen /
> Ich schätze den für hoch der kan hierunten sitzen /
> Da keine Hoffart ist / kein eusserlicher schein
> So nur die Augen füllt / kan seine selber sein

to the Italianate, almost operatic chorus of Egyptian gardeners in Lohenstein's *Cleopatra*, with its high-baroque embellishments on the same conventional *topos*. But when, in the final chapter of Book V of *Simplicissimus*, the unheroic hero bids farewell to the "schnöde arge Welt" in terms apparently reminiscent of the Lutheran hymnbook or a Bach cantata, he warns us not to judge by appearances and jump to false conclusions by deftly preceding the passage in question not with a German authority but with a reference to the Spanish writer.

In other words, the theme was in the air to such an ubiquitous extent that its appearances in German baroque writing are not to be accounted for simply in terms of their obvious or indeed unexpected sources. From Lutheran hymn to Seneca-inspired drama, from stylized or satirical comedy to popular prose fiction the theme of *Schein und Sein* is ever present, and accompanied often by its many corollaries, such as "life is a dream," "the world's a stage," and "the transience of all things."

These themes all came together in what was probably Germany's favorite version of the subject and the one which most clearly reflects the particular nature and complexity of baroque art and literature in the German-speaking countries. This is the traditional notion of the *rusticus imperans* — the poor peasant who, in a drunken stupor, wakes up to find himself a mighty prince (or petty princeling!) for a day. As in a dream, he wallows in his new-found power, wealth, and glory, only to find that he is returned when drunk again to his former humble but befitting station, the victim of the true prince's cruel prank. Familiar to us as the framework story of the tinker Christopher Sly in the "induction" to Shakespeare's *Taming of the Shrew* (1594), and based on Spanish — and, ultimately, oriental — sources, it was made the subject of a homespun comedy by the Lutheran pastor Ludwig Hollonius in 1605 with the significant title *Somnium vitae humanae*.

In 1647 the story was taken up by the gifted Jesuit playwright Jakob Masen (1606-81) in his *Rusticus imperans*, one of the most popular of seventeenth-century Neo-Latin dramas. The inability of Mopsius, the village smith and drunkard, to play his miscast part in the burlesque farce staged by the omniscient ruler becomes in the Jesuit's hands a parable of human life and a sobering reminder of the vanities of the world and the fickleness of fortune. The play is rich in satirical bite and social comment, but central to the tragicomic plight of its unwitting protagonist at every interpretative level are the human being's tendency to be misled by appearances and illusion, and his innate inability to make the right distinctions until his eyes are truly opened. Lightness of touch alone fends off some leading metaphysical questions on the nature of reality and the identity of the individual psyche.[15]

The fact that this Neo-Latin play enjoyed greater success than the vernacular drama is a telling comment on the German cultural situation, but what is equally significant is that the subject was dramatized by authors on both sides of the religious divide that was tearing Germany apart during the first half of the seventeenth century. When calm had been restored and the patterns of German baroque culture were already well established, the *rusticus imperans* story, still topical, was chosen by yet another dramatist, Christian Weise (1642-1708), this time not only to point a moral, but to give his schoolboys practical experience in language and deportment and a useful insight into the attitudes and distinctions revealed through manners and speech.

The range of Weise's comedy, *Wunderliches Schauspiel vom Niederländischen Bauer* (1685), is correspondingly wide, covering as it

does the whole social gamut from courtly affectation to boorish blunt-
ness, and making many an effective point as regards the roles we play
and our tendency to project images as well as to judge by the images of
others. But Weise handles his material with the homely humor of a strict
yet benevolent grammar-school master, and the human comedy of the
work has more in common with Dutch genre painting than with the
chiaroscuro of Caravaggio or Rembrandt, of Gryphius or Masen, in
whose works, whether Catholic or Protestant, the shifting interplay of
light and shadow upon a large-scale canvas could sometimes illumine
deep spiritual dimensions. By comparison Weise's undertaking is
modest, but his handling of it suggests some points worth making. In his
comedy of character, situation, and manners — or, rather, the peasant
Mierten's sorry lack of them — appearances are shown to matter in the
community, while illusions are revealed as a comical and stupid human
foible or as the result of ignorance and upbringing. Meanwhile "reality"
refers less to the underlying or ultimate spiritual truth behind appearances than to the world as it is, viewed honestly and realistically, not
allegorized or idealized. Thus a realistic, almost naturalistic trend, long
evident in Spanish and German picaresque fiction and linking up with
sixteenth-century vernacular writing, reemerged at the very center of
baroque interests in Weise's treatment of the "dreaming peasant."

By and large, however, seventeenth-century German writers and
their readers had few doubts as to the reality of illusion; real life seemed
little else when viewed, as generally it was, *sub specie aeternitatis*. In the
retrospect of death, *Leben* could so easily read *Nebel* that only a proper
attitude to dying could help a person to read the word aright and so come
to the prevailing baroque conclusion: "The sum of all is this: that thou
art a man, than whom there is not any greater instance of heights and
declensions, of lights and shadows, of misery and folly, of laughter and
tears, of groans and death," as Jeremy Taylor puts it in *The Rule and Exercises of Holy Dying* (1651), words which could be paralleled by many a
German writer of the period and which convey the tensions and contrasts
of European baroque writing while reminding one yet again of its indebtedness to Scripture.

The aesthetics of baroque reality and illusion in Germany are thus
as complex and as varied as the thinking that underlies them. The commonplaces of Renaissance aesthetic theory — the "poet-God" and the
"imitation of nature" — proliferated alongside staunchly held convictions
that in the divinely established, eternally instituted order man is God's
creatures, created in His image, and that spiritual well-being is of pre-
ponderant importance and therefore matters more than material wel-

fare and progress. Death being the common gateway to a certainty which, during a man's lifetime, faith alone can supply, a certain *joie de vivre* is noticeably lacking in all but the most devoutly sanguine or poetically shallow of seventeenth-century German writers, i.e., religious poets and mystics such as the Catholic Friedrich von Spee or the Protestant Catharina Regina von Greiffenberg, or the libertine contributors to the *Neukirch Sammlung*.

The mirthlessness of German baroque writing—some comedies, prose, and erotic verse apart—is in clear contrast to the baroque in most other European settings. Exuberant delight in make-believe and illusionism for their own sake was absent: the elegant masquerade of life was a concept foreign to the majority of Germans, and "Amphitryon" was a subject that had to wait till Kleist for German treatment. During the baroque age the Germans' brooding on mortality and death, and their preoccupation with the theme of *Sein und Schein*, comes closer to the mood of Shakespeare's Wittenberg student prince ("Seems, madam! Nay it is; I know not seems") than it does to the delicate enchantments of *The Tempest* or the élan and wit of *L'Illusion comique*.

NOTES

1. On this subject see especially F.-W. Wentzlaff-Eggebert, *Der triumphierende Tod und der besiegte Tod in der Wort- und Bildkunst des Barock* (Berlin and New York: de Gruyter, 1975), and F. van Ingen, *Vanitas und Memento Mori in der deutschen Barocklyrik* (Groningen: Wolters, 1966).

2. Rudolf Lenz, "Die Forschungsstelle für Personalschriften: Aufgaben, bisherige Ergebnisse und Vorhaben," *Wolfenbütteler Barock-Nachrichten*, VI (1979), 271.

3. Geoffrey Rowell, *The Liturgy of Christian Burial* (London: Alcuin Club/S.P.C.K., 1977), pp. 74-80.

4. A. G. Dickens, *The German Nation and Martin Luther* (London: Arnold, 1974), p. 84.

5. See for instance Peter Lahnstein, *Das Leben im Barock: Zeugnisse und Berichte 1640 bis 1740* (Stuttgart: Kohlhammer, 1974), pp. 72, 82, and passim.

6. See the helpful introduction to *Der Protestantismus des 17. Jahrhunderts*, ed. Winfried Zeller (Bremen: Carl Schünemann, 1962).

7. T. S. Eliot's essay "Shakespeare and the Stoicism of Seneca" (1927) remains one of the best, most stimulating treatments of the subject.

8. A subject discussed with insight by Sibylle Rusterholz, *Rostra, Sarg und*

Predigtstuhl: Studien zu Form und Funktion der Totenrede bei Andreas Gryphius, Studien zur Germanistik, Anglistik und Komparatistik, 16 (Bonn: Bouvier, 1974), although the author does not consider the *consolatio* genre in detail or mention this example.

9. See Willi Flemming, *Andreas Gryphius: Eine Monographie* (Stuttgart: Kohlhammer, 1965), pp. 81-95.

10. For detailed treatment of a related *topos* see Peter Rusterholz, *Theatrum Vitae Humanae*, Philologische Studien und Quellen, 51 (Berlin: Erich Schmidt, 1970).

11. John Dryden, *Of Dramatic Poesy*, ed. George Watson (London: Dent, 1962), p. 82.

12. For my fuller survey of the European context, see Peter N. Skrine, *The Baroque: Literature and Culture in Seventeenth-Century Europe* (London: Methuen, 1978; New York: Holmes & Meier, 1979), pp. 33-38.

13. The "Spanish Epoch" in Germany is expertly surveyed in the introduction to Gerhart Hoffmeister, *Die spanische Diana in Deutschland*, Philologische Studien und Quellen, 68 (Berlin: Erich Schmidt, 1972), pp. 11-22; see B. Becker-Cantarino's essay in this volume.

14. Guevara's international success and importance as a stylistic model are considered in interesting detail in Ernest Grey, *Guevara: A Forgotten Renaissance Author*, International Archives of the History of Ideas, Series Minor, 4 (The Hague: Martinus Nijhoff, 1973).

15. See most recently Jean-Marie Valentin, *Le théâtre des Jésuites dans les pays de langue allemande (1554–1680)*, European University Studies, Series I, 255 (Bern: Peter Lang, 1978), pp. 821-25.

SELECTED BIBLIOGRAPHY

Secondary Literature

Adriani, Götz. *Deutsche Malerei im 17. Jahrhundert.* Köln: DuMont, 1977.

Burger, Heinz Otto. *Dasein heißt eine Rolle spielen.* München: Hanser, 1963.

Dickens, A. G. *The German Nation and Martin Luther.* London: Arnold, 1974.

Dryden, John. *Of Dramatic Poesy.* George Watson, ed. London: Dent, 1962, p. 82.

Flemming, Willi. *Andreas Gryphius: Eine Monographie.* Stuttgart: Kohlhammer, 1965, pp. 81-95.

Forster, Leonard. "Der Geist der deutschen Literatur im 17. Jahrhundert." In *Kleine Schriften zur deutschen Literatur im 17. Jahrhundert* (= *Daphnis*, 6, Heft 4). Amsterdam: Rodopi, 1977, pp. 7-30.

——. "Lipsius and Renaissance Neostoicism." In *Festschrift for Ralph Farrel.* Bern: Peter Lang, 1977, pp. 201-20.

Franz, Günther. *Der Dreißigjährige Krieg und das deutsche Volk: Untersuchungen zur Bevölkerungs- und Agrargeschichte.* 3rd rev. ed. Stuttgart: Fischer, 1961.

Gaede, Friedrich. *Humanismus Barock Aufklärung: Geschichte der deutschen Literatur vom 16. bis zum 18. Jahrhundert.* Bern: Francke, 1971.

Grey, Ernest. *Guevara: A Forgotten Renaissance Author.* International Archives of the History of Ideas, Series Minor, 4. The Hague: Martinus Nijhoff, 1973.

Hoffmeister, Gerhart. *Die spanische Diana in Deutschland.* Philologische Studien und Quellen, 68. Berlin: Erich Schmidt, 1972.

Kirchner, Gottfried. *Fortuna in Dichtung und Emblematik des Barock.* Stuttgart: Metzler, 1970.

Lahnstein, Peter. *Das Leben im Barock: Zeugnisse und Berichte 1640 bis 1740.* Stuttgart: Kohlhammer, 1974.

Langer, Herbert. *Kulturgeschichte des 30jährigen Krieges.* Stuttgart: Kohlhammer, 1978.

Lenz, Rudolf. "Die Forschungsstelle für Personalschriften: Aufgaben, bisherige Ergebnisse und Vorhaben," *Wolfenbütteler Barock-Nachrichten,* VI (1979), 271.

Mauser, Wolfram. *Dichtung, Religion und Gesellschaft im 17. Jahrhundert: Die Sonette des Andreas Gryphius.* München: Fink, 1976.

Plard, Henri. "Le Roi d'un jour: Esquisse d'une généalogie de *Jeppe paa Bjaerget.*" *Etudes Germaniques,* 10 (1955), pp. 229-46.

Rowell, Geoffrey. *The Liturgy of Christian Burial.* London: Alcuin Club/ S.P.C.K., 1977.

Rusterholz, Peter. *Theatrum Vitae Humanae.* Philologische Studien und Quellen, 51. Berlin: Erich Schmidt, 1970.

Rusterholz, Sibylle. *Rostra, Sarg und Predigtstuhl: Studien zu Form und Funktion der Totenrede bei Andreas Gryphius.* Studien zur Germanistik, Anglistik und Komparatistik, 16. Bonn: Bouvier, 1974.

Skrine, Peter. N. *The Baroque: Literature and Culture in Seventeenth-Century Europe.* London: Methuen, 1978. New York: Holmes & Meier, 1979.

Valentin, Jean-Marie. *Le théâtre des Jésuites dans les pays de langue allemande (1554–1680).* European University Studies, Series I, 255. Bern: Peter Lang, 1978, pp. 821-25.

van Ingen, Ferdinand. *Vanitas und Memento Mori in der deutschen Barocklyrik.* Groningen: Wolters, 1966.

Wentzlaff-Eggebert, F.-W. *Der triumphierende Tod und der besiegte Tod in der Wort- und Bildkunst des Barock.* Berlin and New York: de Gruyter, 1975.

Wiley, Basil. *The Seventeenth-Century Background.* London: Chatto & Windus, 1934. Rpt. Harmondsworth: Penguin, 1962.

Zeller, Winfried, ed. *Der Protestantismus des 17. Jahrhunderts.* Bremen: Carl Schünemann, 1962.

15

Courtly and Anticourtly Literature

Erika A. Metzger and Michael M. Metzger

During the seventeenth century, life in German-speaking Europe, as revealed in its literature, painting, music, architecture, and other cultural artifacts, was dominated by two major forces: religion and absolutist princely courts. But just as Christianity in Germany was divided between Catholicism and Protestantism, and each of these split again by doctrinal factions, neither did the princely court appear as a unified social and cultural phenomenon. More than three hundred secular and ecclesiastical princes ruled Germany then, ranging in power and significance from the emperor in Vienna over such large duchies as Bavaria and Württemberg; electorates like secular Saxony and Brandenburg and archepiscopal Mainz, Cologne, and Trier; down to the tiny domains of the numerous Imperial Knights (*Freiherren*) of western Germany. Although the majority of these rulers did not have the power or means to emulate the emperor, or later the king of France, by organizing their household or state apparatus along similarly splendid courtly lines, many courts of Germany became, especially through the economic and political decay of the cities, dominant social and political centers, to say nothing of their political significance, with which, however, the present essay cannot deal to any extent.[1]

Because absolutist rulers needed to strengthen their bureaucracies for the centralization of political power within their territories and desired to make their courts representative of that power, the court, the locus of the princely government and household, was expanding in size and significance during most of the seventeenth century. Commensurate with their means, but often enough beyond them, princes commissioned sumptuous palaces with formal gardens, chapels, opera houses, and libraries, and also the paintings, statues, and tapestries to decorate them, the operas, plays, pageants, and musical works to be performed in them. In many ways, "baroque" culture in Germany was propagated chiefly by the princely courts.

Many typical examples of the "courtly" phase in European art can still be studied today, for example, in such architectural monuments as Bernini's colonnades in Rome, the Trianon at Versailles, the Hofburg and the Belvedere palace and gardens at Vienna, the archepiscopal residence at Würzburg, or the Zwinger in Dresden. None of these is imaginable without the development of absolutist government, the concentration of wealth and political power in the hands of the ruler, who flaunted them to the awe of the world to reassure his allies and daunt his potential enemies. Although the aesthetic and political vocabulary of courtly culture in Germany originated mainly in Italy, Spain, and France, German artists and artisans, courtiers and officials proved themselves ready to adopt the new forms. In music, following the lead of such courtly composers as Monteverdi (1567-1643) and Purcell (1659-95), German musicians such as Schütz (1585-1672), Handel (1685-1759), and Bach (1685-1750) created, in their operas, suites, and oratorios, a musical tradition rooted in the adornment of a very specific courtly situation, the need to heighten the numerous occasions of the prince's life through a work of art. At courts both large and small, voluminous amounts of occasional poetry and commemorative paintings served the same purpose. It is in this obvious, functional sense that we might apply the term courtly to certain kinds of literature, such as the allegorical masques performed at court or, to cite a British example, poems like Richard Crashaw's "To the Queen's Majesty" or "Upon the King's Coronation."[2]

The word courtly (German *höfisch*; French *courtois*) means "belonging to a court," "events occurring at a court," and "typical of life at court." It also refers to the manners of courtiers and their ethical code. European courtly literature of the sixteenth and seventeenth centuries not only documents these aspects of courtly life, but also prescribes the ideals of behavior for the courtier. In his study of the courtly culture of France, Norbert Elias describes its poetic concept as that of a literature of representation, its strongest impulse being to shape all human feeling into a system of rigid courtly rationality, at whose center was the monarch. Germany, however, with its decentralized system of many small courts, differed from France in multiplying and diversifying the meanings of courtly and anticourtly. As Elias sees the situation in Germany, "especially in the west, even the households of the lower nobility, such as counts, were conducted like courts in many respects, and since all power was not concentrated in a single court in Germany, these miniature courts, even down to those of the wealthier rural gentry, had a much greater social and cultural significance than did their counterparts in France."[3]

Germany did not have a Versailles. It has therefore been suggested that the Habsburg court at Vienna was a model for major parts of Germany. Thus, Günther Müller characterized the seventeenth century as "the epoch of the Habsburgs." But this is not applicable to all regions of Germany, since many Austrian and German nobles lived on their estates, coming to Vienna, if at all, only for brief visits and not, as was the case in France, to stay at the court and become more and more dependent on the king. Gottfried Wilhelm Leibniz (1646–1716) touched upon this problem in comparing the development of the French and German languages:

ohngeachtet die Frantzösische Sprache aus der Lateinischen entsprossen, (welche bereits so wohl mit Regeln eingefasset) und sonsten von mehrer Zeit her als die Unsere von gelehrten Leuten bearbeitet worden, auch nur einen Hoff als den Mittel-Punct hat, nach dem sich alles richtet; welches uns mit Wien auch um des willen noch nicht wohl angehen wollen, weil Oesterreich am Ende Teutsch-landes, und also die Wienerische Mund-Art nicht wol zum Grunde gesetzet werden kann, da sonst, wann ein Kayser mitten im Reiche seinen Sitz hätte, die Regel der Sprache besser daher genommen werden könnte.[4]

In spite of the polycentric and heterogeneous nature of court life in Germany as compared with the unitary national states of France and England, a universal courtly ideology is clearly discernible in the seventeenth century. This results from practical facts of court life and the influence of the Renaissance tradition of didactic writing about the court. The canonical authors in this tradition were Niccolò Machiavelli (1469–1527), Baldassare Castiglione (1478–1529), Antonio de Guevara (1480–1545), Justus Lipsius (1547–1606), and Baltasar Gracián (1601–58). The court was seen as a microcosm of the larger universe, the perception of which had been radically altered since the end of the fifteenth century. The geocentric, hierarchically structured idea of the world, in which analogy seemed to exist between the universe, society, and the divinely willed place of humans in both, had been shattered by the discoveries of Copernicus and Galileo that the Earth is but one of a number of planets that revolve around the sun. The discovery of the New World also displaced Europe from its former conceptual centrality. Moreover, Europe was constantly tormented by wars, devastating plagues, and economic crises that were brought about by an increasingly monetary system of commerce. Thus, in the seventeenth century, old certainties had given way to the idea that the world had unexpected and perilous dimensions, that people's fate was governed not by Divine Will but by random, mechanical forces beyond their control and without a humane purpose or morality.

The court, too, was seen as a lawless universe whose sole principle was the attainment of power and influence, to which the only avenue was the favor of the prince. The wheel of fortune, a raging sea, a savage forest full of wild animals: these are characteristic metaphors of the age for the court, where a courtier might be elevated in his prince's esteem at one moment and thrust into disgrace and banishment in the next. All people lived there by the fickle whim of the prince, the sun around which this universe revolved. Of course, the chance that a person might be raised from obscurity to distinction through good fortune was also what made princely households so fascinatingly attractive as domains of a law of reward and punishment unto itself. The ideal of the courtly man, the *cortegiano*, who could not only survive but even prevail under these uncertain circumstances, prescribed very specific properties: loyalty, discretion, equanimity, rationality, and perseverance. Pessimistic Neo-stoicism displaced the Christian, knightly values that had characterized medieval feudalism. For the courtier, the most characteristic gesture was the concealment of his true situation and his feelings about it behind an imposing facade of splendor and well-being in keeping with the magnificence that the regent wished his court to reflect.

The expansion of princely bureaucracies brought about, for several decades at least, a loosening of the exclusiveness of court life. Whereas the court had traditionally been the domain of a territory's nobility, the skills demanded by a new age in politics, such as expertise in Roman law and in the rhetoric of legal argumentation, brought into princely chanceries and households university-trained lawyers whose origins were in the bourgeoisie. Such scholars had, by custom, enjoyed many of the social prerogatives of the lower gentry. Hence, there was no social obstacle to their free intermingling with courtiers of the traditional nobility. A fruitful interchange arose at many courts between the two groups, with bourgeois bureaucrats emulating the courtly graces of the nobles, and the nobles sending their sons to the universities with increasing frequency so that they would be able to hold their own in technical aspects of political life. The wide dispersion of the works of such authors as Guevara and Gracián resulted in great part from the need of members of the bourgeoisie, aspiring to careers at court, to learn how to behave in a realm previously closed and unknown to them. The noble-bourgeois elite of the princely bureaucracies brought courtly and humanistic values together to establish a community of practical, philosophical, and aesthetic interests that were powerfully instrumental in the creation of the courtly literary culture of the baroque period.[5] This was especially true of Heidelberg, Braunschweig-Wolfenbüttel, and the courts of Silesia, where the officials from such cities as Breslau played a dominant role.

Even within the domain of the courtly values, however—and such phenomena can be observed throughout Europe—this ideology did not go unchallenged. Paradoxically, among the splendors of the baroque court, in the midst of the cynical Machiavellism of its politics, behind the magnificence of its cultural and artistic facade, there were protests against these very attributes. Urban ostentation is to be replaced by rural simplicity, hypocrisy and cunning by sincerity and love, the terrifying complexity of the present by the idyllically patriarchal relationships of a bucolic Golden Age. These yearnings are the hallmarks of what has come to be known as the "anticourtly" tendency in baroque culture, providing a creative counterweight to the dominant themes of courtly cultural expression.

It is not safe or easy to generalize about the tension between courtly and anticourtly values, since they appear in varying constellations within literature. Some works are entirely courtly in character, while others consistently depict clear alternatives to these values. But many writers, understandably enough, evidently felt a poignant ambivalence regarding the court. Such works as the *Aviso de privados* (*Advice to Courtiers*) of Antonio de Guevara, for example, combine very pragmatic advice to the courtier on how to gain favor at court and overcome the practical difficulties of a princely household with laments on the emptiness and gilded misery of court life, the pleasures of a simple life of withdrawal in the country, and the necessity of embracing the redeeming doctrines of Christianity before it is too late.[6]

As a literary theme, the matter of anticourtly literature can be traced back at least to such Roman poets as Horace and Virgil, in whose works the carefree ease of the countryside was contrasted with the corrupting intrigues of the city and the emperor's court. Christian asceticism, too, reinforced such an attitude. But which specific factors impelled certain courtiers, writers, and artists to cultivate and express such an attitude, while others did not? For the age of Louis XIV of France, Norbert Elias finds the anticourtly attitude at its strongest not among the bourgeoisie, but among those nobles who were deprived of their feudal political and military power by the king and yet were dependent upon him for their survival and continued influence, being forced to subject themselves to the restrictive discipline of the royal household.[7] For such writers, the anticourtly themes provided an ideological and aesthetic safety valve, a way of asserting artistic and intellectual independence while remaining politically and economically subservient, the expression of a sentiment that did not endanger the very real benefits derived from the nobleman's dependence on the king.

This sociological explanation, that the anticourtly attitude was characteristic for those whose chances at court were less than brilliant, might also be applicable to the situation in Germany, although, if we wish to determine the courtly or anticourtly bias of a work, the role of the courts in the author's biography must be carefully assessed. But certainly the widespread rejection of courtly values which was typical for the mid-eighteenth century, when many of the anticourtly ideas were repeated and amplified, may well be directly attributable, as Alberto Martino has recently suggested, to the sharply reduced opportunities that presented themselves to university graduates due to a saturation with officials of princely bureaucracies throughout Germany.[8] Thus, there is strong sociological evidence for a correlation of the anticourtly position with social and economic disaffection. Yet, this is certainly not the sole cause for the occurrence of these values in art and literature. The anticourtly motifs may well have been used also for reasons of artistic effect, or as a compensatory gesture of feeling. We can find the anticourtly attitude manifested as a permanent ethos of opposition and as a fleeting sentiment of aesthetic escape. The prime example of the latter type of occurrence was the pastoral farm maintained at the court of the later French kings at Versailles, where the queen and her courtiers masqueraded as simple peasants.

Two German paintings might best illustrate the coexistence of the courtly and anticourtly in the seventeenth century. It is difficult to imagine greater differences in theme and representation than are to be found in a comparison of the *Allegorical Glorification of the Great*

Michael Willmann, *Allegorical Glorification of the Great Elector*, 1682. Canvas, 162 x 200 cm. Verwaltung der Staatlichen Schlösser und Gärten Berlin.

Elector, painted in 1682 by Michael Willmann (1630-1706), with the contemporary *Landscape with Herds and a Background of Ruins* by Johann Heinrich Roos (1631-85).[9] Holding the palm frond of peace in his hand, the Great Elector of Brandenburg, Friedrich Wilhelm (1620-88), the only figure to gaze outward to the beholder, commands the center of Willmann's painting with somber dignity. Seated in an interior, he is surrounded by allegorical figures of the arts and sciences, who avert their eyes before him in awe or gaze at him in adoration. Above his head fly cherubs, one trumpeting the Elector's fame to the world, the other crowning him with a wreath. The dark tableau is illuminated by a blaze of light from a figure representing Orphic poetry; this radiance falls most fully upon the Elector. The centrality of the figure of the ruler, his seeming apotheosis into a mythic realm, and his dual pictorial function as historical personality and emblem of the attributes of political power make this, whatever its aesthetic shortcomings may be, a decisively courtly painting. On one level, Willmann created a mere flattering contrivance, but the functional effect of the picture is the projection of the awesome majesty of the ruler, receiving tribute from all sources of wisdom and beauty in the world. What then must mere mortals owe him as homage?

The painting by Roos represents a bucolic idyll, whose foreground and middle field are dominated by groups of cattle and sheep in rather melancholy attitudes of innocent stateliness. The figures of a man and woman at their ease in nature are minute by comparison. The landscape is framed by verdant hills and trees and illuminated by a radiant evening sky reflected in a shimmering pond in the background. But the main axis of the picture, along which the eye of the beholder is intended to move, runs from the animals in the foreground to a group of ruins overgrown

Johann Heinrich Roos, *Landscape with Herds and a Background of Ruins*, ca. 1660–70. Canvas, 123.5 x 153.5 cm. Staatsgalerie Stuttgart.

with vegetation and silhouetted against the sky in the background. The picture's elements are organized so that timeless nature is contrasted with the fate of human artifice at the hands of time. In its celebration of rural peace and innocence and its explicit moralizing, the painting seems to exemplify the anticourtly values.

Unlike the terms court and courtly, which were widely found in baroque texts, anticourtly is a modern coinage, used by such scholars as Günther Müller, Erika Vogt, Erik Lunding,[10] Norbert Elias, and Alberto Martino to describe and interpret phenomena not adequately defined by concepts like "criticism of the courtly," "bourgeois," or such terms current in the seventeenth century as *altdeutsch* or *teutsch gesinnt*. Before discussing specific literary examples of the courtly and anticourtly trends, it will be useful to contrast their central ideas, especially as they affect the ideology and content of literary works. Günther Müller demonstrated this opposition as it is reflected in the seventeenth century's conceptions of God, Eros, and Time.[11]

In the courtly view, God is seen as being analogous to the absolute monarch, whereby are stressed the qualities of omnipotence, omniscience, the inscrutability of the divine will (which is a law unto itself), and indifference to the joys and sufferings of mere mortals. Anticourtly writers depict God as a benevolent Father to Man, whose soul is His temple and who lives in a close, inner relationship to Christ.

The physical aspect of Eros dominates in its courtly manifestations. As often as not, love is used to encompass political goals. Love is a daemonic, destructive force, and the frenzy of desire can be the downfall of great men. The relationship between men and women is frankly sexual, a struggle to gain domination, either by persuasion or coercion, an enslavement of the lover by the beloved. The beauty of women is celebrated through similes of precious stones and metals, rare flowers and perfumes, so that they are seen as coveted or prized possessions rather than as living, sentient persons. Anticourtly love, on the other hand, is predominantly spiritual, closely connected with constancy, loyalty, and Christian love or agape. The woman is seen as a helper and friend to the man, equal with him in her humanity.

To the courtly mind, time and the transiency of people within it is the great adversary, the founding element of an essentially tragic view of life. Courtly feasts and regal pomp; the massive, representative aspect of baroque architecture; the extensiveness of princely gardens; indeed, the accumulated learnedness of the baroque novel and drama and their lengthy rhetorical gestures: all of these are but bulwarks against the sense of fleeting time, before which all human works must vanish into dust. Hence, the moment—into which must be compressed as much meaning and vitality as possible in order, for an instant, to stop time—takes on such a deep significance. Extension and depth in space may, at least seemingly, impede time's inexorable movement. In the anticourtly scheme of things, time and transiency, though felt with equal keenness, are the great vindicators, laying the vanity of people and their works into ruin. The present time is only a part of eternity, a moment which must be overcome in order for the eternal, divine truths to be unfolded.

The courtly categories are strongly shaped by humanistic skepticism, Stoic philosophy, and the nihilism implicit both in Machiavellianism and the new scientific thinking. Seen from our perspective, the courtly attitude is indeed the more "modern" view, which helps to account, perhaps, for the intellectual and emotional kinship felt by many readers of the twentieth century with the baroque. The anticourtly attitude, as its recurrent celebration of a bygone Golden Age already implies, is more nostalgic, indeed reactionary, in its values, which are anchored in essentially religious conceptions of normative morality derived from both Christian and pre-Christian sources.

Since courtly and anticourtly sentiments can be perceived in many if not most of the literary documents of the baroque period in Germany, any listing of examples for either tendency cannot pretend to be even remotely exhaustive. It is the intent of this essay to present a domain of concerns in the literature of this period together with criteria to help determine which of these tendencies dominates in any work with which the reader might be dealing. Keeping this reservation in mind, however, certain examples of marked courtly and anticourtly intention and function are readily to be identified.

Especially in the early part of the century, occasional poetry is the most immediately courtly literary form. Thousands of poems celebrating princely victories, visits, weddings, births, and funerals are extant, both in anthologies of the time and in pamphlets. These poems span the entire century and frequently are useful as historical documents. They range from the encomium, "An den Regierenden Hertzogen zu Wirtemberg / . . . H. Johan-Friderichen /" (1618), by Georg Rudolf Weckherlin (1584-1643),[12] to the ode on Prince Eugene of Savoy by Johann Christian Günther (1695-1723), "Auf den zwischen Ihro Kayserl. Majestät und der Pforte An. 1718 geschlossenen Frieden," which celebrates Eugene's victories over the Turkish armies.[13] The courtly tradition of the Renaissance brought on the reawakening of interest in occasional poetry, and almost every poet of the seventeenth century wrote such verses. Among the most famous authors of casual poetry or *Gelegenheitsgedichte* in Germany were Weckherlin, Martin Opitz (1597-1639), Simon Dach (1605-53), Johann Rist (1607-67), and Benjamin Neukirch (1665-1729). David Schirmer (ca. 1623-83), librarian to the Elector of Saxony and writer of masques and opera libretti, was a precursor to the numerous *Hofdichter*, such as Johann von Besser (1654-1729), Johann Ulrich König (1688-1744), and Rudolf von Canitz (1654-99), all of whom we find active at various courts by the turn of the eighteenth century. Around 1650, the celebration of family events by commissioning poems became extremely fashionable among the urban bourgeoisie. The composition of these texts soon became the work of poetasters, so that occasional poetry sank into total literary disrepute.[14]

According to Martin Opitz, tragic drama deals with the mighty and their downfall. By this definition, tragedy is the most courtly genre during the seventeenth century. It is not surprising that those poets for whom the conflict between the imperatives of worldly power and divine morality were significant expressed their concerns on the stage of tragedy. This is the underlying problem of such plays as *Belisarius* (1607) by Jakob Bidermann (1578-1639); *Leo Armenius* (1647) and *Carolus Stuardus* (1650) by Andreas Gryphius (1616-64); and *Agrippina* (1665), *Ibrahim Sultan* (1673), or *Sophonisbe* (1680) by Daniel Casper von Lohenstein (1635-83), to name only a few. In these dramas, interest centers not on the fates of the historical individuals but on the emblematic significance of the tragic paradigm of the fates of people in the treacherous world of the court, the seat of power and intrigue.

Whereas the tragedies of Gryphius or Lohenstein were probably performed only before bourgeois or academic audiences, and thus must be considered courtly mainly because of their concern with the world of the court, there was also a dramatic literature that had a specifically courtly function corresponding to that of occasional lyrical poetry — namely, masques, ballets, pageants, and cantatas written in celebration of events at court, such as the pastoral, *Die Sinnreiche Liebe Oder Der Glückselige Adonis und Die Vergnügte Rosibella* (1673) by Johann Christian Hallmann (1647-1716), which he wrote in honor of the wedding of Emperor Leopold I.

Perhaps the most intrinsically courtly literary form of all is the compendious "heroic-galant" novel in its various manifestations, such as *Des Christlichen Teutschen Groß-Fürsten Herkules Und Der Böhmischen Königlichen Fräulein Valiska Wunder-Geschichte* (1659 et seq.) by Andreas Heinrich Buchholtz (1607–71); *Die Durchleuchtige Syrerin Aramena* (1669–73) and *Octavia, Römische Geschichte* (1677–1707) by Anton Ulrich von Braunschweig-Wolfenbüttel (1633–1714); *Assenat* (1670) by Philipp von Zesen (1619–89); *Die Asiatische Banise* (1689) by Heinrich Anshelm von Zigler und Kliphausen (1663–96); and, possibly the quintessential work of its kind, *Großmüthiger Feldherr Arminius* (1689 ff.) by Daniel Casper von Lohenstein. These works are courtly not only in their contents, telling through multistranded plots of the adventures and love stories at imaginary and historical courts, but they are frequently written by members of the nobility; in the case of Anton Ulrich, indeed, by a reigning monarch. Frequently thousands of pages in length, the novels had a function far beyond mere entertainment. Carefully planned and based on exhaustive study of historical sources and sometimes supplied with lengthy annotations, they served as encyclopedic sources on history, statecraft, warfare, manners, morals, and rhetoric. Meant to be read repeatedly and intensively, these books were intended by their authors to exemplify the ideals of truly heroic rulers, their consorts, and their courtiers. The positive characters possess the virtues of steadfastness, bravery, stoicism, and faith, whereas the negative characters are deceitful, intemperate, excessively passionate, and, ultimately, thwarted in their aims. Thus, the virtues and the vices over which they triumph are almost always relativized in terms of the pragmatic values of the court and the harmonious relationship of monarch and subjects, of the heroic leader and the loyal and resourceful followers.

Anticourtly literature is characterized most sharply by its criticism of the court, though not necessarily of the ruler, and by the negative view of court life that it presents, often preaching the need for withdrawal from court and "the world" in general. Its perspective is frequently that of what Walter Benjamin called "the branded courtier."[15] The reasons for retreat are ethical and religious. Accordingly, the exponent of the anticourtly attitude envisions a viable existence away from the vices of court in the country, a desert hermitage, or an island. The following poem by Friedrich von Logau (1604–55) is a typical example:

Das Dorf

Mein Gut besucht ich nächst; das Feld war voller Segen;
Sonst war mirs nicht so gut als in der Stadt gelegen.
Mein Tisch der war ein Brett. Mein Bette konnte gehen [ein Wagen],
Ich hatte frommen Trank [Wasser]. Zur Speise hatt ich stehen

Ein Kind, ein solches Kind, worüber, wanns geboren,
Die Mutter fröhlich singt [ein Ey]. Ich hatte mir erkohren
Den Platz, der zur Musik den ersten Grund uns giebet [die Tenne].
Und dennoch war mir wohl, und alles fiel [sic] geliebet,
Weil Ruh mir wohlgefiel. Das Zanken der Parteyen,
Der Ueberlauf des Volks, des Hofes Schwelgereyen,
Verleumdung, Neid und Haß, Druck, Heucheley und Höhnen,
Die ausgeschmückten Wort und fälschliches Beschönen
Die hatten hier nicht Statt. Hier war ich ganz mein eigen,
Und konnt all meine Müh zu meinem Besten neigen.
O Feld! o werthes Feld! ich will, ich muß bekennen,
Die Höfe sind die Höll, der Himmel du, zu nennen![16]

The anticourtly mode partook much of à la mode criticism of society at large, i.e., the satirical chastising of the Germans for their readiness to adopt Spanish, Italian, and French fashions in dress and speech, coupled with evocations of the pristine "Germanic" qualities of an earlier age. This criticism applied especially to the courts, as they were the main sources of an international, courtly culture, the courtiers distinguishing themselves precisely by their different manners and language from the common populace, which, however, strove to imitate them wherever possible. Hence Johann Michael Moscherosch's famous complaint:

Fast jeder Schneider   will jetzund leyder
Der Sprach erfahren sein   vnd redt Latein:
Wälsch vnd Frantzösisch   halb Japonesisch /
Wan er ist doll vnd voll   der grobe Knoll.

Der Knecht Matthies   spricht bonä dies /
Wan er gut morgen sagt   vnd grüst die Magd:
Die wend den Kragen   thut jhm danck sagen /
Spricht Deo gratias   Herr Hippocras.

Ihr böse Teutschen   man solt eüch peütschen /
Das jhr die Mutter-sprach   so wenig acht.
Ihr liebe Herren   das heist nicht mehren;
Die Sprach verkehren   vnd zerstören.[17]

Even the philosopher Gottfried Wilhelm Leibniz wrote in this vein, lamenting that "auf des Teutschen Kopf muß stehn ein fremder Hut," and "man lobt das teutsche Geld, wenn man des Teutschen lacht."[18]

The nostalgic aspect of the anticourtly tendency, which hearkened back to an egalitarian, pastoral state of natural felicity, also implied rejection of the existing social structures and criticism of the unjustified privileges enjoyed by the nobility. This is felt strongly, for example, in Grimmelshausen's *Simplicissimus*, which, despite its major concerns with other questions, must be counted among the intrinsically anticourtly works. Such criticism of the social structure foreshadowed tendencies that only came to a full development a century later in the literature of the "Storm and Stress."

The anticourtly complex is not restricted to any specific genre, although it is more frequently encountered in lyrical poetry than in the drama or novel. Thus, there are such anticourtly poems as Weckherlin's "An den Hofe,"[19] "ZeitVerderber" by Hans Aßmann von Abschatz (1646–99),[20] or the satirical poems of Joachim Rachel (1618–99). The epigram was especially well suited to the scathing criticism of such writers as Logau, who produced hundreds of epigrammatic poems; for example:

Hofhunde

Heuchler und Hunde belecken die Teller;
Jene sind Schmeichler, und diese sind Beller;
Diese bewahren, bey denen sie zehren;
Jene verzehren die, welche sie nähren.[21]

Through their antipodal relationship to the world of the court and the critical ideas often expressed in them, works with a bucolic setting, such as pastoral dramas (*Schäferspiele*) and novels (*Schäferromane*), are almost by definition anticourtly, at least in Germany. Especially popular in this respect was the pastoral drama *Il Pastor Fido* by the Italian Giovanni Battista Guarini (1538–1612), which was translated by both Christian Hofmann von Hofmannswaldau (1617–79) and Abschatz. In 1629, a translation appeared of Sir Philip Sidney's (1554–86) *Arcadia*, which had a great influence on the development of the German novel, inspiring, together with Spanish and Italian pastorals, many of the bucolic motifs to be found in later works.

Although anticourtly themes can, as we have seen, occur in isolation, especially in shorter forms, they are more usually to be found interacting dialectically with courtly ideas. This is the case, for example, in *Papinianus* (1659) by Andreas Gryphius or, in quite a different medium, in the novel, *Die Kunst- und Tugend-gezierte Macarie* (1669, 1673) by Heinrich Arnold Stockfleth (1643–1708) and Maria Catharina Stockflethin (1633?–1692). Since anticourtly motifs recurred in literature from Roman times onward, especially in periods when courts were culturally dominant, their use became part of literary convention, so that, quite aside from their function as sociological indicators, they must be seen to have been used also as literary devices. The courtly vs. anticourtly dialectic was a commonplace in Europe since the Renaissance, as can be observed readily, for example, in the plays of Shakespeare.

But beyond and perhaps within these conventionalized occurrences there is also an existential quest for a right judgment about which system of values is the most appropriate: is it the modern, materialistic, ultimately nihilistic courtly system, which seems to promise a better life in the present? Or is the nostalgic, idealistic, humane, anticourtly system, which seems to appeal more to those concerned with peace of mind and the salvation of the soul in the hereafter? In the works of many authors we encounter what Erik Lunding has termed an "oscillation" between both systems. This phenomenon is to be found, for example, in the works of Georg Philipp Harsdörffer (1607-58), Hans Jakob Christoffel von Grimmelshausen (1622?-76), Gryphius, and Abschatz. As Lunding puts it: "The poet assumes a character in a time in which everyone was playacting."[22] The possibilities of such an oscillation, the poet's speaking through several personae—none of which necessarily expresses his own, possibly more detached view—is contained in Harsdörffer's comment in his *Poetischer Trichter* (1653): "Der Hof prachtirt mit vollem Stoltz / ist weder Himmel oder Höll / weil man noch die Tugend belohnet / noch die Laster bestraffet / Wird von Guevarra mit einem Feurer verglichen / da man noch zu nahe noch zu ferne von seyn sol."[23]

Aspects of the work of the Silesian poet Daniel von Czepko (1605-60) may serve to illustrate this observation. Czepko is best known for his religious poetry, epigrams expressing a personal piety strongly influenced by the German mystical tradition of Eckhart and Tauler. In his early life, he had practiced law, and returning from western Germany to his native Silesia spent several years as a tutor and companion on the estates of various members of the local nobility. He married the daughter of a wealthy physician and spent the years from 1636 to 1658 writing poetry and managing the estates that his wife had brought into the marriage. After the death of his wife, Czepko served the duke of Brieg as a court official, meeting his death while on a diplomatic mission. Thus, Czepko participated both in the world of the court and in conscious withdrawal from it into the country. Although the courtly/anticourtly topos in his works is certainly subsidiary to other concerns, both aspects are present. We find defenses of Machiavellianism despite moral scruples:

Auff einen Anti-Machiavellisten.
Zum Hüten, nicht zum wüten.

Wo dir der von Florentz ein Gottes Lästrer ist,
    Der so viel Ränck' und List im Herrschen auffgeschrieben,
Wie wird dem, der getaufft, der seine Lehr erkiest:
    Die grösten sind: die, was er hat geschrieben, üben.[24]

Then there are poems such as "An den Hoffmann, wie er die Freyheit erlangen könne. Überwinde dich," in which, very much in the temper of the courtly manuals of Guevara, the courtier is told how to deal justly and morally with his duties at court, from which he cannot flee to a bucolic idyll:

Hast du die Macht in dir, die Macht, die du itzt hast,
    Aus ungefärbter Pflicht ohn Nachtheil zu begeben,
So wirstu täglich seyn der Freyheit liebster Gast,
    Und kanst viel freyer noch als selbst dein König leben.[25]

Such expressly "courtly" poems assume the pragmatic world of political reality as the stage upon which people must, willy-nilly, act, and they advise caution and morality insofar as circumstances permit, not abandonment of the cares of courtly life.

Exemplary anticourtly texts, on the other hand, can be found in Czepko's *Coridon und Phillis*, in which a nobleman, returning to his beloved country seat, condemns at great length the corruption he saw in the cities and the court:

Geht zu Hofe, die ihr wolt,
Kaufft für Laster euern Sold,
Gebt die Nahmen, falsch zu werden:
Werffet wie ein altes Kleid
Von euch Treu und Redlichkeit,
Hasset Ruh und liebt Beschwerden.
. . .
Nein! Zu Hoffe komm ich nicht,
Es ist wieder meine Pflicht,
Keinen wüst ich zu betrügen:
Keinem wüst ich, solte man
Mich umb Schulden halten an,
Einen Pfennig abzulügen.[26]

Already Erik Lunding asked whether such an oscillation between courtly and anticourtly values is not contrary to human psychology, a question he answered by saying that "this curious symbiosis" does not reflect a real split in the author's ego, "since courtly literature is representational art independent of inner experience and as such has but little connection with the creative ego."[27] In the case of a writer like Czepko, whose creative impulses as a religious poet embrace and transcend the sociological domains of both the courtly and the anticourtly, this statement seems especially applicable. It may also provide further insight into the function of the courtly/anticourtly dialectic of Opitz, Gryphius, Grimmelshausen, Hofmannswaldau, or Lohenstein. None of them can be regarded as a committed propagandist for one side or the other, although this tension can be perceived in the works of all of them. If it is not too rash to try to localize the center of their diverse creative egos, these writers were all most deeply concerned with the pitiful transiency and fallibility of humans in this world and the possibility of their redemption in the next. For these concerns, the worldly knowledge of the courtly and the utopian hope of the anticourtly were powerfully mediating metaphors.

In closing, it is interesting to note that, at about the time that Günther Müller was developing his ideas on the courtly and anticourtly tendencies in baroque German literature, C. G. Jung published his epoch-making study of the process of individuation, *Psychological Types*, in the course of which he gave as examples historical personalities who fit into his basic categories of extroversion and introversion. Jung demonstrated the persistence of this typology in the personalities and problematics of classical and medieval philosophy and the symbolic expression they found, as well as in such later figures as Luther, Zwingli, Schiller, and Nietzsche. The seventeenth century in Germany, however, is not represented by any such typical figures in Jung's study, and this is not surprising, since the development of knowledge about this period was still very much in its beginnings. The idea might be worthy of pursuing, that the courtly/anticourtly controversy is an important symbolic expression and criterion of psychological typology for the seventeenth century, the "curious symbiosis" of the two tendencies in so many significant authors being identifiable as an aspect of the struggle for social and moral orientation, for psychological individuation. These writers were searching for what Morris Philipson calls "a socially available system of symbols," the "symbols that satisfy [the poet's] need for 'wholeness,' permitting him to recapitulate in his own development, now undertaken consciously, the structure of the unconscious development of the histories of culture."[28]

NOTES

1. See the essay by Michael M. Metzger and Erika A. Metzger in this volume, pp. 000-000.
2. *The Complete Poetry of Richard Crashaw*, ed. George Walton Williams (New York: New York University Press, 1972), pp. 47, 453.
3. Norbert Elias, *Die höfische Gesellschaft* (Neuwied: Luchterhand, 1969), p. 62, note 2.
4. Leibniz's comment is in *Das Zeitalter des Barock: Texte und Zeugnisse*, ed. Albrecht Schöne, 2nd ed. (München: Beck, 1968), p. 50. Passage translated by the authors.
5. Alberto Martino, *Daniel Casper von Lohenstein: Geschichte seiner Rezeption. Band I, 1661-1800* (Tübingen: Niemeyer, 1978), pp. 153 ff.; Italian original: I (Pisa, 1975).
6. See the introduction to the German translation (1600) of Guevara's *Aviso de privados*: Aegidius Albertinus, *Institutiones vitae aulicae oder HofSchul*, ed. Erika A. Metzger and Michael M. Metzger, Nachdrucke deutscher Literatur des 17. Jahrhunderts, 23 (Bern, Frankfurt, and Las Vegas: Lang, 1978), pp. 7-60.
7. Elias, pp. 320-94.
8. Martino, pp. 419 ff.
9. Götz Adriani, *Deutsche Malerei im 17. Jahrhundert* (Köln: DuMont, 1977), pp. 103, 140.
10. See Günther Müller, "Höfische Kultur der Barockzeit," in Hans Naumann and Günther Müller, *Höfische Kultur* (Halle: Niemeyer, 1929); Erika Vogt, *Die gegenhöfische Strömung in der deutschen Barockliteratur* (Leipzig: Weber, 1932); Erik Lunding, "German Baroque Literature: A Synthetic View," *German Life and Letters*, 13 (1949/50), 1-12.
11. Müller, pp. 87-135.
12. Weckherlin's poem is in *Epochen der deutschen Lyrik, 1600-1700*, ed. Christian Wagenknecht (München: Deutscher Taschenbuch Verlag, 1969), p. 36.
13. Günther's ode is in *Das Zeitalter des Barock*, p. 348.
14. See Wulf Segebrecht, *Das Gelegenheitsgedicht* (Stuttgart: Metzler, 1977).
15. Walter Benjamin, *Ursprung des deutschen Trauerspiels* (Frankfurt a.M.: Suhrkamp, 1969), p. 156.
16. Friedrich von Logau, *Sinngedichte*, ed. C. W. Ramler and G. E. Lessing, in Gotthold Ephraim Lessing, *Sämtliche Schriften*, ed. Karl Lachmann and Franz Muncker, 3rd ed. (Stuttgart: Göschen, 1891), VII, 286.
17. *Das Zeitalter des Barock*, p. 53.
18. *Schwund- und Kirchenbarock*, ed. Herbert Cysarz, vol. III of *Barocklyrik*,

Deutsche Literatur in Entwicklungsreihen, Reihe Barock (rpt. Darmstadt: Wissenschaftliche Buchgesellschaft, 1964), p. 86.

19. Weckherlin's "An den Hofe" is in *Epochen der deutschen Lyrik, 1600–1700*, p. 169.

20. Hans Aßmann von Abschatz, *Poetische Übersetzungen und Gedichte*, ed. Erika A. Metzger, Nachdrucke deutscher Literatur des 17. Jahrhunderts, 3 (Bern, Frankfurt, and Las Vegas: Lang, 1970), "Vermischte Gedichte," p. 91.

21. Logau, *Sinngedichte*, p. 180.

22. Erik Lunding, p. 9.

23. Georg Philipp Harsdörffer, *Poetischer Trichter* (rpt. Darmstadt: Wissenschaftliche Buchgesellschaft, 1969), III, 265.

24. Daniel von Czepko, *Weltliche Dichtungen*, ed. Werner Milch (rpt. Darmstadt: Wissenschaftliche Buchgesellschaft, 1963), p. 368.

25. Czepko, p. 369.

26. Czepko, pp. 163, 166.

27. Lunding, p. 9.

28. Morris Philipson, *Outline of a Jungian Aesthetics* (Evanston, Ill.: Northwestern University Press, 1963), pp. 11–12.

In a final note the authors wish to thank the Staatsgalerie Stuttgart and the Verwaltung der Staatlichen Schlösser und Gärten, Berlin, for permission to reproduce photographs of their pictures in this volume.

SELECTED BIBLIOGRAPHY

Primary Sources

Abschatz, Hans Aßmann von. *Poetische Übersetzungen und Gedichte*, Erika A. Metzger, ed. Nachdrucke deutscher Literatur des 17. Jahrhunderts, 3. Bern, Frankfurt, and Las Vegas: Lang, 1970.

Albertinus, Aegidius. *Institutiones vitae aulicae oder HofSchul*, Erika A. Metzger and Michael M. Metzger, eds. Nachdrucke deutscher Literatur des 17. Jahrhunderts, 23. Bern, Frankfurt, and Las Vegas: Lang, 1978.

Crashaw, Richard. *The Complete Poetry of Richard Crashaw*. George Walton Williams, ed. New York: New York University Press, 1972.

Cysarz, Herbert, ed. *Schwund- und Kirchenbarock*. Vol. III of *Barocklyrik*. Deutsche Literatur in Entwicklungsreihen. Reihe Barock. Rpt. Darmstadt: Wissenschaftliche Buchgesellschaft, 1964.

Czepko, Daniel von. *Weltliche Dichtungen*, Werner Milch, ed. Rpt. Darmstadt: Wissenschaftliche Buchgesellschaft, 1963.

Gryphius, Andreas. *Gesamtausgabe der deutschsprachigen Werke*, Marian Szyrocki and Hugh Powell, eds. 8 vols. Tübingen: Niemeyer, 1963 ff.

Harsdörffer, Georg Philipp. *Poetischer Trichter*. Rpt. Darmstadt: Wissenschaftliche Buchgesellschaft, 1969.

Logau, Friedrich von. *Sinngedichte*, C. W. Ramler and G. E. Lessing, eds. In Gotthold Ephraim Lessing, *Sämtliche Schriften*. Karl Lachmann and Franz Muncker, eds. 3rd ed. Vol. VII. Stuttgart: Göschen, 1891.

Schöne, Albrecht, ed. *Das Zeitalter des Barock: Texte und Zeugnisse*. 2nd ed. München: Beck, 1968.

Wagenknecht, Christian, ed. *Epochen der deutschen Lyrik, 1600–1700*. München: Deutscher Taschenbuch Verlag, 1969.

Secondary Literature

Adriani, Götz. *Deutsche Malerei im 17. Jahrhundert*. Köln: DuMont, 1977.

Brunner, Otto. *Adeliges Landleben und europäischer Geist*. Salzburg: Müller, 1949.

Elias, Norbert. *Die höfische Gesellschaft*. Neuwied: Luchterhand, 1969.

Kiesel, Helmuth. *"Bei Hof, bei Höll": Untersuchungen zur literarischen Hofkritik von Sebastian Brant bis zu Friedrich Schiller*. Studien zur deutschen Literatur, 60. Tübingen: Niemeyer, 1979.

Lunding, Erik. "German Baroque Literature: a Synthetic View." *German Life and Letters*, 13 (1949/50), 1–12.

Martino, Alberto. *Daniel Casper von Lohenstein: Geschichte seiner Rezeption. Band I, 1661–1800*. Tübingen: Niemeyer, 1978. Italian original: I, Pisa, 1975.

Müller, Günther. "Höfische Kultur der Barockzeit." In Hans Naumann and Günther Müller, *Höfische Kultur*. Halle: Niemeyer, 1929.

——. *Deutsche Dichtung von der Renaissance bis zum Ausgang des Barock*. Darmstadt: Wissenschaftliche Buchgesellschaft, 1957.

Philipson, Morris. *Outline of a Jungian Aesthetics*. Evanston, Ill.: Northwestern University Press, 1963.

Rötzer, Hans Gerd. *Der Roman des Barock, 1600–1700*. München: Winkler, 1972.

Segebrecht, Wulf. *Das Gelegenheitsgedicht*. Stuttgart: Metzler, 1977.

Uhlig, Claus. *Hofkritik im England des Mittelalters und der Renaissance*. Berlin and New York: de Gruyter, 1973.

Vogt, Erika. *Die gegenhöfische Strömung in der deutschen Barockliteratur*. Leipzig: Weber, 1932.

16

The Mystical Quest
for God

Joseph B. Dallett

"I am my beloved's, and his desire is toward me." When Hermann Hugo (1588–1629) chose this verse from the (Vulgate) Song of Songs (7:10) for a motto in the third part of his singularly successful emblem book, *Pia Desideria*,[1] he made his customary selection of nuggets from the Fathers and Doctors of the church and later exegetes to elucidate his poetic recreation of the Scriptural text. Among these excerpts was the following analogical representation from a commentary on Canticles — I quote the contemporary German translation of Carolus Stengelius:

Man findet etliche Bilder / welche also künstlich von erfahrnen Mahlern entworffen seind / das auff welcher seiten man selbige ansihet / vermeinet man allzeit sie haben jhre Augen auff die anschawenden gewendet. Solche Bildtnussen zwar / als vil an ihn gelegen / seind allzeit zu jeglichem gewendet / welche im selben Zimmer gefunden werden / darinn sie seindt: so aber einer gar nit vermerckt das er von jhnen angesehen werde / kompt solches nit her von jhnen / sonder vil mehr von dem jenigen / welcher sein angesicht abwendet: Deßwegen alsbald er sich zu jhnen wenden wirdt / wirdt er zugleich mercken das sie zu jhme gewendet seind: Gleichfals soll man darfür halten / das desgleichen was in vnser sach geschehe.[2]

The analogy helps somewhat in imagining not only the omnipresence of God and His tireless concern for people despite the latter's inattentions, but also the instantaneity of the gazes exchanged when the individual finally catches sight of the divine onlooker.

Hugo's own verses stress individual rather than collective experience. He focuses on a personification of the solitary soul; its (her) encounters with God, keyed to the largely first-person-singular Scriptural mottoes, unfold like chapters in a love affair. If the tripartite structure of the work reflects a traditional standardization of the stages in the interior development of a contemplative mystic (purification or purgation, illumination, union), the feelings voiced in the poetic text of the emblems are subjective ones; they reinforce and are reinforced by the individuality of the accompanying pictures. The illustrations, at least in those editions of the work with woodcuts by Christoffel van Sichem,[3] depict the soul as a girl in confrontation with a boy who is the Lord, quite human except for his halo and wings (he is even to be seen on the throne of heaven in the penultimate woodcut, the source of a belt of light striking the girl seated on the ground below). The subtitles of the three main sections of the work, though technical terms from mystical exercises—the "groans," "desires," and "sighs"[4] of the (successively) "penitent," "holy," and "loving" soul—remind us that this quest for God is governed by the affections, the very word used on the title page for the prose extracts from the "Holy Fathers" that accompany each elegy.

Mystical experience is intensely private; its universal history, for all the testimonies that exist, will never be written. For the mystic way often ends, as it begins, in silence. Indications of the practice of mysticism may take fictional guise (like the half-veiled poetic account of mystical union in the spiritual autobiography, *Philotheus*, 1665, of Laurentius von Schnüffis, 1633-1702),[5] but not every work of imaginative literature dealing with mysticism has a mystic for its author—nor does every manual or directory for the practitioner of meditation. In what is called speculative mysticism, where the intellect rather than feeling leads, God may be conceived abstractly as an infinite Nothing, union with which requires a negation of self and an abandonment of all earthly qualities and values; reason is itself here finally transcended; ultimate fullness of being comes with a merger that cannot be labeled personal experience.[6] The ineffability of such a merger can be discussed in theory and projected poetically, just as in the far more accessible sphere of love mysticism what might seem self-evident can become a high mystery. Witness the example in *La Croix de Jésus* (1647) by Louis Chardon (1595-1651). In a kinaesthetic ecstasy, it is recalled, Bernard of Clairvaux sought to embrace Jesus on the cross, when Jesus "detached His bleeding hands . . . as if to forestall" his lover: "One could not distinguish whether it is Jesus who leans upon Bernard's loving bosom, or Bernard who swoons and languishes upon Jesus' breast."[7] For the highest forms of rapture, God is often declared to be the initiator, but even the first step taken by the mystic presupposes God's attendance, if not cooperation.

Mystic union is said by some to anticipate the beatific vision enjoyed by the blessed in heaven, who see God, in St. Paul's phrase, "face to face" (1 Cor. 13:12); but by others, to fall short of that in its liability to interruption.[8] (Indicatively, the closing poem in Hugo's *Pia Desideria* mingles impatience with fulfillment, quite in keeping with the last verse of Canticles, "Make haste, my beloved . . . ," as the soul urges her departing lover to return with all speed.) Mystics report that the bliss which accompanies the presence of God often yields to the despair and agony of a separation from Him, what the English Benedictine, Venerable Augustine Baker (1575-1641), termed "the great desolation."[9] And with many there is a tension between their awareness of God's singular grace and their own unworthiness.[10] It has been said that a distinguishing feature of German baroque mysticism is "ein Ton außerordentlichen Selbstbewußtseins" making God dependent on humans.[11] This generalization should not be pressed. A felt affinity with the humanity of Christ is usually matched in Christian belief by an appreciation of his unique dual nature and role as redeemer. Still, for some, the incarnate life of Christ calls for an inner quasi recapitulation. Jakob Böhme (1575-1624) warns that "putting on" Christ necessitates going "durch seinen gantzen Proceß, von seiner Menschwerdung an bis zu seiner Himmelfahrt" in a perpetual "dying" to the "vanity of the soul."[12] Particularly the death and resurrection of Christ prefigures the profound spiritual change required of the believer. An identification with Christ crucified has left some mystics visibly stigmatized; stigmata are recorded for saints in the baroque age,[13] during which, incidentally, as part of the renewed cult of St. Francis, the stigmatization on Mount Alverna was often represented in the fine arts.[14]

Similarly, for those who partake of the sacrament of the Eucharist or Holy Communion the self-sacrifice of Christ on the cross is intimately internalized.[15] Understandably, many mystics rely on this sacrament for sustenance. Yet mysticism can pose a challenge to all institutionalized channels of grace when the individual turns directly to God, just as the notions of the inner Word and the indwelling Spirit of God threaten the singular position of Holy Scripture as definitive revelation. Theoretically, all believers could practice mysticism, but its consistent pursuit is at variance with many human activities and dispositions. Nevertheless, civilizations around the world, past and present, have produced mystics, and comparisons between them can make sense.[16]

Given the arduousness of the mystic endeavor, one would not want to restrict the term "mysticism" to what Heiko A. Oberman calls "high mysticism"—"when the soul suffers in sheer receptivity and passivity by the divinely infused contemplation, is transformed in spiritual marriage, and finally absorbed into God, gazing upon God Himself or upon the Holy Trinity."[17] Gottfried Arnold (1666-1714), who defines "mystische Theologie" in a similar way in his *Historie und Beschreibung der mystischen Theologie* of 1703, also acknowledges a much looser sense, as pertaining to what is holy and inspired, an inward life of "true" religion.[18] If this latter definition is too vague, a definition of mysticism like G. Born's in differentiating it from spiritualism is too strict: "Geht die Mystik von der im Grunde immer schon gegebenen Einheit des Menschen mit Gott aus, so ist dieses dem Spiritualismus versagt. Für diesen ist zwischen Gott und Mensch eine Kluft, die nur von Gott durch den . . . Geist überbrückt werden kann."[19] For the view that God is Himself remote, indeed inaccessible, has been the premise of many mystics, the starting point of their upward journey to Him;[20] and even on the assumption of God's immanence in the soul as in all creation, ignorance of or indifference to His presence makes for as effective a barrier to union as the *Kluft* in the above sketch of spiritualism. Moreover, mysticism can by no means be said to exclude the operations of the Spirit.[21] In addition, there is in German theological scholarship a precedent for combining *mystisch* and *Spiritualismus* in one term showing the proximity of some forms of spiritualism, at least, to mysticism.[22] If we are speaking about lives, then surely "mystic" is equally applicable to the Catholic convert, Angelus Silesius (1624-77)—so given to contemplation that Daniel Schwartz, S.J., declared he deserved (with Dionysius the Carthusian) to be called "Doctor ecstaticus"[23]—and to the Lutheran pastor, Johann Casper Charias (born in Berlin in 1639). "Er war in der Vereinigung mit Gott und inwendigen Erfahrung weit gekommen," wrote Erasmus Hoffmann in 1672 about Charias. Although Charias had been hounded out of his pastorate in Kampen by the rigidly orthodox Konsistorium in Amsterdam, he could rejoice in his own untimely death: "er ging," Hoffmann reported, "mit einem Halleluja ein in die ewige Freude."[24]

It is my aim here to present facets in the religious life of seventeenth-century Europe without avoiding all that might more properly be called "spirituality" or "piety" than "mysticism." At the same time, I do not share the opinion that practical mysticism was at a low ebb in the Holy Roman Empire during the baroque period, and I offer a little support for my view. The "mere" diffusion of texts of a mystical character—to which I devote some space—is itself not proof of mystical behavior, but still helpful for understanding the situation at large. This is marked by a (partly international) flow of persons no less than of books and ideas. I illustrate certain literary themes that correspond to conceptions often voiced in devotional life. A systematic survey of German baroque literature in the mystical tradition is beyond the scope of this essay.

My purview is confined geographically to parts of Western Europe. An ideal treatment of the subject in a European framework would take account of the religious life and mystical traditions of those Europeans of the Mohammedan and Jewish faiths in the time period under scrutiny, as well as the Socinians* or Unitarians (above all in Poland, Holland, and Prussia). For practical reasons the compass must be narrowed. I deal only with Trinitarian Christianity—but not even with its Eastern Orthodox exponents.

To some observers, the Holy Roman Empire in the seventeenth century produced hardly any "genuine" mystics. Carl Richstaetter, with Catholic Europe uppermost in his mind, offers this census: "Unter den 90 eigentlichen Mystikern, die für das 16., 17. und 18. Jahrhundert genannt werden, findet sich kaum noch der eine oder andere deutsche Name."[25] And Marie-Luise Wolfskehl, interested above all in literary expressions of the mystic orientation, writes:

Wirkliche Mystik findet sich in diesem Jahrhundert der Hochflut geistlicher Dichtung nur sehr selten, dagegen gibt es unzählige Fälle, in denen das mystisch-erotische Ideengut aus lehrhaften oder sinnbildmäßig spielerischen oder auch nur rein künstlerisch ästhetischen Gesichtspunkten verwendet ist.[26]

The Jesuit poet Friedrich Spee (1591-1635) would seem to be one who made it under the wire for these scholars: Wolfskehl sees his art as having an "echte Erlebnisgrundlage,"[27] while Richstaetter endorses a designation of Spee as "the last German mystic."[28] However, elsewhere Richstaetter treats fellow Jesuits such as Wilhelm Nakatenus (1617-70) and Venerable Philipp Jeningen (1642-1704), as well as the Capuchin Father, Martin von Cochem (1634-1712), as people of intense spirituality.[29] Severin R. v. Lama has drawn attention to a fair number of visionaries and ecstatics among the religious of baroque Austria, both men and women, including Archduchess Margareta (1567-1633), who

---

*They believed in the doctrines of the sixteenth-century Italian religious reformers Laelius and Faustus Socinus, who denied the divinity of Christ.

died as a nun in Montserrat; Marie Hueber (1653-1705), a Franciscan tertiary in Brixen, whom one Father Kürnigl witnessed levitating in tree-tops; and, also in Brixen, the Poor Clare, Anna Kislin (d. 1600), whose heavenly bridegroom was frequently seen at her side as she washed the church linens.[30]

One can certainly infer from the spread of religious orders like that of the Discalced Carmelites, whose raison d'être is contemplation, that in Germany mysticism was being cultivated seriously. One moving force was the Spaniard Thomas of Jesus (ca. 1564-1627), who invented a type of "priory for solitaries"[31] known as the *desierto* to encourage fasting and mental prayer in effective isolation. He set up some half-dozen convents in France and Belgium and one in Cologne (in 1614).[32] Dominicus à Jesu Maria (1599-1630), of the same order, was the inspiration for the founding, by the emperor, of convents in Vienna (1622) and Munich (1629).[33] Discalced Carmelite nunneries also spread to Germany via France and Belgium, where two former companions of St. Teresa herself were active.[34] If such missionary efforts strengthened the institutionalized power of the church in question, the interior life of the religious in the very orders called on to proselytize was also guarded.[35]

Without reference to national origin, Richstaetter generalizes as follows about his own order: "die ignatianische Aszese, nicht zuletzt in der Gesellschaft Jesu, [hat] eine große Zahl von Mystikern gebildet."[36] The Spaniard Ignatius Loyola (ca. 1491-1556), founder of the order and author of its fundamental handbook of inward religious training, the *Spiritual Exercises*, was himself both a mystic and a consummate administrator.[37] Life in the Society of Jesus definitely made room for contemplation. The *Spiritual Exercises* direct the devotee's "inner, spiritual senses" in what may be described as smoothly graduated steps towards the discovery of and participation in the divine will, facilitating, even for the "ordinary" religious life progress (in Fridolin Marxer's words) "gleichsam *in einer nahtlosen Einheit* zu den sublimen Höhen der mystischen Schau."[38] Spee's own contribution to the genre of the meditative manual, his *Güldenes Tugend-Buch* (Cologne, 1649), despite differences of tone, structure, and form (it incorporates, for instance, about twenty poems that also appear in the *Trutznachtigall*, Cologne, 1649),[39] has been characterized by Alois M. Haas as "eine klassische Anleitung zur christlichen Meditation im jesuitisch-ignatianischen Verstand und eine Art Kompendium christlicher Aszetik."[40] Its modern editor, Theo G. M. van Oorschot, is hesitant to label Spee a mystic, partly through an unwillingness to extrapolate a *mystische Haltung* from the mystical cast of Spee's poetry, partly because a direct connection with medieval German mystics cannot be established.[41] But the familiarity of Jesuits in Spee's day with a wide range of mystical authors writing in or translated into Latin can scarcely be denied.[42]

Latin was of course a significant vehicle for the international transmission of mystical writings. It was in Latin translation, for example, that the works of St. John of the Cross were first issued by a press in Germany (French, Italian, and Dutch translations had preceded this publication, to be sure, and it included the Spanish originals of the three poems, "Llama de amor viva," "Noche oscura," and "Cántico espiritual").[43] A copy of this edition (Cologne, 1639) was one of the books willed by Abraham von Franckenberg (1593-1652) to his friend, the poet Johannes Scheffler (rebaptized Angelus Silesius the next year);[44] the same edition was later used by the chiliast Quirinus Kuhlmann (1651-89) for his sensitive German rendition of portions of the incomparable poetry of St. John of the Cross ("In einer dunkler nächte").[45] The Latin translation by the Carthusian Laurentius Surius (1522-78), from Lübeck, of the writings of the Flemish mystic Jan van Ruysbroeck (1293-1381) gave them fresh currency from 1552 on (a reprint of 1609 was also part of Franckenberg's legacy to Scheffler),[46] and later provided the basis for the High German translation of Ruysbroeck that was edited by Gottfried Arnold in 1701. Surius also Latinized works of several High German mystical writers, among them Johannes Tauler (ca. 1300-1361); here he used the recent German edition of 1543 prepared by his friend, the Flemish Jesuit Petrus Canisius (1521-97).[47] But Tauler had already broken into print as far back as 1498 with an edition of eighty-four sermons in the German original.[48]

A telling example of the ever-widening diffusion of a vernacular medieval mystical text is that of the anonymous treatise known as the *Theologia Deutsch* (ca. 1400), first seen through the press on the eve of the Reformation (1516; revised 1518) by Martin Luther.[49] In the subsequent history of the imprints of this work Protestants are conspicuous. From 1516 on, new printings appeared (often repeatedly) in every single decade down to the middle of the eighteenth century. In the sixteenth century there were Dutch, Low German, Latin, and French translations (and more of the same, except for Low German, in the next century). Swedish followed in 1617 (Uppsala; reworked in 1718); an English manuscript version is dated 1628, the oldest English edition extant, 1648; a Danish translation came out in Oslo in 1665. An expanded paraphrase in Latin was written in 1541-42 by the historian and radical spiritualist Sebastian Franck (1499-1542), for whom the original was the best post-Biblical witness to the freedom of God to inspire people anew.[50] Franck's French-Swiss counterpart in the area of religious toleration, Sebastian Castellio (1515-63), published both a Latin and a French translation of the *Theologia Deutsch* (Basel, 1557; Antwerp, 1558). Valentin Weigel (1533-88), Lutheran pastor in Zschopau (in the margravate of Meissen), explicated parts of the work in 1571 in his "Kurtzer Bericht vnd Anleitung zur Teutschen Theologey" (which first appeared in the collection *Philosophia Mystica*, 1618). Editors of the *Theologia Deutsch* include the revered Lutheran churchman Johann Arndt (1555-1621); Philipp Jakob Spener (1635-1705), the leading light of German Pietism; and the apologist for contemporary spirituality, Pierre Poiret (1646-1719), from Metz. As early as 1605 (Arndt's second edition) the *Theologia Deutsch* was issued together with three books of *The Imitation of Christ*; in 1621 it was combined with Tauler sermons as well and some smaller pieces — a "package" similar to that brought out sixty years later by Spener. A Lyons printer combined Castellio's Latin version with a catechetical piece by the Flemish Benedictine Ludovicus Blosius (1506-66), abbot of Liessies and a noted master teacher of spiritual conduct. An Ulm imprint of 1722 united the *Theologia Deutsch* and the pseudo-Tauler *Medulla animae* with Ruysbroeck's *Buch . . . von der Vollkommenheit der Kinder Gottes*.

By the middle of the sixteenth century a general trend was underway that carried right through the baroque era: the exploitation and assimilation of earlier mystical literature by devotional and edificatory writers in Germany, both Catholic and Protestant. Paul Althaus, Sr., first analyzed in detail the capacious receptivity of Protestants such as Andreas Musculus (1514-88), Martin Moller (1547-1606), and Johann Arndt to medieval mystical texts (formulations, images) in shaping their own prayer books, hymnals, and treatises — and the parallel to this spiritualizing tendency in works by their Catholic contemporaries.[51] As Hans-Henrik Krummacher has emphasized, this new "Mut zu einem Universalismus" (Zeller)[52] did not mean for most of the Lutheran theologians and writers in question any rejection of the orthodox tenets of their faith; still, it was in good measure owing to the new acquaintance with medieval mysticism that a *verinnerlichte Frömmigkeit* now arose in Lutheran circles.[53] If the piety of so-called *Reformorthodoxie* went hand in hand with "pure" Lutheran doctrine, the Pietism of Spener, too, in the later seventeenth century, preserved important aspects of this doctrine intact.[54] But Pietism differed from orthodoxy in its emphasis on

Leben—inward life and charity as the "practice of piety"—rather than on *Lehre*.[55] Spener's religious development owed much to Arndt's *Vier Bücher vom wahren Christentum*.[56] This work, highly influential throughout the baroque age, together with the *Guía espiritual* (Rome, 1675) of the Quietist Miguel de Molinos (ca. 1640-97),[57] sparked the conversion of August Hermann Francke (1663-1727),[58] whose Pietist movement centering in Halle finally routed supporters of the older orthodoxy.[59]

Jakob Böhme, of Görlitz (Silesia), ran into orthodox Lutheran opposition upon the circulation of his first work, *Morgenröte im Aufgang*,[60] but his voluminous writings, most published posthumously, very soon enjoyed wide currency (in Dutch and English translations as well as the original German)[61] and gained a following among the heterodox. (A number of holograph manuscripts by Böhme remained the property of a succession of little groups of celibate devotees of the *Theosoph* right down to the time of the confiscation of their archives by the Nazis.)[62]

Theoretical, instructional, hagiographic, and confessional texts by various baroque authors had multiplied greatly by the end of the century, a large number being listed in the *Mystiker-Verzeichnis* in Poiret's *Théologie réelle* (1700) and *Bibliotheca mysticorum selecta* (1708).[63] Poiret's "geistiger Erbe,"[64] Gerhard Tersteegen (1697-1769), interestingly combined concern for tiny coteries of spiritual charges (like the handfuls of brethren of the *Pilgerhütten* at Otterbeck, Mülheim, and Barmen)[65] with a catholicity of ˜enthusiasm for recorded mystical experience from every quarter. This universalism shines through his casebook in high mysticism, *Auserlesene Lebensbeschreibungen Heiliger Seelen* (1733-53). His criteria for exclusion cannot have been any holy soul's place in time, nationality, social rank, religious denomination, or sex, so broad is the selection of the materials showing the *mannigfaltige Austheilungen* of God's grace (title page), though the choice does reflect a wish to bring out the true inward nature of the best of Roman Catholic mysticism. But the poet Tersteegen's special liking for Angelus Silesius is clear from his charming use of epigrams from the *Cherubinische Wandersmann* as epitaphs for a number of the individual "lives." The careful bibliographical notes on the compiler's primary sources illuminate the history of their printings in impressive detail.

Mysticism presupposes and authenticates God's continuous revelation of Himself, not only as confirming the old, but as imparting something new. An early visionary experience of Jakob Böhme's, giving insight into the dynamic process of God's eternal birth from within Himself and of creation, must have seemed to him altogether novel as divine dispensation;[66] yet here God's primal motion is shown to be one of self-revelation. Similarly, Böhme's idea of the heavenly virgin Sophia (Wisdom) as the "body of the Holy Trinity" has (whatever its antecedents) the ring of a fresh disclosure; but Sophia is for Böhme precisely the mode of God's revelation of Himself and His miracles.[67] Furthermore, Böhme viewed the world of nature — the "outflowing" Word or breath of God made visible — as unceasingly revealing itself and its qualities through its own language: "Ein jedes Ding hat seinen Mund zur Offenbarung."[68] In so far as the name of a thing gives away its inner being, *Natursprache* is no metaphor; but Böhme also stressed, here following Paracelsus (1493-1541), that outward physical characteristics contain the "signature" of a thing by which we read its essence. Nature, however, is equally an eternal principle "in God," giving birth "in großem Sehnen und Aengsten" so that God can pass from eternal Nothingness to life.[69] No less does the emergence of sweet beauty, flowers and fruits, from the dark earth and hard stem require fierce, bitter opposing force; for "kein Ding ohne Widerwärtigkeit mag ihm selber offenbar werden."[70] So, too, with man: good issues out of painful struggle or violent conflict under the stimulus of evil; life out of death. There is passivity, to be sure, in man's receiving righteousness from the divine Sophia, but his activity comes about through acceptance of this righteousness by his free will; paradoxically, free will is released only on the resignation of the personal will. "When this occurs the free will can unite with the newly introduced love essence making a new substance or conjunction . . ."[71]

Böhme's originality as a thinker is no more at question than his manifold indebtedness to earlier philosophers, theologians, and writers on the practical arts.[71a] In the matter of the will (its relation to grace was a standing problem in mystical theology) an interesting parallel to Böhme occurs in Ruysbroeck, who, on the one hand, considers *der eigene wille* a disturbing factor akin to self-love, and recommends its elimination through practice,[72] but elsewhere says it is the will, made "good" by grace, which frees us from self ("indem er uns über uns selbst erhebet / so verbindet und vereiniget er uns mit Gott in dem beschaulichen leben"). "Crowned with eternal love," the good will is equatable with "GOttes reich / in welchem GOtt durch die gnade regieret"; in short, a treasured capacity.[73]

Whatever the sequence, some form of cooperation by God and man appeared inescapable. When Valentin Weigel states in his 1570 tract, "Von der Bekehrung des Menschen," that man's rebirth occurs "nicht violenter, sondern voluntarie," he is referring to God no less than to man; for "Gott will vnd mag [kann] nicht ohne den Menschen, vnd der Mensch mag vnd will nicht ohne Gott."[74] Actually, man's part comes down to an abdication of the will—in Weigel's quotation from the *Theologia Deutsch*, "Ein bloses lautter Leiden"—a nonaction comparable to being created, not a *Mitwircken*; but all of God's "Reitzen, Treiben, Zihen vnd Warnung innwenndig vnd auswenndig" is of no avail as long as man is indisposed to accept *Seeligkeit* from God.[75] However, in close, indeed literal adherence to the "Predigt über Matthäus" by Tauler, *Leiden* in the sense of *Gelassenheit* is aligned with inner suffering, *Vnterdruckung, Elendigkeit, Demut, Gedult, Niedrigkeit*—all a sort of schooling or *Übung* punctuated by prayers for persistence (*Verharrung im Leiden*).[76] The goal is life in death, as Weigel observes elsewhere: "Denn die waare Gelassenheit ist ein Absterbung vnd Vergessen seiner selbst. Do man todt ist der gantzen Creatur, da lebet Gott ewiglich."[77]

Weigel worked for the Lutheran church, yet its institutional aspect was false in his eyes. Justification before God, he felt, can only come about from within, as one identifies with the suffering, dying Christ. In the dialogue, *De Christianismo*, Weigel's spokesman, the Auditor, asks, "Wenn wir nicht mit Christo solten getödet werden vnd gekreutziget, was were vnser Glaube, was wer die Taufe vnd Nachtmal nutze? Sein Tod were in vns vmbsonst vnd verloren."[78] The words of Romans 6 that are here echoed should be spoken "aus Hertzensgrunde," for it is in the heart that the Word is planted "mit dem Finger Gottes"; there Christ dwells "durch die Liebe eingewurtzelt" in essential union ("wesentliche Vereinigung") with us.[79]

The cross, the axis of the Christian faith, is a vital image in seventeenth-century poetry, where it can become the very gesture of living. As John Donne asks:

> Who can deny mee power, and liberty
> To stretch mine armes, and mine owne Crosse to be?
> Swimme, and at every stroake, thou art thy Crosse[80]
> . . . . .

The crucifixion of Jesus—what Catharina Regina von Greiffenberg calls "die allergrausamste und erbärmlichste Creutzigung meines Erlösers"[81]—

is the subject of innumerable works of poetic devotion, often with the very kind of sincere empathy and imaginative concentration that Blosius counsels in meditation.[82] In literature as in prayer and hymnody there is frequent focus on the wounds and life-giving blood ("Die wesentliche Gnad / vermängt in diesen Säfften / | wir sichtbar nun vor uns in Blut-Rubinen sehn")[83] and also on the heart of Jesus. The latter-day heirs of this tradition include Nikolaus Ludwig Graf von Zinzendorf (1700–60) and members of the Brüdergemeine of Herrnhut. In hymns composed in the 1740s for their own use they extolled the wounds, above all the lateral wound, of Christ, for which such metaphors were devised as *das charmante höhlgen, Schloßcanal,* and *Taubenfächlein* (the last a derivative of Canticles 2:14: "O my dove, that art in the clefts of the rock . . .").[84] The soul's refuge in the wounded side of her "bridegroom" is a recurrent theme of the sacred songbook by Angelus Silesius and (the composer) Georgius Josephus, *Heilige Seelen-Lust.* The affinity of *Wundenmystik* and the spiritual marriage, all too baldly put, underlies the argument of the *Cherubinische Wandersmann,* V, 372 ("Die Braut soll wie der Bräutigam sein"): "Ich muß verwundet sein. Warum? weil voller Wunden | Mein ewger Bräutigam, der Heiland, wird gefunden. | . . ."[85]

With the devotee's own death the possibilities of the *unio mystica* in the guise of marriage are enhanced, as in the Latin ode, "Genovefa," by Jacob Balde (1603–68); here the expiring saint's longing for death surprisingly defrauds it as she enters Christ's company as bride.[86] Catharina Regina von Greiffenberg can picture her nineteen-year-old friend, Barbara Susanna Eleonora von Regal (struck dead by lightning in 1687), as a victim of God's *Liebs-Pfeil,* destined for eternal life as "holde JEsus-Braut."[87] In the poetic and prose texts written in 1660 by Andreas Gryphius (1616–64) for the funeral of the fifteen-year-old Mariane von Popschitz, the deceased likewise becomes the chosen bride of Christ. While Gryphius does not grant her this status on earth, he says: "Eben so hat man verspüret daß der HERR die Seele unserer nunmehr seeligsten Jungfrauen M a r i a n e mit gleicher Begierde entzündet / daß Sie nach nichts als Dem verlanget / der einig nach Jhr getrachtet."[88] It remains for Angelus Silesius to remind his reader that God Himself plunges into death out of love for human beings ("Die Lieb ist ein Magnet, sie ziehet mich in Gott, | Und was noch größer is, sie reißet Gott in Tod"), and that for them as well as God death is the means of life: "Gott selber, wenn er dir will leben, muß ersterben; ç Wie, denkst du, ohne Tod sein Leben zu ererben?"[89]

NOTES

1. Hermann Hugo, *Pia Desideria Emblematis, Elegiis & affectibus SS. Patrum Illustrata* (Antwerp, 1624).

2. Hermann Hugo, comp., *Gottselige Begirde aus lautter sprüchen der Heyligen Vättern*, trans. Carolus Stengelius (Augsburg, 1627).

3. Van Sichem's woodcuts first appeared in 1628.

4. Alois M. Haas, "Geistlicher Zeitvertreib: Friedrich Spees Echogedichte," in *Deutsche Barocklyrik*. ed. Martin Bircher and Alois M. Haas, pp. 14, 41, n. 39.

5. Cf. Dieter Breuer, *Der "Philotheus" des Laurentius von Schnüffis*.

6. Cf. Alois M. Haas, "Die Problematik von Sprache und Erfahrung in der deutschen Mystik," in Werner Beierwaltes et al., *Grundfragen der Mystik*, pp. 73–104.

7. Louis Chardon, O.P., *The Cross of Jesus*, I, 230.

8. On the (virtual) continuity of "spiritual marriage" as against "spiritual betrothal" in St. Teresa see E. Allison Peers, *Studies of the Spanish Mystics* I, 151–52.

9. Augustine Baker, O.S.B., *Holy Wisdom; or, Directions for the Prayer of Contemplation*, ed. Dom Gerard Sitwell, p. 482.

10. Karl-Heinz zur Mühlen, *Nos extra nos. Luthers Theologie zwischen Mystik und Scholastik*, Beiträge zur Historischen Theologie, 46 (Tübingen: Mohr [Siebeck], 1972), pp. 63 ff.

11. Manfred Windfuhr, *Die barocke Bildlichkeit und ihre Kritiker. Stilhaltungen in der deutschen Literatur des 17. und 18. Jahrhunderts*. Germanistische Abhandlungen, 15 (Stuttgart: Metzler, 1966), p. 212.

12. Jacob Böhme, *Christosophia, oder Der Weg zu Christo*, "Das erste Büchlein, Von wahrer Busse," vol. IV of his *Sämtliche Schriften*, ed. Will-Erich Peuckert, p. 19 (separately paginated).

13. Severin R. v. Lama, *Am tiefsten Quell: Mystik in Österreich*, pp. 270, 295, 339.

14. Pamela Askew, "The Angelic Consolation of St. Francis of Assisi in Post-Tridentine Italian Painting."

15. Cf. sonnets 177 ff. in Catharina Regina von Greiffenberg, *Geistliche Sonette, Lieder und Gedichte*, ed. Heinz-Otto Burger (Darmstadt: Wissenschaftliche Buchgesellschaft, 1967).

16. A recent, attractive book "Translated, drawn, and handwritten" by Frederick Franck is of interest to the student of German baroque mysticism for its juxtaposition of verses by Angelus Silesius ("this Western Zen poet") and sayings from the religious literature of the Far East: *The Book of Angelus Silesius, with Observations by the Ancient Zen Masters* (New York: Knopf, 1976).

17. Heiko A. Oberman, "*Simul Gemitus et Raptus*: Luther and Mysticism," in

The Reformation in Medieval Perspective, ed. Steven E. Ozment, pp. 222-23.

18. Gottfried Arnold, *Historie und Beschreibung Der Mystischen Theologie*, (Leipzig: Sam. Benj. Walther, 1738), pp. 24 ff.

19. G. Born, "Geist, Wissen und Bildung bei Thomas Müntzer und Valentin Icklsamer" (diss. Erlangen 1952), pp. 13-14; quoted in Werner O. Packull, *Mysticism and the Early South German-Austrian Anabaptist Movement, 1515-1531*, p. 189, n. 76.

20. Evelyn Underhill, *Mysticism: A Study in the Nature and Development of Man's Spiritual Consciousness*, p. 98.

21. Richard T. Murphy, O.P., in the introduction to Louis Chardon, *The Cross of Jesus* (above, n. 7), p. xxi, says: "the Thomistic doctrine on the spiritual life makes the operation of the gifts of the Holy Spirit a *sine qua non* for the mystical act and the mystical state."

22. Cf. Heinrich Bornkamm, *Mystik, Spiritualismus und die Anfänge des Pietismus im Luthertum*, p. 11 (on "Spiritualismus" as the more inclusive term and on "spiritualistische Mystik"). The term *mystischer Spiritualismus* occurs, for example, in Martin Schmidt, "Epochen der Pietismus-forschung," in *Pietismus und Reveil*, ed. J. van den Berg and J. P. van Dooren, p. 77

23. Angelus Silesius, *Sämtliche poetische Werke in drei Bänden*, ed. Hans Ludwig Held, I, 346.

24. Casper C. G. Visser, "Die mystisch-pietistische Strömung in der niederländisch-lutherischen Kirche in der zweiten Hälfte des 17. Jahrhunderts," in *Pietismus und Reveil*, ed. J. van den Berg and J. P. van Dooren, pp. 175-76).

25. Carl Richstaetter, *Christusfrömmigkeit in ihrer historischen Entfaltung*, p. 207, n. 2.

26. Marie-Luise Wolfskehl, *Die Jesusminne in der Lyrik des deutschen Barock*, p. 17.

27. Wolfskehl, p. 87.

28. Richstaetter, p. 447.

29. Richstaetter, pp. 444-46, 463-66, 480-84.

30. Lama, pp. 173-74, 257, 276.

31. E. Allison Peers, *The Mystics of Spain*, p. 24.

32. Peers, *Studies of the Spanish Mystics*, II, 219-22; G. Mesters, "Karmeliten," *Lexikon für Theologie und Kirche*, V (1960), col. 1368.

33. G. Mesters, "Dominicus a Iesu Maria," *Lexikon für Theologie und Kirche*, III (1959), col. 481.

34. Benedict Zimmerman, "Carmelite Order," p. 368.

35. E. W. Zeeden, "La vie religieuse dans les pays catholiques de langue germanique à la fin du XVIᵉ siècle," in *Colloque d'histoire religieuse (Lyon, octobre 1963)*, p. 72: "Auch die Kapuziner hielten das meditative Element

für so wichtig, dass sie dort, wo höchste Aktivität geboten war, z.B. bei der Begründung der Schweizerischen Ordensprovinz 1581 und der damit verbundenen volksmissionarischen Arbeit nur ein Viertel der etwa 45 Ordensleute in die Seelsorge entliessen und mindestens die Hälfte für die reguläre geistliche Lebensführung in den Klöstern zurückhielten."

36. Richstaetter, p. 266.

37. On Loyola's mysticism, see Richstaetter, p. 266; also Fridolin Marxer, *Die inneren geistlichen Sinne: Ein Beitrag zur Deutung ignatianischer Mystik.*

38. Marxer, p. 160.

39. Emmy Rosenfeld, *Neue Studien zur Lyrik von Friedrick von Spee*, pp. 33 ff.

40. Haas, p. 13 (see n. 4, above).

41. Friedrich Spee, *Güldenes Tugend-Buch*, ed. Theo G. M. van Oorschot, pp. 704-5.

42. Joseph de Guibert, *The Jesuits, Their Spiritual Doctrine and Practice*, trans. William J. Young, ed. George E. Ganss, pp. 215 ff.

43. Leonard Forster and A. A. Parker, "Quirinus Kuhlmann and the Poetry of St. John of the Cross," *Bulletin of Hispanic Studies*, 35 (1958) 6.

44. M. Hildburgis Gies, *Eine lateinische Quelle zum "Cherubinischen Wandersmann" des Angelus Silesius*, p. 132 and n. 2.

45. Forster and Parker, pp. 3 ff.

46. Gies, p. 132 and n. 1.

47. Richstaetter, p. 153; Guibert, pp. 199-200.

48. George Huntston Williams, "Popularized German Mysticism as a Factor in the Rise of Anabaptist Communism," in *Glaube, Geist, Geschichte*, ed. Gerhard Müller and Winfried Zeller, p. 291 and n. 3.

49. All bibliographical data on the *Theologia Deutsch* come from Georg Baring, *Bibliographie der Ausgaben der "Theologia Deutsch" (1516–1961).*

50. Steven E. Ozment, *Mysticism and Dissent: Religious Ideology and Social Protest in the Sixteenth Century*, pp. 33-34.

51. Paul Althaus, d., A. *Forschungen zur Evangelischen Gebetsliteratur.*

52. Winfried Zeller, comp., *Der Protestantismus des 17. Jahrhunderts*, p. xxi.

53. Hans-Henrik Krummacher, *Der junge Gryphius und die Tradition*, pp. 497-98.

54. Cf. Johannes Wallmann, "Wiedergeburt und Erneuerung bei Philipp Jakob Spener: Ein Diskussionsbeitrag," in *Pietismus und Neuzeit: Jahrbuch 1976*, ed. A. Lindt and K. Deppermann, pp. 25, 28.

55. Johannes Wallmann, "Pietismus," *Evangelisches Staatslexikon*, II (1975), col. 1815.

56. Johannes Wallmann, *Philipp Jakob Spener und die Anfänge des Pietismus*, pp. 22, 46, 51; Spener edited Arndt's work in 1674, sixty-nine years after its first appearance (p. 239).

57. Cf. Karl Vossler, *Poesie der Einsamkeit in Spanien*, pp. 155-74.

58. Erhard Peschke, "Die Bedeutung der Mystik für die Bekehrung August

Hermann Franckes," in *Zur neueren Pietismusforschung*, ed. Martin Greschat, p. 300.

59. Wallmann, "Pietismus," col. 1816.

60. Arlene Adrienne Miller, "Jacob Boehme from Orthodoxy to Enlightenment" (diss. Stanford 1971), p. 2.

61. Werner Buddecke, *Die Jakob Böhme–Ausgaben*, 2. Teil, *Die Übersetzungen*, passim.

62. Wolfram Buddecke, "Die Jakob-Böhme–Autographen: Ein historischer Bericht," pp. 61–87.

63. Max Wieser, *Peter Poiret*, pp. 225–38.

64. Wieser, p. 23.

65. W. Zeller, "Tersteegen," *Evangelisches Kirchenlexikon*, 1962 ed.

66. Cf. Roland Pietsch, "Jakob Böhmes Gottesbegriff."

67. Ernst Benz, *Der vollkommene Mensch nach Jacob Boehme*, pp. 18, 21 ff.

68. Jakob Böhme, *De signatura rerum*, quoted in Wolfgang Kayser, "Böhmes Natursprachenlehre und ihre Grundlagen," p. 557.

69. Jakob Böhme, *Drei Prinzipien*, 7, 31; quoted in Erwin Metzke, "Von Steinen und Erde und vom Grimm der Natur in der Philosophie Jacob Böhmes," in his *Coincidentia oppositorum*, ed. Karlfried Gründer, p. 133.

70. Cf. Metzke, pp. 152, 148.

71. Miller, p. 190.

71a. Cf. Hans Bayer, "Die empraktischen Sprachkategorien von Jacob Böhmes Weltdeutung," *Zeitschrift für deutsche Philologie*, 96 (1977), Sonderheft, pp. 170–201.

72. Jan van Ruysbroeck, "Von einigen der vornehmsten Tugenden," chap. 4, "Von verläugnung des eigenen willens . . . ," in his *Schriften*, pp. 24 ff.

73. Ruysbroeck, "Spiegel der ewigen Seligkeit," chap. 16, in his *Schriften*, p. 80 (separately paginated).

74. Valentin Weigel, *Zwei nützliche Tractate, der erste von der Bekehrung des Menschen . . .*, ed. Winfried Zeller, 3. Lieferung, *Sämtliche Schriften*, ed. Will-Erich Peuckert and Winfried Zeller, pp. 18 and 16.

75. Weigel, p. 17.

76. Weigel, *Zwei nützliche Tractate, . . . der andere von Armut des Geistes oder wahrer Gelassenheit . . .*, p. 56.

77. Weigel, p. 81.

78. Weigel, *Dialogus de Christianismo* (1584), ed. Alfred Ehrentreich, 4. Lieferung, *Sämtliche Schriften* (1967), p. 112; this work was first published in 1616 (p. 159).

79. Weigel, *Dialogus de Christianismo*, pp. 38, 36.

80. John Donne, "The Crosse," quoted in Barbara Kiefer Lewalski, *Protestant Poetics and the Seventeenth-Century Religious Lyric*, p. 255.

81. Greiffenberg, sonnet 147, in her *Geistliche Sonette, Lieder und Gedichte* (above, n. 15).

82. Blosius, *Regel des geistlichen Lebens*, fol. C^v.

83. Greiffenberg, sonnet 147 (see n. 15, above).

84. Jörn Reichel, *Dichtungstheorie und Sprache bei Zinzendorf*, *Der 12. Anhang zum Herrnhuter Gesangbuch*, p. 56.

85. Angelus Silesius, *Sämtliche poetische Werke*, ed. H. L. Held, vol. III, *Cherubinischer Wandersmann; Sinnliche Beschreibung der vier letzten Dinge*, p. 182.

86. Cf. Friedrich-Wilhelm Wentzlaff-Eggebert, *Deutsche Mystik zwischen Mittelalter und Neuzeit, Einheit und Wandlung ihrer Erscheinungsformen*, pp. 196 ff.

87. See Martin Bircher, "Unergründlichkeit, Catharina Regina von Greiffenbergs Gedicht über den Tod der Barbara Susanna Eleonora von Regal," in *Deutsche Barocklyrik*, ed. M. Bircher and A. M. Haas, pp. 188-89.

88. Andreas Gryphius, *Magnetische Verbindung* . . . , in *Trauerreden des Barock*, ed. Maria Fürstenwald, p. 176. Cf. Friedrich-Wilhelm Wentzlaff-Eggebert, *Der triumphierende und der besiegte Tod in der Wort- und Bildkunst des Barock*, pp. 122-45.

89. Angelus Silesius, *Cherubinischer Wandersmann*, II, 2 (p. 43), and I, 33 (p. 10).

SELECTED BIBLIOGRAPHY

Primary Sources

Angelus Silesius. *Sämtliche poetische Werke in drei Bänden*. Hans Ludwig Held, ed. 3rd ed. München: Hanser, 1952.

Arnold, Gottfried. *Historie und Beschreibung Der Mystischen Theologie / Oder Geheimen Gottesgelehrtheit / wie auch der alten und neuen Mysticorvm*. Leipzig: Sam. Benj. Walther, 1738.

Baker, Augustine, O.S.B. *Holy Wisdom or Directions for the Prayer of Contemplation*. The Digest made by Fr Serenus Cressy, O.S.B., from the treatises of Fr Baker, first published under the title *Sancta Sophia* in 1657. Dom Gerard Sitwell, ed. The Orchard Books. London: Burns & Oates, 1964.

Blosius, Ludovicus. *Regel des geistlichen Lebens. Allen Christen zu einem guten anfang vnnd fortgang in einem rechtgeistlichen eingezogenen leben vast nutzlich. Durch den hochwürdigen Herrn Ludwig Blosium Abbatem Laetiensem beschriben / vnd vom Latein ins Teutsch gebracht durch Philippum Dobereiner*. [n.p.] 1569.

Böhme, Jacob. *Sämtliche Schriften*. Faksimile-Neudruck der Ausgabe von 1730 in elf Bänden. Will-Erich Peuckert, ed. Stuttgart-Bad Cannstatt: Friedrich Frommann Verlag Günther Holzboog, 1955-61.

Chardon, Louis, O.P. *The Cross of Jesus.* Vol. I, trans. Richard T. Murphy. Cross and Crown Series of Spirituality, 9. St. Louis and London: Herder, 1957.

Franck, Frederick, comp. *The Book of Angelus Silesius, with Observations by the Ancient Zen Masters.* New York: Knopf, 1976.

Greiffenberg, Catharina Regina von. *Geistliche Sonette, Lieder und Gedichte.* Heinz-Otto Burger, ed. Darmstadt: Wissenschaftliche Buchgesellschaft, 1967.

Gryphius, Andreas. *Magnetische Verbindung Des Herrn Jesu / und der in Ihr verliebten Seelen Als die Seeligst-erblichene Leiche Der weyland Hoch-Edelgebohrnen / Höchst-Tugend Zucht und Ehrenreichen Jungfrauen / Jungfr. Marianen gebohrnen von Popschitz / Den XXIII. Wintermonats / des MDCLX. Jahres. auß Dero Väterlichen und Bruderlichen Hoch-Adelichen Rittersitz Gröditz Zu Ihrer Beerdigung abgeführet. Der Höchstansehlichen Versammelung vorgestellet Von Andrea Gryphio. Gedruckt zur Steinau an der Oder / bey Johann Kuntzen. In Trauerreden des Barock.* Maria Fürstenwald, ed. Beiträge zur Literatur des 15. bis 18. Jahrhunderts, 4. Wiesbaden: Steiner, 1973, pp. 163–95.

Hugo, Hermann, comp. *Gottselige Begirde aus lautter sprüchen der Heyligen Vättern Zuesamen gezogen Vnd mitt schönen figuren Zieret durch R. P. Hermannum Hugonem. S.J. Verteütscht Durch R.P.F. Carolum Stengelium Ord. S. Ben. Getruckt, in Augspurg Anno 1627.* [Colophon:] . . . bey Mattheo Langenwaldter.

——. *Pia Desideria Emblematis, Elegüs & affectibus SS. Patrvm Illustrata, Avthore Hermanno Hvgone Societatis Iesv. Ad Vrbanum VIII. Pont. Max. Sculpsit Christophorus à Sichem, pro P.I.P. Typis Henrici Aertssenii, Antverpiae M.DC.XXVIII.*

Joannis Evangelista, Guardian of Louvain. *Scheidung der Seel und deß Geists Oder Innerliches Augsteigen der Braut / durch die Staffeln der Keuschen Lieb . . . Als der ander Theil oder Anhang des Buchs Vom Reich Gottes in der Seel. . . .* Sulzbach: Abraham Liechtenthaler, 1569.

Kuhlmann, Quirinus. *Dèr Kühlpsalter.* Robert L. Beare, ed. 2 vols. Neudrucke Deutscher Literaturwerke, N.F. 3, 4. Tübingen: Niemeyer, 1971.

Ruysbroeck, Jan van. *Des Ehrwürdigen Vaters D. Johannis Rusbrochii, Weiland Canonici Regularis Augustiner Ordens / und Prioris des Klosters Grünthal / Doctor Ecstaticus, Bestehend auß allen desselben sehr Gottseligen Schrifften / . . . Vormahls von dem P.F. Laurentio Surio, einem Carthäuser zu Cölln auß dem Holländischen ins Lateinische / Nun aber zum gemeinen nutz Alles ins Teutsche treulichst übersetzet / von G. J. C. Und mit einer Vorrede herauß gegeben / von Gottfried Arnold. Offenbach am Mayn / Druckts Bonaventura de Launoy, Ysenburg- und Büdingischer Hof-Buchdr. Im Jahr 1701.*

Spee, Friedrich. *Güldenes Tugend-Buch.* Theo G. M. van Oorschot, ed. Vol. III of *Sämtliche Schriften.* Historisch-kristische Ausgabe in drei Bänden.

Emmy Rosenfeld, ed. *Deutsche Barock-Literatur*. München: Kösel-Verlag, 1968.

Weigel, Valentin. *Sämtliche Schriften*. Will-Erich Peuckert and Winfried Zeller, eds. Lieferungen 1-7. Stuttgart-Bad Cannstatt: Friedrich Frommann Verlag Günther Holzboog, 1962-78.

Secondary Literature

Althaus, Paul d. Ä. *Forschungen zur Evangelischen Gebetsliteratur*. Gütersloh: Bertelsmann, 1927.

Askew, Pamela. "The Angelic Consolation of St. Francis of Assisi in Post-Tridentine Italian Painting." *Journal of the Warburg and Courtauld Institutes*, 32 (1969), 280-306.

Baring, Georg. *Bibliographie der Ausgaben der "Theologia Deutsch" (1516–1961): Ein Beitrag zur Lutherbibliographie*. Bibliotheca Bibliographica Aureliana, 8. Baden-Baden: Heitz, 1963.

Bayer, Hans. "Die empraktischen Sprachkategorien von Jacob Böhmes Weltdeutung." *Zeitschrift für deutsche Philologie*, 96 (1977). Sonderheft, pp. 170-201.

Benz, Ernst. *Die Vision. Erfahrungsformen und Bilderwelt*. Stuttgart: Klett, 1969.

——. *Der vollkommene Mensch nach Jacob Boehme*. Stuttgart: Kohlhammer, 1937.

Bircher, Martin, and Alois M. Haas, eds. *Deutsche Barocklyrik: Gedichtinterpretation von Spee bis Haller*. Bern and München: Francke, 1973.

Bornkamm, Heinrich. *Mystik, Spiritualismus und die Anfänge des Pietismus im Luthertum*. Vorträge der theologischen Konferenz zu Gießen, 44. Folge. Gießen: Töpelmann, 1926.

Breuer, Dieter. *Der "Philotheus" des Laurentius von Schnüffis: Zum Typus des geistlichen Romans im 17. Jahrhundert*. Deutsche Studien, 10. Meisenheim am Glan: Hain, 1969.

Buddecke, Werner. *Die Jakob Böhme–Ausgaben: Ein beschreibendes Verzeichnis*. 2. Teil, *Die Übersetzungen*. Arbeiten aus der Staats- und Universitätsbibliothek Göttingen, Hainbergschriften, N.F. 2. Göttingen: Häntzschel, 1957.

Buddecke, Wolfram. "Die Jakob-Böhme-Autographen: Ein historischer Bericht." *Wolfenbütteler Beiträge*, 1 (1972), 61-87.

Faivre, Antoine, and Rolf Christian Zimmermann, eds. *Epochen der Naturmystik. Hermetische Tradition im wissenschaftlichen Fortschritt. Grands Moments de la Mystique de la Nature. Mystical Approaches to Nature. . . .* Berlin: Schmidt, 1979.

Forster, Leonard, and A. A. Parker. "Quirinus Kuhlmann and the Poetry of St. John of the Cross." *Bulletin of Hispanic Studies*, 35 (1958), 1-23. Rpt. in

Leonard Forster, *Kleine Schriften zur deutschen Literatur im 17. Jahrhundert. Daphnis*, 6, Heft 4 (1977), 235-261.

Galle, Jürgen. "Das Genoveca-Motiv in der Lyrik: Die lateinische Ode Jacob Baldes und ihre deutschen Versionen im 17. Jahrhundert." In *Europäische Tradition und deutscher Literaturbarock: Internationale Beiträge zum Problem von Überlieferung und Umgestaltung*. Gerhart Hoffmeister, ed. Bern and München: Francke, 1973, pp. 117-34.

Gies, M. Hildburgis. *Eine lateinische Quelle zum "Cherubinischen Wandersmann" des Angelus Silesius: Untersuchungen der Beziehungen zwischen der mystischen Dichtung Schefflers und der "Clavis pro theologia mystica" des Maximilian Sandäus*. Breslauer Studien zur historischen Theologie, 12. Breslau: Müller & Seiffert, 1929.

Gnädinger, Louise. "Die spekulative Mystik im *Cherubinischen Wandersmann des Johannes Angelus Silesius.*" *Studi germanici* (NS), 4 (1966), 29-59; 145-90.

Guibert, Joseph de. *The Jesuits, Their Spiritual Doctrine and Practice: A Historical Study*. Trans. William J. Young. George E. Ganss, ed. 1964. Rpt. St. Louis: The Institute of Jesuit Sources, 1972.

Haas, Alois M. "Die Problematik von Sprache und Erfahrung in der deutschen Mystik." In Werner Beierwaltes, Hans Urs von Baltasar, and Alois M. Haas. *Grundfragen der Mystik*. Kriterien, 33. Einsiedeln: Johannes Verlag, 1974, pp. 73-104.

Kabisch, Eva-Maria. *Untersuchungen zur Sprache des "Kühlpsalters" von Quirinus Kuhlmann: Eine exemplarische Analyse*. Diss. Freie Universität Berlin 1970. Berlin: privately printed, 1970.

Kayser, Wolfgang. "Böhmes Natursprachenlehre und ihre Grundlagen." *Euphorion*, 31 (1930), 521-62.

Krummacher, Hans-Henrik. *Der junge Gryphius und die Tradition: Studien zu den Perikopensonetten und Passionsliedern*. München: Fink, 1976.

Lama, Severin, R. v. *Am tiefsten Quell: Mystik in Österreich*. Wien: Bergland, 1964.

Lewalski, Barbara Kiefer. *Protestant Poetics and the Seventeenth-Century Religious Lyric*. Princeton, N.J.: Princeton University Press, 1979.

Marxer, Fridolin. *Die inneren geistlichen Sinne: Ein Beitrag zur Deutung ignatianischer Mystik*. Dissertatio ad Lauream in Facultate Theologica Pontificiae Universitatis Gregorianae 1962. Freiburg, Basel, Wien: Herder, 1963.

Mesters, G. "Dominicus a Iesu Maria." *Lexikon für Theologie und Kirche*, III (1959).

Metzke, Erwin. "Von Steinen und Erde und vom Grimm der Natur in der Philosophie Jacob Böhmes." In *Coincidentia oppositorum: Gesammelte Studien zur Philosophiegeschichte*. Karlfried Gründer, ed. Forschungen und Berichte der Evangelischen Studiengemeinschaft, 19. Witten: Luther-Verlag, 1961, pp. 129-57.

Miller, Arlene Adrienne. "Jacob Boehme from Orthodoxy to Enlightenment." Diss. Stanford 1971.

Oberman, Heiko A. "*Simul Gemitus et Raptus*: Luther and Mysticism." In *The Reformation in Medieval Perspective*. Steven E. Ozment, ed. Modern Scholarship on European History. Chicago: Quadrangle Books, 1971, pp. 219-51.

Ozment, Steven E. *Mysticism and Dissent: Religious Ideology and Social Protest in the Sixteenth Century*. New Haven, Conn., and London: Yale University Press, 1973.

Packull, Werner O. *Mysticism and the Early South German-Austrian Anabaptist Movement, 1525-1531*. Studies in Anabaptist and Mennonite History, 19. Scottdale, Pa., and Kitchener, Ontario: Herald Press, 1977.

Peers, E. Allison. *The Mystics of Spain*. Ethical and Religious Classics of the East and West, 5. London: Allen & Unwin, 1951.

——. *Studies of the Spanish Mystics*. 2nd rev. ed. 3 vols. London: S.P.C.K.; New York: Macmillan, 1960.

Peschke, Erhard. "Die Bedeutung der Mystik für die Bekehrung August Hermann Franckes." In *Zur neueren Pietismusforschung*. Martin Greschat, ed. Wege der Forschung, 165. Darmstadt: Wissenschaftliche Buchgesellschaft, 1977, pp. 294-316.

Pietsch, Roland. "Jakob Böhmes Gottesbegriff." *Zeitwende: Die neue Furche*, 47 (1976), 100-112.

Reichel, Jörn. *Dichtungstheorie und Sprache bei Zinzendorf: Der 12. Anhang zum Herrnhuter Gesangbuch*. Ars poetica, Texte und Studien zur Dichtungslehre und Dichtkunst, Studien, 10. Bad Homburg, Berlin, Zürich: Gehlen, 1969.

Richstaetter, Carl. *Christusfrömmigkeit in ihrer historischen Entfaltung: Ein quellenmässiger Beitrag zur Geschichte des Gebetes und des mystischen Innenlebens der Kirche*. Köln: Bächem, 1949.

Rosenfeld, Emmy. *Neue Studien zur Lyrik von Friedrich von Spee*. Collana Universita' Commerciale "L. Bocconi." Lingue e Letterature straniere, 13. Milan: Istituto Editoriale Cisalpino, 1963.

Schwartz, Ernst Thomas, Jr. "The Metaphysical Tradition of the *Cherubinische Wandersmann*." Diss. Maryland 1972.

Stählin, Traugott. *Gottfried Arnolds geistliche Dichtung: Glaube und Mystik*. Veröffentlichungen der Evangelischen Gesellschaft für Liturgieforschung, 15. Göttingen: Vandenhoeck & Ruprecht, 1966.

Underhill, Evelyn. *Mysticism: A Study in the Nature and Development of Man's Spiritual Consciousness*. 12th ed. 1930; rpt. New York: Dutton, 1961.

van den Berg, J., and J. P. van Dooren, eds. *Pietismus und Reveil; Referate der internationalen Tagung: Der Pietismus in den Niederlanden und seine internationalen Beziehungen, Zeist 18.-22. 1974*. Kerkhistorische Bijdragen, 7. Leiden: Brill, 1978.

Vossler, Karl. *Poesie der Einsamkeit in Spanien.* München: Beck, 1940.

Wallmann, Johannes. *Philipp Jakob Spener und die Anfänge des Pietismus.* Beiträge zur historischen Theologie, 42. Tübingen: Mohr (Siebeck), 1970.

———. "Pietismus." *Evangelisches Staatslexikon,* 1975 ed.

———. "Wiedergeburt und Erneuerung bei Philipp Jakob Spener: Ein Diskussionsbeitrag." In *Pietismus und Neuzeit: Jahrbuch 1976.* A. Lindt and K. Deppermann, eds. Bielefeld, 1977.

Wentzlaff-Eggebert, Friedrich-Wilhelm. *Deutsche Mystik zwischen Mittelalter und Neuzeit: Einheit und Wandlung ihrer Erscheinungsformen.* 3rd ed. Berlin: de Gruyter, 1969.

———. *Der triumphierende und der besiegte Tod in der Wort- und Bildkunst des Barock.* Berlin and New York: de Gruyter, 1975.

Wieser, Max. *Peter Poiret: Der Vater der romanischen [sic] Mystik in Deutschland: Zum Ursprung der Romantik in Deutschland.* Mystiker des Abendlandes. München: Müller, 1932.

Williams, George Huntston. "Popularized German Mysticism as a Factor in the Rise of Anabaptist Communism." In *Glaube, Geist, Geschichte: Festschrift Ernst Benz zum 60. Geburstag.* Gerhard Müller and Winfried Zeller, eds. Leiden: Brill, 1967, pp. 290-312.

Windfuhr, Manfred. *Die barocke Bildlichkeit und ihre Kritiker. Stilhaltungen in der deutschen Literatur des 17. and 18. Jahrhunderts.* Germanistische Abhandlungen, 15. Stuttgart: Metzler, 1966.

Wolfskehl, Marie-Luise. *Die Jesusminne in der Lyrik des deutschen Barock.* Gießener Beiträge zur deutschen Philologie, 34. Gießen: Otto Kindt, 1934.

Zeeden, E. W. "La vie religieuse dans les pays catholiques de langue germanique à la fin du XVIe siècle." In *Colloque d'histoire religieuse (Lyon, octobre 1963).* Grenoble: Commission internationale et sous-commission française d'histoire ecclésiastique comparée, 1963, pp. 63-80.

Zeller, Winfried, comp. *Der Protestantismus des 17. Jahrhunderts.* Klassiker des Protestantismus, 5; Sammlung Dieterich, 270. Bremen: Schünemann, 1962.

———. "Tersteegen." *Evangelisches Kirchenlexikon: Kirchlich-theologisches Handwörterbuch.* 1962 ed.

Zimmerman, Benedict. "Carmelite Order." *The Catholic Encyclopedia,* 1908 ed.

zur Mühlen, Karl-Heinz. *Nos extra nos: Luthers Theologie zwischen Mystik und Scholastik.* Beiträge zur historischen Theologie, 46. Tübingen: Mohr (Siebeck), 1972.

IV

The Rise
of the Modern Genres

17

The European Novel in Seventeenth-Century Germany: A Decade of Research (1970–80)

Gerhart Hoffmeister

Does the *German* baroque novel actually exist? It is possible to deny this on the ground that the novel of the seventeenth century in Germany was a European invention. The European pastoral, picaresque, courtly, and sentimental novels of the period had provided, at least during the first half of the century, the models for German authors to translate, adapt, and assimilate before they ventured out on their own, though still looking back to the past for inspiration from their great European predecessors and masters. The German novel came of age with Grimmelshausen's *Simplicissimus* (1669) and Lohenstein's *Arminius* (1689 ff), to mention just a couple of the most outstanding works, heirs to two quite distinct traditions, the picaresque and the courtly novel.

By shifting our emphasis from "German" to "baroque" we can actually state with conviction that the German *baroque* novel — referring to works in the grand style with complicated plots, those "wildgewordene Realenzyklopädien," as Eichendorff put it — is much too exclusive a term to cover the astonishing variety of literary products of the century that are still being rediscovered and reedited for modern readers in Germany and the United States. Although most of them probably deserve to be forgotten, there are superbly readable gems among them worth a revival. It may come as a surprise, however, that the seventeenth-century

novel did not figure in the poetics of the day, nor did their authors readily put their own name on the title page, unless it was a courtly novel.
This apparent low esteem has to do with the novel's nonacceptance into
the classical canon of rhymed poetic genres, due to its content, which was
thought to endanger readers' morals—a view illustrated by the vehement
attacks of Protestant pastors such as Gotthard Heidegger, who claimed
"wer Romans list / der list lügen" (6, p. 71), because of the lies,
dissoluteness, and eroticism to be found in the secular love and adventure novels since Heliodorus's *Aithiopika*. No wonder, then, that the
polemics centered on the bestseller of the sixteenth century, *Amadis de
Gaull*, which—next to the popular chapbooks (*Faustus, Hans Clawert,
Lalebook, Ahasverus*, etc.), Fischart's *Geschichtsklitterung* modeled on
Rabelais's *Gargantua and Pantagruel* (1532 ff.) and Jörg Wickram's
novels, echoes of the courtly romance in a chronicle manner—was the
only fiction of note available to the upper class. That was not much to
build on, and the only choice German authors had was either to look for
inspiration in foreign literatures or to write something better than the
dangerous or even devilish *Amadis*, marketed in French since the 1540s
and in German since 1569 (51, 67, 78). It was above all a question of laying proper foundations for the development of German literature, foundations on which "Stuben / Kammeren und Palläste" were going to be
built, as Justus Schottelius put it (14, p. 1244).

The statistics available confirm that German writers started almost
from scratch, translating one novel or perhaps two per year, first from
Spanish, then increasingly from French. Between 1614 and 1669, 59
translations of foreign novels were made and 29 original works were
published. From the *Simplicissimus*-year of 1669 until 1724 translations
fell behind sharply: 151 were produced in contrast to 315 original novels.
All in all, within a period of 110 years more than 550 novels were
printed—quite an achievement, considering the zero start and the fact
that the majority of the middle class could neither read nor write until
well into the early 1800s. On the other hand, it is a rather small number
in the light of the approximately five hundred novels turned out in 1802
alone (53, p. 114). Until the 1730s patrons of the arts exerted their
beneficial influence only at the courts, where a learned civil-service class,
often of noble lineage, furnished the authors as well as the readers.

A quick glance at Hans Gerd Rötzer's chronology ("Werk-
chronologie," 65, pp. 135 ff.) will tell us something about the literary
discoveries and predilections of the age. It is the picaresque genre above
all that made a deep and lasting impression on the German literary
scene: *Lazarillo de Tormes* was translated in 1614 and 1617; *Guzmán de*

Alfarache in 1615; Cervantes's *Rinconete y Cortadillo* four years after its publication in 1617 (16), and his *Don Quijote,* part I up to chapter 23, in 1648 (26); and *La Pícara Justina* was adapted in 1620. Immediately following in importance is the pastoral novel: Montemayor's *Diana* was translated by Hans Ludwig von Kuffstein in 1619 and republished as well as extended by Harsdöffer in 1646 (5, 37); d'Urfé's *Astée* was translated in 1619; and Sidney's *Arcadia* in 1629 and again in 1638. The courtly novel appeared next on the scene: Barclay's *Argenis* (1621) was translated by Martin Opitz in 1626; Philipp von Zesen's versions from the French had been appearing since 1644 and Wilhelm von Stubenberg's from the Italian courtly novel since 1650 (21). The European sentimental novel is represented by several adaptations reaching from Juan de Flores's *Historia de Grisel y Mirabella* (ca. 1495, translated by Christian Pharemund in 1630) to Diego de San Pedro's *La Cárcel de amor* (1492, translated by Kuffstein in 1624) (9) and *Arnalte y Lucenda* (1491, adapted by Augspurger in 1642).

The critical step from close translations and freer adaptations to independent prose works was apparently first taken in a short pastoral novel, *Amoena und Amandus* (abbreviated title, 1632), followed by several other pastorals (titled, in abbreviated form: *Coelinde und Corimbo,* 1636; *Leoriander und Perelina,* 1642; *Ferrando und Dorinde,* 1644), until an original of major importance was published, Zesen's *Adriatische Rosemund* (1645). This novel is a blend of the pastoral, the courtly, and the sentimental traditions, and inasmuch as it portrays a lady suffering from unrequited love (47), it represents a conscious effort to replace foreign models of erotic content by a "keusche libesbeschreibung" (preface). Andreas Heinrich Bucholtz repeated this attempt in his *Des Christlichen Teutschen Groß-Fürsten Herkules Und Der Böhmischen Königlichen Valiska Wunder-Geschichte* (1659-60), which still uses the structure, style, and motifs of the *Amadis* but successfully overcomes its eroticism and fantastic adventures by emphasizing chaste marriages linked to historical events. *Amadis*, a product of the Spanish *reconquista*, with its roots in fifteenth-century reality, had been turned into a narrative of the perfect Christian knight, a mirror for princes in seventeenth-century courts.

I

Traditionally the courtly-historical novel has been identified with the baroque novel in general (60, pp. 21 ff.). It has been the ideal type and standard in comparison with which everything else did not amount to much. Only recently has this abstract view been superseded by more detailed investigations that emphasize the diversity even within this group of novels, without losing sight of their common features. It is not our intention to summarize these again since this has been done expertly and frequently (54, 65, 76), but we want to point out some qualities essential in this context. The courtly novel originated in France with Bishop Jean Pierre Camus (1584-1652), with the native Lothringian John Barclay (1582-1621), followed by Sieur de Gerzan (fl. 1669), Jean Desmarets de Saint Sorlin (1595-1676), Madeleine de Scudéry (1607-1701), and Sieur de La Calprenède (1609-63). Their works reflect the growing centralization of power under the reign of Louis XIII and Cardinals Richelieu and Mazarin as well as the influence of the Hôtel de Rambouillet, with its new ideal of *préciosité* in style and morals after 1618.

Adapted to German tastes by Opitz, Zesen, Stubenberg, and others, the courtly novel became the literary expression of the absolutist ruling class, combining affairs of state with love in the sphere of the court, its plots based on the "byzantine" principle of Heliodorus: "alles in verwirrung fallen zu laßen, und dann unverhofft herauß zu wickeln," as Leibniz put it (8, p. 68). A process of multiplying loving couples gave rise to a complicated net of plots, subplots and intermezzi resembling the many layers of an onion (8, p. 57). No wonder, then, that Thomasius refers to the "gesunden und delicaten Speisen des heroisch-höfischen Staats- und Liebesromans" (8, p. 48), distinguishing it from other, less appealing novelistic possibilities because of its being a mirror of morals and divine justice.

The courtly novel as theodicy—this is also the message of the most important theoretical document of the age come down to us, Sigmund von Birken's preface to Herzog Anton Ulrich's *Aramena* (1669): "Da lernen wir den allweißen, gerechten, gütigen, allmächtigen und wahrhaften Gott, aus seinen werken, aus der wunderbaren Regirung, aus denen über die Tyrannen und Boshaften verhängten Straffen, aus beschirmung und belohnung der Gottliebenden und Tugendhaften, und aus der erfüllung seiner Verheisungen erkennen." A few years later, in a letter to Anton Ulrich (1713), Leibniz was to draw a close parallel between the creator God and the novelist: "Gleichwie E. D. [Eure Durchlaucht] mit Ihrer Octavia noch nicht fertig, so kan Unser Herr Gott auch noch ein paar tomos [Bände] zu seinem Roman machen . . .

niemand ahmet unsern Herrn besser nach als ein Erfinder von Romanen" (8, pp. 67 ff.). Birken, writing about Anton Ulrich's *Aramena*, which presents twenty-seven couples in almost four thousand pages, is well aware of the social implications of this work written by an aristocrat for the aristocratic reader "oder doch leute . . . die mit solchen personen kundschaft gepflogen haben." Therefore he calls this type of novel "rechte Hof- und Adels-Schulen," "einen Hof- und Welt-Spiegel" (8, p. 14).

As examples of theodicy and mirrors for princes, Anton Ulrich's works apparently fulfill the ideal of the courtly baroque novel. Or do they? In a recent study, Fritz Martini has discovered the realism of the early enlightenment in Anton Ulrich, who depicts his protagonists from a psychological viewpoint at the expense of the rule of providence (52, pp. 62 ff.). According to Elida M. Szarota (73), Lohenstein's *Arminius* (1689 ff.) does confirm this trend in its own way since this paradigm of baroque literature, with all its pejorative connotations to the reader schooled in classicist literature, turns out to be a mirror of the political and military events of the age. This is, in spite of its historical costume, making of it a roman à clef that in a single chapter (I, 7) presents every major phase of the Thirty Years War from the Battle at the White Mountain to the Peace of Westfalia. Fascinating is Szarota's confrontation of Lohenstein and Leibniz as well as her pointing out the debate between the Cartesian Timon and the Catholic dogmatist Druys (II, 2). As a precursor of the enlightenment, Lohenstein's Timon demands freedom of religion in the name of reason. A final contrastive analysis between Anton Ulrich's *Aramena* and *Arminius* manifests the latter's late-baroque structure, which gives up antithetical devices in favor of techtonic synthesizing methods.

The same year, 1689, saw the publication of Heinrich Anselm Zigler's *Asiatische Banise*, the most successful of the courtly novels, since it is relatively short and straightforward in its plot construction as well as "leicht und gewöhnlich" in its style (preface). But the courtly genre had passed its zenith, as becomes apparent through this work's lack of a convincing metaphysical world view and its author's conscious efforts to ironize the technique, the plot, the structures, and the views of the courtly novel, perhaps under the influence of Cervantes (Sancho Pansa = Scandor, see 30, p. 147). His emphasis of traditional motifs for the sake of entertainment gives many an episode a certain melodramatic flavor. With some justification, Zigler's novel can be read as an example of the disintegration of this novel type into an adventure story. A further indication of such a development is that Zigler's plot was quickly claimed by the puppet stage, the itinerant comedians, and the opera (43, 54).

II

While the world of the courtly novel is governed by God's providence, and anything evil or ugly disappears from the predestined solution of the happy end, the opposite is true of the picaresque novel, where everything is ugly, mean, and depressive. This difference seems to exclude any links with the courtly novel, but surprisingly enough, it is nothing but the other side of the coin, the result of escaping into an unreal world with either a utopian character of ideal perfection (courtly novel) or an exaggerated description of the baseness of human nature and the imperfections of the world. Both types are "nichts anderes als unterschiedliche Interpretationen einer idealen teleologischen Weltlehre; einerseits ihre Affirmation, andererseits nicht gerade ihre Negation, aber doch der Hinweis auf die Schwierigkeit ihrer Realisation im Machtbereich der Fortuna" (65, p. 62; 17).

Much has been written about the origin of the picaresque genre and various theories have been advanced concerning its so-called normative features (18, 22, 61). Essential for our present context is the fact that the picaro was born in Spain under specifically Spanish circumstances, as a reaction to the stylized novel of chivalry (*Amadis*) and as an expression of anger and accusation against the traditional Christian society by suppressed Jewish *conversos* who were not granted equality (19, 24, 65). In Spanish literature the picaresque novel is not a shallow story of roguery; on the contrary, even in the case of the very early *Lazarillo de Tormes* (1554), it is a literary document of harsh social criticism, written either from motives of an Erasmian reform spirit (*Lazarillo*) or of direct accusations by a deprived minority (*Guzmán*). Moreover, not only the first impression of a humorous story but also the claim of primitive episodic structuring is misleading, because on closer inspection it has been ascertained that these Spanish originals have been built according to consciously used techtonic principles, either the device of gradation toward a climax (*Lazarillo*, see 74) or of syllogistic compactness (*Guzmán*, see 66).

What happened when these models were transplanted to Germany in the early 1600s? In spite of their utter absence from the official poetics and polemics of the learned poets of the day, they were immediately successful, because these adaptations seemed to continue the tradition of the popular chapbooks of the sixteenth century and at the same time acted as a counterpoise to the heroic but much-maligned *Amadis* series. However, they are considerably different from their originals, a difference that is already being expressed through the labels *novela picaresca* and *Schelmenroman* (novel of roguery or pranks). In intent, structure, and social perspective, these German transformations, from Albertinus's *Gusman* (1615) to Küefuß's *Der Ander Theil Lazarilli von Tormes* (1653), amount to far-reaching "falsifications" of the originals.

As outcasts, the Spanish Lazarillo and Guzmán fight for their existence and acceptance in a so-called Christian society ruled by prejudice and aristocratic notions of pure blood. This is a struggle on an immanent social level with strong criticism of the established church and upper class. *Lazarillo*, however, was transposed into a story exemplifying the rule of *fortuna*, the emphasis shifting from society to the protagonist's salvation. After a loosely knit sequence of episodes, which disregards the compositional clasps of the Spanish version, an *Adieu Welt* was added on to the German continuation (1653) for the first time (66, p. 51). By and large, the German *Lazarillo* could now be read as a comic story of a hero who defeats *fortuna*, a reading reinforced by the chapbook tradition and the French *roman comique*, which often served as an intermediary between the Spanish and German novels (50).

A second example is *Guzmán de Alfarache* (1599), the archtypal *novela picaresca* by Mateo Alemán. According to Rötzer's recent interpretation, it is built like a classical drama (66, pp. 96 ff.) and in the manner of a syllogistic argument (pp. 86 ff.) that leads from the definition of sin via many daily sins (*engaño*) to repentance (*desengaño*). Albertinus, the German adapter, transformed this complex dialectical process into a dualistic concept of sin (part I) and mercy (II) and conceived the hero as an example of salvation, thus turning the original realistic social novel into a dogmatic manual, a complement to the Jesuit plays (66, p. 100). Frewdenhold's *Gusman*-continuation of 1626 made things even worse, at least from a structural point of view, because as a travel report with a pronounced undulatory movement it could be continued ad infinitum.

In sum, the German *Lazarillo* and *Gusman* represent the first examples of the *Schelmenroman*, a form of the adventure novel with funny highlights, recounting the vita of a quick-witted and usually amusing rogue. Whereas the *novela picaresca* concentrates on the satirical criticism of society, these adaptations escape into the religious dualism of this world and the next. While the Spanish novel unmistakably ends on an unhappy or ambiguous note, the German and for that matter other European adaptations (Lesage's *Gil Blas*, 1715 ff., and Defoe's *Moll Flanders*, 1722) usually have a happy ending, providing a theoretical justification for "upward social mobility," as Bjornson put it (22, p. 15). The European rogue rises socially from a vulgar picaro and foundling without true access to higher society (Lazarillo) via aristocratic pretenses (in Quevedo's *Buscón*, 1626) and dreams of gentility fulfilled (Moll Flanders) to a hero with a noble soul who becomes a country gentleman (Gil Blas) or recovers his status as a genuine nobleman (Smollett's Roderick Random, 1748) (22). Whereas a presupposed identity between *la novela pícaresca* and the novel of roguery (*Schelmenroman*) has often been used as a starting point for serious discussion of the picaresque genre, on closer inspection it turns out that a loose structure allowing for countless episodic additions is characteristic of the adaptations only. And yet both branches of the picaresque novel, *la novela pícaresca* and the *Schelmenroman*, have at least this in common: despite official contempt they contributed as much to the acceptance of novels as serious literary forms as did their courtly counterpart; they made vulgar heroes popular, and they led to the breaking down of artificial barriers between the grand and the plain style (22).

Finally, the question arises as to how Grimmelshausen's *Simplicissimus*, the most outstanding and readable novel of the seventeenth century in Germany, fits into this complex background. Often this work has been interpreted as the first German novel of education (*Bildungsroman*, see 29, 31). Simplicissimus appears to broaden his range of experience step by step and to discover himself (*nosce te ipsum*, Book V, chapter 23). But his development cannot be described in terms of a psychological maturing, and the category of self-propelled perfectibility, so essential to the *Bildungsroman* since Goethe's *Wilhelm Meister*, is completely lacking. Rather, Simplicissimus is treated as a guinea pig of *fortuna*, his function being to unmask the world in its inconstancy (see the frontispiece); thus he emerges as an exemplary figure not far removed from a rogue such as Till Eulenspiegel, who also changes his roles constantly. In *Simplicissimus*, the tradition of the chapbooks meets with the picaresque influence, though Grimmelshausen did not model his hero on the Spanish picaro but on what was available to him in German adaptations, above all Albertinus's *Gusman*. According to Rötzer, who has presented the most convincing comparative analysis of the two works, *Gusman* determines *Simplicissimus* in several ways: in the Catholic viewpoint of the Tridentinum (Church Council of Trent, 1545-63), in the plan of salvation—which Grimmelshausen changed from Albertinus's dualistic sequence of sin, instruction, salvation into a dialectic of instruction, sin, salvation—and in the intended interpretation according to the medieval fourfold level of meaning as well as Simplicissimus's function as an exemplary, predetermined figure leading the way out of this world. This is contrary to the picaro's struggle for survival in a hostile society (66), but in keeping with mystical-ascetic writings of the Middle Ages and the baroque. It should be added that the picaresque structure in *Simplicissimus* does not exclude the discovery and methodical application of other structural principles of a unifying character, e.g., an astrological superstructure as analyzed in detail by Günther Weydt (79) and since then an occasion for bitter contention between Weydt and Blake L. Spahr (72, 80) Discovering several structural layers in this novel reinforces the impression that we are dealing with a masterpiece of "classical" dimensions.

III

From a European perspective the pastoral novel belongs to the courtly romance (27,I, 208), since the structure and the motifs of the courtly-chivalric novel (*Amadis*) were integrated into the plots of, among others, Jorge de Montemayor's *Los siete libros de la Diana* (1559) and Sir Philip Sidney's *The Countess of Pembroke's Arcadia* (1590; 1593). Both works could be read as courtly romans à clef, but whereas Montemayor transformed the courtly sphere into a bucolic setting, Sidney disguised noble knights as shepherds. These two novels were followed by Honoré d'Urfé's *Astrée* (1607-27), its protagonist Celadon acting as the paragon of *honneste amitie* (virtuously gallant love), the ideal of a *précieux* circle of friends, lovers, and intellectuals who followed the prescriptions of the French *salons* (cf. Hôtel de Rambouillet). In rapid succession these three works were translated in the early 1600s.

Since Germany did not produce any famous successors in this genre of the epic pastoral, one might wonder whether it left any traces at all, apart from the foundation of the "Académie des vrais amants" in 1618 by some German aristocrats. Certainly, these adaptations paved the way toward the imitation of the courtly novel, with which they had merged to a considerable degree. For example, following the *Amadis*, Montemayor's *Diana* provided a first model for a relatively complicated plot based on the principle of entanglement and disentanglement, which was soon to become the prominent feature of the high-baroque novel. In my dissertation on the "Spanish Diana in Germany" (37), I established that at least in the instance of Kuffstein's translation a considerable effort was made to make the *Diana* more palatable to courtly circles by inserting moral observations on the conduct of the shepherds and by elaborating on Spanish court customs. This Kuffstein did in an apparent reaction to the often crude and down-to-earth attitudes in bourgeois and even rustic literature of the previous century (36). It has also been proved that Kuffstein—in conjunction with Albertinus, Ulenhart (the Cervantes adapter), and Opitz—fashioned a prose style typical of the early baroque period, a style still acceptable to the Nürnberg patrician Harsdörffer in 1646 and beyond him to Austrian readers in 1690, when the last edition of Kuffstein's *Diana* appeared in Linz. Literary echoes of his translation are to be found in the Nürnberg group of the Pegnesische Blumenorden (37, pp. 168 ff.). The topographical realism of Montemayor and his successor Gaspar Gil Polo (*Diana enamorada*, 1564) became a standard feature of pastoral poetry everywhere in Europe.

Nevertheless, it is remarkable that the European pastoral had far less effect on the general framework of German pastorals than on specific motifs and structural devices, though it is incorrect to claim (57, pp. 152 ff.) that German pastorals are lacking in any epic plot development—considering works from *Amoena und Amandus* (1632) via Tobias Nißlen's (De la Grise's) *Der unglückseelige Misoneur* (1681) to Salomon Gessner's *Daphnis* (1754; see 7; 39). Two quite different types of pastoral literature were developed in Germany: the prose eclogue in the tradition of antiquity and the Italian Renaissance (*Prosaekloge* according to Klaus Garber [28], formerly labeled *Gesellschaftsschäferei* by Heinrich Meyer [58] on the one hand, which has little if anything in common with the novel genre (e.g., Opitz, *Schäfferey von der Nimfen Hercinie*, 1630), and on the other hand the *Individualschäferei* (Heinrich Meyer). The latter breaks with the European pastoral tradition in that it tells only one couple's love story with an unhappy ending, concealing real-life experiences behind bucolic costumes. A comparative analysis between the courtly romance and this individualized new type has been made by Arnold Hirsch in 1934 (35) and Volker Meid in 1974 (54), with conflicting results on whether these short novels are products of the middle class or the landed or even courtly aristocracy (34). For example, in regard to *Amoena und Amandus, Leoriander und Perelina* (1642), or Jakob Schwieger's *Die verführete Schäferin Cynthie* (1660), one has to treat their social context with caution, because it appears that their authors were following d'Urfé's model more closely than previously thought, at least in respect to their protagonists (32; 65, pp. 58 ff.).

IV

Almost up to the very present there has existed in the view of modern baroque scholarship only one representative novel type, namely, the courtly type, which includes the pastoral. Diametrically opposed to this genre is the picaresque novel, which, with its naturalistic description of lowly life, has been recognized and discussed as the counterpart to the grand novel. All those works that did not fit in either category have usually been put into a group of their own, the so-called "bürgerlich-höfische Mischformen" (54, 65), a perfectly suitable label in the light of the two other socially determined major branches, but misleading in our view since this classification does not take account of the European tradition or of the specific features of this mixed group. Therefore we would prefer to call them sentimental in character.

Since the German baroque novel is of European extraction, any attempt at a valid classification can neither bypass the European genesis of the models nor fail to demonstrate the intermediary steps through which they were received in Germany. Scholarship from the early 1900s has taken note of the existence of *la novela sentimental* in Spain, France, and Italy (64, 77). Hans Gerd Rötzer, well versed in Spanish literature, as recently as 1972 drew attention to the fact that structural elements of the chivalric (*Amadis*) as well as the sentimental novel fused with the European pastoral, but he did not pursue this matter any further (65, p. 47), so we are still faced with the claim by Max von Waldberg in 1906 (77) and Fritz Brüggemann in 1935 (2) that the European sentimental novel did not exert any appreciable influence on German literature until around 1750, the dawn of *Gefühlskultur* (Brüggemann). Literary historians have not dealt with this problem, and thus we can present only a few outstanding examples and some preliminary connections in the final pages of this survey.

During the last decade I have come across three sentimental love stories with unhappy endings: Silvio Piccolomini's *De duobus amantibus historia de Eurialo et Lucretia* (1444), Diego de San Pedro's *La Cárcel de amor,* adapted by Hans Ludwig von Kuffstein, and *Die Unglückselige Liebes- und Lebens-Geschichte des Don Francesco und Angelica* (1667).

Silvio Piccolomini's (later Pius II) Neo-Latin novella seems to have inaugurated the rise of the sentimental and tragic love story, having assimilated stylistic and structural elements from the Tristan romance (twelfth century France), Dante (*Vita nuova*, 1293), and Boccaccio (*Fiammetta*, 1343). Under Silvio's influence, which blended with the indigenous chivalric strain, *la novela sentimental* came into being in the 1490s in Spain; about a dozen novels were grouped together and labeled thus by Menéndez y Pelayo (56), among which those by Juan de Flores and Diego de San Pedro count as the leading examples.

Having flourished in Spain, the new literary vogue of composing courtly but unhappy love novels spread to Germany either through direct translations from Spanish or through French intermediaries (e.g., Christian Pharemund, *Aurelio und Mirabella*, 1630). Diego de San Pedro's *La Cárcel de amor* in fact replaced Silvio's story as the representative novel of this type. Sometimes referred to as the "Werther of the fifteenth century" (69, pp. 87 ff.) and considered as one of the most popular books of the sixteenth century in Europe, it was translated about twenty times into various languages, but only once into German, in 1624, a rather late date which is symptomatic of the cultural lag of a German courtly revival delayed by the Reformation and its aftermath. With the cultural leadership role of the courts restored in the 1600s, Kuffstein's *Gefängnüß der Lieb*, a courtly-sentimental love story with letters interspersed, turned into one of the favorite books of the seventeenth century because of its representations of courtly decorum and its value as a manual for letter-writing. Eight editions (between 1624 and 1675), along with praise by J. H. Schill (in 1644) and Birken (8, p. 13), and finally a comical adaptation by itinerant actors (46) attest to its success.

The Spanish origin of the sentimental novel proper—reinforced by such works as the *Celestina* (1499), a tragically ending dialogue novel translated by Germans three times between 1520 and 1624 (23), and Montemayor's *Diana*—should not tempt us to underestimate the French contribution in this area. German aristocrats and learned men were usually able to read French much better than Spanish in the seventeenth century, and they may have come across sentimental romances such as Hélisenne de Crenne's *Les Angoysses douloureuses qui procédent d'amours* (1538, based on her own life, on Boccaccio's *Fiammetta*, and perhaps on Silvio), or Théodose Valentinian's *Histoire de l'amant resuscité de la mort d'amour* (1555, modeled on Diego de San Pedro). Around 1600 there appeared, as precursors to d'Urfé's *Astrée*, a series of *Tragiques amours* that provided a paradigm for succeeding sentimental long novels (Scudéry) as well as for the tragic short ones of the later century (e.g., Mme de La Fayette, *La Princesse de Clèves*, 1678; Mme d' Aulnoy, *Histoire d'Hypolite*, 1690).

The reading of the sentimental novels, whether they were originally Italian, Spanish, or French before being adapted to the German tongue, is attested among others by Jörg Wickram, whose character Cario Ruffion refers to *La Celestina* (15, pp. 13 ff.; incidentally, Wickram was the first German novelist to produce a sentimental love story based on the mésalliance of bourgeois men and noble ladies in *Gabriotto und Reinhard*, 1551). To my great surprise, moreover, I detected a reference to Silvio in *Amoena und Amandus*, supposedly an individualized German pastoral that breaks away from the European tradition and accordingly could not properly be classified. Similarly unclassifiable was Zesen's *Adriatische Rosemund*, this hybrid between the courtly and pastoral tale, but closely linked to *Amoena* and beyond this to Silvio. If we add to those *Leoriander und Perelina*, Balthasar Kindermann's *Kurandors Unglückselige Nisette* (1660), and Johann J. Bekkh's *Elbianische Florabella* (1667), we have assembled several "pastoral" novels that have assimilated essential features of the sentimental genre. Other works of pastoral and even nonpastoral extraction could be joined to this group, such as Tobias Nißlen's *Unglückseeliger Misoneur* and above all *Don Francesco und Angelica*.

Taking the above-mentioned *Individualschäfereien* out of the category of makeshift *Mischformen* necessitates a clarification on our part of what traits actually constitute the sentimental novel (4, preface):

1. In the first place, "sentimental" in this context is not being used in a contemptuous modern sense, nor is it a question yet of the subjective or psychological-analytic element of the post-Goethean period with an emphasis on narcissistic amour-propre. It refers solely to the voguish taste of the Renaissance and the baroque for melancholy moods and loves, for tenderly passionate emotions of a conventional kind and with a topoi-like character. Sentimentality in that age was equivalent to a certain *morbidezza*, a fashionable emotional weakness or softness in the expression of sentiments.

2. An essential component of the sentimental novel is the mésalliance of two lovers, one belonging to the higher aristocracy, the other to the lower nobility or even the middle class.

3. Either the lady does not yield to her suitor or she seeks a man's favors without success. In his turn, to remain free he might rely on his con-

cept of honor or on other reasons such as his education, rank, denomination, and social career. "Honor" gets the better of love.

4. The passionate lover, usually the female, falls victim to the conventional mores represented either by her lover or her parents (44). Sometimes a loving couple sacrifice themselves. In contrast to the idealized courtly novel this novel turns into an anti-fairy tale (Tristan and Iseult).

5. From the very beginning, love, a cosmic power that raises its followers beyond the legitimate ties of rank and moral code, propels the story toward an unhappy ending, anticipated through forebodings of separation, and a final farewell. "Wer nicht weinen kan, der kan auch nicht lieben" (*Don Francesco*, p. 377) could serve as the motto of this genre, since it signals the shifting emphasis from an external plot to the world of emotions.

6. The plot is developed in a linear, not in a syllogistic or "byzantine" courtly fashion. This is possible because the love story of only one couple is being told, or at most a triangular configuration is presented, on account of an intruding rival. Parts of the action are often linked through letters, which may either cheer up the soul or destroy it, depending on their content.

7. Often the lover meets both his greatest love and his greatest enemy in the same family: father, brother, or husband. "Was für ein Verhengnüs aus einem Geblüt / von einerley Geburt und Eltern / seinen ärgsten Feind und allergröste Freundin in der gantzen Erden zu finden" (*Don Francesco*, p. 223; this is the Cid-motif).

8. These novels often seem to be based on autobiographical experiences and can be read as romans à clef.

9. In contrast to the prevailing view that there was a lack of short novels in seventeenth-century Germany (75), these works are short, confirming our contention that they form a group of their own, the sentimental genre.

V

Did these 500-odd novels of various types in the baroque age contribute anything to the rise of the later German novel? We know that Lohenstein's *Arminius* was denigrated by the Gottsched school and that Grimmelshausen was not rediscovered until well into the middle of the nineteenth century. The pastoral novel quickly lost favor with the reading public by the age of Goethe. Earlier scholarship has claimed that the dawning of a new age of *Gefühlskultur* around 1750 took place without any roots in the previous century. Norbert Miller supports this view even today (59), while Herbert Singer (70, p. 2) asserts his belief in "eine konsequente Fortentwicklung des höfischen Romans von Lohenstein und Ziegler bis zu Gellert oder gar Wieland." I am convinced that new literary movements never quite break with a previous period but usually carry over major portions of their predecessors' tools, motifs, and structural devices, though not without retooling them, not without adapting these devices and beliefs to the needs of the new spirit of the time.

The baroque world view based on metaphysical principles of church dogmatism (asceticism) and of providence manifested in the rule of *fortuna* underwent a process of disintegration toward the end of the century. This development can easily be verified by a reading of Johann Beer's and Christian Reuter's novels, the last remarkable examples of the picaresque novel before the twentieth century, though one should not underestimate the continued influence of the picaresque structure on intervening works, e.g., Goethe's *Wilhelm Meister*. Beer and Reuter are well on the way toward composing novels of adventure for their readers' entertainment, novels that express a delight in this world and display a subjective narrative technique hitherto unknown. The political novels by Christian Weise and Johann Riemer actually demonstrate how one can get on in this world.

One example each from the courtly and the sentimental tradition should suffice here to show how baroque concepts survived in a transformed fashion well into the eighteenth century. We have already mentioned that Zigler's *Asiatische Banise*, in its extreme depiction of passionateness and its inclusion of a donquijotesque figure such as Scandor, verges on a parody of the preceding courtly novel. Zigler inaugurated an epigonic school of *Banise* writers whose two dozen authors put their model's motifs and structural devices to good use in works such as Johann Rost's *Unglückselige Atalanta* (1708), Florander's *Unvergleichliche Darine* (1730) and Adamantes's *Die wohlprobirte Treue* (1716). Most of the paraphernalia of the courtly tradition, from Heliodorus and *Amadis* to the high baroque, recur in these works, but they are stereotyped and trivialized through sensationalism, without the least concern for decorum and social or stylistic levels, not to mention metaphysical beliefs. Motifs of the traditional novel (abduction, comedy of errors, emperor as libertine, falsified letters, magic tricks, rival brothers, etc.) are popularized by being transposed into the milieu of robbers or rowdy students (43). This trend was continued until the *Ritter- und Räuberroman* flourished in the late 1700s, at the same time when a revised version of Zigler's *Asiatische Banise* appeared in a fragmentary form (1788) that sentimentalized the original style considerably (55). The importance of these Zigler followers lies in the fact that they kept conventional epic motifs alive, though on a trivial level; the following generations of the Storm and Stress and romantic writers would revive the motifs and rid them of that trivial flavor.

A second example illustrating our contention of continuity refers to the sentimental novel. In two ways these novels seem to be significant for the eighteenth century. First, as novels of mésalliance, which is obviously a topic taken up by the playwrights of the *Empfindsamkeit* and the *Sturm und Drang*. Second, a confrontation between specific examples such as *Don Francesco und Angelica* and Gellert's *Schwedische Gräfin* (1747-48) may help to throw further light on this problem, since in both instances motifs of the traditional adventure novel cause sentimental reactions in the respective protagonists, which in turn shifts the emphasis of the story to the inward plot carried by interspersed letters. In both cases happiness in love and marriage is thwarted by political intrigues contrived in the courtly sphere. Thus the evil court is juxtaposed with a utopian world in which ideals of moral behavior seem to be realized. But in both novels the Stoic ideal of controlling one's emotions breaks down in the face of tragedy, which leads to frequent expression of tears and tender feelings.

SELECTED BIBLIOGRAPHY

Primary Sources

1. Anton Ulrich, Herzog von Braunschweig. *Die Durchleuchtige Syrerin Aramena*. Parts I-IV. Blake L. Spahr, ed. Nachdrucke deutscher Literatur des 17. Jahrhunderts, 4. Bern: Lang, 1975.

2. Brüggemann, Fritz, ed. *Der Anbruch der Gefühlskultur in den fünfziger Jahren*. Deutsche Literatur in Entwicklungsreihen XIV, 7. 1935. Rpt. Darmstadt: Wissenschaftliche Buchgesellschaft, 1966.

3. Bucholtz, Andreas H. *Des Christlichen Teutschen Gross-Fürsten Herkules und der Böhmischen Königlichen Fräulein Valiska Wunder-Geschichte*. Parts I-II. Ulrich Maché, ed. Nachdrucke deutscher Literatur des 17. Jahrhunderts, 6. Bern: Lang, 1973.

4. *Don Francesco und Angelica* (1667). Gerhart Hoffmeister, ed. Tübingen: Niemeyer, 1982-83 (forthcoming).

5. Harsdörffer, Georg Ph. *Diana von H. J. De Monte-Major* (1646). Rpt. Darmstadt: Wissenschaftliche Buchgesellschaft, 1969.

6. Heidegger, Gotthard. *Mythoscopia romantica oder Discours von den so benanten Romans* (1698). Walter E. Schäfer, ed. Bad Homburg: Gehlen, 1968.

7. Kaczerowsky, Klaus, ed. *Schäferromane des Barock.* Reinbek: Rowohlt, 1970 (= RK 530-31).

8. Kimpel, Dieter, and Conrad Wiedemann, eds. *Theorie und Technik des Romans im 17. und 18. Jahrhundert.* I: *Barock und Aufklärung.* Deutsche Texte. Tübingen; Niemeyer, 1970.

9. Kuffstein, Hans Ludwig von. *Carcell de Amor oder Gefängnüß der Lieb* (1624). Gerhart Hoffmeister, ed. Nachdrucke deutscher Literatur des 17. Jahrhunderts, 7. Bern: Lang, 1976.

10. Lohenstein, Daniel Casper von. *Grossmüthiger Feldherr Arminius.* Parts I-II. Elida M. Szarota, ed. Nachdrucke deutscher Literatur des 17. Jahrhunderts, 5. Bern: Lang, 1973.

11. Opitz, Martin. *Die Übersetzung von John Barclays Argenis.* George Schulz-Behrend, ed. Stuttgart: Bibliothek des literarischen Vereins, 1970.

12. ———. *Arcadia der Gräffin von Pembrock* (1643). Stuttgart, 1970. Rpt. Hildesheim: Olms, 1971.

13. Schöne, Albrecht, ed. *Das Zeitalter des Barock.* Die deutsche Literatur, Texte und Zeugnisse, 3. München: Beck, 1963. 2nd ed. 1968.

14. Schottelius, Justus G. *Ausführliche Arbeit von der Teutschen Haubt-Sprache* (1663). Deutsche Neudrucke, Reihe: Barock. Tübingen: Niemeyer, 1967.

15. Wickram, Jörg. *Der verlorne Sohn.* Hans Gerd Roloff, ed. *Sämtliche Werke*, IX. Berlin: de Gruyter, 1971.

16. Ulenhart, Niclas. *Historia von Isaac Winckelfelder und Jobst von der Schneid* (1617). Gerhart Hoffmeister, ed. München: Fink, 1982-83.

Secondary Literature

17. Alewyn, Richard. "Der Roman des Barock." In *Formkräfte der deutschen Dichtung vom Barock bis zur Gegenwart.* Hans Steffen, ed. Göttingen: Vandenhoeck, 1963. 2nd ed. 1967, pp. 21-34.

18. Alter, Robert. *Rogue's Progress: Studies in the Picaresque Novel.* Cambridge, Mass.: Harvard University Press, 1964.

19. Bataillon, Marcel. *Le roman picaresque.* Paris: La Renaissance du livre, 1931.

20. Beck, Werner. "Die Anfänge des deutschen Schelmenromans: Studien zur frühbarocken Erzählung." Diss. Zürich 1957.

21. Bircher, Martin. *Johann Wilhelm von Stubenberg (1619-63) und sein Freundeskreis.* Berlin: de Gruyter, 1968.

22. Bjornson, Richard. *The Picaresque Hero in European Fiction.* Madison: University of Wisconsin Press, 1977.

23. Briesemeister, Dieter. "Zu Christoph Wirsungs deutscher Celestina-übersetzung (1520 und 1534)." In *Sprache, Literatur, Kultur, Romanistische Beiträge*. D. Briesemeister, ed. Bern: Lang, 1974, pp. 50-57.

24. Castro, Américo. "Perspectiva de la novela picaresca." *Revista de la Biblioteca, Archivo y Museo*, 12 (1935), 123-143. Trans. in *Pikarische Welt*. Heidenreich, ed. (see below).

25. Carnap, Ernst C. "Das Schäferwesen in der deutschen Literatur des 17. Jahrhunderts und die Hirtendichtung Europas." Diss. Frankfurt a. M. 1939.

26. Colon, Germá. *Die ersten romanischen und germanischen Übersetzungen des Don Quijote*. Bern and München: Francke, 1974.

27. Faber du Faur, Curt von. *German Baroque Literature*. A Catalogue in the Yale University Library. 2 vols. New Haven, Conn., and London: Yale University Press, 1958-69.

28. Garber, Klaus. *Der locus amoenus und der locus terribilis: Bild und Funktion der Natur in der deutschen Schäfer- und Landlebendichtung des 17. Jahrhunderts*. Köln and Graz: Böhlau, 1974.

29. Gerhard, Melitta. *Der deutsche Entwicklungsroman bis zu Goethes "Wilhelm Meister."* Halle: Niemeyer, 1926. 2nd ed. Bern: Francke, 1968.

30. Geulen, Hans. *Erzählkunst der frühen Neuzeit: Zur Geschichte epischer Darbietungsweisen und Formen im Roman der Renaissance und des Barock*. Tübingen: Rotsch, 1975.

31. Gundolf, Friedrich. "Grimmelshausen und der 'Simplicissimus.' " *Deutsche Vierteljahrsschrift für Geistesgeschichte und Literaturwissenschaft*, 1 (1923), 339-58.

32. Heetfeld, Gisela. "Vergleichende Studien zum deutschen und französischen Schäferroman." Diss. München 1974.

33. Heidenreich, Helmut, ed. *Pikarische Welt: Schriften zum europäischen Schelmenroman*. Darmstadt: Wissenschaftliche Buchgesellschaft, 1969.

34. Heiduk, Franz. "Die Liebesbeschreibung von Amoena und Amandus." *Jahrbuch der deutschen Schillergesellschaft*, 17 (1973), 136-53.

35. Hirsch, Arnold. *Bürgertum und Barock im deutschen Roman*. 1934. Rpt. Köln and Graz: Böhlau, 1957.

36. Hoffmeister, Gerhart. "Courtly Decorum: Kuffstein and the Spanish Diana." *Comparative Literature Studies*, 8 (1971), 214-23.

37. —— *Die spanische Diana in Deutschland: Vergleichende Untersuchungen zu Stilwandel und Weltbild des Schäferromans im 17. Jahrhundert*. Berlin: Erich Schmidt, 1972.

38. ——. "Antipetrarkismus im deutschen Schäferroman des 17. Jahrhunderts." *Daphnis*, 1 (1972), 128-41.

39. ——. "Gessners *Daphnis*—Das Ende des europäischen Schäferromans." *Studia neophilologica*, 44 (1972), 128-41.

40. ——. ed. *Europäische Tradition und deutscher Literaturbarock: Interna-*

tionale Beiträge zum Problem von Überlieferung und Umgestaltung. Bern: Francke, 1973.

41. ———. "Grimmelshausens 'Simplicissimus' und der spanisch-deutsche Schelmenroman." *Daphnis,* 5 (1976), 275–94.

42. ———. *Spanien und Deutschland: Geschichte und Dokumentation der literarischen Beziehungen.* Berlin: Erich Schmidt, 1976; transl. Madrid, 1980.

43. ———. "Transformationen von Ziglers 'Asiatischer Banise': Zur Trivialisierung des höfisch-historischen Romans." *German Quarterly,* 49 (1976), 181–90.

44. ———. "Engel, Teufel oder Opfer: Zur Auffassung der Frau in der sentimentalen Erzählung zwischen Renaissance und Aufklärung." *Monatshefte,* 69 (1977), 150–58.

45. ———. " 'Aristoteles und Olympias'—Christian Thomasius' dynamischer Entwurf eines heroi-komischen Kurzromans (1688)." *Argenis* 2 (1978), 249–61.

46. ———. "Kuffstein und die Komödianten." *Daphnis* 1982 (in press)

46a. ———. "Andreas Hartmans 'Comoedia des Amadis' (1587)." *Daphnis,* 9 (1980), 463–75.

47. Ingen, Ferdinand van. "Philip von Zesens 'Adriatische Rosemund': Kunst und Leben." In *Ph. von Zesen 1619–1969.* F. van Ingen, ed. Wiesbaden: Franz Steiner, 1972, pp. 47–122.

48. ———. "Johann J. Bekkhs 'Elbianische Florabella.' " In *Europäische Tradition und deutscher Literaturbarock.* G. Hoffmeister, ed. (see above), pp. 285–304.

49. Jaumann, Herbert. "Bürgerlicher Alltag im barocken Schäfferroman? Gattungsgeschichtliche Thesen zu 'Damon und Lisille.' " In *Schäferdichtung.* Wilhelm Voßkamp, ed. Dokumente des internationalen Arbeitskreises für deutsche Barockliteratur, 4. Hamburg: Hauswedell, 1977, pp. 39–58.

50. Koschlig, Manfred. "Das Lob des 'Francion' bei Grimmelshausen." *Jahrbuch der deutschen Schillergesellschaft,* 1 (1957), 30–73.

51. Maché, Ulrich. "Die Überwindung des Amadisromans durch A. H. Bucholtz." *Zeitschrift für deutsche Philologie,* 85 (1966), 542–59.

52. Martini, Fritz. "Der Tod Neros. Suetonius, Anton Ulrich von Braunschweig, Sigmund von Birken oder: Historischer Bericht, erzählerische Fiktion und Stil der frühen Aufklärung." In *Festschrift Käthe Hamburger.* F. Martini, ed. Stuttgart: Klett, 1971, pp. 22–86.

53. Martino, Alberto. "Barockpoesie, Publikum und Verbürgerlichung der literarischen Intelligenz." *Internationales Archiv für Sozialgeschichte der deutschen Literatur,* 1 (1976), 107–45.

54. Meid, Volker. *Der deutsche Barockroman.* Sammlung Metzler, 128. Stuttgart: Metzler, 1974.

55. ———. "Ziglers 'Asiatische Banise' 1689 und 1788: Zur Wirkungsgeschichte

des Barockromans." *Argenis*, 2 (1978), 327-40.

56. Menéndez y Pelayo, Marcelino. "Tratado histórico sobre la primitiva novela española." In *Orígines de la novela*, II, 1. Madrid: Bailly & Balliere, 1925.

57. Meyer, Heinrich. "Schäferroman." In *Reallexikon der deutschen Literaturgeschichte*. Merker und Stammler, eds. Berlin: de Gruyter, III, 1925-26, 150 ff.

58. ———. "Der deutsche Schäferroman des 17. Jahrhunderts." Diss. Freiburg 1928.

59. Miller, Norbert. *Der empfindsame Erzähler: Untersuchungen an Romananfängen des 18. Jahrhunderts.* München: Hanser, 1968.

60. Müller, Günther. "Barockroman und Barockromane." *Literaturwissenschaftliches Jahrbuch der Görres-Gesellschaft*, 4 (1929), 1-29.

61. Parker, Alexander, *Literature and the Delinquent: The Picaresque Novel in Spain and in Europe 1599-1753.* Edinburgh: University Press, 1967.

62. Rausch, Ursula. "Philipp von Zesens 'Adriatische Rosemund' und Chr. F. Gellerts 'Leben der schwedischen Gräfin von G. Eine Untersuchung zur Individualitätsentwicklung im deutschen Roman." Diss. Freiburg 1961.

63. Reichardt, Dieter. *Von Quevedos 'Buscón' zum deutschen 'Avanturier.'* Bonn: Bouvier, 1970.

64. Reynier, Gustave: *Le Roman sentimental avant l'Astrée.* Paris: Librairie Armand Colin, 1908.

65. Rötzer, Hans Gerd. *Der Roman des Barock, 1600-1700: Kommentar zu einer Epoche.* München: Winkler, 1972.

66. ———. *Picaro—Landtstörtzer—Simplicissimus: Studien zum niederen Roman in Spanien und Deutschland.* Darmstadt: Wissenschaftliche Buchgesellschaft, 1972.

67. Schäfer, Walter E. "Hinweg nun Amadis und deinesgleichen Grillen! Die Polemik gegen den Roman im 17. Jahrhundert." *Germanisch-romanische Monatsschrift*, N. F. 15 (1965), 366-84.

68. Schweitzer, Christoph E. "Spanien in der deutschen Literatur des 17. Jahrhunderts." Diss. Yale 1954.

69. Serrano-Poncela, S. "Dos 'Werther' del Renascimiento español." *Asomante*, 5 (1949), 87-103.

70. Singer, Herbert. *Der deutsche Roman zwischen Barock und Rokoko.* Köln: Böhlau and Graz: 1963.

71. Spahr, Blake L. *Anton Ulrich and "Aramena": The Genesis and Development of a Baroque Novel.* Berkeley: University of California Press, 1966.

72. ———. "Grimmelshausens 'Simplicissimus': Astrological Structure.' " *Argenis*, 1 (1977), 7-29.

73. Szarota, Elida M. *Lohensteins "Arminius" als Zeitroman: Sichtweisen des Spätbarock.* Bern: Francke, 1970.

74. Tarr, Frederick C. "Literary and Artistic Unity in the 'Lazarillo de

Tormes.' " *PMLA*, 42 (1927), 404-21. Rpt. in Heidenreich (see above).

75. Voßkamp, Wilhelm. *Romantheorie in Deutschland: Von Martin Opitz bis F. von Blankenburg*. Stuttgart: Metzler, 1973.

76. Wagener, Hans. *The German Baroque Novel*. New York: Twayne, 1973.

77. Waldberg, Max von. *Der empfindsame Roman in Frankreich*. Vol. I, 1. Straßburg and Berlin: Trübner, 1906.

78. Weddige, Hilkert. *Die "Historien vom Amadis Auss Franckreich": Dokumentarische Grundlegung zur Entstehung und Rezeption*. Wiesbaden: Franz Steiner, 1975.

79. Weydt, Günther. *Nachahmung und Schöpfung im Barock: Studien um Grimmelshausen*. Bern: Francke, 1968.

80. ———. "Und sie bewegen sich [leider?] doch! Zu B. L. Spahrs—und G. Lemkes—Zweifeln an der Planetenstruktur des 'Simplicissimus.' " *Argenis*, 2 (1978), 3-18.

18

The Changes of the Moon:
Lyric Poetry—Tradition
and Transformation

George C. Schoolfield

As a lover herself, albeit largely unrequited, the moon is a friend to lovers: in classical mythology, Selene/Luna is distinguished by her devotion to the shepherd Endymion, forever asleep on Mount Latmus. An epigram by Philodemos (ca. 110–40/35 B.C.) in the *Greek Anthology* (V, 123) makes her tutelary function quite clear:

> Two-horned child of night, friend of night-vigils, shine, Selene,
>> Shine, casting your light through well-pierced windows.
> Gaze on golden Callistion: the watching of works of lovers
>> Is not begrudged to you, an immortal.
> You will bless both her and me, know it, Selene;
>> For did not Endymion set your soul afire?

Also, more simply, the moon is the illuminator of the night, the time of love. In one of Propertius' (ca. 50 B.C.–?) best known poems (I, 3:31–33), she rouses the poet's beloved, Cynthia:

> And so at last the moon, come gliding past various windows,
>> The sedulous moon with its lingering light,
> Made her open her tight-shut eyes with its gentle beams.

(Cynthia herself bears one of the moon's many names, from Mount Cynthus on Delos, the birthplace of Apollo and Artemis/Diana.) In Propertius, too, the moon is asked to tarry over the lovers' initial embrace, thus creating a preternaturally long night (III, 20:14); and, when the moon refuses to "descend so often from the skies," its recalcitrance bodes ill for love (II, 28:37).

Yearning or disappointed, a lover customarily calls on the moon for help; in Theocritus' (ca. 300–ca. 260 B.C.) second idyll, the "Pharmaceutria," the lovelorn girl addresses the moon as she brews her philtres:

> So, shine sweetly,
> O Selene; for I shall sing to you, quiet goddess,
> And to Hecate infernal . . .

Dido, on the other hand, reverses the order of divinities in her invocation (*Aeneid*, IV, 510–11), calling first on "triform Hecate" and then the "triple-faced maidenhood of Diana." A jealous Tibullus (ca. 55–19 B.C.) accuses Pholoe of having been bewitched by some old woman's moon-charm ("incantation [*cantus*] tries to draw the moon down from her chariot," I, 8:21), and, in the *Heroides* (VI: 85), Ovid's (43 B.C.–ca. A.D. 13) Hypsipyle charges her successful rival Medea with having used a moon-charm to win Jason's love, "to draw the reluctant moon from its course." Finally, in Ausonius's (ca. A.D. 310–90) *Cupid Crucified*, "Luna bicornis," "the two-horned moon," is among the unhappy ladies who want revenge of Cupid's son; the poet of late antiquity implies that Luna's sadness comes from her inability to wake the object of her affection—she wanders through the "fields of air" as once she did over the rocks of Mount Latmus, "accustomed to strive after sleeping Endymion." Small wonder that Ariosto's (1474–1533) Astolfo, visiting the moon in the *Orlando Furioso*, finds it a place of "le lacrime e i sospiri degli amanti" (the tears and the sighs of love; canto XXXIV, stanza 74), or that Sir Philip Sidney (1554–86), in *Astrophel and Stella* (stanza 31), talks of the sad steps and wan face of the moon, caused by "That busy archer." Surely, he tells the moon, "thou feel'st a lover's case."

Customarily, the poet showers praise on the moon; he hopes for aid, or at least consolation, in return. In "À la lune," Jean Passerat (1534–1602) flatters the goddess by listing her attributes:

> O bel oeil de la nuit, ô la fille argentée
> Et la soeur du soleil et la mère des mois,
> O princesse des monts, des fleuves et des bois,
> Dont la triple puissance en tous lieux est vantée.[1]

(Oh fair eye of the night, oh the silvered daughter
And the sister of the sun, and the mother of months,
Oh princess of mountains, of rivers and woods,
Whose triple power is praised everywhere.)

The "triple puissance" is worth noting; Passerat means the three major aspects of the lunar deity — as Selene/Luna, the light-giver proper, as Artemis/Diana, the huntress on earth, and as Hecate, infernal and particularly helpful to those seeking redress of amatory wrongs. Having made his bow to myth, Passerat enjoins the moon to take pity on his "âme . . . tourmentée" and to send a dream to his proud mistress which will show her his "peine." The moon is a handy go-between.

Of a somewhat more practical turn of mind, the Flemish poet Justus de Harduwijn (1582–1636) celebrates the moon's illuminative ability:

O nacht-goddine schoon / o nacht-blinckende Maene /
Die met een silver-schijn aerd ende zee bebleckt /
Als door s'nachts duysterheydt uwen licht-waeghen treckt /
En u moor-perden fris beposten s'hemels baene.[2]

(Oh fair goddess of the night, oh night-shining moon
Who lights sea and earth with a silver shine
When through the gloom of night your light-chariot passes
And your black horses, fresh, gallop the stages of heaven's road.)

This is a prelude to asking the moon to put on her "vol-aensicht" (full face) and to lead him to his beloved, for whom he suffers love's "onrust en ellende" (unrest and misery), and in quest of whom he has wandered up and down the street. (Both Passerat and Harduwijn — and how many other poets — have a bad case of the petrarchistic ailment, the *nósos*, of love.)[3] After all, the moon will understand his plight, having had to behave in the same restless way herself. Harduwijn here refers to the preceding sonnet in his collection, where he has told the story of the moon's devotion to Endymion.

To be sure, the moon can be enjoined to conceal its light, as in Ronsard's (1524–85) *Amours de Marie* (sonnet 25):

Cache pour ceste nuit ta corne, bonne Lune!
Ainsi Endymion soit tousjours ton amy,
Ainsi soit-il tousjours en ton sein endormy,
Ainsi nul enchanteur jamais ne t'importune.[4]

(Hide for this night your horn, good moon!
Thus Endymion may always be your friend,

Thus he may always be asleep at your breast,
Thus no sorcerer may ever disturb you.)

Creeping into a "hostile camp" for love, he needs darkness.

The same request is frequently a starting point for a second kind of moon poetry; scolding or even insolent, such poetry is written, to use the title of Mary Coleridge's nineteenth-century poem, "In Dispraise of the Moon."[5] The moon is chided for being too good at its job — bright light hinders "les larcins d'amour" (the thefts of love). Philippe Desportes (1546–1606) presents this argument in "Contre une nuit trop claire"; if the moon had in fact loved Endymion, she would have known the true requirements of lovers.[6]

Desportes is oblique in his criticism, but Giambattista Marino (1569–1625) resorts to direct insult, no doubt for comic effect — the moon prevents him from tending to his "affari amorosi." The sonnet begins with a catalogue of the moon's qualities, transposed into the negative:

Né tu pietosa dea, né tu lucente,
né pura, né gentil, né bella sei,
Luna perversa, a' caldi preghi miei
rigida e sorda e, qual mai sempre, algente.[7]

(You are neither a pitying goddess, nor a shining one
Nor pure nor gentle nor fair,
Perverse Moon, by my hot prayers
Unmoved and deaf, and, as ever, freezing.)

Indeed, the moon should not be in the sky, but in hell, "con la perduta gente (with the cursed folk); as his mythological burden, Marino employs not the Endymion story but the scabrous tale of how the moon lost her virginity to Pan, and his parting shot is a mocking reference to the *cantus* or invocation, put into a *protasis/apodosis* (an "if/then" sentence): if the moon "comes out" to earth, from the embrace of that "crooked god," the poet hopes that "every Thessalian magician" will disturb her. Marino thus paraphrases 11.790–91 of Seneca's (ca. 4 B.C.–A.D. 65) *Medea*, where the moon descends, "tormented by Thessalian threats." (The Thessalians were notorious makers of moon charms.) It may well be that Marino's sonnet is a conscious parody of Ronsard's, turning praise into dispraise. The poems have in common not just importunate sorcerers, but also the Pan story, which Ronsard brings up as evidence that the moon, too, has known passion.

The dispraise of the moon may also take a quite different tack. It is proposed that the moon is "inconstant" (Shakespeare) or a "false fire" (Sir John Davies, 1569-1626) — that its light cannot be depended upon, as it waxes and wanes or is hidden by clouds. Jean-Antoine de Baïf (1532-89) prefers trustworthy Venus, the star of evening, to the moon, "qui cache sa clarté" (who hides her brilliance),[8] and the pseudonymous "Skogekär Bergbo" of the petrarchistic Swedish sonnet-cycle, *Venerid* (ca. 1650, published 1680), likewise complains that the moon's light is too easily obscured and that the moon, besides, is forever changing size and color:

> Gör månan något ljust, det varar inte länge,
> och mest om nattetid — nu full, nu åter ny,
> nu mindre än som halv, nu silver, nu som bly.
> Och ofta när han skin i vägen molnen hängia.[9]

> (If the moon makes something bright, it does not last long,
> And [is] mostly at night — now full, now new again
> Now still less than half, now silver, now like lead,
> And often when he shines, clouds hang in the way.)

The *pointe* for which "Skogekär" prepares us is that "Venerid's" bright eyes will light his way in the northern darkness.

Some poets use the Endymion myth to suggest that the moon, kissing an unconscious lover now and then, is either haughty or chilly, or both; the poet, of course, wants his fiery and constant passion to be contrasted with the moon's occasional gestures of love. Francisco de la Torre (whose poems were published in 1631) calls the moon "altiva y arrogante" (proud and arrogant),[10] forgetful of her "sweet lover"; Lope de Vega (1562-1635) has Clytie — the sea-nymph changed into a heliotrope by her love for Apollo — tell Endymion that he does not know how well off he is. Talking in his sleep, the shepherd has complained that the moon, busy with her epicycle, has neglected him; Clytie retorts that, since he has been refrigerated by the moon's cool love, he suffers far less than she:

> Oyóle Clicie, y dijo: "Por qué lloras,
> pues amas a la Luna, que te enfría.
> ¡Ay de quien ama al sol, que solo abrasa!"[11]

> (Clytie heard him and said: "Why do you weep
> For you love the moon, who chills you.
> Woe betide the lover of the sun, that only burns!")

Or the moon—again in a conceit that juxtaposes fire and, at best, tepidity—is charged with being too languid in her love; in the *Amours de Cassandre* (1552), Ronsard says that the "Lune a l'oeil brun, Déesse aux noirs chevaux" (Moon with the dark eye, goddess with the black steeds) lingers with her unconscious shepherd on Latmus, merely fondling him, but the poet wants the night to be foreshortened, so that the dawn, his love, will come.[12] Ronsard here makes a clever combination of three major tropes of the love lyric: the "long night," *not* asked for by the lover—a reverse of the Ovidian formula, "Run slowly, horses of the night" (*Amores,* I, 13:40); the night of torment of the lonely bed, as in Ovid's "What shall I say it is that makes my cot seem so hard" (*Amores*, I, 2:1-2) and in Janus Secundus's (1511-36) "Oh little bed, bearing the weight of your master without a sweet companion" (*Elegies*, II, 8:1-2); and Petrarch's (1304-74) paronomastic equation of the beloved with the dawn, "Laura ora" / "L'aurora" (*Canzoniere,* 291). And, to top off his combinatory brilliance, Ronsard has put these tropes within the framework of an incantation to the moon.

Apart from these two main divisions, of praise and dispraise, in the erotic application of the moon, there are other usages. The beloved may be called the moon, while the lover is the tide subject to her; thus Charles Best's (1570-1627) "The Moon":

> Look how the pale queen of the silent night
> Doeth cause the ocean to attend upon her . . .
> So you, that are the sovereign of my heart,
> Have all my joys attending on your will.[13]

Or the lover may call himself the moon, placed in thrall to the beloved's sun, as in Anton Maria Salvini's (1653-1729) sonnet 240:

> Luna son' io, che intorno a te m'aggiro,
> Almo Sol di bellezza, e mio gran Nume.[14]

> (I am the moon, who revolves around you,
> Grand Sun of beauty, and my great divinity.)

More simply, the beauty of the beloved is said to resemble that of the moon, or to surpass it. The compliment is at least as old as the Song of Songs (6:10): "Who is she that looketh forth in the morning, / Fair as the moon, / Clear as the sun." Less the generalizer than Solomon, Horace compares the color of Chloris's skin to the moon, "shining thus with her white shoulder, / as the bright moon shines on the sea at night"

(*Carmina,* II, 5:18-20). Such comparisons were quite popular among the Neo-Latin poets of the sixteenth century: Laelius Capilupus (1497-1563) tells "Delia" she is appropriately named, shining as she does with lunar grandeur, and his brother Hippolytus (1511-79) assures "Galatea" that — dancing with her friends on the banks of the Po, a veritable moon among the stars — she might lend her brilliance to the moon itself.[15]

This uncomplicated flattery is taken up on the threshold of the German baroque by poets who — like the Capilupi — wrote both in Latin and their mother tongue. Paul Schede Melissus (1534-1602), for example, tucks the *blanditia* (a caress with smooth words) into one of his handful of vernacular poems: "Deß tag's bist mir ein helle Son / Deß nachts ein klarscheinender Mon."[16] The Zincgref anthology containing Melissus's German verse also has a curtal sonnet, "Sol, luna, oculi," of Caspar Kirchner (fl. 1624), who measures the sun and moon against his beloved's eyes, and has the heaven's orbs come off second best:

> Jhr beyde / Sonn / und Mon / der Welt zwey klare Augen /
> Was könnet Jhr doch mehr / den nur den grossen Saal
> Dess Himmels reitten durch, und scheinen uberall?

Martin Opitz (1597-1639) opens a sonnet with the same suggestions, to which the virtue of constancy has been added:

> Ich gleiche nicht mit dir deß weißen Mondens Liecht:
> Der Monde fellt und steigt; du bleibst in einem Scheine:
> Ja nicht die Sonne selbst; die Sonn' ist gantz gemein /
> Gemein' auch ist ihr Glantz; du bist gemeine nicht.[17]

Opitz made an even more striking use of the moon in his elegy, "Indem die Sonne sich hat in das Meer begeben." The speaker of the poem compares himself to Pan, crying out for Delia, the moon, who has descended into the woods, "durch den Schlaff erwuscht [erwischt]":

> Pan aber schläffet nicht.
> Er geht / er rufft / er schreyt mit sehnlichem Verlangen /
> Daß seine Stimm erklingt durch pusche / Berg und Thal . . .
> Dem Pan antwortet nur der blosse Wiederschal.[18]

Opitz had known the Pan story since his school days, from Vergil's adduction of it in the *Georgics* (III, 391-94): "You, oh Luna, were lured by Pan, the Arcadian god, / Pan, calling into the deep forest, nor did you spurn his cries." However, like Sannazaro in one of his Latin epigrams ("Pan poured forth long laments on the Tegaean rock, / captured, oh moon, by your shining form"),[19] Opitz leaves Pan unrequited, in torment. The little classical narrative provides the poem with a special piquancy: identifying himself with Pan (the maker of the pipes), the poet hints at his own creative art; furthermore (even though the poem closes with a reference to the "Thür" of the beloved, thus putting the elegy into the subgenre of the *paraclausithyron*, the poem of "weeping beside the door"), he implies that he may have some chance, as Pan did, of overcoming Delia's resistance. Simultaneously, he gives Pan's cries an air of wild excess ("er rufft / er schreyt"), even as he makes the beloved seem both unusually desirable (the moon herself!) and unusually cold.

Coming late into the world of the Renaissance-baroque lyric, German poets were able to find some fresh nuances in patterns of moon poetry which, by rights, should already have been exhausted. Paul Fleming's "An den Mohn"[20] was written in the middle 1630s, sometime during his trip to Russia and Persia.[21] Its Salibande is Elsabe Niehus, whom he had met in Reval on his way east.

> Du / die du standhafft bist in deinem Unbestande /
> Steig' / Hekate / herab; ich singe dir ein Lied /
> ein Lied von meiner Zier / die itzt auch nach dir sieht /
> ob ich schon bin sehr weit von ihr und ihrem Lande.
>
> Komm / Berezynthie / zu dieses Strohmes Rande /
> an dem ich geh' herum / da meine Hoffnung blüht /
> du weißt es / Delie / was itzt mit ihr geschicht:
> Du weißt es / wie es steht ümm meine Salibande.
>
> Komm / Föbe / Tag der Nacht / Diane / Borge-liecht /
> Warsägrin / Lieder-Freund; komm / Lune / säume nicht;
> Die gantze Welt die schläfft. Ich wache dich zu loben.
>
> Strohm-Fürstinn / Jäger-Frau / Nacht-Auge / Horn-Gesicht' /
> Herab; Itzt fang ich an / das süsse Lob-Gedicht'.
> Und kömmst du nicht herab / so hör es nur dort oben.

The poet tries, by means of an incantation, to bring the moon down from its height; favorable to lovers, it will serve as a bond of an unspecified sort between the speaker and distant Salibande. The tone of the *cantus* is one neither of despair nor of torment; the lover is convinced that Salibande—like himself—gazes at the moon ("die itzt auch nach dir sieht"), and three lines later he makes no bones about his optimism ("da meine Hoffnung blüht"). The moon, he believes, is well-informed about Salibande's condition (twice "Du weißt es," in anaphora). Does he hope that the moon, descending, will tell him about the distant girl? It is of course a convention of the moon poem that the moon remains silent.

The *cantus* by Fleming requires a string of imperatives, which are carefully distributed throughout the poem, one in the sonnet's first quatrain ("Steig . . . herab"), one in the second ("Komm"), three in the first tercet ("Komm," "komm," "säume nicht"), and, in the conclusion, "Herab" and "so hör." Typically, the *cantus* lists some of the qualities of the moon; here, the poem opens in medias res with the wordplay "stand-hafft"/"Unbestand," which captures attention through its very ambiguity (the moon is constant in its course no matter how it waxes and wanes; or, the moon is constant only in its inconstancy). But the process of praise by means of line-filling description is immediately broken off; in its stead, Fleming begins a series of proper names for the moon, again laid out in a crescendo: "Hekate" in the first quatrain, "Berezynthie" and "Delie" in the second—but these are only a preparation for the sestet, where the name series is first interrupted and then replaced by *pronominationes*, substitutions of epithets for names.

Fleming's catalogue of names and sobriquets (fourteen in all)[22] pursues the example of the peroration in Daniel Heinsius's *Lof-Sanck van Bacchus* (11. 631-41),[23] where Heinsius makes an extensive display of his onomastic skill ("O Sabon, Indiaen, Osiris, ende Pan/ Denys, Hymenean, Euasta, Sinne-breker,/ Lenaee, Ligyre, ghy Snorcker, ghy Groot-spreker," etc.). Opitz translated the encomium into German and gave a sampling of the lines in question in chapter 6 of the *Buch von der deutschen Poeterey*, "Von der Zuebereitung und ziehr der worte." Certainly, the exigencies of the Alexandrine line and the sonnet's rhyme scheme have had something to do with the order of Fleming's list; yet the progression does not depend wholly upon requirements of meter and rhyme.

That Fleming names "Hekate" at the outset provides a signal of his awareness (which he means to share with his audience) of the incantatory tradition, a tradition of poetic sorcery, in which he works. (In the same way, authors of fountain poems introduce a catch-phrase from Horace's ode to the Bandusian spring—usually a version of "splendidior vitro," clearer than crystal—to call the classical ancestry to mind.) "Berezynthie" reinforces the suggestion of the uncanny that "Hekate" has made. In a lapsus memoriae caused perhaps by qualities "Hekate" holds in common with Cybele (aid to oracles, and inspirer of trances or ecstasies), Fleming gives an appellation taken from Cybele's haunt, Mount Berecynthus.[24] "Delie," from the home island of Apollo and his sister, shifts to the light-bringing function of the deity, as do the subsequent "Föbe" and "Diana" and "Lune," as well as the accompanying "Tag der

Nacht" and "Borge-liecht." "Strohm-Fürstinn'" and "Jäger-Frau" offer essentially terrestrial qualities. They can be taken as a reduction of what Catullus says in "We Are in the Faith of Diana" (*Carmina*, 34):[25] "mistress of the mounts / and of the greening woods / and of the hidden groves / and of the sounding rivers"; or Horace in *Carmina*, I, 21:5: "delighted in streams and the leaves of groves." But Fleming then returns to the light-bringing moon with his last composites, "Nacht-Auge" and "Horn-Gesicht." Despite what our modern sensibilities might suggest to us, neither "Borge-liecht" nor "Horn-Gesicht" need be pejorative. The former renders Catullus's "You are called Luna with spurious light" in the Diana hymn, and the latter echoes that most solemn of Horatian sources, the *Carmen Saeculare:* "two-horned queen of the stars."

Fleming's "newe worte" for the moon, then, are not particularly inventive (they are by no means as striking as the examples of denominative ingenuity Opitz provides from Ronsard, Joseph Scaliger, and Heinsius), and they stick rather closely to traditional aspects and activities of the moon divinity. Two, however, because they expand the meaning of the poem, are of particular importance: the opening epithets of line 10, "Warsägrin" and "Lieder-Freund." "Warsägrin" refers, of course, to the moon as "Hecate Trivia," or "Diana Trivia," the goddess of crossways, the patronness of prophecy, an aspect frequently mentioned—for example, by Catullus in his hymn, by Vergil's Dido, and by Seneca's Medea, where "Trivia's swift chariot," the moon "with pale and mournful face," appears in the first line of the wronged woman's final charm (11. 787– 842). The moon's oracular talents are not adduced just for adduction's sake: the poem's speaker would like to find out what the fate of the love affair with Salibande will be. As for "Lieder-Freund," Fleming goes counter to classical (and humanistic) practice: Apollo traditionally held that role—"Phoebus who gave me inspiration and the art of song and the name of poet," Horace says in a locus classicus (*Carmina*, IV, 6:29-30). But Fleming accords the honor to Apollo's sister with good reason: it is she who has been the object of the poetry of the lovelorn, and their magician accomplices, over the centuries.

The sonnet promises much in the way of song; for the moon, the poet will sing "ein Lied / ein Lied von meiner Zier" (with the key noun emphasized by an *anadiplosis*, the repetition of the closing word[s] of one line at the beginning of the next), he wakes to praise the moon, "um dich zu loben," and, in the penultimate line, he announces that he will begin at last: "Itzt fang ich an / das süsse Lob-Gedicht'." What he has in mind is an extensive song in which both Salibande (the "Zier") and the moon are to be extolled. But it is an intentional irony of the poem that the promised song is never sung, or rather, the moon gets a portion of *her* praise in this sonnet-preamble, while Salibande's lot is never dealt out. As a matter of fact, the poet's praise of the moon appears not to have been effective; the moon is reluctant to descend, and there is a kind of impotent exasperation in the final line. And there is, as well, another indication of self-mockery: the poet is not only a failed singer of the *cantus* — he may also be much less the confident lover than he has let on. The poem opens, it will be remembered, with the joke about inconstancy, and the moon knows more about Salibande than, at present, the poet does.

In its declamatory tone and its use of elementary but impressive rhetorical figures and ornaments (anaphora, anadiplosis, pronominatio, the *figurae etymologicae* [use of words with the same root] on "standhafft," "Lied," "loben"), "An den Mohn" is a typical product of the earlier German baroque, Faber du Faur's "Realm of Martin Opitz." Yet the poem has extraordinary qualities — not the least of them the strain of ambiguity in the poet's attitude toward the moon, toward Salibande, and toward the very *cantus* tradition in which he so consciously writes.[26] Fleming's Latin epigram, "Ad Lunam," unabashedly berates the moon for its celestial behavior, its waxing and waning.[27] In "An den Mohn" Fleming creates an emotional tenor that is, happily, indeterminate. Measured against the standards of the age, Fleming's poetry — at its best — contains a remarkable range of implication. The polyhistor Daniel Georg Morhof's tribute to Fleming (from 1682) was richly deserved: "in Wahrheit / es stecket ein unvergleichlicher Geist in ihm / der mehr auff sich selbst als auff fremder Nachahmung beruht."[28]

David Schirmer's "Sie Liebet Ihn," like the whole of the *Rosen-Gepüsche* in which it appears, continues the manner of the so-called Leipzig school,[29] for which Fleming had become an admired model. Schirmer regarded "Sie Liebet Ihn" as a showpiece; he placed it near the beginning of both editions of his collection:[30]

> Funckelt ihr göldnen Himmels-Sternen!
> blitzet ihr hellen Nacht-Laternen!
> Jauchtzet ihr Stralen an der Sonnen!
> rauschet ihr kühlen Wasser-Bronnen;
> Asterie will sich zur liebe verdammen /
> die keusche Brust fühlet die blinckenden Flammen;
> Tugend und Gunst
> mehret die Brunst /

welche die rauchenden Geister anbrennet.
Hertzgen und Mund
stehen verwund /
dass sich Asterie selber nicht kennet.

Brummende Donner / Hagel-Spitzen /
Feuer-bestraltes Wetter-Blitzen /
Krachende Wolcken / Harte Schläge /
fliehet Asterien aus dem Wege /
beräumet die Weißlichte Strasse dort oben /
Asterie bleibet unsterblich erhoben.
bleiche nun ganz /
Luna / dein Glantz
wird die verdüsterten Augen verlassen.
Hinde / spann an /
zeichne die Bahn /
ihre Hand kömmet den Zügel zufassen.

Fahre nun wohl aus deinen Tächern
Zu den vergöldten Liebs-Gemächern /
Sage / du wollest aller Enden
Venus gebutzten Leib beschänden.
Erzehle / wie Paris mit Freuden-Gethöne
dir geben den Apffel / das Zeichen der Schöne.
Melde darbey /
Sylvius sey /
Welcher ihn könne durch Tugend erwerben.
Kömst du / mein Glück /
Wieder zurück /
Will ich dein willigster Diener ersterben.

The poem's title imparts the discovery Asterie has just made and of which, evidently, she has told the poet. The poem itself is an expression of what the speaker imagines Asterie's subsequent reactions — and nature's — to be. The whole of the nocturnal sky must rejoice at Asterie's emotional ignition; as for Asterie, her chaste breast (an important phrase) feels the "glittering flames," and she can no longer recognize herself — she is transformed. That she wishes to "condemn herself" to love, and that her "heart and mouth" have been wounded — these are phrases indicating (as the poem's title does) an abandonment of the (male) one-sidedness of passion customary in the petrarchistic pattern; the "suffering" of desire has been extended to the female partner.

After further sound-and-lighting effects (Schirmer, the court poet, creates a whole theatrical performance), the metamorphosis continues.

Like a rocketship, Asterie has taken off for a trip to the heavens. The tur-
bulent elements of the thunderstorm are ordered to clear out of the
Milky Way, and to open a path for Asterie's literal elevation to immortality. (As Janus Secundus told Julia, and Ronsard told Hélène, a poet's
love confers immortality; Schirmer goes his predecessors one better by
placing Asterie among the heavenly bodies.) In what is, arithmetically,
the center of the poem, the moon itself is commanded to grow pale
before Asterie's beauty; the imperatives, having first been sent to the
plural entities of the nocturnal sky, are now directed to the moon, the
queen of the night. Schirmer's moon, in fact, is instructed to abdicate; its
shine will leave its darkened eyes, and its place in the lunar chariot will
be taken by Asterie. Luna's (i.e., Diana's) companion animal, the hind,
changing mistresses, is ordered to guide Asterie still farther through the
skies; Asterie's hand will take the chariot's reins.

That Asterie slides into the driver's seat is not just an easy compliment, another way of saying that she is fairer than the moon. (And
perhaps chaster as well: the reader has already been told about her
"chaste breast.") Nonetheless, she is supposed to have undergone a
radical change at the very beginning of her ascent, a take-off to which
the puzzling opening of the final strophe would seem to return: "Fahre
nun wohl aus deinen Tächern . . ." Logically, Asterie should have long
since left roofs ("Tächer"/"Dächer") behind. But the word does not
mean "house roofs" here. In *Die Geharnschte Venus*, Caspar Stieler
(1632–1707) writes (IV, 4): "Das Wolken-Dach war mit der Nacht um-
zogen,"[31] and, in a later anthology, a poem by Gottlieb Stolle
(1673–1744) has the line: "Schwärtzt sich gleich das Wolken-
Dach . . ."[32] The "Tächer" are layers of clouds,[33] and Asterie (the
climactic recipient of the poem's many imperatives) is instructed to shed
her coverings, to get undressed. Her beauty wholly revealed, she will
then announce that she can put Venus herself to shame, "Venus
gebutzten Leib beschänden."

De Baïf's "Dizain," mentioned above, is in effect a poem about the
rivalry between the moon and Venus, the evening star; in Schirmer,
Asterie, the moon's substitute, takes up the contest. Arriving at the
golden chambers of love, she must tell the story of the judgment of Paris,
but with a new twist—she will win the prize. (In the contest, of course,
both Asterie and Venus have to be nude; that Schirmer calls Venus
"gebutzt" means that the goddess is a worthy opponent, "shining" or
"bright."[34]) Having got the apple, Asterie must deliver a third part of the
message: Sylvius (the speaker of the poem names himself at last) will win

the apple from her in his turn, "durch Tugend." But are we to take Sylvius's "virtue" seriously? After all, "Tugend," in the first strophe's coupling of it with "Gunst" (the favor which Asterie feels for her admirer), served to fan her passion, her "Brunst." Furthermore, what Sylvius thinks he is going to get has nothing to do with virtue, as virtue is commonly understood. In the classical world, the "apple" meant sexual attentions—Propertius gives "apples" to Cynthia as she lies on her couch (I, 3:24).[35] Sylvius trusts that Asterie—no longer a better moon but a better Venus—will bestow the fruit upon him. Should anyone in the audience have missed the point, Schirmer repeats it in the poem's final sentence, all the while maintaining a surface decorum. Like the concluding line of Fleming's sonnet, it is a protasis/apodosis, but a good deal more hopeful. If Asterie now deigns to return to earth, Sylvius—calling himself "I" for the first time, in this poem about revelation—will gladly "perish" as her willing servant: it must be remembered that "ersterben" frequently refers to the *mors parva*, the *piccola morte*, of coition.

In its art of seduction, "Sie Liebet Ihn" bears a resemblance to the verses of a Caroline poet, Sir Francis Kynaston (1587–1642), "To Cynthia. On her changing."[36] Cynthia is told that she should not try to live up to her moon name ("Cynthia, though thou bearst the name / Of the pale Queen of the Night . . ."). Instead of carrying on an unconsummated affair with a sleeping shepherd, she would do well to recall that she is but a mortal whose "glories" will fade ("There is no cause nor yet no sence / That dainty fruits should rot / Though the tree die, and wither, whence / The Apricots were got"). Yet Schirmer's poem outdoes Kynaston's: by the imaginative variant upon the moon invocation in the cascade of imperatives, by the extravagant (and extravagantly amusing) sweep of Asterie's astronautics, and by the blend of delicacy and boldness with which Schirmer makes the lover's plea.

Elsewhere in Schirmer's *Rosen-Gepüsche*, a moon poem of the traditional sort is to be found, where the *cantus* is used to ask the moon to tarry, and so to make the night longer, while the poet enjoys the company of his "schwartz-braunes Venus-Kind" (her brunette beauty is set up against the moon's "Silber-Wangen," her palpable generosity against the chastity of "der reine Mond"):

Wie? wilstu / blasses Bild / den müden Tag ereilen?
  Halt doch den Wagen an.
Verzeuch ein wenig noch / Diana / dein verweilen.
  Verrenne dir die Bahn.

> Halt doch den Ziegel fest in deinen weißen Armen.
> Lass deine Hinde stehn.
> Weil ich in Liebes Glut ietzunder soll erwarmen
> Und bey den Kräutern gehn.[37]

The request is repeated in the first of the two moon poems[38] among the two hundred sonnets of Johann Georg Schoch (1634-ca. 1690), a native of Leipzig and still another cultivator of the city's playful eroticism. The sonnet "Er nimmt mit dem Mond wiederumm abschied" is, in essence, a combination of two appeals to the moon—to be love's witness and to grant a long night:

> Bleib Luna / bleib doch noch ein wenig bey uns stehen /
> Und sieh nur / wie wir uns so freundlich können küssen /
> Du / und die stille Nacht / soll unser Liebe wissen.
> Bleib / biß der Haus-Hahn wird den hellen Tag ankrehn /
>   Und die gekühlte Lufft die Felder überwehn.
> Bleib / bleib; Wie hast du dich so schleinig [schleunig] uns entrissen?
> Du wirst Endymion vielleicht umfangen müssen
> Und wirst auff Latmien zu gleicher Freude gehn?
>   So werd ich gleich mit dir auch wieder Abschied nehmen /
> Weil ich zugleich mit dir hieher gekommen bin.
> Doch warte! Nim mich mit! Wo eilst du doch so hin?
>   Wir kommen wiederumb an diesem Fenster-Rehmen [Rahmen]
> Zusammen auff die Nacht. so bald wir sie empfinden;
> Da solst du mich gewiß / hier eben wieder / finden.

If the tropes are well worn, so are the structural features; the moon is given a set of directives, which, as usual, she ignores. The sonnet's octave has six imperatives, as well as two questions (the second a double one); the sestet has two more imperatives (the appeal to the moon to take the lover along, now that the appointed hour of love has passed) and still another question ("Wo eilst du doch so hin?"). Yet the poem is less encumbered than its predecessors with classical allusion and verbal ornamentation: although the obligatory mythological reference (to Luna's departure, in order to visit Endymion) is still present, the memorable central image of the octave has been taken directly from nature: the cock will crow, and the cool wind will blow across the fields, as though to dispel the sultry eroticism of the night. In addition, surprisingly little attention is paid to the beloved; instead, the poet sets the greater store by the friendship of the moon, with whom he comes and goes, and whose company he wants at the next rendezvous. The relationship with the moon is a closer one than in Fleming (where the poet orates to the moon as deity) and Schirmer (where the moon is replaced by the beloved).

The second of Schoch's poems has a title that serves as a connecting text, "An den Mond / als Er Ihn nicht wieder fand." The lover has come back, the moon has not:

> Wo steckst du / Zynthie? Bist du denn wieder fort?
> Ist dir denn schon der Thau in Lamppen-Napff geschwommen /
> Darvon dein Liechter-Docht so zeitlich ausgeglommen?
> Kein Stern ist mehr zu sehn / die Nacht ist alle port /
> Seit mich die Katharis mit ihr an so ein Ort /
> An so ein Ort / da nichts / als stete Nacht / genommen /
> Dahin du nimmermehr mit deinen Sternen kommen.
> Da durfft ich Sie: Doch halt; Ich sage mehr kein Wort.
> Ach solt ich doch nur stets in diesem fünstern [Finstern] seyn!
> Ihr frohes Augen-Liecht das geb mir satten Schein /
> Wenn gleich kein blasser Mond und keine Sonne wären.
> Ihr Himmel-gleicher Mund ist meiner Seele Haus /
> Da geht sie tausend-mahl in küssen ein-und-aus;
> Da kan ich den Hymet von ihren Lippen zehren.

As in the preceding poem, there is a homely touch: the dew has crept up the wick of the moon's lamp and put out her light. At first glance, we may think of the moon's nourishing dew, so often mentioned in poems of tribute: Vittoria Colonna's (1492-1547) "il latte puro . . . quasi rugiada" (the pure milk . . . as if dew), and Sir Walter Raleigh's "Praised be the dews, with which she moists the ground."[39] Yet Schoch does not mean to allude, except quite incidentally, to what Fontanella called "la crescente virtù" (the power of causing growth) of the moon.[40] Instead, he has a slyer intent — following Desportes, Ronsard, Marino, he knows that when the moon goes out, the time has come for "thefts of love."[41] In fact, he compounds the darkness: the first quartet's "die Nacht ist alle port" ends with an orthographical and phonetic distortion of the French "de toutes parts," i.e., everywhere, and in the second quartet the stars have vanished, too.

With all lights out, the scene has been set for a gallant obscenity: Katharis has taken the lover to a place (repeated in anadiplosis, like Fleming's "ein Lied / ein Lied," here to underscore the naughty meaning) where night is eternal, into the special *locus amoenus* celebrated by Hofmannswaldau (1617-79) and his imitators, into "das süsse Sorgengrab" of Johann von Besser's (1654-1729) "Die Schooss der

Geliebten." (Indeed, could the dew that put out the candle have been something like Hofmannswaldau's infamous "Wollust-Thau"?) Schoch spares his readers' blushes by means of an *aposiopesis* (theoretical halt or breaking off): "Da durfft ich Sie. Doch halt, Ich sage mehr kein Wort." However, he does say more, turning the wish for a long night of love into a double-entendre ("Ach solt ich doch nur stets in diesem fünstern seyn"), only to return to respectability with the petrarchistic metaphor of illumination: her eyes will give him light enough. But he descends once again into daring implications before the conclusion. Albeit an "originally mystical conceit,"[42] the soul kiss is a commonplace in the risqué *basia* poetry of the Renaissance (see Janus Secundus, *Basium* 13). The honey ("Hymet," so-called after the famous bees of Greece's Mount Hymettus) which the poet greedily drinks from his beloved's lips may also have a second, bawdy import.

Schoch's second sonnet runs into the same dead end of inventive pornography (or, at any rate, Quintilian's *cacemphaton*: "language distorted into an obscene meaning by evil usage") as does so much other German poetry about love from the baroque century's latter part. Even the grandiose opening of Caspar Stieler's "Nacht-Glücke" collapses without hesitation into the literally priapic:

> Willkommen, Fürstin aller Nächte!
> Prinz der Silber-Knechte /
> Willkommen / Mohn / aus düstrer Bahn
> Vom Ozean!
> Diß ist die Nacht, die tausend Tagen
> Trozz kann sagen:
> Weil mein Schazz
> Hier in Priapus' Plazz
> Erscheinen wird / zu stillen meine Pein.
> Wer wird / wie ich / wol so beglükket sein?[43]

In the eighteenth century, and beyond,[44] traces of the earlier *cantus* can still be readily discerned: the rakish classical allusion (the young, "Leipzig" Goethe's "Und nun zieht sie mich hernieder / Wie dich einst Endymion"),[45] the plaintive query (the old Goethe's "Willst du mich sogleich verlassen?"), the lover's distress (Hölty's "Wenn der silberne Mond durch die Gesträuche blickt, / . . . Wandl ich taurig von Busch zu Busch"), and the notion that the moon is, somehow, love's go-between (Brentano's "So oft der Mond mag scheinen, gedenk ich dein"). Nonetheless, in this later and infinitely more sentimental time, a much larger world of lunar possibilities has been entered, of which Fleming had given an inkling with his "Lieder-Freund," Schoch with the companion moon of his first sonnet. Klopstock added a new appellation for the moon to the old imperative address: "Eile nicht, bleib, Gedankenfreund!" For the mature Goethe, the moon was the agent of enormous and unspecific emotional release: "Lösest endlich auch einmal / Meine Seele ganz." And, a little sourly, Schopenhauer wrote, in *Die Welt als Wille und Vorstellung* (III, 30): "Der Mond stimmt uns erhaben."

NOTES

1. Jean Passerat's poem is in *Anthologie poétique française, XVIe siècle*, ed. Maurice Allem (Paris: Garnier/ Flammarion, 1965), II, 151.
2. Justus de Harduwijn, *De weerlücke liefden tot Roose-mond*, ed. O. Dambre (Culemborg: Tjeenk Willink-Noorduijn, 1972), pp. 74–75.
3. Hans Pyritz's discussion of the ailment of love in Petrarch and petrarchism remains basic reading: *Paul Flemings Liebeslyrik: Zur Geschichte des Petrarkismus* (Göttingen: Vandenhoeck, 1963), pp. 125 ff.
4. Pierre Ronsard, *Oeuvres complètes*, ed. Gustave Cohen (Paris: Gallimard, 1950), I, 131.
5. The pair of opposites, "moon praise/moon dispraise," resembles the parallel and larger phenomenon of "petrarchism/antipetrarchism"; see Jörg-Ulrich Fechner, *Der Anti-Petrarkismus: Studien zur Liebessatire in barocker Lyrik* (Heidelberg: Winter, 1966).
6. Philippe Desportes, *Diverses amours et autres oeuvres meslées*, ed. Victor E. Graham (Geneva: Droz; Paris, Minard, 1963), p. 39.
7. Giuseppe Guido Ferrero, ed., *Marino e i Marinisti*: (Milan and Naples: Ricciardi, 1953), p. 335.
8. Jean-Antoine de Baïf, *Oeuvres en rime* (Paris: Lemerre, 1881), I, 352.
9. "Skogekär Bergbo," *Venerid*, ed. Bertil Sundborg (Stockholm: Sällskapet Bokvänner, 1951), p. 135 (sonnet 12).
10. Francisco de la Torre, *Poesías*, ed. Alonso Zamora Vicente (Madrid: Espasa-Calpe, 1944), p. 75 (sonnet 28).
11. Lope de Vega, *Obras poeticas*, ed. José Manuel Blecua (Barcelona: Planeta, 1969), I, 32–33 (sonnet 16).
12. Pierre Ronsard, *Oeuvres complètes*, I, 66.
13. Charles Best's poem is in *The Oxford Book of Sixteenth Century Verse*, ed. E. V. Chambers (Oxford: Oxford University Press, 1970), p. 818. Sir Walter Raleigh's (ca. 1552-1618) long poem to Queen Elizabeth—who by her vaunted chastity and brilliance inspired much moon poetry—employs the same configuration: cf. "The 11th and Last Book of the Ocean to Cynthia," in *The Poems*, ed. Agnes M. C. Latham (Boston: Houghton Mifflin, 1929), p. 111.

14. Anton Maria Salvini, *Sonetti* (Florence: Tartini & Franchi, 1728), p. 240.

15. The poems of Laelius and Hippolytus Capilupus are in *Delitiae CC italorum poetarum, huius superiorisque aevi illustrium*, ed. Janus Gruterus, (Frankfurt a.M.: Rosa, 1608), I, 665 ("Ad Galateam") and I, 669 ("Ad Deliam").

16. The poem by Paul Schede Melissus is cited in *Martini Opicii Teutsche Poemata und Aristarchus Wieder die Verachtung Teutscher Sprach, Item Verteutschung Danielis Heinsij Lobgesangs Jesu Christi, und Hymni in Bachum Sampt einem anhang Mehr auserleszener geticht anderer Teutscher Poeten* (Straßburg: Zetzner, 1624), p. 165; the Kirchner poem is on p. 184. Schede has a much more complex Neo-Latin poem, "Ad Lunam," a *genethliacon* (poem written to celebrate a birth) for Johannes Posthius, in *Schediasmata* (Paris: Sittartus, 1586), I, 431-32. It uses the moon as "Lucina," the goddess of childbirth.

17. Martin Opitz, *Weltliche Poemata Zum Viertenmahl vermehret und ubersehen herraus geben* (Frankfurt a.M.: Goetze, 1644), II, 379 (sonnet 37).

18. Ibid., II, 304.

19. Martin Opitz, *Opera omnia latine scripta nuper edita* (Venice: Aldus, 1535), p. 47 ("De Luna et Pane"); p. 36 ("De Endymione et Lune") has a slumbering Endymion (again a somniloquist) who is mortally jealous of Pan's success.

20. Paul Fleming, *Teutsche Poemata* (Lübeck: Jauchen [ca. 1642]), p. 632.

21. Liselotte Supersaxo, *Die Sonette Paul Flemings: Chronologie und Entwicklung* (Zürich diss.; Singen: Steinhauer, 1956), p. 151, thinks the poem was written on the banks of the Volga: "Als Entstehungszeit kommen die Monate Juli und August des Jahres 1636 in Frage."

22. The article on "Diana" in the *Großes Vollständiges Universal-Lexikon aller Wissenschaften und Künste* (Halle and Leipzig: Zedler, 1732-50), VII, 758-61, lists 146 "vornehmste Zunahmen" for the divinity!

23. *Bacchus en Christus: Twee Lofzangen van Daniel Heinsius*, ed. L. Ph. Rank, J. D. P. Warners, and F. L. Zwaan (Zwolle: Tjeek Willink, 1965), pp. 176-78.

24. The *ratio decori*, "decoration's sake," may also have helped to make Fleming choose "Berenzynthie"; cf. Joachim du Bellay's striking ingressus to the sixth sonnet in *Les antiquités de Rome*: "Telle que dans sa char la Berecynthienne . . ."

25. The hymn that catalogues aspects of the moon (or associate deities) has a long history: Homeric hymns 27 (to Artemis) and 32 (to Selene); Catullus's "Dianae sumus in fide"; Horace's *Carmen Saeculare* (to Apollo and Diana) and his little Diana ode (III, 22), used by the Jesuit Jakob Balde (1604-68) as the starting point for an ode to the Virgin of Ettal (*Carmina*, III, 2). In

Neo-Latin poetry, a major monument is Michael Marullus's (d. 1500) hymn to the moon (*Carmina*, ed. Alessandre Perosa [Zürich: Artemis, n.d.], pp. 145-47). The Marinist Girolamo Fontanella's (1612-1643/44) "Alla Luna" (Ferrero, *op. cit.*, 865-67) and Ben Jonson's (1573?-1637) "Hymn to Diana" are among the vernacular examples.

26. Manfred Beller, "Thema, Konvention, und Sprache der mythologischen Ausdrucksformen in Paul Flemings Gedichten," *Euphorion*, 67 (1973), 157-88, has a brief comment on Fleming's "An den Mohn": "Mir scheint . . . der Reiz gerade in der Spannung zwischen dem Pathos der Anrufung und der ironischen Schlußwendung zu liegen" (pp. 175-76).

27. Fleming's "Ad Lunam" is in *Lateinische Gedichte*, ed. J. M. Lappenberg (Stuttgart: Literarischer Verein, 1863), pp. 264-65.

28. Daniel Georg Morhof, *Unterricht Von Der Teutschen Sprache und Poesie, deren Uhrsprung, Fortgang und Lehrsätzen* (Kiel: Reumann, 1682), p. 426.

29. A. J. Harper has a sober and enlightening account in "Leipzig Poetry after Paul Fleming — a Reassessment," *Daphnis*, 5 (1976), 145-70.

30. *David Schirmers Erstes [-Vierdtes] Rosen-Gepüsch* ([Leipzig]: Wittigau, 1653), pp. 2-4; *David Schirmers Poetische Rosen-Gepüsche* (Dresden: Löfler, 1657), pp. 3-4. In his *David Schirmer—A Poet of the German Baroque* (Stuttgart: Heinz, 1977), pp. 37-39, A. J. Harper emphasizes the poem's verbal skill: "It is the metrical and general virtuosity of the linguistic expression rather than the theme which makes the poem of interest."

31. Caspar Stieler, *Die Geharnschte Venus oder Liebes-Lieder im Kriege gedichtet* (Hamburg: Pfeiffer, 1660), p. 130.

32. Gottlieb Stolle's poem is in *Des Schlesischen Helikons auserlesene Gedichte* (Liegnitz: Rohrlach, 1699, 1700), II, 132.

33. The Dutch Renaissance poet, P. C. Hooft (1581-1647) chooses the etymologically related "deken" ("cover") to express a similar idea: "Amaryllis, de deken sacht / Van de nacht, / Met sijn blaeuwe wolken buijen, / Maeckt de starren sluimerblint . . ." ("Amaryl the gentle cover / Of the night / With its blue cloud fetter / Makes the stars slumber-blind . . .", *Erotische Gedichten*, ed. C. C. van Stockum (Zutphen: Thieme, 1956), p. 42.

34. Caspar Stieler, *Der Teutschen Sprache Stammbaum und Fortwachs, oder Teutscher Sprachschatz* (Altdorf: Meyer, 1691), I, 264, gives "politus" as a meaning of "gebutzt." Also, since Venus is the evening star, could the word include a punning suggestion of "sternbutz[e]"?

35. Cf. Gaston Vorberg, *Glossarium Eroticum* (Hanau: Müller und Kiepenheuer, 1965), pp. 325, 509. See also the late baroque's breast metaphor, "Liebes-Äpffel" ("Die süsser sind als die / so Abels Mutter aß," as Christian Hölmann, 1677-1744, put it), and the interest of Sir Francis

Kynaston in Cynthia's "Apricots" (see below).

36. Sir Francis Kynaston, *Leoline and Sydanis: An Heroick Romance of the Amorous Adventures of Princes; Together with Sundry Affectionate Addresses to his Mistress, under the Name of Cynthia* (London: Hearne, 1642), pp. 148-49. (The poem is meant, we are told, to persuade Cynthia to cease mourning for her mother's death.)

37. Schirmer, *Rosen-Gepüsche* (1657), p. 414.

38. *Johann Georg Schochs neu-erbaueter Poetischer Lust- und Blumen-Garten* (Leipzig: Kirchner, 1660); the sonnets appear on pp. 74-76 of the book's second part, "Johann Georg Schochs Erstes [-Ander] Hundert Liebes-Sonnet," which has its own pagination.

39. Vittoria Colonna, *Le Rime* (Rome: Salviucci, 1840), p. 249 (sonnet 89); Raleigh, *op. cit.*, p. 111.

40. For Fontanella, see note 25.

41. In Shakespeare's *The Rape of Lucrece*, Tarquin does his lustful work in utter darkness, having put his foot on the candle by the bed.

42. Gerhart Hoffmeister, *Petrarkistische Lyrik* (Stuttgart: Metzler, 1973), pp. 27-28; see also Gerhart Hoffmeister, "Barocker Petrarkismus: Wandlungen und Möglichkeiten der Liebessprache in der Lyrik des 17. Jahrhunderts," in *Europäische Tradition und deutscher Literaturbarock: Internationale Beiträge zum Problem von Überlieferung und Umgestaltung,* ed. Gerhart Hoffmeister (Bern and München: Francke, 1973), pp. 37-54. After having described "My fluttering soul, sprung with the pointed kiss . . ." in his notorious "The Imperfect Enjoyment," Lord Rochester (1647-90) destroys the elegant metaphor by what (to say the least) is excessive specificity.

43. Caspar Stieler, *Die Geharnschte Venus*, p. 202. The poem's hermaphroditic start illustrates a problem German poets have had with the moon, feminine in classical mythology and the classical and Romance tongues, masculine in German grammar and folklore. Bürger refers to it in "Auch ein Lied an den lieben Mond": "Ich weiß nicht recht / Wie ich dich heißen soll? / Mann oder Weib?" Could it be that German poetry's moon image becomes more "masculine" as the baroque (so heavily indebted to the classics and to Romance models) is left behind?

44. From Klopstock on, moon poetry burgeons in Germany (or, as Brecht's Babusch says in an altogether different connection, "Mond gibt's genügend"). See the anthologies of Brigitte Neske, *Das Mondbuch: Der Mond in der deutschen Dichtung* (Pfullingen: Neske, 1958), and Edgar Nies, *Der Mond in der deutschen Lyrik* (Hollfeld: Bange, n.d.). Neither contains any of the baroque's moon poems.

45. Matthias Claudius's sentimentalization of the Endymion story (in "Ein Brief an den Mond") may be more symptomatic of the new age and its attitudes — Endymion is a lost child, searched for by the moon.

SELECTED BIBLIOGRAPHY

Secondary Sources

Alewyn, Richard, ed., *Deutsche Barockforschung: Dokumentation einer Epoche*. Köln and Berlin: Kiepenheuer & Witsch, 1965. (Contains *i.a.*: Fritz Strich, "Der lyrische Stil des 17. Jahrhunderts," pp. 21-53 [first printed 1916]; Albrecht Joseph, "Sprachformen der deutschen Barocklyrik," pp. 284-311 [first printed 1930]; Wolfgang Kayser, "Der rhetorische Grundzug von Harsdörffers Zeit und die gattungsgebundene Haltung," pp. 324-35 [first printed 1932].)

Beckmann, Adelheid, *Motive und Formen der deutschen Lyrik des 17. Jahrhunderts und ihre Entsprechungen in der französischen Lyrik seit Ronsard*. Tübingen: Niemeyer, 1960.

Beißner, Friedrich, "Deutsche Barocklyrik." In Hans Steffen, ed., *Formkräfte deutscher Dichtung vom Barock bis zur Gegenwart*. Göttingen: Vandenhoeck, 1963.

Bircher, Martin, and Alois M. Haas, eds., *Deutsche Barocklyrik: Gedichtinterpretationen von Spee bis Haller*. Bern and München: Francke, 1973.

Browning, Robert M., *German Baroque Poetry 1618-1723*. University Park and London: Pennsylvania State University Press, 1971.

Capua, A. G. de, *German Baroque Poetry: Interpretive Readings*. Albany: State University of New York Press, 1973

Cohen, J. M., *The Baroque Lyric*. London: Hutchinson University Library, 1963.

Conrady, Karl Otto, *Lateinische Dichtungtradition und deutsche Lyrik des 17. Jahrhunderts*. Bonn: Bouvier, 1962.

Cyzarz, Herbert, *Deutsches Barock in der Lyrik*. Leipzig: Reclam, 1936.

Capua, A. G. de, *German Baroque Poetry: Interpretive Readings*. Albany: State University of New York Press, 1973.

Fechner, Jörg-Ulrich, *Der Anti-Petrarchismus: Studien zur Liebessatire in barocker Lyrik*. Heidelberg: Winter, 1966.

Forster, Leonard, *The Icy Fire: Five Studies in European Petrarchism*. Cambridge: The University Press, 1969.

Gellinek, Janis Little, *Die weltliche Lyrik des Martin Opitz*. Bern and München: Francke, 1973.

Gillespie, Gerald, *German Baroque Poetry*. New York: Twayne, 1971.

Haller, Rudolf, *Geschichte der deutschen Lyrik vom Ausgang des Mittelalters bis zu Goethes Tod*, pp. 37-183 ("Das Jahrhundert des Barock"). Bern and München: Francke, 1967.

Harper, Anthony J., *David Schirmer—A Poet of the German Baroque*. Stuttgart: Heinz, 1977.

———, "Rebirth in Poetry: Renaissance Verse-Reform and the German Lyrik of the Seventeenth Century." In *Time and Change*: Essays on German and European Literature, Anthony J. Harper, ed. Frankfurt: Rita G. Fischer Verlag, 1982, pp. 5-28.

Heiduk, Franz, *Die Dichter der galanten Lyrik: Studien zur Neukirch'schen Sammlung*. Bern and München: Francke, 1971.

Herzog, Urs, *Deutsche Barocklyrik: Eine Einführung*. München: C. H. Beck, 1979.

Hoffmeister, Gerhart, *Petrarkistische Lyrik*. Stuttgart: Metzler, 1973.

——, ed., *Europäische Tradition und deutscher Literaturbarock: Internationale Beiträge zum Problem von Überlieferung und Umgestaltung*. Bern and München: Francke, 1973.

Nelson, Lowry, Jr., *Baroque Lyric Poetry*. New Haven and London: Yale University Press, 1961.

Moret, André, *Le lyrisme baroque en Allemagne: Ses origines, ses idées, ses moyens d'expression*. Lille: Bibliothèque universitaire, 1936.

Pyritz, Hans, *Paul Flemings Liebeslyrik: Zur Geschichte des Petrarkismus*. Göttingen: Vandenhoeck, 1963. (Reprint of 1932 edition).

Ziemendorff, Ingeborg, *Die Metapher bei den weltlichen Lyrikern des deutschen Barock*. Nendeln/Liechtenstein: Kraus, 1967. (Reprint of 1933 dissertation.)

19

*The Development
of the Vernacular Drama*

Barton W. Browning

A broad general shift in both popular and learned tastes accompanied
the advent of seventeenth-century German drama. During the fifteenth
and sixteenth centuries there had been, roughly speaking, three major
dramatic forms: the popular stage, the religious pageant, and the
pedagogical exercise. On the popular level the common public played in
and enjoyed *Fastnachtsspiele* such as those written by Hans Sachs.
Although the Reformation marked the onset of the passion play's
demise, these religiously oriented spectacles were still able to draw large
casts and crowds from the general populace.[1] The pedagogical stage,
which began primarily as an institution of the humanists, produced
Latin classics for a severely limited audience.[2] Over the course of the sixteenth century these scholars developed their own Neo-Latin pieces along
with occasional German works, yet the actors were students and the
major emphasis of their productions remained practical training in
language skills and the declamatory arts. As compared to the growing
strength and concentration of the English stage, Reformation Germany's
dramatic efforts appear diffuse and decidedly amateur.

The seventeenth century brought with it two significant modifica-
tions of these earlier dramatic forms and one new import. On the
popular level the newly arrived English players soon captured the interest
of the crowd and easily outshone the clumsy indigenous productions.[3]
The major religious drama of the seventeenth century, the Jesuit drama,

labored under a similar burden of playing in a foreign tongue but solved
its problems in a more decorous fashion.[4] The Jesuit stage in essence
adapted the humanists' use of Latin drama as an instructional device.
Since the aims of the order extended beyond the education of an intellectual elite, their dramas sought a broader audience and soon expanded
into some of the most elaborate spectacles of a century that reveled in
elaborate display. In addition to its primary instructional purpose, the
Jesuit stage always reflected missionary aims, an early example of *Kunst
als Waffe*. The third major development in seventeenth-century German
drama were those plays composed for the stage of the Protestant gymnasium, the self-aware vernacular drama with artistic aspirations. This
Protestant school stage gave birth to the major works of seventeenth-
century German theater, and in these institutionally related dramas German writers made their lasting contributions to baroque dramatic
literature.

In light of the fact that the leading exponents of the vernacular
drama were Silesian and wrote for the Silesian school stage, this genre
has become known as *das schlesische Kunstdrama*, the last term,
Kunstdrama, also setting it apart from the popular drama of the day.[5]
This stage was, nonetheless, quite responsive to its companion dramatic
trends. The drastic action and high-pitched emotional fury of the
English actors left their mark in the tragedies of Gryphius and flowered
again in Lohenstein's bloody spectacles. In Breslau the Protestant gym-
nasia felt pressured to compete with the startling visual effects of the
Jesuit stage, and the perennial conflict between tyrant and martyr so
characteristic of Jesuit drama found an appropriate adaptation in the
works of the Silesian dramatists. Influences also flowed in the other
direction. Gryphius's dramas, for example, were picked up and played
by wandering troupes, albeit in a form trimmed to the taste of a less
fastidious audience.[6] In short, the *Kunstdrama* was actively involved in
the total seventeenth-century dramatic spectrum.

The genesis of the *Kunstdrama* is, in its narrowest sense, quite clear:
these dramas were written for the Protestant gymnasium where future
generations of government officials and learned professionals received
their pre-university training.[7] The major authors of this genre had
themselves played in their schools' productions and thus wrote for the
stage with a practical knowledge of its advantages and limitations. Their
plays are by no means closet dramas; these pieces were written to be
played.[8]

As heir to one line of the sixteenth-century pedagogical stage, the

Protestant school drama provided a welcome relief from the rote memorization of classical texts. Furthermore, the students "werden behertzt in dem Reden / höflich in den Geberden / fähig in dem Verständniß / üben das Gedächtniß und arten sich [*entwickeln sich dazu*] höheren Verrichtungen vorzustehen."[9] Long before the end of the sixteenth century the Straßburger Akademietheater had distinguished itself through its presentations of classical and Neo-Latin dramas,[10] but it was only in the wake of Opitz's defense of the vernacular that serious German dramatists finally joined their colleagues in Italy, France, England, and Holland in adopting their native tongue for the stage.

The *Kunstdrama* was, of course, not meant for a popular audience, and its function as a school production had certain implications. Writers' attempts to emulate classical models in both form and linguistic refinement are unmistakable. As exemplary authors the tragedian Seneca and his forebear Euripides replaced the sixteenth-century favorites Plautus and Terence.[11] In line with the seriousness of their undertaking, students declaimed their roles in an elevated diction with elaborate rhetorical ornamentation, that is, in the obligatory *stilus gravis*. The simple, direct narration of the sixteenth century was replaced by involved circumlocutions or periphrases. As Opitz suggested, one must "ein ding nicht nur bloß nennen / sondern mit prächtigen hohen worten umbschreiben."[12] From their classical models the writers also inherited a preference for sententious phrases, or *Lehrsprüche*, which were viewed as nothing less than "des Trauerspiels Grundseulen"[13] These pithy formulations of general wisdom were highly esteemed, and such florilegia as Männling's *Lohensteinius sententiosus* (Breslau, 1710) testify both to the general interest in resonant maxims as well as to Lohenstein's preeminence in their construction. In the dramas themselves, the modern reader often finds that lengthy stichomythic exchanges tend to obscure the expressive value of individual *sententiae*. Throughout the extended debate scenes of the *Kunstdrama,* figures hurl resounding phrases back and forth in an attempt to overwhelm, not so much through accuracy as through sheer weight of numbers. As Albrecht Schöne wryly stated: "Wer verstummt, unterliegt."[14]

A negative influence of the school stage can be seen in a certain polyhistorical eagerness to press as much information as possible into a given dramatic text. Dramas served not only as exercises in theatrical argumentation but also as wide-ranging surveys of the ancient or the exotic world. What could not be fitted into the script found a home in the extensive footnotes that followed. Lohenstein's plays are filled with

learned references, and his footnotes occasionally run longer than the
dramas themselves. Another danger arose from the understandable
desire to ensure every student a role. Weise, who was immediately connected with the school itself, filled the cast of his *Masaniello* with eighty-
two actors. The numerous roles in Lohenstein's *Epicharis* may also
reflect something of this practice: twenty-two individual characters close
the first act with each reciting in succession a single line.

In terms of language the prototypical poetic line of seventeenth-
century German verse, the Alexandrine, carried the day in the drama as
well. This six-foot iambic line with its strong caesura in the middle corresponded admirably well to the antithetical style of the age. Yet, as is
the case with the English heroic couplet, the German Alexandrine can
rapidly become monotonous, and a certain amount of rhetorical finesse
is necessary to carry the sweep of an entire passage. When read carefully,
the opening lines of Gryphius's *Papinian* give an impression of how skillful recitation could enhance the effect of a drama while simultaneously
underscoring its basic theme.[15]

In the choruses, which were known as *Reyen*, as well as in visionary
and mad scenes, writers had considerably greater metric freedom. Both
Gryphius and Lohenstein achieve remarkable effects when they slip the
restraints of the Alexandrine mold. Whereas in the later writers the
Reyen tend to become ever more self-sufficient — the critical importance
of the choruses has been a commonplace since Benjamin's study[16] —
Gryphius keeps these interludes bound relatively closely to the action of
his plays. Even so, some stand out because of their evocative power, as in
the memorable chorus from *Cardenio und Celinde*, where the
treacherous situation of a sinfully tempted soul is described as follows:

> Es ist nicht ohn / wer auff Morast sich wagt /
> (Wie schön er überdeckt mit immer frischen Grase
> Das unter ihm doch reist gleich einem schwachen Glase)
> Hat (doch zu spät) die kühne Lust beklagt
> Er sinckt / wenn ihn nicht Rettung stracks erhält
> Bald über Knie und Brust / in die verschlämmten Pfützen /
> Die Stimme schleust [*schließt*] der Koth / der Stirnen kaltes schwitzen
> Verwischt der Schilff darunter er verfällt.[17]

Later critics of the *Kunstdrama* and of seventeenth-century
literature in general often centered their attacks on precisely those
stylistic excesses that had made the fame of baroque poets in their own

age. While bemoaning the elaborate metaphorical compilations of the *Kunstdrama*, they deplored the seemingly enigmatic tirades of the dramatists as mere bombast or *Schwulst*.[18] There is little doubt that many of their criticisms were justified. Newer studies in rhetoric and emblematics have, nonetheless, done much to make the Silesian authors' dramatic diction more accessible.[19] Studies in emblematic imagery have proved particularly helpful in deciphering the puzzling metaphors that appear from Opitz on through Hallmann and Haugwitz. Drawing upon widely known interpretations of "natural" phenomena, dramatists compressed their images into compact metaphors that, in typical seventeenth-century fashion, were then accumulated in longer series. Hallmann writes:

> den scharffen Adlers-Augen
> Kann nicht der Sonnen-Gluth die edle Krafft aussaugen /
> Dem Salamander raubt die Flamme nicht den Geist;
> Und ob der rothe Blitz mit hundert Keilen schmeiß't /
> Wird doch der Lorber-Baum im minsten nicht verletzet.[20]

As was the case in lyric poetry, such a series depends not so much upon the aptness of its individual images as upon their collective weight. The desired result stems from the total impact of an accumulation of images all pointing in a similar direction.[21]

As a background to the impressive linguistic constructs of the *Kunstdrama*, the Protestant school stage was able to provide considerable technical resources. While the Breslau schools could never hope to obtain the generous financial support the Jesuit stage enjoyed in Munich or Vienna—the 1659 Viennese production of Avancini's *Pietas Victrix* marked a high point in Jesuit staging—their movable scenery and basic stage machinery could create striking visual effects. The diary of Elias Major, rector of the Elisabethanum in Breslau from 1631-69, provides first-hand information on the location, staging, and number of performances during his tenure.[22] The school stage itself was generally divided into a larger front section and a smaller back portion that was concealed by a curtain. Scenes were played alternately on the front and rear stages, and the suspicion seems justified that some occasional weak scenes existed merely to allow a change in the rear stage decorations.[23] Gryphius makes ample use of this stage division in the later version of *Carolus Stuardus*, where the back stage opens during Poleh's mad scene to reveal the imminent fate of the conspirators, the successful crowning of Charles II, etc. Gryphius also uses the central curtain in his *Cardenio* for a stage effect that captures perfectly his major theme, the vanity of worldly existence. Both the delightful garden and the beautiful Olympia undergo a sudden transformation: "Der Schaw-Platz verändert sich plötzlich in eine abscheuliche Einöde / Olympie selbst in ein Todten-Gerippe / welches mit Pfeil und Bogen auff den Cardenio zielet."[24] The later dramatists use the rear stage for similar or even more extravagant effects. In his *Mariamne* Hallmann brings eight successive visionary scenes to torture Herodes's guilty conscience, while Lohenstein includes a fire-spewing altar and an earthquake in his *Sophonisbe*, and in *Agrippina* instructs that a ship break apart and sink into the sea before the eyes of the chorus and the properly astounded audience.

In a century where dramatic artifice permeated both art and architecture, it is hardly surprising that drastic stage effects came to play an important dramatic role. The search for maximum impact in both language and staging was, however, neither merely cheap theatrics nor, as in the case of the wandering troupes, a desire to pack the house. Much of the drastic action of the *Kunstdrama* was, in fact, imbedded in a theoretical context that required and even demanded dramatic extremes.

As is usual, Martin Opitz provides the theoretical touchstone here, and as is equally common, he is transmitting primarily the views of his critical predecessors. Following Scaliger, Opitz defines the subjects of tragedy as "Königlichem Willen / Todtschlägen / verzweiffelungen / Kinder- und Vätermörden / brande / blutschanden / kriege und auffruhr / klagen / heulen / seuffzen und dergleichen."[25] In this passage Opitz accurately anticipates the content of Lohenstein's plays and reinforces the exclusion of middle- and lower-class characters from the tragic realm. A more substantial discussion comes in his introduction to Seneca's *Trojan Women*. Tragedy reflects the fate of those who rely upon *Fortuna*, "die in allem jhren thun und lassen auf das blosse Glück fussen."[26]

As Schings has indicated, Opitz goes on to define tragedy as a means of dealing with the essential unpredictability of the world.[27] Having viewed the "Mißligkeit des Menschlichen Lebens" through tragedy, and having recognized on the intellectual level how the world's snares have entrapped others, people can steel themselves against life's empty allures. With the fall of Troy and its brave defenders still before their eyes, they can learn on the emotional level to bear personal calamities more steadfastly. This repeated exposure to the suffering of others has a double goal: the recognition of human finitude combined with the realization that a person's eternal self cannot be touched by shifts in material fortune. Optiz's theories and Lohenstein's dramas inculcate this lesson through negative examples; the martyr heroes of Gryhpius and of the Jesuits display their *constantia* as a positive model.[28] At its most effective, tragedy could thus provide a certain consolation in the face of the world's apparently inevitable evils.

In order to enhance the "Erstaunen / oder Hermen und Mitleiden"[29] and thereby to increase the impact of the tragic depiction, swings of fate were purposely exaggerated. The farther and swifter the fall of the mighty, the greater the impression. Despite critical caveats banning torture and execution scenes, the striking outrages of the traveling players soon joined the dramatic arsenal of the *Kunstdrama*. Aristotle's mixed hero, who was neither eminently good nor evil, found his place usurped by figures at both extremes. A tragic hero, according to Harsdörffer, "sol ein Exempel seyn aller vollkommenen Tugenden."[30] Gryphius's martyr heroes radiate this purity as their unshakable constancy allows them to triumph in the face of the most extreme cruelties their opponents can conceive. The tyrant meanwhile serves as the exemplary opponent and as the prime warning against the evils of inconstancy. Thus Gryphius's Chach Abas, Lohenstein's Soliman, and Hallmann's Herodes all prove to be stamped from the same mold.

Aside from the Latin productions of the Jesuit stage, Germany was able to offer little in the way of serious drama until the close of the Thirty Years War. The North German pastor Johann Rist (1607-67) composed numerous plays and festival pieces, yet only a few have survived, and Rist was never able to establish a dramatic tradition. As was the case in other genres, it was Martin Opitz (1597-1639) who set the tone for the drama, not so much through original creation as through translation and skillful adaptation. His version of *The Trojan Women* (1625)[31] confirmed Seneca's role as the basic model for German tragedy and provided the stylistic example for subsequent dramatists, including the most prominent poet of the age, Andreas Gryphius.

Over the centuries Andreas Gryphius (1616-64) has dominated critical discussions of seventeenth-century German drama. His preeminence in lyric poetry, his undeniable rhetorical skills—no other author of the age could match Gryphius in the richness and aptness of his metaphorical inventions—and his religious and ethical convictions have ensured his primacy. German baroque drama begins, in essence, with his first tragedy, *Leo Armenius* (1650). Drawing upon his familiarity with both the Dutch and Jesuit stage, Gryphius dramatizes the fall and assassination of the Byzantine emperor Leo Armenius. Leo's role is problematic because his own right to the throne is unclear,[32] but the overtones of martyrdom that accompany his demise point clearly toward the pattern that Gryphius later followed in *Catharina von Georgien* (1657), *Carolus Stuardus* (1657 and 1663), and *Papinianus* (1659). These three dramas all center on a single martyr figure, whether it be a martyr in the conventional sense as with Catharina, a martyr in the political sense as with Charles I, or a martyr in the defense of justice as with Papinian. All three of these characters overcome their earthly attachments and go to their deaths with a certain defiant anticipation. In a gesture reminiscent of Christ, Carolus even turns down offers of aid that might have saved him.[33] While Papinian dies protecting the sanctity of a secular concept (the law), the manner of his death and the proximity of his stance to an exemplary attitude of Christian Neo-Stoicism place him solidly in the martyr's role.

Two dramas in particular, *Catharina* and *Cardenio*, reflect the range of Gryphius's tragedies, *Catharina von Georgien, Oder Bewehrete Beständigkeit*, presents Gryphius's martyr concept in its purest form. Forced to choose between renouncing her religion and marrying the King of Persia or suffering a terrible death, Catharina embraces the latter. Although her torture and execution are related in painful detail — at the middle of the century physical outrages are described rather than shown — her spiritual victory is manifest. The ever-present intriguer figure meets an end befitting his villainy, while the stricken conscience of the wavering tyrant Chach Abas provides a torture far more effective than those visited upon Catharina. In a final apparition, Catharina's charred corpse pronounces the inevitable doom of Chach Abas and his land.

Cardenio und Celinde, Oder Unglücklich Verliebete (1657), makes it clear that Gryphius was both aware of theoretical quibbles and willing to disregard them. In the preface he concedes that his characters are of too low a station for a proper tragedy and that even his language is "nicht viel über die gemeine."[34] The result, however, was a play that became his most popular and most influential tragedy. The seemingly random forces of chance whip the impetuous Cardenio back and forth in his ill-fated love for Olympia,[35] while Celinde burns with a diseased and insatiable passion for Cardenio. In the end, Cardenio and Celinde retire from the world to devote themselves to the contemplation of earthy vanity. Olympia, safely ensconced in a marriage sanctioned by Lutheran theology, reminds Cardenio that her beauty is only transitory. If he were to open her grave three months after her death, "was jhm der Sarg wird zeigen / In den man mich verschloß / das schätz er vor mein eigen."[36] The entire drama thus serves as a *memento mori* and at the same time brings lively dramatic contrast and even tension into a tradition that often tended toward epic narration.

Gryphius's efforts in the area of comedy produced three major works: the social and literary parody *Peter Squentz* (1657), the mock encounter of two braggart soldiers in *Horribilicribrifax* (1663)—here Gryphius also pilloried the dreadful language mixture of the day—and the dual play *Verlibtes Gespenste* and *Die gelibte Dornrose* (1660), wherein individual acts from the two pieces are played alternately. Gryphius's best-known comedy, *Absurda Comica, Oder Herr Peter Squentz*, is a satiric depiction of a village schoolmaster's attempts to play the Pyramus and Thisbe tale before a group of nobility. The actors' reward is ultimately based on the number of errors in their production. Hans Sachs and the dramas of the *Meistersänger* provided the obvious butt for this parody. Despite many similarities, it is almost certain that Gryphius was not directly acquainted with Shakespeare's treatment of the same theme in *A Midsummer Night's Dream*.[37]

Tragedy in the highest style was the sole dramatic concern of Daniel Casper von Lohenstein (1635–83). The encyclopedic interests of this Breslau official are reflected in the learned discourses he appended to the notes following his dramas. Trained in the law, Lohenstein filled his footnotes with sources and commentaries lined up like legal precedents. In both dramatic form and diction, Lohenstein was clearly indebted to Gryphius, even though he relied less on Dutch models and turned more toward French and classical sources.[38] What emerged from this apparently rather scholarly approach was some of the most extreme dramatic action of an age filled with extremities.

Lohenstein's first drama, *Ibrahim Bassa* (1653), is usually lumped together with his last production, *Ibrahim Sultan* (1673), under the rubric of "Turkish" dramas. His "Roman" tragedies, *Agrippina* and *Epicharis* (both 1665), are flanked by his "African" plays, *Cleopatra* (1661 and 1680) and *Sophonisbe* (1680).[39] Lohenstein's secular treatment of his subjects clearly distinguishes him from his elder colleague. Gryphius's programmatic subtitles already reflect transcendent values; Lohenstein's plays bear only the names of their protagonists. With the disappearance of the transcendent security that had informed Gryphius's heroes, one finds Lohenstein's protagonists playing vigorously active roles. Passive endurance fades from the scene as his characters employ their full resources of power and cunning to maintain themselves and their positions.[40]

Immediate political power becomes a primary concern, and a new figure, the domineering female protagonist, emerges at the center of the struggles. The *Machtweib* joins the tyrant and the martyr as a staple dramatic figure. Feminine beauty incites the dramatic action in all six plays, and as Just has pointed out, eros mingles with politics to produce the dramas' dominant motivating forces.[41] As with Gryphius's characters, figures subject to their passions—Nero, Masanissa, Ibrahim Sultan—are seen as weak or tyrannical, while exemplary characters— Augustus, Scipio—bear the torch of reason. Moving between these two poles are the female characters, whose complexity and puzzling shifts have posed a major problem for critics. Sophonisbe, for example, shifts her allegiances back and forth several times between her husband Syphax and the conquering Masanissa, and interpretations of her position have ranged from attributions of sheer political opportunism to views of her as victimized by the overriding forces of history or even of fate itself, her case being only a single stage in the inevitable transfer of world power from Africa and Rome to Austria.[42]

Lohenstein's critical reputation still suffers from the attacks of eighteenth-century critics who took little pleasure in the abstruse and often enigmatic metaphors that fill his verse. For the nineteenth century, worse still were the extreme violence and overt sexuality permeating his plays. Both Cleopatra and Sophonisbe deliberately employ their sexual attraction as a weapon in their struggles. Agrippina, the mother of Nero, attempts to consolidate her waning power by seducing her emperor son. Having brought out the entire arsenal of petrarchistic and emblematic imagery, along with a generous display of her natural charms, she fails only at the last moment because of an untimely intrusion. Nero subsequently turns upon his mother and has her assassinated, whereupon he returns to view her corpse with an unsettling mixture of satisfaction and desire. In the companion piece *Epicharis*, which was often played on alternate days, Lohenstein argues the case for and against tyrannicide. Whereas Gryphius had rejected the possibility of harming a figure who was a "ruler by divine right," Lohenstein has Epicharis lead the conspiracy against Nero and ultimately die as a martyr for her political goals. The final acts of the play bring what must be the most exhaustive catalogue of torture and executions in all of seventeenth-century literature.

Critical interest in Lohenstein has grown rapidly in recent years, and the volume of material dealing with his works has begun to approach that treating the somewhat more predictable Gryphis. Johann Christian Hallmann (1640-1704)? will most probably not experience a similar revival. Although his name is usually mentioned primarily in reference to the decline of the *Kunstdrama*, Hallmann was quite productive, and the forthcoming critical edition will allow a more highly differentiated view of his achievements.[43] His *Mariamne* (1670) still has something of the dynamic force of the earlier tradition, but Hallmann's talent is derivative and cannot consistently match the linguistic or intellectual vigor of his predecessors. By increasing the variety of nondramatic elements in his plays—musical interludes, ballet, fireworks, etc.—Hallmann undoubtedly responded to the tastes of his time but also contributed thereby to the dissolution of the austere form Gryphius had initiated. Sadly enough, by the end of the century Hallmann was reduced to rewriting his plays into a more popular operatic form.[44]

August Adolf von Haugwitz (1645–1706) clearly deserves his reputation as the weakest writer working in the tradition of the *Kunstdrama*. His *Maria Stuarda* (1683) and his *Soliman* (1684) are only pale reflections of his predecessors' achievements.[45] Haugwitz's humdrum verse offers little excitement, and his dramatic efforts merely underscore the increasing exhaustion of the *Kunstdrama* as the century drew to its close.

On a different artistic level, Christian Weise (1642–1708), rector of the gymnasium in Zittau, exemplifies both the strengths and weaknesses of the school stage in its most immediate sense. Separated from Gryphius and Lohenstein by both interests and inclination, Weise anticipates the spirit of the approaching Enlightenment as the grand dramatic themes of the high baroque give way to a more direct pedagogical interest in educating the "political man," the well-balanced and capable official. Weise's sixty-one dramas testify to the heavy demands on his creative talents; each year he wrote and produced a biblical, a historical, and a "free" drama, usually a comedy, which were performed on three successive days.[46] His use of prose provides a distinct break with the aesthetic demands of the *Kunstdrama*, as does his reintroduction of the clown, *Pickelhering*. Even his tragedy *Masaniello* (1684) includes a comic figure, a mixture of genres that would have been unacceptable to earlier theoreticians and practitioners alike. Weise's greatest dramatic gift lay in the writing of comedy. His reworking of the Peter Squentz theme in *Tobias und die Schwalbe* (1682) and his *Bäurischer Machiavellus* (1679) can still be read with pleasure.

Serious drama becomes a rare commodity toward the end of the century. One of the true creative talents of the era, Christian Reuter (b.1665) is best known for his student comedies *Die Ehrliche Frau zu Plißine* (1695) and *Frau Schlampampe* (1696), both of which are based on a feud he had started with his landlady during his Leipzig university days.[47] Despite his clear indebtedness to Molière, Reuter fills his plays with local color. His lusty prose and sharp wit shine in individual scenes, but overall his dramas tend to the looser forms of the *Wanderbühne*.

Were it not for the ever-popular troupes of traveling actors and the healthy and flourishing operatic scene,[48] the German theatrical landscape around 1700 would have been extremely barren. Both the themes and the linguistic pomp of Gryphius and Lohenstein had fallen on hard times and soon would be out of favor entirely. Gottsched tells of a 1724 conversation with the director of a traveling troupe who stated that they would not play Gryphius because no one would attend a play in verse and certainly not a play without a clown. What the troupe presented, instead of the outmoded *Kunstdrama,* were: "Lauter schwülstige und mit Harlekins Lustbarkeiten untermengte Haupt- und Staatsaktionen, lauter unnatürliche Romanstreiche und Liebesverwirrungen, lauter pöbelhafte Fratzen und Zoten . . ."[49] Gottsched also emphasizes that this was one of the better companies of the day.

The richness and depth that German drama offered shortly after the middle of the seventeenth century had thus fallen into a hopelessly mixed and formless sprawl. Gottsched's French-oriented theatrical reforms were undoubtedly necessary. Yet in retrospect it becomes evident that a serious, artistically aware German drama first found its tongue in the seventeenth century. In the rapidly approaching age of Goethe, German vernacular drama was soon to find its full and authentic voice.

NOTES

1. See Heinz Kindermann, *Das Theater der Antike und des Mittelalters*, vol. I of *Theatergeschichte Europas* (Salzburg: Otto Müller, 1966), pp. 243-73.

2. C. Kaulfuß-Diesch, "Schuldrama," *Reallexikon der deutschen Literaturgeschichte* (1928-29).

3. On the English players see the article, "The English Comedians in Germany," by Gerhart Hoffmeister in this volume.

4. For the general background of the Jesuit stage see Willi Flemming, *Geschichte des Jesuitentheaters in den Landen deutscher Zunge* (Berlin: Gesellschaft für Theatergeschichte, 1932), and the recent study by Jean-Marie Valentin, *Le Théâtre des Jesuites dans les pays de langue allemande (1554-1680)*, 3 vols. (Bern and Frankfurt a.M.: Lang, 1978).

5. Willi Flemming established this term in the first volume of his basic six-volume edition of German baroque drama: *Das schlesische Kunstdrama,*

Deutsche Literatur in Entwicklungsreihen, Reihe Barock, *Barockdrama*, I (Leipzig: Reclam, 1930), 10–54. Erik Lunding followed suit in *Das schlesische Kunstdrama: Eine Darstellung und Deutung* (Copenhagen: Haase, 1940).

6. See, for example, the *Papinian* version contained in vol. III of Flemming's series—*Das Schauspiel der Wanderbühne* (Leipzig: Reclam, 1931), pp. 138–201.

7. On the integration of theater and rhetorical training see Wilfried Barner, *Barockrhetorik: Untersuchungen zu ihren geschichtlichen Grundlagen* (Tübingen: Niemeyer, 1970), pp. 291–302. Also of interest is the section "Schule und Literatur" in *Stadt-Schule-Universität-Buchwesen und die deutsche Literatur im 17. Jahrhundert*, ed. Albrecht Schöne (München: Beck, 1976), pp. 173–310.

8. See Max Hippe, "Aus dem Tagebuch eines Breslauer Schulmannes im siebzehnten Jahrhundert," *Zeitschrift des Vereins für Geschichte und Altertum Schlesiens*, 36 (1901), 159–42, and Gerhard Spellerberg, "Szenare zu den Breslauer Aufführungen Gryphischer Trauerspiele," *Daphnis*, 7 (1978), 235–65.

9. Georg Philipp Harsdörffer, *Poetischen Trichters zweiter Theil* (1648; rpt. Hildesheim and New York: Olms, 1971), p. 81.

10. Günter Skopnik—*Das Straßburger Schultheater, sein Spielplan und seine Bühne*, Schriften des wiss. Instituts der Elsaß-Lothringer im Reich an der Univ. Frankfurt, N.F. 13 (Frankfurt a.M., 1935)—brings the most detailed study of this stage.

11. See Paul Stachel's classic study, *Seneca und das deutsche Renaissancedrama: Studien zur Literatur- und Stilgeschichte des 16. und 17. Jahrhunderts*, Palaestra, 46 (Berlin: Mayer und Müller, 1907).

12. Martin Opitz, *Buch von der Deutschen Poeterey*, ed. Richard Alewyn (Tübingen: Niemeyer, 1936), p. 32.

13. Harsdörffer, p. 81.

14. Albrecht Schöne, *Emblematik und Drama im Zeitalter des Barock*, 2nd ed. (München: Beck, 1968), p. 151.

15. Andreas Gryphius, *Trauerspiele*, I, ed. Hugh Powell, vol. IV of *Gesamtausgabe der deutschsprachigen Werke* (Tübingen: Niemeyer, 1964), 171.

16. Walter Benjamin led the way in emphasizing the significance of the *Reyen* in his *Ursprung des deutschen Trauerspiels* (1928; rpt. Frankfurt a.M.: Suhrkamp, 1972).

17. Gryphius, *Werke*, V, 131.

18. Manfred Windfuhr, *Die barocke Bildlichkeit und ihre Kritiker: Stilhaltungen in der deutschen Literatur des 17. und 18. Jahrhunderts* (Stuttgart: Metzler, 1966), pp. 339–467.

19. Two of the best works on baroque rhetorical practices are by Barner (see note 7) and by Joachim Dyck, *Ticht-Kunst: Deutsche Barockpoetik und rhetorische Tradition*, Ars poetica, 1 (Bad Homburg: Gehlen, 1966). For

further literature on emblematics see the article by Peter Daly in this volume.

20. Schöne quotes this prime example from *Theodoricus* in his *Emblematik*, p. 94 (see note 14).

21. Karl Otto Conrady catalogues this and similar techniques for baroque lyric in his *Lateinische Dichtungstradition und deutsche Lyrik des 17. Jahrhunderts* (Bonn: Bouvier, 1962).

22. The relevant passages are cited by Hippe (see note 8). For a more general view of staging and stage practices, see Heinz Kindermann, "Protestantisches Schultheater," in his *Theatergeschichte Europas*, III, 408-40.

23. Willi Flemming, *Andreas Gryphius und die Bühne* (Halle: Niemeyer, 1921), pp. 127-314.

24. Gryphius, *Werke*, V, 148.

25. Opitz, *Poeterey*, p. 20.

26. Martin Opitz, *Weltliche Poemata*, I, ed. Erich Trunz (Tübingen: Niemeyer, 1967), 314-15.

27. Hans-Jürgen Schings, "Consolatio tragoediae: Zur Theorie des barocken Trauerspiels," in *Deutsche Dramentheorien*, ed. Reinhold Grimm (Frankfurt a.M.: Athenäum, 1971), I, 1-44.

28. Ibid., pp. 25-28. For the historical development of tragic theory in Germany and particularly during the baroque era, see David E. R. George, *Deutsche Tragödientheorien vom Mittelalter bis zu Lessing: Texte und Kommentare* (München: Beck, 1972), pp. 85-132.

29. Harsdörffer (see note 9, above), p. 83.

30. Harsdörffer, p. 84.

31. Dates given for the dramas are those of the first published version. On Opitz's translation of *Antigone* see the standard essay by Richard Alewyn, *Vorbarocker Klassizismus und griechische Tragödie: Analyse der Antigone-Übersetzung des Martin Opitz* 1926; rpt. Darmstadt: Wissenschaftliche Buchgesellschaft, 1962).

32. Cf. Gerhard Kaiser's discussion of *Leo Arminius* in his extremely useful edition, *Die Dramen des Andreas Gryphius: Eine Sammlung von Einzelinterpretationen* (Stuttgart: Metzler, 1968), pp. 3-34. For general literature on Gryphius see Eberhard Mannack, *Andreas Gryphius*, Sammlung Metzler, 76 (Stuttgart: Metzler, 1968).

33. Albrecht Schöne, "Carolus Stuardus," in *Die Dramen des Andreas Gryphius: Eine Sammlung von Einzelinterpretationen* (Stuttgart: Metzler, 1968), ed. Gerhard Kaiser, pp. 149-50. Schöne makes a strong case in this article for the "post-figural" identification of Carolus Stuardus with Christ. See also his *Säkularisation als sprachbildende Kraft: Studien zur Dichtung deutscher Pfarrersöhne*, 2nd ed. (Göttingen: Vandenhoeck und Ruprecht, 1968).

34. Gryphius, *Werke*, V, 99.

35. Hans Jürgen Schings emphasizes the role of Providence in Gryphius's

thought in *Die patristische und stoische Tradition bei Andreas Gryphius: Untersuchungen zu den Dissertationes funebres und Trauerspielen* (Köln and Graz: Böhlau, 1966). Hans Turk follows his lead in *Die Dramen des Andreas Gryphius*, ed. Gerhard Kaiser, pp. 73-116 (note 33, above). See also Hans Wagener's and Peter Skrine's interpretations of *Cardenio* in this volume.

36. Gryphius, *Werke*, V, p. 166.

37. Eberhard Mannack, "Andreas Gryphius' Lustspiele — ihre Herkunft, ihre Motive und ihre Entwicklung," *Euphorion*, 58 (1964), 2.

38. See above all Bernhard Asmuth, *Lohenstein und Tacitus: Eine quellenkritische Interpretation der Nero-Tragödien und des Arminius-Romans* (Stuttgart: Metzler, 1971).

39. Klaus Günther Just edited the plays in this order (*Türkische Trauerspiele, Römische Trauerspiele, Afrikanische Trauerspiele*) as vols. 292-94 of the Bibliothek des literarischen Vereins in Stuttgart (Stuttgart: Hiersemann, 1953-57).

40. Cf. the literature survey in Bernhard Asmuth's *Daniel Casper von Lohenstein*, Sammlung Metzler, 75 (Stuttgart, Metzler, 1971), pp. 24-51.

41. Klaus Günther Just, *Die Trauerspiele Lohensteins: Versuch einer Interpretation* (Berlin: Erich Schmidt, 1961).

42. The major positions in this debate are marked by Wolfgang Kayser, "Lohensteins Sophonisbe als geschichtliche Tragödie," *Germanisch-Romanische Monatsschrift*, 29 (1941), 20-39, and by Rolf Tarot, "Lohensteins *Sophonisbe*," *Euphorion*, 57 (1963), 72-96. Gerhard Spellerberg brings the strongest support for the fate theory in *Verhängnis und Geschichte: Untersuchungen zu den Trauerspielen und dem "Arminius"-Roman Daniel Caspers von Lohenstein* (Bad Homburg: Gehlen, 1970).

43. Johann Christian Hallmann, *Sämtliche Werke*, ed. Gerhard Spellerberg (Berlin: de Gruyter, 1975 ff.).

44. Johann Christian Hallmann, *Mariamne*, ed. Gerhard Spellerberg (Stuttgart: Reclam, 1973), pp. 178-85.

45. The only modern edition of a Haugwitz drama is that of Robert Heitner: Adolf August von Haugwitz, *Schuldige Unschuld oder Maria Stuarda* (Bern and Frankfurt a.M.: Lang, 1974).

46. Cf. Walther Eggert, *Christian Weise und seine Bühne* (Berlin and Leipzig: de Gruyter, 1935) and the more recent study by Gotthardt Frühsorge, *Der politische Körper: Zum Begriff des Politischen im 17. Jahrhundert und in den Romanen Christian Weises* (Stuttgart: Metzler, 1974). See also the new Weise edition, Christian Weise, *Sämtliche Werke*, ed. John D. Lindberg (Berlin: de Gruyter, 1971 ff.).

47. For literature on Reuter see Wolfgang Hecht, *Christian Reuter*, Sammlung Metzler, 46 (Stuttgart: Metzler, 1966).

48. Cf. the immense popularity of Heinrich Postel (1658-1705) and the Hamburg opera; see Gloria Flaherty, *Opera in the Development of German*

Critical Thought (Princeton, N.J.: Princeton University Press, 1978), pp. 10-65.

49. Johann Christoph Gottsched, *Sterbender Cato: Ein Trauerspiel,* 10th ed. (Leipzig: Teubner, 1757), sig. A3^V.

SELECTED BIBLIOGRAPHY

Primary Sources

Flemming, Willi, ed. *Barockdrama.* 6 vols. Deutsche Literatur in Entwicklungsreihen. Reihe Barock. Leipzig: Reclam, 1930-33.
Gryphius, Andreas. *Gesamtausgabe der deutschsprachigen Werke.* Marian Szyrocki and Hugh Powell, eds. 8 vols. Tübingen: Niemeyer, 1963-72.
Hallmann, Johann Christian. *Sämtliche Werke.* Gerhard Spellerberg, ed. Berlin: de Gruyter, 1975 ff.
Lohenstein, Daniel Casper von. *Türkische Trauerspiele; Römische Trauerspiele; Afrikanische Trauerspiele.* Klaus Günther Just, ed. Bibliothek des literarischen Vereins in Stuttgart, 292-94. Stuttgart: Hiersemann, 1953-57.

Secondary Literature

In addition to the standard bibliographic aids three works are particularly useful for German baroque drama and dramatists:

Dünnhaupt, Gerhard. *Bibliographisches Handbuch der Barockliteratur.* Stuttgart: Hiersemann, 1980.
Gabel, Gernot Uwe. *Drama und Theater des deutschen Barock: eine Handbibliographie der Sekundärliteratur.* Hamburg: n.p., 1974.
Heiduk, Franz. "Bilbliographischer Abriß." In Erdwin Neumeister, *De poetis germanicis.* Franz Heiduk, ed. Bern and München: Francke, 1978, pp. 271-504.

Alewyn, Richard. *Vorbarocker Klassizismus und griechische Tragödie: Analyse der Antigone-Übersetzung des Martin Opitz.* 1926. Rpt. Darmstadt: Wissenschaftliche Buchgesellschaft, 1962.
Asmuth, Bernhard. *Daniel Casper von Lohenstein.* Sammlung Metzler, 75. Stuttgart: Metzler, 1971.
———. *Lohenstein und Tacitus: Eine quellenkritische Interpretation der Nero-Tragödien und des Arminius-Romans.* Stuttgart: Metzler, 1971.
Barner, Wilfried. *Barockrhetorik: Untersuchungen zu ihren geschichtlichen Grundlagen.* Tübingen: Niemeyer, 1970.
Benjamin, Walter. *Ursprung des deutschen Trauerspiels.* 1928. Rpt. Frankfurt a.M.: Suhrkamp, 1969 and 1972.

Dyck, Joachim. *Ticht-Kunst: Deutsche Barockpoetik und rhetorische Tradition. Ars poetica*, 1. Bad Homburg: Gehlen, 1966.

Flemming, Willi. *Andreas Gryphius und die Bühne*. Halle: Niemeyer, 1921.

———. *Andreas Gryphius: Eine Monographie*. Stuttgart, Kohlhammer, 1965.

Gillespie, Gerald. *Daniel Casper von Lohenstein's Historical Tragedies*. Columbus: Ohio State University Press, 1965.

Hecht, Wolfgang. *Christian Reuter*. Sammlung Metzler, 46. Stuttgart: Metzler, 1966.

Heckmann, Herbert. *Elemente des barocken Trauerspiels: Am Beispiel des "Papinian" von Andreas Gryphius*. Darmstadt: Gentner, 1959.

Hink, Walter. *Das deutsche Lustspiel des 17. und 18. Jahrhunderts und die italienische Komödie*. Stuttgart: Metzler, 1965.

Just, Klaus Günther. *Die Trauerspiele Lohensteins: Versuch einer Interpretation*. Berlin: Erich Schmidt, 1961.

Kaiser, Gerhard, ed. *Die Dramen des Andreas Gryphius: Eine Sammlung von Einzelinterpretationen*. Stuttgart: Metzler, 1968.

Kindermann, Heinz. *Das Theater der Barockzeit*. Vol. III of *Theatergeschichte Europas*. Salzburg: Otto Müller, 1967.

Lunding, Erik. *Das schlesische Kunstdrama: Eine Darstellung und Deutung*. Copenhagen: Haase, 1940.

Mannack, Eberhard. *Andreas Gryphius*. Sammlung Metzler, 76. Stuttgart: Metzler, 1968.

Schings, Hans-Jürgen. *Die patristische und stoische Tradition bei Andreas Gryphius: Untersuchungen zu den Dissertationes funebres und Trauerspielen*. Köln and Graz: Böhlau, 1966.

———. "Consolatio tragoediae: Zur Theorie des barocken Trauerspiels." In *Deutsche Dramentheorien*, Reinhold Grimm, ed. Frankfurt a.M.: Athenäum, 1971.

Schöne, Albrecht. *Emblematik und Drama im Zeitalter des Barock*. 2nd ed. München: Beck, 1968.

———. ed. *Stadt-Schule-Universität-Buchwesen und die deutsche Literatur im 17. Jahrhundert*. München: Beck, 1976.

Stachel, Paul. *Seneca und das deutsche Renaissancedrama: Studien zur Literatur- und Stilgeschichte des 16. und 17. Jahrhunderts*. Palaestra, 46. Berlin: Mayer und Müller, 1907.

Skopnik, Günter. *Das Straßburger Schultheater, sein Spielplan und seine Bühne*. Schriften des wiss. Instituts der Elsaß-Lothringer im Reich an der Univ. Frankfurt, N.F. 13. Frankfurt a.M., 1935.

Szarota, Elida Maria. *Künstler, Grübler und Rebellen: Studien zum europäischen Märtyrerdrama des 17. Jahrhunderts*. Bern and München: Francke, 1967.

———. *Geschichte, Politik und Gesellschaft im Drama des 17. Jahrhunderts*. Bern and München: Francke, 1976.

Szyrocki, Marian. *Andreas Gryphius: Sein Leben und Werk*. Tübingen: Niemeyer, 1964.

Wentzlaff-Eggebert, Friedrich-Wilhelm. "Die deutsche Barocktragödie: Zur Funktion von 'Glaube' und 'Vernunft' im Drama des 17. Jahrhunderts." In *Formkräfte der deutschen Dichtung vom Barock bis zur Gegenwart*. Hans Steffen, ed. Göttingen: Vandenhoeck, 1963, pp. 5-20.

Windfuhr, Manfred. *Die barocke Bildlichkeit und ihre Kritiker: Stilhaltungen in der deutschen Literatur des 17. und 18. Jahrhunderts*. Stuttgart: Metzler, 1966.

20

*The Tradition of the Baroque**

Alberto Martino

Continuity or discontinuity in the tradition of the baroque? Ever since the question was first posed by literary historians both theses have had their supporters, and both with plausible arguments. For it is sufficient to consider one or another of the concepts of poetic or rhetorical theory, one group or another of stylistic elements, certain authors rather than others, one literary genre as opposed to another, in order to reach quite opposite conclusions. The result of one's analysis is already present in the choice of concepts, stylistic phenomena, authors, and texts to be examined. The subjectiveness of this choice is increased by the general uncertainty as to what exactly is meant by the baroque in literature and what are its chronological delimitations. Systematic contributions to the history of the reception of seventeenth-century writers are few, and this inevitably leads to a generalization of results obtained from the limited documentary material subjectively selected.

When referred, moreover, to the tradition of the whole of literary baroque, the continuity-discontinuity alternative is meaningless. No literary movement, especially one that has lasted all of a century, disappears overnight. No new literary movement is completely new, for even the most revolutionary is linked to the one before in numberless ways. But it is true also that no literary movement endures, in its totality, without change. And then, one might ask, continuity or discontinuity in terms of whom? The poets and writers? The reading public? (Which?) Critical and

*Translated from the Italian by Arthur Whellens.

literary historians? How can the reactions of such different "consumers" of a work of literature be homogeneous and synchronous? In order to avoid the vicious circle of proving with appositely selected documents a thesis chosen a priori, and at the same time to avoid the danger of discovering self-evident truths, we must approach the problem from the outside. The problem, that is, must be seen in the light of an analysis of the numerous extraliterary phenomena linked to the appearance of baroque poetry and its reception by the contemporary public. For the survival of the baroque tradition and the extent of this survival must depend largely on the stability and invariability of these phenomena and on the degree to which they are changed and transformed.

Baroque "poetry of art" (*Kunstdichtung*) is something of a hothouse flower, produced by complex processes of transformation and restructuring in society and by deep cultural "chemistry."[1]

The development of territorial principalities and of the modern absolute state—sovereign and centralizing—was accompanied by the formation of a large and influential bureaucracy, to which were given, as the feudal system was dismantled, ever greater duties in administration, finance, the law, and diplomacy. The prince recruited the members of this bureaucracy from the patrician and middle classes for two reasons: first, a question of political prudence—the nobles could certainly not be expected to carry out honestly and zealously a policy which deprived their class of authority; second, because for the most part only the patrician and middle classes, which had an uninterrupted tradition of strict university studies, could provide qualified officials and in particular the doctors of Roman law who were to form the ruling class of the new state bureaucracy.

The recruitment of the upper echelons of the state administration from the patrician and middle classes, and at times from more humble ones, gave rise to great social mobility and paved the way for a fusion of noble culture with the humanistic and late-humanistic culture of the learned, and for social integration between the nobility and the middle-class intelligentsia. The nobles found themselves deprived of the right of feud and therefore of political power, impoverished by the devaluation of the revenue from the land, and replaced by jurists in the most important positions in the court and territorial administration. So to stem the influence of the middle-class intelligentsia and in order not to be completely excluded from the exercise of power and from well-paid administrative posts, they were forced to frequent the schools and universities, and here they assimilated the ideals of Roman law and middle-class humanism. For their part, the middle-class intellectuals, appointed for life by the prince (up to about the mid-sixteenth century jurists were normally engaged for short periods as consultants on specific legal questions, or to carry out certain administrative duties and diplomatic missions), took up permanent residence at court, where they came into contact with the values of the chivalric-noble tradition.

The balance between counselors of middle-class origin and those of noble origin was reestablished thanks to the gradual penetration of nobles with a university training in law into the Councils of State. The *Landstände** imposed on the princes the "law of indigenousness," that is, the obligation to assign the most important posts in the territorial administration to officials born in the territory and not belonging to the lower classes. Thus there was formed a community of interests between middle-class officials and noble officials, and with this the beginning of a cooperation between bureaucracy and the nobles and therefore a process of social integration and uniformity.

This process, aided by the bestowal of noble titles on middle-class officials and by their marriages with daughters of the old aristocracy, this meeting between the chivalric, courtly culture of the feudal nobility and the humanistic or late-humanistic culture of the learned class, already begun in the schools and universities, took place at court. The court, however, did not accept the earlier cultural traditions passively; it rooted out of the humanistic culture all "democratic" and middle-class elements and profoundly transformed the chivalric, courtly culture, putting in place of the ideal of liberty and freedom of action that of absolute submission to the prince. In this way a culture was formed in which humanistic and courtly ideals were indeed present as constituent elements, but molded and suited to the political needs of the court, the center of power.

This court culture (though the real creator was, in the long run, the prince) was produced by an elite of officials, of both noble and middle-class origin, possessing the same rhetorical and legal training and the same familiarity with history and philology. Its function was to extol the aristocratic, courtly values (first and foremost "courtesy," which includes them all), and to justify, glorify, and represent the sacred and absolute nature of power. The same function was performed by poetry, which too was produced to a large degree by officials of the imperial, territorial, or

---

*Feudal body or provincial diet, since the 1200s representing knights, clergy, towns, etc.

court bureaucracy with a legal background. This court or municipal bureaucracy—together with those sectors of the nobility, patriciate, or middle class that attended court or that had frequented the grammar schools or *Ritterakademien** and the universities—formed the reading public of baroque poetry. The profound cultural, spiritual, and social homogeneity that existed between author and public accounts for those peculiarities of style and contents which make baroque poetry understandable for the initiated and obscure for the common reader.

Baroque poets wrote for a public able to decipher cryptograms, anagrams, and chronograms, understand the niceties of recondite emblematic allusions, appreciate complicated allegories, hyperboles, conceits, far-fetched comparisons, unusual metaphors, and the sapient use of rhetorical figures and images; a public able to take pleasure in virtuosities of language and lexical affectation, to catch the references to meters, forms, tropes, and topoi of Greek and Latin poetry, and of the verse of Petrarch and Marino; an audience that would enjoy learned digressions and understand the many references to mythology, history, and philosophy; that could find its way through the intricate mazes of the stories narrated and participate in stage disputations and the casuistry of passions; a public that could recognize behind the ancient masks their contemporaries and in exotic tales the happenings of the court they knew so well; a public with a taste for the rhetorical and the emblematic—in short, a learned poetry for a learned audience centered ideally round the court: such is baroque poetry.

The ideal of polymathy (much learning), common to writers and public and linked to a cultural training based on rhetoric, was derived from the desire of the literati to form a caste that would rise above the common people, above the middle class, and approach the nobility. Only learning could legitimize the desire for an elite and constitute the shibboleth of the *nobilitas litteraria*, which they declared equal, if not superior, to the nobility of blood. The authors of the seventeenth century stated quite openly that they wrote not for the ordinary, unlearned man, but for a cultural and aristocratic elite.

As long as the expansion of the administration, caused by the formation of territorial states and of the absolute state, maintained elevated social mobility and allowed almost all the middle-class intelligentsia to be absorbed into the ruling classes, then poetry main-

---

*Schools for young noblemen, 1500s to 1800s.

tained its role as a transmitter of learning and as representation and glorification of the absolute power of the prince, and maintained, too, its formal rhetorical and decorative connotation.

But toward the end of the seventeenth century and the beginning of the eighteenth, social mobility (as far as the intellectual elite is concerned) came to an almost complete halt. The reasons for this were the regression of the bureaucracy, the process by which the absolute state became more and more aristocratic (now only the nobles could reach the highest posts in the administration), and the progressive impenetrability of the upper class, which was now becoming a caste to itself. The intelligentsia—forced out of the positions of power, threatened with unemployment, relegated to inferior posts in the administration, and deprived of former privileges (for example, university graduates were no longer considered on a par with nobles)—reacted by questioning the constituted authority and its culture, by embracing the ideals and culture of the middle classes (which in the eighteenth century were in great numerical and economic expansion), and by developing typically middle-class ideologies (illuminism, Pietism, sentimentalism).[2]

In literature, the middle-class intellectuals advocated writing works with moralizing and consolatory contents, representations of private, everyday life, so as to interest the readers of the rising middle class, which was now seen as the reading public par excellence. Spontaneity and simplicity of form, clarity and perspicuity of style and language were what the writer must first of all aim at. Truth, nature, and reason were affirmed as constituting the "beautiful" in poetry. The books of rhetoric written for schools and universities condemned the use of emblems, conceits, wit, hieroglyphics, flowers of speech, and realia. They taught a style devoid of all affectation and embellishment, extremely simple and ordered, as concrete and spontaneous as the language used in everyday life. The "moral reviews"—*Moralische Wochenschriften*)—of immeasurable importance in the formation of the reading public in the mid-eighteenth century—propagated and promoted the same stylistic ideals, attacking the "gothic" style of the writers of the so-called second Silesian school, considered to be the essence of bad taste and characterized by the names of "Bombast," "Galimathias," "Phöbus," and "Schwulst." Poetic theories were founded on the axiom that poetry must imitate Nature, and that Beauty, Truth, Reason, and Nature are one. The Pietists, who believed that language, style, and poetry were spontaneous expressions of feeling, played an important part in discrediting the artificial, cerebral poetry of the baroque.

The passage of the intelligentsia from pro-aristocratic to pro-
middle-class positions caused a complete reversal of the aesthetic, poetic,
and stylistic norms that regulated the production and reception of a
work of art. It is clear that readers initiated by illuministic manuals of
rhetoric into the cult of simplicity and linguistic transparency, and
taught by the Pietists to look upon all elaborateness and linguistic artifice as an expression of spiritual emptiness and insincerity, were no
longer able to appreciate a style overburdened with ornament, artifice,
and syntactic complexities. To the subjective inability to appreciate
baroque language was added the objective impossibility of deciphering
it, owing to a lack of knowledge of baroque rhetoric, particularly of
emblems, the most characteristic element of the baroque poetic code
(435 emblem books were published in Germany in the century of baroque, that is, between 1618 and 1723; from 1732 to 1800 only 71).

One may ask why the ruling class, the heir of the class formed in the
period of great social mobility (1500-1690) by the intermixing of the
feudal nobility with the intellectuals, did nothing to save a literature
which it had itself produced and which was the expression of its ideals. In
order to justify its monopolization of power (taking advantage of the fact
that the absolute state was becoming more and more aristocratic), and in
order to increase its social prestige, the ruling class had widened to the
utmost the gap between itself and the other classes, not only by refusing
further "misalliances" and isolating itself in the manner of a caste, but
also by exaggerating its aristocratic tendencies, surrounding itself with
luxury and adopting the customs, language, and culture of France. In
the period from 1690 to 1770 the ruling class spoke French, wrote in
French, and read, almost exclusively, French works or works in French
translation. German literature and culture were scorned and ignored.
The days were long gone when ruling princes and dukes, along with
princes, counts, and barons of the Empire and the lower nobility col-
laborated with the middle-class intelligentsia in developing German
language and literature. It is only in the field of music and the plastic
and figurative arts that the upper aristocracy, the nobles, and the senior
clery continued to act as *Kunstträger* (tastemaker). It is no coincidence
that in these arts, especially in architecture, the baroque continued to
flourish and indeed reached its height in the mid-eighteenth century,
that is, in the period of the birth and development of middle-class
literature.

Although the overturning of aesthetic ideals and poetic norms occurred quite quickly (it was anticipated in attacks by Christian Weise,

Curiöse Gedanken von Teutschen Briefen, 1691, by Gotthard Heidegger in *Mythoscopia romantica*, 1698, and by Christian Wernike in *Überschriffte*, 1697, 1701, but actually took place in the brief lapse of time between the appearance of *Discourse der Mahlern*, 1721-23, and the publication of *Critische Dichtkunst*, 1730, by Gottsched), the rejection of the baroque literary tradition by the public and the poets themselves was progressive and much less radical. In the first place, the disappearance of the public which had been the "receiver" of baroque poetry was gradual, as was gradual the appearance of the new middle-class reading public, formed by the stylistic ideals of the Enlightenment. Furthermore, though it was possible, owing to the social changes described above, to deny almost overnight the value of baroque poetry, to affirm new aesthetic principles, and to dictate new poetic norms, it was not so easy to create a literature in keeping with the new principles and norms, capable of taking the place of baroque and offering valid models to be imitated by the new generations of poets.

That the baroque tradition was still flourishing some decades after its condemnation by the literary critics is proved by the many re-editions of some of the most representative baroque writers. All the works of Lohenstein were republished—some in several editions—between 1701 and 1748, the year in which the publisher Johann George Löwe even attempted to launch a complete edition of the works of the author of *Arminius* (only one volume of the *Sämmtliche Poetische Schriften* planned by Löwe appeared). Editions of the *Asiatische Banise* by Heinrich Anshelm von Zigler und Kliphausen were published in 1707, 1716, 1721, 1728, 1733, 1738, 1753, and 1764. To this work, which numbered among its readers Goethe and Lessing, Jung-Stilling and Karl Philipp Moritz, a best-selling sequel was written by Johann Georg Hamann (five editions between 1724 and 1766). The seven volumes of the famous collection of baroque poetry, the so-called *Neukirchsche Sammlung* (1695-1727) were republished altogether about twenty times between 1706 and 1754. In 1728 and 1744 there were new editions of *Herkules und Valiska* (1659-1660) by Andreas Heinrich Bucholtz, which Jung-Stilling read and which, together with *Octavia* by Anton Ulrich von Braunschweig, constituted the early reading of the "fine soul" (Susanna Katharina von Klettenberg, 1723-74) described in the sixth book of *Wilhelm Meisters Lehrjahre*.

The catalogues of private libraries also show that interest in baroque literature was not dead. In the patrimonial inventories of citizens of Tübingen who died in the decade from 1750 to 1760 we find two copies of *Arminius* by Lohenstein and two copies of Anton Ulrich von Braunschweig's *Aramena*³ (in his review *Theresie und Eleonore* in 1767 Joseph von Sonnenfels was still recommending these two books to young girls). In the patrimonial inventories of citizens of Frankfurt on the Main who died around 1750 we find, as far as baroque literature is concerned, works by Angelus Silesius, Hofmannswaldau, Opitz, A. Gryphius, Lohenstein, Zigler's *Asiatische Banise* and Bucholtz's *Herkules und Valiska* and *Herkuliskus und Herkuladisla*.⁴ In the libraries of lawyers, doctors, theologians, and notables of Bremen who died between 1731 and 1778 were to be found works by Zesen, Fleming, Opitz, A. Gryphius, Lohenstein, Hofmannswaldau, Rist, Schirmer, and Moscherosch.⁵

Lohenstein was imitated by poets such as Brockes and Günther in their first attempts at poetry; his works aroused the first poetic urge in an Enlightenment poet like Haller, and Heinrich Zschokke as a schoolboy enjoyed reading *Arminius*.

On the other hand, the apologists of the new stylistic and poetic ideals at first found themselves on the horns of a dilemma: should only French classical works be recommended (together, perhaps, with Greek, Latin, and English works in French translations), or should a recommended reading canon include, besides the French, selected works of the baroque literary tradition? In the first case it would be impossible to educate the taste of the largest reading public (the prerequisite of a knowledge of French would narrow the scope to the upper middle class). In the second case, the attempts to impose a clear, simple style and to discredit the affected style of baroque writers would be foiled.

In the catalogue of an ideal female library suggested in Bodmer's *Discourse der Mahlern* we find, among numerous French works and translations, the writings of only three German authors — Opitz, Canitz, and Besser, the nearest to the ideals of classicism. The Hamburg review *Der Patriot* recommends the female public to read only French poetry and prose and the French translation of *The Guardian* (Erdmann Neumeister's *Geistliche Cantaten* and Brockes's *Irdisches Vergnügen in Gott*, being classified among "works of devotion," are allowed). *Vernünftige Tadlerinnen*, the review published at Leipzig by Gottsched, is less strict in its recommended reading list. In the number of 10 January 1725 the reading of *Arminius*, *Octavia*, and *Asiatische Banise* is permitted for the purity of the language. However, in the number of 27 June of the same year *Arminius*, *Octavia*, and *Asiatische Banise* are listed among the books to be eschewed, together with *Clélie*, *Artamène*, *ou le Grand Cyrus*, *Les Aventures de Télémaque*, *Argenis*, *Herkules und Valiska*, *Orlando Furioso*, *Pastor Fido*, *Aramena*, and *Die getreue*

Sclavin Doris (A. Bohse). In another number, would-be poets are advised to read Opitz and Gryphius (because they, unlike Lohenstein and Hofmannswaldau remained unsullied by marinism), and the writings of Christian Weise, Canitz, and Besser.

With the appearance of a literature in keeping with the stylistic, ideological, and philosophical ideals of the Enlightenment, the dilemma, still insoluble in the period 1720-40, between the rejection of the baroque tradition and therefore the renunciation of a link with literature in German (the only exception being Opitz, considered a classicist) and the maintaining of some slight contact with the baroque, was solved. There was an end, too, to another equivocation—that of the recourse to works, like those of French classicism, which corresponded to the stylistic and poetic ideals of the Enlightenment but were antithetical in contents, being, on the contrary, nearer to those of the baroque literary tradition and its ideology.

This is shown by the titles suggested for reading in 1746 by *Der Mahler der Sitten*, the second edition of *Discourse der Mahler*. The literature of French classicism, widely represented in the *Discourse*, is now almost nonexistent (authors such as Corneille, Racine, Molière, La Rochefoucauld, and Boileau are omitted). Pride of place is given instead to the new German poets, Pyra, Lange, Haller, Hagedorn, Gleim, and Liscow; to the exponents of new middle-class realism (Defoe, Marivaux, Fielding); and to the classics of the Enlightenment thought (Voltaire, Montesquieu, Pope). Clearly, the attraction of French classicism lay only in the style and had nothing to do with its aristocratic ideology. And clearly, too, the polemic against baroque literature was not a question of style only, but, above all, a polemic against its aristocratic ideology and its hierarchic conception of life and society. In number 66 of *Mahler der Sitten*, dedicated to a criticism of the *Helden-briefe* by Hofmannswaldau, the ornate baroque imagery is accused of lending credibility to the "repugnant principles" of class inequality, and in number 68 Amthor's poem "Monarch!" is described as "unterthänig." Similarly, in *Vergleichung zwischen Lohensteins Arminius und Heideggers Apollo Auricomus* (1732) Bodmer had seen in the spirit of "subjection" that moves the characters of *Arminius* and in the "courtesy" that guides their actions the greatest defects of the romance.

In addition to effects from the spread of English and French middle-class literature, and, from 1748, the poetry of Klopstock, the baroque literary tradition also suffered from the emergence of the aesthetic of sentimentalism.[6]

For classicist aesthetics and poetics, the baroque was indeed a diseased literary taste (*Schwulst, literarische Pest*), a perversion and corruption of style, caused by lack of discipline and control, and by the insane desire to surpass classical models, but it was, nonetheless, a literary phenomenon the writings of which were a constant source of examples of how not to write. In terms of sentimentalist aesthetics, however, the baroque was simply not poetry, crammed as it was with elements that inhibited empathy and emotion (learning, conceits, metaphors, hyperboles, emblems, realia, allegory, antithesis, and amplification).

Readers raised on sentimentalism (or "emotionalism") did not read to improve themselves or their style, or for the intellectual pleasure deriving from a complex labyrinthic structure and the unraveling of enigmas, or from the perception of resemblances and differences between the poetic imitation and the thing imitated. They read in order to be moved by the vicissitudes of people like themselves; they wanted to identify with characters like themselves. Sentimentalism (emotionalism) changed not only aesthetic canons, but the function of reading and the mentality of the reader. And indeed the spread of the aesthetic of emotionalism coincided with the beginning of the *Leserrevolution* that marked the change from intensive reading (repeated reading of a small number of books) to extensive reading (unrepeated reading of a large number of books).[7]

So when, from 1750-55 onward, the Dubosian* aesthetic of emotionalism spread throughout Germany, silence began to descend on baroque literature. Richardson was the fashion. In the second half of the eighteenth century, almost every library, were it middle or upper class, noble or aristocratic, possessed the novels of Richardson, or at least one of the innumerable imitations, reworkings, translations, or sequels. And in these libraries, next to Richardson stood works by Fielding, Goldsmith, Sterne, Marivaux, and Prévost.

The baroque romance, favored especially by the female reading public in the early eighteenth century, together with other baroque genres, had already disappeared from private libraries by the second half of the century. The large library of Goethe's father contained only one work of baroque poetry, Rammler and Lessing's edition of Friedrich von Logau's *Sinngedichte* (Leipzig, 1759). In the library of the landgrave Caroline of Assia (1721-74) there was not one single example of German baroque literature; in that of her mother, Duchess Caroline von Pfalz-

---

*Abbé Jean-Baptiste Dubos (1670-1742) wrote *Réflexions critiques sur la poésie et la peinture,* 1719 ff.

Zweibrücken-Birkenfeld (1704–74), we find only the *Weltliche Poemata*
by Opitz. Baroque poetry was completely absent in the library of Baron
Ludwig Carl von Weitolshausen (1724–83). Baroque literature (apart
from the religious *Lieder* of Joachim Neander) did not figure among the
books of Maria Schramm Misler (1734–77), a member of a distinguished
Hamburg family and a Pietist like von Weitolshausen.[8]

Baroque literature was poorly represented, too, in the circulating
libraries, which appeared in Germany in the second half of the eighteenth century. *Argenis* by John Barclay, *Arminius, Herkules und
Valiska,* and *Asiatische Banise* are in the 1777 catalogue of the
"Hofmeisterische Lees Bibliothec in Zürich an der Roosengasse"; *Asiatische Banise, Argenis, Arminius, Römische Octavia,* the seven volumes
of the *Neukirchsche Sammlung,* and the four-volume edition of Opitz's
Teutsche Gedichte edited by Daniel Wilhelm Triller were to be found in
the circulating library founded by Johann Georg Binz in Vienna at the
end of 1789.[9]

The lack of interest in baroque poetry is reflected in school anthologies as well. The first school anthology of German poetry, edited by
Michael Denis in 1762, contained not one single example of baroque
poetry. The second anthology (edited by Ignaz Weitenauer, 1768) contained some Opitz and Logau (this was certainly due to their rehabilitation by Ramler and Lessing). But baroque poetry disappeared not only
from the reading public's attention; it was ignored even by critics and
literary historians. Generally speaking, the manuals of literary history of
the late eighteenth century dismiss baroque literature with a farrago of
illuministic critical commonplaces dating from 1722 to 1740, and with
biographical and bibliographical information so erroneous as to reveal
complete unfamiliarity with the poetry in question and profound
ignorance regarding the most important sources of biography, bibliography, and literary history of the seventeenth and early eighteenth century. For example, Christian Friedrich Daniel Schubart, in the few lines
dedicated to baroque romance in *Vorlesungen über die schönen
Wissenschaften für Unstudierte* (1777), attributes the romances of
Bucholtz to Happel. In writing of baroque tragedy he considers Gryphius
an imitator of Lohenstein. Johann August Eberhard attributes to
Lohenstein the novels by Bucholtz. For Carl Joseph Bouginé, in his
Handbuch der allgemeinen Literargeschichte (1790), the author of the
second part of *Arminius* is Benjamin Neukirch.[10]

To be sure, attempts were made to salvage the baroque tradition.
Lessing and Ramler contributed with their above-mentioned edition of

Logau's epigrams. Mendelssohn and Herder dared to praise the style of *Arminius* by Lohenstein, the poet who for years had provided examples of "bad taste" for illuminist critics, so much so that *lohensteinisch* became a synonym for *schwülstig*. Friedrich Justus Riedel made an attempt, admittedly faltering, at a historical understanding of Lohenstein.[11] Most important of all, Herder was unflagging in his study of seventeenth-century literature. He pointed out to his contemporaries the merits, in terms of the German language and poetry, of Opitz, Weckherlin, Fleming, Gryphius, Lohenstein, Logau, and Dietrich von dem Werder, and included in his collection of *Volkslieder* works by Simon Dach, Opitz, Moscherosch, Weckherlin, Fleming, Zincgref, Morhof, Robert Robertin, and Heinrich Albert. He published and translated works by Johann Valentin Andreae and Jacob Balde.[12] So it was probably Herder who brought to the attention of the Romantics this literary period, generally despised and forgotten.

The Romantics were deeply interested in all aspects of seventeenth-century literature. Real or supposed affinities, their Catholicism, the search for the popular roots of German culture and of the German nation, the cult of the past, their enthusiasm for history and philology—all this led them to regard baroque poetry with greater attention. And though the poets and critics of Romanticism could in no way achieve a complete understanding of seventeenth-century poetry (they were hindered by their conception of the essentially "popular" nature and "national" role of all true poetry, by the cult of originality, spontaneity, and imagination, and by their rejection of the artificial, the cerebral, and the learned in art), yet they succeeded in bringing to the awareness of their contemporaries this forgotten period of German poetry.

Brentano edited *Trutz Nachtigall* (Berlin, 1817) and *Güldenes Tugend-Buch* (Koblenz, 1829) by Friedrich Spee; Tieck included in his *Deutsches Theater* (Berlin, 1817) works by Opitz, Gryphius, and Lohenstein; Achim von Arnim echoed the theme of *Cardenio und Celinde* by Gryphius in his *Halle und Jerusalem*; in *Des Knaben Wunderhorn* Brentano and Arnim included many songs by seventeenth-century poets. And Brentano and Arnim, again, were enthusiastic readers of Böhme, Spee, Angelus Silesius, Gryphius, Reuter, Moscherosch, and of the *Simplicissimus*.

Seventeenth-century literature is widely illustrated through excerpts by all the great Romantic literary historians: Franz Horn (*Geschichte und Kritik der deutschen Poesie und Beredsamkeit*, 1805), August Wilhelm Schlegel (*Über dramatische Kunst und Literatur*, 1809-11), Friedrich

Schlegel (*Geschichte der alten und neuen Literatur,* 1815), Friedrich
Bouterwek (*Geschichte der neueren Poesie und Beredsamkeit,* 1817),
Tieck (*Deutsches Theater,* 1817; "Über das deutsche Drama," 1825;
"Über die geschichtliche Entwicklung der neueren Bühne," 1831), Lud-
wig Wachler (*Vorlesungen über die Geschichte der deutschen National-
literatur,* 1818), and Eichendorff (*Geschichte des Dramas,* 1854;
Geschichte der poetischen Literatur Deutschlands, 1857).[13]

But the Romantics did not only "rediscover" the tradition of German baroque. They also "discovered" the great Spanish baroque
literature, and by means of excellent translations integrated it firmly in
the living German tradition. The causes of the revival of literary baroque
in the Biedermeier period, much favored by the "restoration" of the absolute state, are to be found in both the Romantic rediscovery of German
literary baroque and the grafting of the *Siglo de Oro* literature onto
German poetry. Melchior Diepenbrock's collection, *Geistlicher Blumen-
strauss aus spanischen und deutschen Dichtergärten* (Sulzbach, 1829),
which had considerable influence on the Catholic poets of the Biedermeier period, is a symbol of this fusion of German and Spanish baroque
tradition.[14]

The revival of baroque religious poetry (Abraham a Sancta Clara,
Angelus Silesius, Gryphius) was notable not only among Catholics
(Annette von Droste-Hülshoff) but also in Protestant circles (Mörike).[15]
Furthermore, in Gotthelf we find a reappearance of the "calenders" and
of the baroque *Hausväterliteratur.*[16] Catholic Austria, where the
baroque had never completely disappeared, produced some of the
loftiest expressions of the tradition—the "Wiener Volkstheater"[17] and
the drama of Grillparzer.

While the restoration tendencies between 1815 and 1848 greatly
favored the reception of the baroque tradition, liberal-bourgeois and
democratic trends—before and after 1848—hindered it. From Gervinus
to Heinrich Kurz, from Koberstein to Goedeke, literary history of a
liberal and democratic bias condemned the "courtier" nature of baroque
poetry—its dependence on foreign models, its rhetorical and bombastic
style—and was scandalized by its immorality.

Seventeenth-century literature was treated no better by late-
nineteenth-century historians such as Wilhelm Scherer, Erich Schmidt,
and Felix Bobertag. Not even Carl Lemcke (*Von Opitz bis Klopstock,*
Leipzig, 1871) whose aim was to do "historical justice" to the literature
from Opitz to Klopstock, was able to perceive the essence of baroque
poetry, conditioned as he was by his dislike of rhetoric, his idea of poetry

and art as plastic representations of the individual and the realm of the imagination, and by his moral and political prejudices. When writing of Lohenstein, he is struck by the idea of the affinity between baroque art and poetry, but he goes no further than to state, rather waspishly, that both are dominated by bombast and emphasis.

And yet it was the recognition of the affinity between baroque poetry and art that was to lead the way to a revaluation of seventeenth-century literature. Certainly, the discovery of baroque art was fundamental in this process of revaluation, and the rediscovery had not yet come about when Lemcke was writing—but it was not far off.

The reversal of the negative judgment on the baroque in the plastic and figurative arts—which had been uninterrupted from Winckelmann's *Gedanken über die Nachahmung der griechischen Werke in der Malerei und Bildhauerkunst* (1755) to Jakob Burckhardt's *Cicerone* (1885), and from Wilhelm Lübke's *Geschichte der Architektur* (1855, 1870) to Jaro Springer's *Allgemeine Kunstgeschichte* (1887)—may be said to have taken place at the end of the 1880s, when Cornelius Gurlitt published his monumental *Geschichte des Barockstiles* (1887–89), Robert Dohme his *Geschichte der deutschen Baukunst* (1887), Heinrich Wölfflin his *Renaissance und Barock* (1888), and Carl Just his *Velazquez und sein Jahrhundert* (1888).[18]

It is true that the art historians' rediscovery of the baroque—now considered an independent period in the history of art, with its own characteristics, and not an inferior product, the last stage of the decadence and perversion of the Renaissance—was preceded by neobaroque tendencies in architecture, in furniture making, and in interior decoration and design. These fashions began to flourish in Europe in the 1860s and were much nourished by the aristocracy and the upper middle class. In Paris during the second empire, in Berlin in the "Gründerjahre" and in Vienna in the first few decades of the reign of Franz-Josef, neobaroque taste spread in the furnishing of palaces, in the construction of public buildings, and in portraiture. 1867 marked the beginning of the decisive conversion of Ludwig II to neobaroque with the construction of the castles of Linderhof and Herrenchiemsee. After the unification of Italy, the house of Savoy contributed greatly to the diffusion of the neobaroque.[19]

The imperial and dynastic need for representation, the revival of the idea of the "divine right" of the monarchy, the alliance between the crown and the upper classes—such were the main nonartistic factors in the spread of neobaroque in Europe. But the diffusion was due also to a change in artistic sensibility and in the way of "seeing things." This is shown by the parallel between the birth and development of neobaroque and the birth and development of Impressionism. Both took place in the same period, between 1867 and 1886.[20]

Neobaroque fashion and the reception of Impressionist painting are certainly at the bottom of the revaluation of the baroque by art historians from 1887 onward. But the developments in the field of art and the history of art had almost no effect on literary taste and the history of literature. For many years, literary historians were not aware of the "discovery" of the baroque, and continued to call seventeenth-century literature "Renaissance literature" and to condemn it as a corruption and perversion of classical style. They were not even aware of what Nietzsche says of baroque art in *Menschliches, Allzumenchliches* (1878–79; see "Religiöse Herkunft der neueren Musik," "Vom Barock-stile"),[21] where we find profound and prophetic insights into baroque as "counterrenaissance," as the style of the counter-Reformation;[22] into the rhetorical and dramatic (theatrical) nature of baroque style; baroque as a phenomenon common to all arts; insights into the independent value and particularity of baroque, which must be acknowledged, not dismissed out of hand; and into its periodic recurrence at the decline of every great (classical) art. Nor had the historians of literature noticed the transposition of the concept of baroque from the plastic and figurative arts to literature when in *Renaissance und Barock* Wölfflin himself compared the Renaissance style of Ariosto's *Orlando Furioso* with the baroque of Tasso's *Gerusalemme Liberata*.

It was not until 1914 that a contribution (which passed completely unnoticed) by Valdemar Vedel was published on "Den digteriske Barokstil, omkring ear 1600,"[23] and the first volume appeared of Karl Borinski's[24] *Die Antike in Poetik und Kunsttheorie*, subtitled "Mittelalter, Renaissance und Barock." In the same year Josef Nadler completed the third volume (published only in 1918, owing to the war) of *Literaturgeschichte der deutschen Stämme und Landschaften*, in which he defines as baroque the Austro-Bavarian literature of the seventeenth century. Also in 1914, Oskar Walzel wrote an essay on "Barock in der Dichtung von heute," published the following year under the title "Deutsche Vorkriegsdichtung,"[25] in which he points out the stylistic and spiritual affinity between certain contemporary writers (Enrica von Handel-Mazzetti, Flaubert, Franz Werfel, Georg Heym) and baroque poets and artists.

Finally, in 1916, Fritz Strich, influenced by Heinrich Wölfflin's

Kunstgeschichtliche Grundbegriffe (1915), published the famous essay, "Der lyrische Stil des 17. Jahrhunderts,"[26] which, rightly or wrongly (wrongly from a purely chronological point of view, rightly if one considers its importance for studies in literary baroque) is usually indicated as the beginning of the modern *Barockforschung*. In it Strich sweeps aside all the ambiguity regarding style and chronology that was the result of considering seventeenth-century poetry as Renaissance poetry, and defines its style as "baroque." Then, faithful pupil of Wölfflin that he is, he bases his analysis on the style. Antithesis and *accumulatio*, continuous movement and continuous change (metamorphosis), parallelism and repetition, polar tension and lack of measure, dissonance and wealth of metaphor—these, for Strich, are the basic connotations of the style of seventeenth-century German poetry. But they are also connotations of more or less eternal "essences," such as "German man," "the German spirit," "the baroque spirit," and "protogermanic poetry" (here Strich seems to betray a deeper influence than Wölfflin's—that of Wilhelm Worringer's *Abstraktion und Einfühlung*, 1908, and *Formproblem der Gotik*), 1911. By manipulating these essences, Strich "discovers" that baroque is a specific national German style; he "discovers" the affinity—already hypothesized by Worringer—between gothic and baroque, the stylistic affinity between baroque lyrics and protogermanic poetry, and, finally, the affinity between baroque and Romanticism.

This kind of speculation and juggling with the eternal essences of the German national spirit, which belongs more to the ideology of Germanism than to philology and literary history, is characteristic of a great deal of the *Barockforschung* of the following decades. Although their heuristic value is nil, these "essences" and "affinities" played a most important role in making baroque literature relevant to the modern audience and therefore prepared the way for a revival of interest among the more cultured readers between the two world wars.

Of all the affinities "discovered" by historians of art and literature intent on contributing to the building of the ideology of Germanism, the most important was baroque's affinity with Expressionism.

One of the first, if not the first, to perceive an affinity of style—and of contents, too—between baroque poetry and expressionist poetry was Oskar Walzel, who refers to Hermann Bahr's essay on "Expressionismus und Goethe"[27] in *Deutsche Vorkriegsdichtung*, mentioned earlier. A few years later, in an essay on "Eindruckskunst und Ausdruckskunst in der Dichtung" (1919), Walzel returned to the problem of the affinity between expressionism and baroque, with explicit reference to Wölfflin's categories, and affirmed that the elements common to both artistic movements are the sudden ecstasies and the raptures, the obscurity and lack of clear outlines, the ascetic moods and the ardent desire for martyrdom. In the same collection (*Zur Einführung in die Kunst der Gegenwart*, 1919) in which Walzel's essay appeared, we find also that of Max Deri, "Naturalismus, Idealismus, Expressionismus," where expressionism is associated with baroque, with Sturm und Drang, and with Romanticism. A few years later Werner Mahrholz in *Literargeschichte und Literaturwissenschaft* (1923) pointed out the affinity between baroque and the present age, and in *Deutsche Dichtung der Gegenwart* (1926) he speaks of "baroque and gothic expressionists" and "baroque or gothic expressionism."

The baroque was closely linked to the spreading nationalist ideology by means of its insertion in a hypothesized tradition of genuinely German art forms (gothic, baroque, Sturm und Drang, Romanticism, Expressionism) and made "modern" by means of rather temerarious comparisons with contemporary artistic movements and philosophic currents (philosophies of life). The baroque thus became an object of great interest to historians of art and literature. The results of this *Barockenthusiasmus* were a large number of monographs and imposing syntheses full of illuminating discoveries. Furthermore, interest for the baroque spread to a wider audience, cultured but not specialized (the most telling proof of this interest is the great number of anthologies of baroque poetry that appeared between the wars).[28] It is true that the roots of the revival of baroque poetry were not altogether uncontaminated, nor were many of its fruits. But what reception, what rediscovery of forgotten traditions is possible without historical and philological deformations and without contamination by contemporary ideologies, be they noble or ignoble?

NOTES

1. I deal extensively with the problem of the genesis of baroque poetry in "Barockpoesie, Publikum und Verbürgerlichung der literarischen Intelligenz," in *Internationales Archiv für Sozialgeschichte der deutschen Literatur*, 1 (1976), 107-45, and in *Daniel Casper von Lohenstein: Geschichte seiner Rezeption*, Band I: 1661-1800 (Tübingen, 1978), 28-174, 397-435.

2. For the relationship between social mobility and the "embourgoisement" of the intelligentsia, and for the problem of the changes in aesthetic, poetic, and stylistic norms, see the two works cited in note 1.

3. Hildegard Neumann, "Der Bücherbesitz der Tübinger Bürger von 1750–1850" (diss. Tübingen 1955).

4. Walter Wittman, "Beruf und Buch im 18. Jahrhundert" (diss. Frankfurt a.M. 1934).

5. Rolf Engelsing, *Der Bürger als Leser: Lesergeschichte in Deutschland, 1500–1800* (Stuttgart, 1974).

6. For the aesthetics of emotionalism and its diffusion in Germany, see the first chapter of my *Geschichte der dramatischen Theorien in Deutschland im 18. Jahrhundert* (Tübingen, 1972), pp. 1–108, and my essay "Emotionalismus und Empathie: Zur Entstehung bürgerlicher Kunst im 18. Jahrhundert," in *Jahrbuch des Wiener Goethe-Vereins, 83* (1979), pp. 117–30.

7. Rolf Engelsing, "Die Perioden der Lesergeschichte in der Neuzeit," in his *Zur Sozialgeschichte deutscher Mittel- und Unterschichten* (Göttingen, 1973), pp. 112–54, 283–92.

8. Martino, *Lohenstein*, pp. 405–11.

9. On the circulating libraries see Georg Jäger, "Die deutsche Leihbibliothek im 19. Jahrhundert," *Internationales Archiv für Sozialgeschichte der deutschen Literatur*, 2 (1977), 96–133, and my essays: "Die deutsche Leihbibliothek und ihr Publikum," in *Literatur in der sozialen Bewegung*, ed. Alberto Martino (Tübingen, 1977), pp. 1–26; "Biblioteche circolanti e produzione letteraria in Germania nell'Ottocento," in *Critical Dimensions*, ed. Mario Curreli and Alberto Martino (Cuneo, 1978), pp. 313–31; *Die Leihbibliothek der Goethezeit*, Exemplarische Kataloge zwischen 1790–1830, ed. mit einem Aufsatz zur Geschichte der Leihbibliotheken im 18. und 19. Jahrhundert von Georg Jäger, Alberto Martino und Reinhard Wittmann, Hildesheim, 1979; "Lekturkabinette und Leihbibliotheken in Wien (1772–1848)," in *Die österreichische Literatur von der Zeit Maria Theresias bis zur Restauration unter Franz I*, ed. Herbert Zeman (Graz, 1979), pp. 119–42; "Die Leihbibliotheksfrage: Zur Krise der deutschen Leihbibliothek in der zweiten Hälfte des 19. Jahrhunderts," in *Die Leihbibliothek als Institution des literarischen Lebens im 18. und 19. Jahrhundert*, ed. Georg Jäger and Jörg Schönert (Hamburg, 1980), pp. 89–163.

10. Martino, *Lohenstein*, pp. 392–94.

11. Martino, *Lohenstein*, pp. 370–78.

12. Volkmar Braunbehrens, *Nationalbildung und Nationalliteratur: Zur Rezeption der Literatur des 17. Jahrhunderts von Gottsched bis Gervinus* (Berlin, 1974), pp. 48–65.

13. Erwin Polt, "Die Wiedererweckung des deutschen Dramas des 16. und 17. Jahrhunderts in der Romantik" (diss. Wien 1930).

14. Friedrich Sengle, *Biedermeierzeit*, I (Stuttgart, 1971), 137–39, 143–44. This first volume and the second (Stuttgart, 1972) of Sengle's monumental work contain invaluable information and profound observations on the

revival of the baroque tradition in the Biedermeier, and important suggestions for a systematic investigation of some of its fundamental aspects.

15. Manfred Koschlig, "Mörikes barocker Grundton und seine verborgenen
     Quellen: Studien zur Geschichtlichkeit des Dichters," *Zeitschrift für Würt-*
     tembergische Landesgeschichte, 34-35 (1975-76), 231-323. Koschlig gives
     a synthesis of this vast work in his article "Die Barock-Rezeption bei Mörike:
     Ein Bericht," *Daphnis*, 7 (1978), 341-59.
16. Werner Hahl brought to my attention the connection between Gotthelf and
     Hausväterliteratur.
17. Otto Rommel, *Barocktradition im österreichisch-bayrischen Volkstheater*,
     6 vols, Deutsche Literatur in Entwicklungsreihen, Reihe XIII: Barock
     (Leipzig, 1935-39), and *Die Alt-Wiener Volkskomödie: Ihre Geschichte*
     vom barocken Welttheater bis zum Tode Nestroys (Wien, 1952).
18. For the revaluation of baroque by the historians of art see the very impor-
     tant essay by Hans Tintelnot, "Zur Gewinnung unserer Barockbegriffe," in
     Die Kunstformen des Barockzeitalters, ed. Rudolf Stamm (Bern, 1956), pp.
     13-91. Hans-Harald Müller's *Barockforschung; Ideologie und Methode:*
     Ein Kapitel deutscher Wissenschaftsgeschichte, 1870-1930 (Darmstadt,
     1973) is also to be recommended for its precision and clarity. As Klaus
     Garber points out in his important history of the reception of Opitz (*Martin*
     Opitz—"der Vater der Deutschen Dichtung": Eine kritische Studie zur
     Wissenschaftsgeschichte der Germanistik, Stuttgart, 1976, pp. 23-35),
     Herbert Jaumann's attempt in *Die deutsche Barockliteratur; Wertung-*
     Umwertung: Eine wertungsgeschichtliche Studie in systematischer Absicht
     (Bonn, 1975) to give the history of the revaluation of the baroque has com-
     pletely failed. Jaumann feels the need to theorize and establish categories,
     but he is in fact incapable of carrying out a historical analysis and of ex-
     amining the connections between social reality and the constitution of and
     the changes in aesthetic and critical judgments. In his book he does nothing
     but juggle with categories and concepts which are indeed worthy of the
     "modernistische Begriffszirkus" that he himself incautiously invokes
     (p. 602) but completely foreign to a serious historical analysis.
19. Tintelnot, "Zur Gewinnung unserer Barockbegriffe," pp. 36-41.
20. Tintelnot, pp. 41-42.
21. Friedrich Nietzsche, *Werke in drei Bänden*, ed. Karl Schlechta (München,
     1966), I, 576-77, 791-92. On Nietzsche and baroque see the forceful obser-
     vations of Wilfried Barner, *Barockrhetorik: Untersuchungen zu ihren*
     geschichtlichen Grundlagen (Tübingen, 1970), pp. 3-21, and Joachim
     Goth's *Nietzsche und die Rhetorik* (Tübingen, 1970), pp. 35-51.
22. Nietzsche likens baroque style to modern music, which, in his opinion,
     is a product of the Counter-Reformation, and which he sees as
     "Gegenrenaissance." See also "Musik—und der grosse Stil," in *Aus dem*
     Nachlaß der Achtzigerjahre (Nietzsche, *Werke*, ed. K. Schlechta, III,
     782-83).

23. Vedel's essay was published in *Edda: Nordisk Tidsskrift for Litteratur forskning*, 2 (1914), 17–40.

24. Borinski had already used the expression "poetic baroque" in 1886 in *Die Poetik der Renaissance*. Wilhelm Dilthey, too, had spoken of "poetischer Barockstil" in studies on seventeenth-century literature written about 1902 but published only in 1927 in the third volume of *Gesammelte Schriften*, ed. Paul Ritter.

25. This appeared in *Zeitschrift für den deutschen Unterricht*, 29 (1915), 449-55.

26. Published in *Abhandlungen zur deutschen Literaturgeschichte: Franz Muncker zum. 60. Geburtstag dargebracht* (München, 1916), pp. 21-53. Now included in *Deutsche Barockforschung*, ed. Richard Alewyn (Köln and Berlin, 1970), pp. 229-59. On this essay and the history of the "first" transposition of the concept of the baroque from the figurative arts to poetry, see Fritz Strich, "Die Übertragung des Barockbegriffs von der bildenden Kunst auf die Dichtung" (in *Die Kunstformen des Barockzeitalters*, pp. 243-65) and Hans-Harald Müller, *Barockforschung*, pp. 118-33.

27. See *Die neue Rundschau*, 3 (1914), 913-26, for Bahr's essay.

28. *Die Deutsche Lyrik des Barock*, Ausgewählt und eingeleitet von Walther Unus (Berlin, 1922), was widely read.

SELECTED BIBLIOGRAPHY

Secondary Literature (not cited in the text or the notes)

Blackall, Eric A. *Die Entwicklung des Deutschen zur Literatursprache, 1700–1775*. Stuttgart, 1966.

Brietzke, Heinz Günter. "Zur Geschichte der Barockwertung von Winckelmann bis Burckhardt (1755-1855)." Diss. Berlin 1954.

Epstein, Hans. *Die Metaphysizierung in der literarwissenschaftlichen Begriffsbildung und ihre Folgen: Dargelegt an drei Theorien über das Literaturbarock*. Berlin, 1929.

Jones, G. L. "Gottsched and the German Poets of the Seventeenth Century." *Forum for Modern Language Studies*, 7 (1971), 282-93.

Kettler, H. K. *Baroque Tradition in the Literature of the German Enlightenment, 1700-1750*. Cambridge, 1943.

Luther, Gisela. *Barocker Expressionismus? Zur Problematik der Beziehung zwischen der Bildlichkeit expressionistischer und barocker Lyrik*. The Hague, 1969.

Mansfeld, Franz. "Das literarische Barock im kunsttheoretischen Urteil Gottscheds und der Schweizer." Diss. Halle-Wittenberg 1928.

Schwind, Peter. *Schwulst-Stil: Historische Grundlagen von Produktion und Rezeption manieristischer Sprachformen in Deutschland, 1624–1738.* Bonn, 1977.

Walzel, Oskar. *Wechselseitige Erhellung der Künste: Fin Beitrag zur Würdigung kunstgeschichtlicher Begriffe.* Berlin, 1917.

——. "Barockstil bei Klopstock." In *Festschrift Max H. Jellinek: Zum 29. Mai 1928 dargebracht.* Wien and Leipzig, 1928, pp. 167–90.

Windfuhr, Manfred. *Die barocke Bildlichkeit und ihre Kritiker: Stilhaltungen in der deutschen Literatur des 17. und 18. Jahrhunderts.* Stuttgart, 1966.